CHRISTIANITY
& Religious Plurality

CHRISTIANITY
& Religious Plurality

Historical and Global Perspectives

Edited by
WILBERT R. SHENK
and
RICHARD J. PLANTINGA

CASCADE Books • Eugene, Oregon

CHRISTIANITY AND RELIGIOUS PLURALITY
Historical and Global Perspectives

Copyright © 2016 Wipf and Stock Publishers. All rights reserved. Except for brief quotations in critical publications or reviews, no part of this book may be reproduced in any manner without prior written permission from the publisher. Write: Permissions, Wipf and Stock Publishers, 199 W. 8th Ave., Suite 3, Eugene, OR 97401.

Cascade Books
An Imprint of Wipf and Stock Publishers
199 W. 8th Ave., Suite 3
Eugene, OR 97401

www.wipfandstock.com

PAPERBACK ISBN: 978-1-4982-8265-9
HARDCOVER ISBN: 978-1-4982-8267-3
EBOOK ISBN: 978-1-4982-8266-6

Cataloguing-in-Publication data:

Names: Shenk, Wilbert R., editor. | Plantinga, Richard J., editor.
Title: Christianity and religious plurality : historical and global perspectives / edited by Wilbert R. Shenk and Richard J. Plantinga.
Description: Eugene, OR: Cascade Books, 2016 | Includes bibliographical references.
Identifiers: ISBN 978-1-4982-8265-9 (paperback) | ISBN 978-1-4982-8267-3 (hardcover) | ISBN 978-1-4982-8266-6 (ebook)
Subjects: LCSH: Christianity and other religions—Congresses. | Religious pluralism—Congresses.
Classification: BR127 E246 2016 (paperback) | BR127 (ebook)

Manufactured in the U.S.A.   10/10/16

Scripture quotations marked NIV are taken from the Holy Bible, New International Version®, NIV®. Copyright © 1973, 1978, 1984, 2011 by Biblica, Inc.™ Used by permission of Zondervan. All rights reserved worldwide. www.zondervan.com The "NIV" and "New International Version" are trademarks registered in the United States Patent and Trademark Office by Biblica, Inc.™

Scripture quotations marked NRSV are taken from the Holy Bible, New Revised Standard Version Bible, copyright 1989, Division of Christian Education of the National Council of the Churches of Christ in the United States of America. Used by permission. All rights reserved.

Scripture quotations marked TNIV taken from the Holy Bible, Today's New International® Version TNIV®. Copyright 2001, 2005 by International Bible Society® . Used by permission of International Bible Society®. All rights reserved worldwide. "TNIV" and "Today's New International Version" are trademarks registered in the United States Patent and Trademark Office by International Bible Society®.

Contents

Contributors | vii
Acknowledgments | ix

Introduction | 1
—Wilbert R. Shenk

PART 1: BIBLICAL AND PATRISTICS PERSPECTIVES

Chapter 1
"Yhwh Our God Yhwh One": Religious Plurality and the Old Testament | 9
—John Goldingay

Chapter 2
Scripture in the Context of Religious Plurality: Aspects of the Patristic Witness and Their Analogies in Contemporary Africa | 31
—Kwame Bediako

PART 2: THE CONSEQUENCES OF CHRISTENDOM BEFORE 1800

Chapter 3
Christians, Social Location, and Religious Plurality | 49
—Wilbert R. Shenk

Chapter 4
Diversity and the Challenge of Difference: Historical Perspective on the Muslim World and Western Impact | 71
—Lamin Sanneh

Chapter 5
Religious Plurality in South Africa: Some Historical Perspectives | 103
—Gerald J. Pillay

Chapter 6
Religious Plurality in East Asia before 1800: The Encounter between Christianity and Asian Religions | 118
—Peter C. Phan

PART 3: CONTEMPORARY AND GLOBAL PERSPECTIVES

Chapter 7
Religious Plurality and the Christian Mission in the People's Republic of China | 159
—Kim-Kwong Chan and Daniel H. Bays

Chapter 8
Christianity in Interaction with the Primal Religions of the World: A Historical and Global Perspective | 181
—Gillian Mary Bediako

Chapter 9
At the Crossroads: Contemporary Indonesian Christianity amid Primal Religions | 208
—Martin L. Sinaga

Chapter 10
Muslim Responses to Plurality in the Last 100 Years | 219
—J. Dudley Woodberry

Chapter 11
Hinduism in the Twentieth Century | 240
—Paul Cornelius

Chapter 12
Keeping Faith: Immigration, Religion, and the Unmaking of a Global Culture | 257
—Jehu J. Hanciles

Chapter 13
The Future of Pluralisms—and Why They Likely Will Fail | 284
—Veli-Matti Kärkkäinen

Chapter 14
Afterword: Looking Back with an Eye to the Conversational Future | 310
—Richard J. Plantinga

Contributors

Daniel H. Bays, Emeritus Professor of History and Director, Hubers Asian Studies Program, Calvin College, Grand Rapids, Michigan

Gillian Mary Bediako, Deputy Rector, Akrofi-Christaller Institute of Theology, Mission and Culture, Akropong-Akuaquem, Ghana

Kwame Bediako, late Founder and Rector of Akrofi-Christaller Institute of Theology, Mission and Culture, Akropong-Akuaquem, Ghana

Kim-Kwong Chan, Executive Secretary, Hong Kong Christian Council, and Honorary Research Fellow, Universities Service Center for Chinese Studies, Chinese University of Hong Kong

Paul Cornelius, Regional Secretary—India, Asia Theological Association, Bangalore, India

John Goldingay, David Allan Hubbard Professor of Old Testament, Fuller Theological Seminary, Pasadena, California

Jehu J. Hanciles, D. W. and Ruth Brooks Associate Professor of World Christianity, Candler School of Theology, Emory University, Atlanta, Georgia

Veli-Matti Kärkkäinen, Professor of Systematic Theology, Fuller Theological Seminary, Pasadena, California

Peter C. Phan, The Ignacio Ellacuria Chair of Catholic Social Thought, Georgetown University, Washington, DC

Gerald J. Pillay, Professor of Church History, Vice-Chancellor and Rector, Liverpool Hope University, Liverpool, UK

Richard J. Plantinga, Professor, Department of Religion, Calvin College, Grand Rapids, Michigan

Lamin Sanneh, D. Willis James Professor of Missions and World Christianity and Professor of History, Yale Divinity School, New Haven, Connecticut; member of the Pontifical Commission of the Historical Sciences and the Pontifical Commission on Religious Relations with Muslims

Wilbert R. Shenk, Senior Professor of Mission History and Contemporary Culture, Fuller Graduate School of Intercultural Studies, Pasadena, California

Martin L. Sinaga, Minister, Simalungun Protestant Church, Lecturer in Jakarta Theological Seminary, and member of the Theological Commission of the National Council of Churches of Indonesia

J. Dudley Woodberry, Dean Emeritus and Senior Professor of Islamic Studies, Fuller Graduate School of Intercultural Studies, Pasadena, California

Acknowledgments

THIS VOLUME ORIGINATED WITH a symposium on religious plurality held in Pasadena, California, April 25-27, 2003. The event was co-sponsored by Calvin College and Fuller Theological Seminary. The initial impetus came from Dr. Joel A. Carpenter, director of Calvin College's Nagel Institute. Dr. C. Douglas McConnell, then dean of the School of Intercultural Studies, now provost, of Fuller Seminary gave encouragement from the beginning. The two institutions underwrote the project by providing generous financial support that enabled the project to be carried out. This moral and financial support is gratefully acknowledged. Publication was delayed due to reasons beyond the editors' control. The substance of these essays is of continuing relevance.

Introduction

Wilbert R. Shenk

THROUGHOUT MUCH OF THE twentieth century, *pluralism* was understood as describing two separate but related issues. Its meaning and usage evolved over time. Writing in 1966, W. A. Visser 't Hooft defined pluralism as "a situation in which various religious, philosophical or ideological conceptions live side by side and in which none of them holds a privileged status."[1] In 1970 Raymond Hammer used the term primarily in the sense of a "multiple-religious situation."[2] He pointed out that Europeans had long assumed that each continental country had one religion, whereas in reality most countries in other parts of the world had multiple religions. Two decades later Martin E. Marty described the religious situation in North America as one of religious pluralism, which "refers both to the wide diversity of religious groups in America and to the polity which grants them equal liberty."[3] That is to say, pluralism now was used to describe a situation characterized by religio-cultural variety as well as ascribing normative value to such variety.

Since the 1960s a theological movement dedicated to reconstructing Christian theology in the light of pluralism has gained influence. Well-known scholars committed themselves to this task. Among the best known have been Wilfred Cantwell Smith, John Hick, and Paul F. Knitter.[4] These scholars boldly contested longstanding convictions and theological

---

1. Visser 't Hooft, "Pluralism," 129. He notes that there is a range of definitions of pluralism and then offers his own succinct statement.

2. Hammer, "Pluralism, Religious," 488.

3. Marty, "Pluralism, Religious," 911.

4. E.g., Smith, *World Theology*. See also Berthrong, "Wilfred Cantwell Smith," and Hughes, *Wilfred Cantwell Smith*, ch. 5; Hick, *John Hick*; Netland, *Religious Pluralism*, esp. ch. 5; and Knitter, *Jesus*.

constructs, challenging theologians to take account of the multiplicity of religions and seek to accommodate all religions within one conceptual system. These views have stirred intense debate that has given rise to a considerable publishing industry devoted to this theme. By now, in the minds of many people, pluralism is synonymous with this particular viewpoint. At the same time, it has become increasingly clear there are inherent problems with this paradigm, thus reflecting the strengths and limitations of modernity.

Douglas John Hall critiqued pluralism for the way it "sacrifices Christian particularity to a detached universalism."[5] While Christians can rejoice in the ending of historical Christendom that maintained its political and religious dominance through a coercive system, the only available alternative is not a synthetic belief that claims to gather all religions into one amalgam. This would be to violate the integrity of each faith tradition. For Christians, faithfulness to the gospel means steadfast witness to the gospel's inherent *skandalon*, or, offense, which confronts every generation and every people across the world.

This symposium emerged out of a sense that the pluralism paradigm was exhausted. The polarization that pluralist claims had engendered left the search for understanding paralyzed. These essays are offered as a contribution toward clarifying and opening up space to explore two important dimensions: 1) the *historiography* of religious plurality and 2) the *missiological* necessity of plurality. The *empirical-historical* situation—what one finds on the ground—must be extricated from the *ideological* program that has dominated this discussion for the past generation. Religious plurality has been a part of human cultures throughout history. But new forces are at work that are accelerating the pace and intensity of change. This calls for great sensitivity and sympathy for peoples and groups caught in this maelstrom that is forcing many to leave their historical homes and cultures and become a part of the greatest human migration in history.

A hallmark of the modern era has been technological innovation in transportation and communication, opening the way for the movement of peoples from their historical homelands to other countries, regions, or continents. Europeans took the lead in large-scale migration starting in the seventeenth century. Following World War II, the pattern of migration became more variegated, with people from Asia, Africa, and Latin America swelling the tide of those who were moving from their traditional homelands to new ones. The pace of migration has continued to accelerate over the past fifty years. People from all over the world have relocated in pursuit of education and employment opportunities or to escape from political and

---

5. Hall, "Confessing Christ," 65.

religious oppression. Naturally, they have taken their cultures—including religion—with them. By the year 2000, Buddhists immigrants from Japan, Korea, China, Taiwan, Vietnam, Cambodia, Thailand, Tibet, and Sri Lanka had settled in Los Angeles County. Diana Eck concludes, "Nowhere can we see the whole panorama of Buddhism as clearly as in Los Angeles. . . . LA is unquestionably the most complex Buddhist city in the world . . . representing the whole spectrum of Asian, and now American, Buddhism."[6]

Modern political theory has promoted a grand experiment in the co-existence of multiple religious faiths and ideologies under a common polity that guarantees the rights of individuals to exercise their convictions. Historians point out that the Constitution of the United States is the first document to establish the equality of all varieties of religion before the law, so that adherents of any faith or ideology are guaranteed equal protection. To do this, framers of the US Constitution devised a secular system of government. If all religions are to be respected, by law, no religion can be given preferential treatment. Accordingly, the US Constitution disallows the government to establish any religion. Although there have been many stumbles along the way, the experiment has been embraced by many other nations. The United Nations' Universal Declaration of Human Rights, adopted in 1948, is an attempt to extend these basic rights to all people, including the right to practice whatever faith they choose. Today, societies around the world are under great strain as their laws and cultural conventions are being challenged to accommodate changing socioreligious landscapes.

In the 1960s, in response to its growing cultural complexity, the Canadian government took the first step to develop a national policy of "multiculturalism." This consisted of three major actions: 1) the Official Languages Act—passed in 1969—recognized French and English as Canada's two official languages; 2) in 1971 the government promulgated its "policy of multiculturalism" as the means of insuring "the cultural freedom of Canadians"; and 3) the Charter of Rights and Freedoms enacted in 1982 asserted "that all Canadians are equal," and it gave "legal protection to the rights of every individual."[7] Reflecting on two decades of experience with Canada's policy of multiculturalism in 1993, Reginald W. Bibby noted that the "infant pluralism" had grown up and Canada now had "not only a *cultural* mosaic but also a *moral* mosaic, a *meaning* mosaic, a *family structure* mosaic, an *educational* mosaic, a *sexual orientation* mosaic. . . . Pluralism has come to

---

6. Eck, *New Religious America*, 148.
7. Bibby, "Mosaics and Melting Pots," 415.

pervade Canadian minds and Canadian institutions."[8] In short, the outcome has intensified individualism and relativism.

Language is dynamic, and the meaning of words evolves over time. Pluralism, like multiculturalism, has acquired an increasingly ideological meaning. J. Andrew Kirk has proposed that the term be rescued by adopting a more rigorous and nuanced definition:

> By religious pluralism I mean any view of religious life and belief which asserts *either* that the most fundamental aspect of all (major) religious traditions are manifestations of the same "ultimately Real" (the monistic thesis of John Hick) *or* that, though incommensurable, each religious tradition encompasses a path to salvation of equal worth and benefit (polymorphism).[9]

Increasingly, scholars have recognized the need to draw a distinction between what Kirk defines as pluralism, on the one hand, and the empirical fact of multiple faiths, on the other. As suggested by the Canadian example, important new issues of public policy are being raised in many countries by virtue of the rapid pluralization of societies that historically have been regarded as homogeneous.

In this volume, *pluralism* is used when dealing with the ideology that all religions are expressions of a common essence. Advocates of pluralism are dedicated to discovering this common denominator, convinced that this will unite peoples in overcoming misunderstanding, prejudice, and hostility. This is the basis for harmony and peace in the world that heretofore has proved so elusive.

We propose an alternative view. *Plurality* accurately describes the situation across the world historically and empirically. In a sense we must first clear the ground and start over. The way forward is to recognize that the world has always been, and continues to be, characterized by religious plurality.[10]

BIBLIOGRAPHY

Berthrong, John. "Wilfred Cantwell Smith: The Theological Necessity of Pluralism." *Toronto Journal of Theology* 5 (1989) 188–205.
Bibby, Reginald W. "Mosaics and Melting Pots in Motion: Reading and Responding to New Times." *Missiology: An International Review* 21 (October 1993) 413–28.
Eck, Diana L. *A New Religious America*. San Francisco: HarperSanFrancisco, 2001.

8. Ibid.
9. Kirk, "Religious Pluralism," 430.
10. See Plantinga, *Christianity and Plurality*.

Hall, Douglas John. "Confessing Christ in the Religiously Pluralistic Context." In *Many Voices, One God: Being Faithful in a Pluralistic World*, edited by Walter Brueggemann and George W. Stroup, 65–77. Louisville: Westminster John Knox, 1998.

Hammer, Raymond. "Pluralism, Religious." In *Concise Dictionary of the Christian World Mission*, edited by Stephen Neill et al., 488. London: Lutterworth, 1970.

Hick, John. *John Hick: An Autobiography*. Oxford: Oneworld, 2002.

Hughes, Edward J. *Wilfred Cantwell Smith: A Theology for the World*. London: SCM, 1986.

Kirk, J. Andrew. "Religious Pluralism as an Epiphenomenon of Postmodern Perspectivism." In *Theology and Religions: A Dialogue*, edited by Viggo Mortensen, 430–42. Grand Rapids: Eerdmans, 2003.

Knitter, Paul F. *Jesus and the Other Names: Christian Mission and Global Responsibility*. Maryknoll, NY: Orbis, 1996.

Marty, Martin E. "Pluralism, Religious." In *Dictionary of Christianity in America*, edited by Daniel G. Reid, 911. Downers Grove, IL: InterVarsity, 1990.

Netland, Harold A. *Encountering Religious Pluralism: The Challenge to Christian Faith and Mission*. Downers Grove, IL: InterVarsity, 2001.

Plantinga, Richard J., ed. *Christianity and Plurality: Classic and Contemporary Readings*. Malden, MA: Blackwell, 1999.

Smith, Wilfred Cantwell. *Towards a World Theology: Faith and the Comparative History of Religion*. Philadelphia: Westminster, 1981.

Visser 't Hooft, Willem Adolf. "Pluralism—Temptation or Opportunity." *The Ecumenical Review* 18 (April 1966) 129–49.

Part 1

Biblical and Patristics Perspectives

Chapter 1

"Yhwh Our God Yhwh One"
Religious Plurality and the Old Testament[1]

John Goldingay

WHAT ATTITUDE DOES THE Old Testament suggest regarding religious plurality? In the first part of this essay I consider varying perspectives on this question that emerge from different parts of the Old Testament. The Old Testament as a whole offers two overarching insights. One is that it is possible to recognize foreign religions as reflecting truth about God from which Israel itself may even be able to learn; but at the same time, the Old Testament sees these religions as always in need of the illumination that can come only from knowing what Yhwh has done with Israel. So the Old Testament does not suggest that one should take a radically exclusivist attitude to other religions, as if they were simply misguided, simply the fruits of human sin, or inspired by demonic spirits. Yet one cannot simply affirm them as if they are just as valid as the Old Testament faith of Israel itself.

The closing sections of the essay suggest why this is so. The narrative nature of Old Testament faith is key to understanding its attitude to this question. The Old Testament is not simply a collection of religious

---

1. This essay is an expansion and revision of a paper written for the 1991 Tyndale Fellowship Conference on Religious Pluralism, itself revised in light of comments by Christopher J. H. Wright as respondent, and published under both our names in Clarke and Winter, *One God, One Lord*, 43–62. Copyright expired; publishing rights have reverted to author.

traditions parallel to those of other peoples, although that is one aspect of its significance. In the story of Israel that led to the story of Jesus Christ, God was doing something of decisive importance for all humanity. The Old Testament's religious tradition is therefore of unique and decisive importance to all peoples because it is part of the Christian story.

PERSPECTIVES FROM CREATION: HUMANITY'S AWARENESS OF GOD AND DISTANCE FROM GOD

Genesis 1–11 assumes that human beings are created in God's image and aware of God. Their disobedience and expulsion from God's garden did not remove the image or the awareness; this is presupposed by their religious observances in act and word (e.g., Gen 4:1, 3, 26). The God they refer to in connection with these observances is identified as Yhwh, though on the usual understanding of Exodus 6 this identification is a theological interpretation of their practice rather than an indication of the name for God they would themselves have used. They acknowledge God as creator, giver of blessing, judge, and protector, and respond to God in offering, plea, and proclamation. The chapters imply an understanding of the religious awareness of human beings in general that corresponds to the understanding of the ethical awareness of human beings expressed in Amos 1–2. They imply a universal lordship and involvement of Yhwh among all peoples that corresponds to that stated in Amos 9:7.

This understanding also bears comparison with that of Proverbs, Ecclesiastes, Job, and the Song of Songs. These works have particularly clear parallels with others from ancient Mesopotamia and Egypt. Sometimes the relationship with these involves direct dependence, as is the case with the "Thirty Sayings" in Proverbs 22–24. Sometimes the parallels are matters of theme, form, emphasis, and mode of treatment, which as such apply also to features of proverbial, skeptical, philosophical, dramatic, and erotic literature from other times and areas. In either case, non-Israelite insight is set in a new context within the religion of Yhwh (cf. Prov 1:7), but the implication of such parallels is that pagan thought has its own insight. The Old Testament pictures God's wisdom involved and reflected in creation (Prov 3:19–20; 8:22–31), and God's breath infused into human beings by virtue of their creation (e.g., Job 32:8). Both ideas suggest a theological rationale for expecting that the nature of the created world and the experience, thought, culture, and religion of the human creation will reflect something of God's truth. The Wisdom literature is thus evidence of the ability of Yahwistic faith to incorporate the insights of other cultures, recognizing its human value while removing from it idolatrous or polytheistic elements. We might thus reflect on the significance of the Wisdom tradition as a starting point for cross-cultural communication of biblical faith and interreligious dialogue.[2]

The picture of all humanity as made in God's image might seem to point in the same direction, though the Old Testament itself does not develop this idea. This lack of reference back to the motif in Genesis 1—as to other aspects of Genesis 1–3—can puzzle Christians for whom these chapters are of key theological significance. Exegetically, the meaning of "the image of God" is much disputed.[3] Further, despite the universal form of the expression, originally its point may have been to reassure Israelites of their human significance as much as directly to make a comment on humanity as a whole. So we may say that the Old Testament indeed presupposes that all humanity was made by God and has some insight into the significance of human life, but it does not use the idea of being made in God's image to express the point.

From the time of Noah, human beings in general are seen as being in a form of covenant relationship with God (Gen 6:18; 9:8–17; cf. the kinship covenant of Amos 1:9). This Noahic covenant undergirds the providential preservation of life on earth. The fundamental idea of "covenant" in Hebrew, as in English, is that of a formalized commitment in relationship; the commitment may be one-sided or more mutual. It would not have raised our eyebrows if the relationship between God and humanity in Genesis 1–2 had been described as covenantal, and it has often been interpreted as implicitly so. The absence of the actual term "covenant" in Genesis 1–2 perhaps suggests that a covenanted relationship is by definition one that needs special protection or undergirding because of known pressures on commitment, such as the human shortcomings that come to expression in Genesis 3–6. It is only when sin has become a reality that commitments need to be the subject of a covenant. It is in any case striking that God enters into such a committed relationship with humanity after the flood on the basis of their shortcomings that had clearly emerged (cf. the explicit argument of Gen 8:21—obscured by NIV).

This is not, however, the kind of special redemptive covenant relationship that Israel later enjoys, with its more explicit committed mutual relationship, which itself turned out to be insufficient to solve the problems unveiled in Genesis 1–11. The human beings in the covenant relationship initiated with Noah are not readmitted to God's garden, and they tend toward resistance of the fulfillment of their human destiny. Indeed, the events

---

2. See Eaton, *Contemplative Face*.
3. But see now Middleton, *Liberating Image*.

that follow the covenant-making in Genesis 9 underline the moral and religious shortcomings of Noah's descendants and give Genesis 1–11, as a whole, a rather gloomy cast. The chapters are a background to the necessary story of restoration that follows.

Both sides to Genesis 1–11 have implications for attitudes toward the religions of our own day. On the one hand, the religions reflect humanity's being made in God's image and being in a form of covenant relationship with God. Books such as Proverbs further reveal an attitude toward other cultures—of which their religions are a significant part—that looks at them as sources of insight and not merely as expressions of lost-ness. On the other hand, Genesis 1–11 suggests that the religions, like all human activity, belong in the context of a world that needs restoration to the destiny and the relationship with God that were intended for them, which God purposed to bring about through the covenant with Israel that culminated in the mission and accomplishment of Jesus. Similarly, books such as Proverbs, Job, Ecclesiastes, and the Song of Songs illustrate the limitations of what can be said on the basis of human experience outside of Yhwh's special involvement with Israel.

The religions can thus be viewed both positively and negatively in relation to the faith of Israel. They are not inherently demonic or merely sinful human attempts to reach God. We can learn from them. Yet they are not equally valid insights into the truth about God. They may provide a starting point and certain areas of common ground but not a finishing point. All human religion is not only inevitably tainted by our fallen life in this earth, but it can also be the very means we use to keep at arm's length the God we choose not to obey. Religion can express our rebellion as well as our response. This, of course, was as true for Israelite religion, as the prophets pointed out, and for Christian religion as for any other faith. Religion always has this duality or ambiguity—a simultaneous seeking after God our creator and fleeing from God our judge.

PERSPECTIVES FROM THE STORIES OF ISRAEL'S ANCESTORS: THE POSSIBILITIES AND LIMITATIONS OF "ECUMENICAL BONHOMIE"[4]

The stories in Genesis 12–50, following the book's opening exposition of the world's created-ness and humanity's turning away from God, speak of special acts and words in relation to Israel's ancestors in connection with a

---

4. Phrase of Wenham, "Religion of the Patriarchs."

special purpose God has for them. In a sense, these later chapters are thus moving from a more inclusive to a more exclusive attitude, but this purpose is one intended to benefit the whole world. Further, the ancestors' words and deeds do not imply the belief that other peoples in Canaan have no knowledge of God—though the ancestors do seem to establish their own places of worship, near those of the Canaanites, rather than making use of Canaanite sanctuaries. Like some other peoples in ancient Western Asia, Israel's ancestors enjoy a particular awareness of God as the God of the father, a God who enters into a special relationship with their leader, and through him guides them in their lives.

In keeping with Genesis 1–11, Genesis 12–50 presupposes that this God is the one whom later Israel worships as Yhwh. It also speaks of this God as *El*, commonly in compound with other expressions in phrases such as *El Elyon* (El Most High; Gen 14:18–22), *El Roi* (El Who Sees Me; 16:13), *El Shaddai* (El Almighty; 17:1; 28:3; 35:11; 43:14; 48:3), and *El Olam* (El Eternal; 21:33). Like its equivalent in other Semitic languages, *'il*, Hebrew *'el*, can be both a term for deity, like *'elohim* (e.g., Exod 15:2; 20:5), and an actual name for God. It is thus sometimes properly transliterated "El," and sometimes properly translated "God" or "god."

Its background as a Canaanite name for "the god par excellence, the head of the pantheon"[5] lies near the surface in Genesis 14, where Melchizedek the priest-king of Salem blesses Abram in the name of his god, "El Elyon, creator of heaven and earth" (Gen 14:19). Abram in turn takes an oath in the name of "Yhwh, El Elyon, creator of heaven and earth" (14:22). Apparently Abram and Genesis itself recognize that Melchizedek—and presumably other people in Canaan who worship El under one manifestation or another—serves the true God but does not know all there is to know about that God. It is in keeping with this recognition that Israel in due course takes over Melchizedek's city of Salem and locates Yhwh's own chief sanctuary there. "Yhwh roars from Zion" (Amos 1:2); indeed, "El, God, Yhwh" shines forth from Zion (Ps 50:1). A similar implication emerges from Abraham's calling on God as Yhwh El Olam in Gen 18:33. El Olam appears only here as a designation of Yhwh, but comparable phrases appear elsewhere to designate Canaanite deities. Such Canaanite texts also more broadly refer to El as one who blesses, promises offspring, heals, and guides in war—like Yhwh. Joseph and the Pharaoh, too, seem to work on the basis that the God they serve is the same God (see Gen 41:16, 39; and cf. the Pharaoh's giving and Joseph's accepting an Egyptian theophoric name and a wife who was a priest's daughter, 41:45).

---

5. Cross, *Canaanite Myth*, 13.

So there are a number of correspondences between Yhwh and El as the Canaanites know him, but these correspondences do not constitute identity. They do not indicate that Canaanite and Israelite faith are identical or equally valid alternatives dependent on where you happen to live. From the perspective of the historical development of religions, it might be feasible to see Yahwism as a mutation from Western Asian religion, as Christianity was a mutation from Judaism, but this does not imply that the mutation is of similar status to its parent; rather the opposite. Canaanite religion had its insight and limited validity, but what God began to do with Abram was something of far-reaching significance, even for the Canaanites themselves. The process was not merely syncretistic in a natural development of human religious insights. In dealing with the ancestors of Israel, the living God, later disclosed as Yhwh, made an accommodation to the names and forms of deity then known in their cultural setting. This does not thereby endorse every aspect of Canaanite El worship. The purpose of God's particular action in the history of Israel is ultimately that God, as the saving and covenantal God Yhwh, should be known fully and worshiped exclusively by those who as yet imperfectly know him as El. The end result of what God began to do through Abram was of significance for the Canaanites precisely because it critiqued and rejected Canaanite religion.

It has been suggested that biblical faith emerged in a context of multiple religious options, but we must understand the religio-cultural context of that time. People did not think in terms of options, and these options were not multiple. Abraham lived in a context of one faith in Babylon and another in Canaan. He was summoned out of the first in order to begin a different narrative. He was then content to live that narrative alongside Canaanites such as Melchizedek, who lived their own narrative. What to do with the difference between these narratives is God's business.

The human perspective changes over time. In the context of pre-modernity, people had one religious option but accepted that other people lived by other narratives. In the context of modernity, people did not allow others to live by different religious options. In the context of postmodernity, everybody has his or her own story.

PERSPECTIVES FROM EXODUS AND SINAI: THE DISTINCTIVE IMPORTANCE OF YHWH'S ACTS OF REDEMPTION

The distinctive foundation of Israelite faith is that the true God, El Most High the creator of heaven and earth, Eternal and Almighty, has acted in a particularly significant way in relation to Israel. God gives concrete expression to the relationship with, and guiding of, the particular people whose story Genesis 12–50 tells, by bringing them out of service to Egypt and into service of Yhwh, entering into covenant with them at Sinai. This God goes on to give them the whole land of Canaan as a secure home. All this happens in fulfillment of specific promises made to their ancestors long before. That gives new content to their understanding of the God they shared with the Canaanites. This new content was anticipated in this God's self-revelation to Moses as Yhwh—even if that name was already known, perhaps even as an epithet of El—and henceforth is reflected in the centrality of the name Yhwh. The deity of these other religions is now more fully known in Israel, ultimately so that this God may be more fully known among other peoples, too. The creator's victory over Sea[6] has been won in history. El's decrees and judgments are delivered on earth at Sinai.

It is still the deity worshiped within these other religions who is more fully known here, and it is apparently assumed that Israel can still learn from these other religions. Many religious observances and concepts in Israel correspond to those of other Western Asian peoples, and for that matter, to those of traditional religions elsewhere. Even though there were parallels with traditional religions at a number of points, Israelite and other religions developed independently. Since priesthood and sacrifice are common human institutions, we need not imagine Israel "borrowing" these ideas from Canaan. In other instances, rituals or practices were borrowed and adapted from contemporary cultures. Perhaps it makes little theological difference which of these routes applies in different instances; either way, God expects Israel to use human instincts in order to think of Yhwh, and to worship Yhwh.

Thus the significance of the exodus is brought out by the reuse of motifs from Canaanite myth expressed in terms of a victory over Sea. The Mesha stone with its reference to the "ban" suggests that Israel's theology and practice of war-making follow the pattern and theology of war elsewhere in Palestine. The Tent of Exodus 25–40 follows Canaanite models for a dwelling of El, in its framework construction, its curtains embroidered with cherubim, and its throne flanked by cherubim. Such adaptation continues with the building of the temple, the religion of the Psalter, and the ideology of kingship—divine and human—reflected there. It continues in the oracles of the prophets, whose admission to the council of Yhwh is an admission to that of El—the phrase comes in Psalm 82—where they overhear El giving judgment, and the visionary symbolism of the apocalypses. Occasional

---

6. Ibid., 88.

specific texts indicate concrete dependence (see Psalm 104). This is not to say that these institutions, ideas, or texts are unchanged when they feature within Yahwism, but that it was able to reach its own mature expression with their aid.

We have noted that the Old Testament treats worship of El offered by Israelites and non-Israelites as worship of the true God. The story of Jonah presupposes that Yhwh alone is God, but it does not picture either the Ninevites or the sailors consciously relating to Yhwh, as Jonah does. Yet their fasting and crying to God (ʾelohim) meets with a response from the one whom Jonah can call ʾelohim, Yhwh, and El.

Indeed, Deuteronomy suggests that worship of other deities by non-Israelites is ordained by God (see Deut 4:19; cf. 32:8–9).[7] This may be an example of the way the Old Testament attributes to Yhwh as sole cause certain phenomena that we tend to attribute to secondary human volition—as it does, for example, in some cases of human lying, or disobedience, or hardening of the heart. If Israelites observed that other nations worshiped their own deities, and if Yhwh was sovereign high God over all, then Yhwh must in some way be responsible for the fact. However, seeing Yhwh as bearing responsibility for all events still leaves a theological question unresolved (cf. Ezek 20:25). There remains a tension between the stance of these Deuteronomic texts and the expectation commonly expressed in the Psalms that all peoples should or will come to acknowledge Yhwh as Lord of all the world. Perhaps the first is an interim acceptance, and the second God's ultimate purpose.

Such interim acceptance has to be interpreted, however, in the light of the later fuller awareness of the inadequacy of such religion. The Bible does not hint that in finally coming to acknowledge Yhwh these peoples' own religion finds its fulfillment. Rather, the acknowledgment of Yhwh exposes the inadequacy of any earlier religious understandings. Once the fullness of Yhwh's self-revelation is earthed in Israel, the way is open to a critique of other gods and religions, and to the expectation that one day all peoples will acknowledge that truth and salvation are to be found in Yhwh alone. They will then either join Israel in worshiping and obeying Yhwh, or face a destiny of judgment and destruction. The progress of history thus does change things. Joshua's renewal of the covenant (Joshua 24) implies that, whatever kinds of polytheistic worship may have been part of Israel's ancestry, polytheism was no longer appropriate in light of Yhwh's great redemptive achievements in relation to Israel. Fresh choices had to be made "today."

---

7. See, e.g., NRSV and NIV marginal comment, following the Qumran ms. and LXX.

This seems consistent with Paul's affirmation of God's apparently differential attitude to human religion at different stages of either history or awareness (Acts 17:27–31). The knowledge of Christ requires repentance even from things God had previously overlooked.

On the other hand, the Old Testament does not explicitly base its condemnations of other peoples on the grounds that they believe in the wrong gods. Condemnation of the nations, where reasons are given, is usually based on their moral and social behavior (see the oracles against the nations; e.g., Amos 1–2; Isaiah 13–23). Condemnation of religious deficiency is reserved for the people of God (cf. Amos 2). The gods of the nations are regarded as simply impotent. Worship of them is not so much culpable as futile. They cannot save. So, whether Jonah's sailors or the Ninevites pray to Yhwh consciously or to whomever they recognize as God, it is Yhwh who saves them. The whole point of much of the mockery of other gods by Elijah—but even more so in Isaiah 40–55—is that when the crucial moment comes, they are ridiculously powerless to save. Worse, they are an encumbrance to their worshipers. It is Yhwh alone who saves.

Deuteronomy 32 does not merely allocate the worship of other deities to different peoples. Yhwh allocates the peoples to these actual deities. These are not merely figments of the peoples' imaginations. They are actual entities under Yhwh's sovereignty. Admittedly they do not always submit to that sovereignty (cf. Psalm 82). Further, whether they do so or not, they have no power of their own—they are merely Yhwh's underlings.

In Old Testament terms, then, the question whether there is salvation in other religions is a non-question. There is salvation in no religion because religions do not save. Not even Israel's religion saved them. It was at best a response to Yhwh, the living God who had saved them. And only this God can save. When the nations come over to Israel, in the prophet's vision, it will not be to say, "Now we realize that your religion is the best one," but to acknowledge, "In Yhwh alone is salvation" (Isa 45:14, 24). When people such as Jethro or Rahab come to acknowledge Yhwh, it is on the basis of a realization that the story they have been told about Yhwh demonstrates this truth. It would be an exaggeration to say that Old Testament faith was not ethnic—it was an ethnic group to which Yhwh reached out. But belonging to the right ethnic group was not enough—the members of this ethnic group needed to make their response to Yhwh. Not belonging to this ethnic group was no bar to making its story one's own, and thus being adopted into it.

On the part of Israelites themselves, the Old Testament rejects worship of any deity alongside the true God (e.g., Exod 20:3). Their confession is, "Yhwh our God Yhwh one" (Deut 6:4): Yhwh is the object of their entire commitment. The worship of El need not contravene this commitment because it is a form of worship of Yhwh. The worship of deities distinguishable from Yhwh does contravene it.

We might then regard adherence to an African traditional religion as a God-given starting point for people on their way to recognizing that the definitive acts of God are found in the story of Israel that comes to a climax in Jesus. It might be possible to take the same stance in relation to a religion such as Islam or to British folk-religion, or to American new age religion, though here the question is complicated by the fact that these are, at least in a formal sense, post-Christian religions that explicitly or implicitly presuppose a conscious rejection of the gospel.

PERSPECTIVES FROM LIFE IN THE LAND: THE SHORTCOMINGS OF BAAL RELIGION

While the Old Testament can be implicitly open to other peoples' understandings of deity, it is by no means consistently so. There is a conflictual dimension to its view of other religions, which also needs to be seen in its context. While Joseph and the Pharaoh of his day presuppose the identification of their deity, the Pharaoh of Moses's day has notoriously forgotten Joseph and refuses to acknowledge the God of Israel. Thus while Moses can accept the identification of Yhwh and El, he must represent the opposition of Yhwh to the Egyptian gods as served by the Pharaoh. The exodus signifies the former's victory over and judgment on the latter (see Exod 12:12). The basis for Yhwh's action here is both a commitment to the descendants of Abraham and a commitment to compassion; the Pharaoh and his gods are opposed to both. A major subplot of the exodus narrative seeks to show the stages by which the Pharaoh is forced to acknowledge Yhwh.[8] No matter how positively we view the openness to other people's experience and worship of God, there are circumstances that demand a conflictual stance. In this case, it was because of rival claims to deity, resistance to God's redemptive work in history, and manifest, unrepentant oppression and injustice.

The worship of Baal—who apparently displaced El as the most prominent god among Israel's neighbors—and of other gods and goddesses, also holds a different status from the worship of El detailed in the Old Testament. Admittedly, there are hints that at certain stages Yhwh could have been worshiped under the name Baal. Baal is an ordinary noun meaning "owner" and could have been used, like 'adon (master) to acknowledge the authority of Yhwh (cf. Hos 2:16). Behind the biblical text itself there may be what Frank

---

8. The train of thought runs through Exod 5:2; 7:5, 17; 8:10, 22; 9:15, 29; 14:18, 25.

Moore Cross calls a conflation of El and Baal in the person of Yhwh.[9] In the Old Testament itself, however, the worship of Yhwh through use of the word Baal is never accepted. Even a name such as Eshbaal (man of Baal, 1 Chr 8:33) is altered to Ishboshet (man of shame; 2 Sam 2:8). Baal religion is seen as a negative influence on Israelite religion. Baal sanctuaries are to be destroyed rather than adapted (Deuteronomy 7 and 12). The Baalistic influence on Israel's religion introduced by Solomon is a perversion. Thus worship of God as El is affirmed and worship of God as Baal is repudiated. Israel does not have to choose between Yhwh and El but does have to choose between Yhwh and Baal (1 Kgs 18:21, cf. Josh 24:14–15).[10]

The Old Testament is not explicit about the basis for this contrast in attitudes to the religion of El and that of Baal. Perhaps the high god El could more easily become the sole God Yhwh than the subordinate Baal could; worship of Baal implied worship of gods other than Yhwh, rather than worship of Yhwh as Baal. The historical power of El was that shown in Israel's key experiences of exodus from Egypt and conquest of Palestine—even if the nature of El, not least as one failing to exercise real control in heaven, would need redefining in the light of those experiences. Baal, too, is involved with war, but his additional involvement with fertility might make it more important for Yhwh to be distanced from Baal, lest questions of fertility become too important within Yahwism and lest the way they are approached within Baalism affects Yahwism. Israel's history recalled the way Baal-worship led the wilderness generation into sexual immorality (Num 25:13), and Hosea attacks the way Israel let itself be influenced by this aspect of Canaanite religion. Yet the nature of Yhwh also gained definition under the influence of Baalism as Yhwh was more explicitly declared to be lord of the crops and was portrayed as Israel's own lover. In coming to describe the relationship between Yhwh and Israel in marriage terms, Hosea thus adopts language and imagery from Canaan even while attacking the theology that the Canaanites expressed by means of it.[11] If we reflect on the contexts in which the conflicts between Yhwh and the gods of Egypt and the Baals of Canaan is characteristically presented, it becomes clear that these had a moral dimension that provides some help for our own evaluation of human religions and cultures.

9. Cross, *Canaanite Myth*, 163.

10. I refer here and elsewhere to the Old Testament's own stance to such questions. Both the Old Testament and archeological discoveries suggest that in its actual practice Israelite religion was much more open-minded than their prophets and scriptures suggest.

11. Cf. Board for Mission and Unity, §28; and Senior and Stuhlmueller, *Biblical Foundation*, ch. 1–5.

The presenting cause of Yhwh's hostility toward the Pharaoh—god himself and representative of the gods of Egypt—is the Pharaoh's oppression of the Hebrews. There is no such conflict and hostility in the narratives of Genesis when first Joseph, and then his brothers, have their long interaction with Egypt. On the contrary, there is a recognition of the God of Joseph by the then Pharaoh (e.g., Genesis 41) in a way echoed later in Daniel. But the exodus Pharaoh, having initiated a state policy of oppression that has political, economic, social, and spiritual aspects, refuses to acknowledge the God of Moses (Exod 5:2). It is this that rouses Yhwh to action—faithful action in the biblical sense of acting against the oppressor and rescuing the oppressed. The destruction of the Pharaoh is thus a declaration of Yhwh's opposition to a religion that sanctions a social order that in turn sanctions inhumanity and oppression.

The more protracted struggle with Baalism, lasting from the very emergence of Israel in Canaan through the ministries of all the preexilic prophets, has similar features. From the specific condemnations of Baalism in the Torah (e.g., Leviticus 18; 20; Deuteronomy 7) to its characterization in prophetic material such as Hosea and Jeremiah, it can be seen to have included practices that were degrading or destructive or both, such as sexual rites and child sacrifice, as well as occult arts. The Old Testament implicitly argues that these were prevalent at the time of Israel's emergence in Canaan in a way that had not been the case in the era of Israel's ancestors. The less conflictual attitude to Canaanite religion in Genesis goes along with the statement that "the iniquity of the Amorites is not yet full" (Gen 15:16), whereas the wrongdoing of the later inhabitants of the land is enough to make the land itself vomit them out (Lev 18:24–28).

In other words, we can discern again a differential response to other religions, related to the kind of social and moral characteristics they foster among their adherents.[12] What Elijah (and Yhwh) so vehemently opposed was not merely the worship of the wrong God—or rather of a no-god, as focused on Mount Carmel—but the hijacking of the whole social, economic, and legal ethos of Israel by the religious vandalism of Jezebel's Phoenician Baalism, as focused in the Naboth incident (1 Kgs 21). The struggle was not simply over what was the right religion but over what was a right and just society for Naboth to live in. Baal religion undergirded—or at least imposed no restraint on—the way Ahab and Jezebel treated Naboth. It could be argued, therefore, that the moral, social, and cultural effects of a major religious tradition do give us some grounds for a discriminating response to

---

12. See the discussion of this point in Wright, *Living as the People of God*, 31–48, and Wright, *Old Testament Ethics*.

it—though this can be as uncomfortable an argument for Christianity as a cultural religion as for any other.

We have noted that the Old Testament is ambivalent about Israel's own means of worship. Sacrifice and temple are accepted, along with monarchy and priesthood, as issuing from human instincts rather than divine initiatives. But women priests are not accepted, and neither is worship by means of an image of God. This last piece is a distinctive feature of Israel's religion of the Old Testament, though one might wish to be clearer why this is so. In popular Christian thinking, the reason for prohibiting images has been the essentially non-physical nature of God, but the Old Testament does not make this point, and arguably both the idea of humanity's being in God's image and the idea of incarnation are difficult to reconcile with it. The Decalogue juxtaposes and interweaves the prohibition on worshiping Yhwh by means of an image with the prohibition on worshiping other gods, and it may imply the conviction that the one easily slides into the other: an image could as easily be of Yhwh or of Baal, so we will be wise to avoid images as part of avoiding Baalism. The argument of Deuteronomy 4 is that a silent, static image cannot represent the essentially dynamic speaking and acting nature of Yhwh, and this fits the polemic of Isaiah 44 and 46 against both domestic images and national images. But 2 Samuel 7 uses parallel arguments against the building of a temple, and then allows it. Christian history certainly illustrates the way images can be a snare, but the Orthodox icon tradition also illustrates how they can be a means of true worship.

Does such openness allow a religion to come to full flowering as Yhwh's nature is more clearly grasped and Yhwh's lordship is more fully acknowledged? Or does it turn the religion into something other than itself and lead to the ignoring of Yhwh's nature and expectations? But we have to come to terms with the fact that we do not know the rationale for a number of God's requirements of Israel in religious affairs, and that a number of these requirements may be culture-relative or simply arbitrary. In deciding about the adapting or avoiding of different humanly devised forms of worship, it seems likely that a significant part is played by tactical considerations regarding what may do more harm than good. Another factor often underlying Yhwh's requirements of Israel is simply the desire that they should look and behave differently, as a means of advertising to them and to other peoples that they are different in the sense of having a distinctive place in God's purpose. The Cornelius story marks the termination of the period when God operates by this principle, though the new period it introduces is not one in which differences between one religion and another can now be ignored but rather one in which they can now be confronted rather than avoided.

PERSPECTIVES FROM THE BABYLONIAN AND PERSIAN PERIODS: THE INTERRELATION OF UNIVERSALISM AND EXCLUSIVISM

The stances taken in the literature that relates to the Babylonian and Persian periods offer further pointers regarding the contextual nature of attitudes to other religions and their adherents. Prophecies in Isaiah 40–55 take a polemical stance over against the Babylonian gods Bel and Nebo, the equivalents of El and Baal. Either Yhwh is God, or they are gods; the possibility of seeing Bel as the name under which the Babylonians worship the one God is not entertained. Yhwh alone is creator, Yhwh alone rules in heaven, Yhwh alone acts in world events, and Yhwh alone reveals the significance of those events (see Isa 40:12–26; 41:1–7, 21–29; 42:5–9; 46; and cf. Jer 10). Babylon and its religion are to be put down. The affirmation that Yhwh creates both light and darkness and is responsible for both prosperity and disaster (Isa 45:7) perhaps sets itself over against the dualism of Babylonian religion.

In its mono-Yahwism and its affirmation of Yhwh's commitment to Israel, Isaiah 40–55 might be seen as the most exclusivist and nationalist section of the Old Testament. Yet alongside this aspect of its stance is a conviction that Yhwh's relationship with Israel is of significance for the whole world, a conviction that has often made these chapters seem the most universalist in the Old Testament. The same two-stranded attitude continues in Isaiah 56–66. Perhaps one implication is that Yhwh offers people alternative scenarios: on the basis of what they see Yhwh doing with Israel, the nations will come to acknowledge that Yhwh alone is God, but they choose whether they do so willingly and joyously, or unwillingly and without profit.

In contrast to Isaiah 40–55, Ezra-Nehemiah and Daniel identify Yhwh as the God of heaven, a title that other peoples within the Persian empire could give to their chief god (see Ezra 1:2; 5:11–12; 6:9–10; 7:12, 21, 23; Neh 1:4–5; 2:4, 20; Dan 2:18–19, 37, 44; in 5:23, "the Lord of heaven"). Daniel, Ezra, and Nehemiah are involved in the service of the Persian court, and like Joseph, Daniel, and his friends, accept a courtly education and foreign names, with their religious implications. At the same time, Ezra and Nehemiah insist on keeping the people of Yhwh separate from the surrounding peoples and their religions, while Daniel insists on the importance of Jews maintaining their distinctive faithfulness to their God and their purity (Dan 1), and also their distinctive worship (Dan 3) and piety (Dan 6).

It is an oversimplification to suggest that the separatist strand to Ezra-Nehemiah characterizes the Second Temple period as a whole, and contrasts with a more inclusive attitude earlier. We have noted that Ezra and Nehemiah are capable of expressing their theology with the help of the terms of the surrounding culture and religion, as Exodus and Hosea do. Exodus, Deuteronomy, and Hosea are separatist in a parallel sense to the one that applies to Ezra and Nehemiah. Isaiah 19 belongs among a number of passages in the prophets that are usually listed as especially inclusivist, and that are usually dated during the Second Temple period. We have noted that Isaiah 40–55, often reckoned the universalist highpoint of the Old Testament, includes the Old Testament's most scathing treatment of other religions. The stance the Old Testament takes to other religions apparently varies not only with the nature of the religion but also with the nature of the power and the pressure exercised by its adherents, but both openness and guardedness seem to feature in all contexts.[13]

PERSPECTIVES FROM THE GREEK PERIOD: THE CREATIVITY OF EXCLUSIVENESS

Similar considerations to the ones we have noted in the previous section arise from the closing scene of the period covered by the Old Testament, related in the visions in Daniel. Like Daniel (see Dan 5:23), the Syrian king, Antiochus, seems to have presupposed that Yhwh could be identified with "the Lord of Heaven," the Syrian high god. In some sense or in some periods, one might have expected Jews to accept this assumption, but the visions in Daniel presuppose that the two are incompatible. To accede to the religious prescriptions of the king would be to abandon one's commitment to the God of Israel. Once more the Old Testament suggests that there is a time or a case for openness to other religions, and a time for recognizing that this risks the flourishing of Israelite religion and the Israelite people.

It is simplistic and misleading for the Anglican document *Towards a Theology for Inter-Faith Dialogue* to say that it is "when Israel is most open to others that she is most creative" while "exclusiveness and isolation . . . have an impoverishing effect."[14] Out of a context of "exclusiveness and isolation," Daniel is rather a creative book. The pluralistic context of Israel's life suggests that Israel's ways of relating to other religions ought to be a resource for us in a situation that is now more like post-exilic Israel's than the Western church has experienced for some time. But to affirm "openness not isolation"[15] is only to simplify down a characteristic scriptural dialectic

---

13. The often-quoted Mal 1:11 is of such uncertain significance that it seems unwise to argue from it.
14. Board for Mission and Unity, *Towards a Theology*, 30.
15. Ibid., 31.

in the opposite direction to the one that the report elsewhere deplores when it does not match its own instincts.[16]

THE NARRATIVE NATURE OF BIBLICAL FAITH

If other religions make a starting point in relating to God but not a finishing point, the fundamental reason lies in the nature of the gospel. Maurice Wiles, for example, offers what he intends as an uncontroversial summary of the essential nature of the Christian faith in terms of convictions about the reality and nature of God; for example, as love.[17] If one understands scriptural faith to focus on such eternal truths about God, then it may be difficult to identify the essential shortcoming in a religion. A religion may have a secure grasp of such truths. There are, after all, other ancient and modern religions that include belief in a God who is just and loving, creator, committed to one's own people, and who expects a response from people in prayer, worship, obedience, and concern for justice. Likewise, one may see the essential nature of Christian faith as involving profound religious experiences. A friend of mine thus speaks of a U2 concert as "church." If so, this will again suggest other criteria for comparing different faiths. In the Old Testament, sacred institutions such as sacrifice, priesthood, monarchy, and temple are pictured as devised by human beings, harnessed with partial success to God's purpose, but inclined to contribute to the paganization of Israel. Some of these institutions may have distinctive theological meaning within Israelite religion, but it would be precarious to base the decisive significance of Israel's faith on its having features of such a kind.

The significance of Israelite religion does not lie in itself or in the number of distinctive features we can chalk up for it in comparison with other religions. This is always a risky business because parallels elsewhere then have a way of emerging. Israel's significance lay in its status as witness to the deeds of the living, active, saving God. This is the repeated thrust of Isaiah 40–55: written in the context of overbearing religious plurality, the prophet did not encourage Israel to compare its religion with the Babylonians' and feel superior, but directed its thoughts to the acts of Yhwh in its actual history and declared, "You are Yhwh's witnesses."

The framework of Old Testament faith, like that of New Testament faith, takes narrative form. It is a declaration about things God has done.

16. Ibid., 46. It is significantly ironic, too, that *Towards a Theology* is capable of what now seems a rather old-fashionedly anti-Jewish tone in the way it downgrades Second Temple Judaism in order to commend the New Testament (see 33, 35, 36).

17. Wiles, *Explorations in Theology*, 61.

It is good news, not a good idea. It states that in the history of Israel and of Jesus, God has acted in love to restore humanity to God and to its destiny. The gospel is the news that God created the world, stayed involved with it when it went wrong, became involved with Israel in order to put it right, commissioned his son to become a Jew himself, let him die, and raised him to a transformed life. Christian faith involves the conviction that this story offers the essential key to what it means to be human.

It is the narrative nature of this gospel that binds together the Old Testament and the New Testament and gives the Old Testament a distinctive place in relation to the Christian gospel. In this sense there cannot be "other Old Testaments" for people with a background in other religions. There is a distinctive sense in which Jesus came as the climax to the story of Israel. This is not to imply that God was simply absent from these other people's stories. Walter Moberly speaks of the story of Israel's ancestors as "the Old Testament of the Old Testament"—it leads into Israel's story as Israel's story leads into the story of Jesus and the church.[18] One might then see Genesis 1–11 as "the Old Testament of the Old Testament of the Old Testament"—the story of the world leads into the story of Israel's ancestors. And we might see the stories of other peoples and other religions as testimonies to God's involvement with them and as declarations of the significance of their stories, analogous to the story of God's involvement with the nations in Genesis 1–11. But the Old Testament itself is still *the* Old Testament.

It is sometimes argued that translation is a fundamentally impossible enterprise. A mediating view on this question is the suggestion that narrative is fundamentally translatable in a way that many other genres are not. Poetry loses in translation, which means the wisdom books, the Psalms, and the prophets lose. Paul's discursive theology also takes a lot of translation, because it takes a lot of interpretation—it is very dense because of its use of metaphor, and it is very contextual. But a story is another matter. Stories lose less in translation. There is then some irony in the fact that while Paul kept in touch with the narrative nature of the gospel, the Church Fathers in their subsequent discursive theological work had a harder time doing so. One fateful development of their centuries was the reworking of the gospel into Greek terms, which is often called a translation into Greek concepts; but it was more than translation. The reworking involved the effective abandonment of the narrative dynamic of Christian faith.

It is as well that the principle of translatability applies especially to narrative, because of the fact that the Bible is dominated by narrative for the reason just suggested. It is not merely a statistical fact but one that reflects

---

18. Moberly, *Old Testament*.

the nature of scriptural faith, as not a collection of concepts—even declarations such as "Yhwh is God" or "Jesus is Lord"—but a story, a piece of news, a gospel. The scriptural narrative becomes a gospel again when its implications are worked out in a context, as happens in different ways within scripture and then in many subsequent different contexts.

It is in this way that "the vital place of mother-tongue Scriptures . . . resides in the fact that by enabling us [to] 'hear in our own language[s] the wonderful things of God . . .' (Acts 2:11), they create resonances and reverberations which make other overlapping recognitions occur."[19] Mother-tongue scriptures enable the articulation of the gospel because they make it possible to work out how that narrative is gospel in a context. It would not be surprising if other religions possess narratives that illustrate the significance of the biblical narrative and illumine the nature of the gospel. They will thus bring blessing to people who share the gospel with people of this culture and make it possible for them as storytellers to respond to that gospel. But they are not the gospel story.

The process of contextualizing the gospel story may also lead to loss of understanding. The Christian church in the West learned to tell that story in a predominantly legal framework. God is judge, human wrongdoing is the breaking of the law, Jesus pays the legal penalty for sin, and that enables believers to be acquitted. This is only a marginally biblical framework for understanding the gospel. It came to be prominent in the Western Church in a particular cultural context, but then it came to have a life of its own. In present Western culture such a legal way of looking at the relationship of God and humanity has less power than it had a millennium ago, but the church has a hard time escaping from this way of telling the scriptural story into a more relational way of explaining the gospel's significance.

In a context of religious plurality, the nature of the gospel is worked out afresh as the biblical story is set alongside another religion's story, or its non-story nature. This means that the people who tell the story appreciate it afresh, as happens when a Ghanaian Christian comes to see Jesus as ancestor or elder brother. It also means that the people who hear the story for the first time see how the story is good news for them in their particularity. It is specifically the context of the biblical narrative that constitutes the context that readers enter in order to participate in its world of meaning and experience. I have heard it suggested that non-Western cultures have retained an awareness of the importance of narrative that modernity encouraged Western cultures to slough off—in the rarified form in which one meets them in

---

19. See K. Bediako's essay in this volume (Chapter 2, 31–45).

theology and philosophy. So communicating the gospel is aided by the fact that the gospel takes narrative form.

THE NARRATIVE NATURE OF BIBLICAL FAITH AND RELIGIOUS DIALOGUE

Awareness of the narrative nature of the gospel thus gives us a point of contact with people living in other religious contexts. But it also distances us from them, because it makes the claim that this narrative is of unique importance. This is so not because of its nature as revelation but because it tells of the key events that determine the way God relates to the world. As a matter of fact, God created the world as a place that was good and not half-finished, to contradict a common modern myth. When humanity then flouted God's word, God determined to "carry" its wrongdoing—the literal meaning of the Hebrew word routinely translated "forgive"; that is, God determined to put up with it, not to be put off by it, to pay the price for it in God's own being in order to keep the relationship going. God did that through Israel's story in a way that came to a climax in the cross, where God went so far as to let Jewish and Gentile humanity do the last thing it could possibly do by way of rejection, by putting God to death; and God carried that too, and thereby frustrated it. God refused to be overcome by it, in either sense of "overcome." God did not give up on the relationship, nor did God agree to stay dead. Jesus's resurrection and his appearing to his disciples is the indication that he rejects both of these.

This story is a revelation of the nature of God, but it is that because it is more fundamentally an account of something God did once-for-all. In other religions, as in Hollywood movies, there might be promises of this story, or prophecies of it, or metaphors for it, or even revelations of it, but there cannot be regular narratives of it, because these narratives need to come from the people who experienced these events and who in the scriptures give their testimony to them.

Religious plurality involves competing narratives. Israel's neighbors had very different narratives from Israel's about the origin of the world, and Genesis 1 seems to have been written to counter these by giving a very different narrative account of deity, the world, and humanity. The New Testament story is intolerant and exclusive in its claim that cross and resurrection are the final and effective expression of God's resistance to being overcome by humanity. The Holy Spirit may indeed be involved in enabling different peoples to perceive and respond to insights about God and about life in the context of many ways of living religiously, but all such possible insights need to be brought into the context of the gospel expressed in the biblical narrative.

In the church in Southern California, for instance, at least in the Anglo-American church, I am particularly aware of two influential narratives. One is the narrative of "my individual spiritual journey." A large local church in Pasadena routinely welcomes people to worship "wherever you are on your journey of faith." Individual students at Fuller Theological Seminary keep spiritual journals, implying the conviction that their journey matters. They have individual spiritual directors, guides on this journey. The other narrative is the story of the United States, its finding of its own freedom—July Fourth, Independence Day, is a very big event; it seems odd that the world's great superpower should make such an issue of its independence—and its receiving a vocation from God to bring democracy to the world.

In relation to the first of these narratives, the church assumes that I and my personal relationship with God is the key to understanding the significance of Christian faith, not noticing that if this were so one would expect the Bible to be more like a book on spirituality. In relation to the second narrative, the church often uncritically accepts the identification of church and nation that is a paradoxical feature of the United States. It formally keeps church and state separate but substantially intertwines them in a way that does not occur in countries where there is still a church-state connection but where church and culture are more overtly separate.

Churches commonly affirm one or other, or both, of those two narratives and do not set them in the context of the gospel narrative to let it test them, broaden them, or refute them. Our situation is thus rather similar to that which occurs in the Old Testament story. Jeremiah, for example, charged that Israel lived by the Canaanites' narrative, expressed in the stories of Baal and Anat, more than by the story of the exodus and Sinai. Israel did not consciously abandon this story but lived as if that other narrative, with its direct potential for understanding the crucial processes whereby the crops grew each year, was the true one.

Instead, we are called to invite people to tell their story and then see how that illumines the gospel and how the gospel illumines it, sets it in a new context, and relativizes it. It is when another narrative threatens to overwhelm the scriptural narrative that we must stand against it. It is then that it becomes demonic.

Both the Old Testament and the New Testament are exclusivist in the sense that they believe in the supreme importance of the history that begins with the promise to Israel's ancestors and the exodus. Both are universalist in the sense that they believe that this history is designed to embrace all peoples; its benefits are not simply for Israel or the church. Thus a passage such as Isa 2:2–4 shares God's dream that at the End all peoples will come to learn from Yhwh in Jerusalem. The situation in Genesis 1–2 is more than restored.

The shortcoming of other religions is that they cannot, and thus do not, focus on this story. Humanity's problem was not merely lack of knowledge concerning the nature of God and humanity but the need for restoration of the relationship between these two, so that humanity may realize its destiny. We needed redemption, not merely revelation. Whatever insight other religions may have on the nature of God and humanity, they lack the key to the restoration of the relationship and the realization of the destiny, because this lies in what God did in Israel and in Christ. Biblical religion is not primarily another set of religious teachings about God but a witness to what God did to save creation. That witness does generate insights about God and creation, some of which are so fundamental to the reality of "the way things are" that they are held in common with the religious understandings of other groups of human beings made in God's image. But merely listing the common beliefs between biblical faith and other religions—like drawing parallels between movies and the gospel—does not dissolve the significance of the Bible as witness to the unique events by which God has acted to restore creation.[20]

Claiming to be witnesses to the one sequence of deeds whereby God acted to redeem the world inevitably smacks of arrogance, as well as being un-postmodern. We can only ask people to look in the direction we are pointing and make their judgment *a posteriori*, not *a priori*. Our problem then will be that the Christian religion has also often proved itself incapable of encompassing the gospel or reflecting it, so that the response of someone who belongs to another religion can understandably be that even if Christianity has rightly diagnosed the human problem, it has still not identified the solution.

CONCLUSION

In his book *Uncompleted Mission: Christianity and Exclusivism*, Kwesi A. Dickson notes that there are "exclusivist" and "open" strands within the Old Testament's attitude to other religions and cultures. He sees the New Testament as taking up the first rather than the second, regrets that modern Christian mission has followed—partly through its involvement with imperialist expansionism—and argues for the opposite stance.[21] I have argued

20. Cf. De Ridder, *Discipling the Nations*, 43–62.
21. Dickson, *Uncompleted Mission*.

that there are good theological reasons why the Old Testament has both exclusivist and open strands, and that we should take this as our model.

BIBLIOGRAPHY

Board for Mission and Unity of the General Synod of the Church of England. *Towards a Theology for Inter-Faith Dialogue*. London: CIO, 1984.

Clarke, Andrew D., and Bruce W. Winter, eds. *One God, One Lord: Christianity in a World of Religious Pluralism*. Grand Rapids: Baker, 1992.

Cross, Frank Moore. *Canaanite Myth and Hebrew Epic: Essays in the History of the Religion of Israel*. Cambridge, MA: Harvard University Press, 1973.

De Ridder, Richard R. *Discipling the Nations*. Grand Rapids: Baker, 1971.

Dickson, Kwesi A. *Uncompleted Mission: Christianity and Exclusivism*. Maryknoll, NY: Orbis, 1991.

Eaton, John. *The Contemplative Face of Old Testament Wisdom in the Context of World Religions*. Philadelphia: Trinity, 1989.

Middleton, J. Richard. *The Liberating Image: The Imago Dei in Genesis 1*. Grand Rapids: Brazos, 2005.

Moberly, R. W. L. *The Old Testament of the Old Testament: Patriarchal Narratives and Mosaic Yahwism*. Minneapolis: Fortress, 1992.

Senior, Donald, and Carroll Stuhlmueller. *The Biblical Foundations for Mission*. Maryknoll, NY: Orbis, 1983.

Wenham, Gordon J. "The Religion of the Patriarchs." In *Essays on the Patriarchal Narrative*, edited by A. R. Millard and D. J. Wiseman, 161–95. Winona Lake, IN: Eisenbrauns, 1983.

Wiles, Maurice F. *Explorations in Theology* 4. London: SCM, 1979.

Wright, Christopher J. H. "The Authority of Scripture in an Age of Relativism: Old Testament Perspectives." In *The Gospel in the Modern World: A Tribute to John Stott*, edited by Martyn Eden and David F. Wells, 331–48. Leicester: Intervarsity, 1991.

———. *An Eye for an Eye*. Downers Grove, IL: InterVarsity, 1983.

———. *Living as the People of God: The Relevance of Old Testament Ethics*. Leicester: InterVarsity, 1983

———. *Old Testament Ethics for the People of God*. Downers Grove, IL: InterVarsity, 2004.

Chapter 2

Scripture in the Context of Religious Plurality
Aspects of the Patristic Witness and Their Analogies in Contemporary Africa

Kwame Bediako

SCRIPTURE AS VERNACULAR: THE MOTHER TONGUE AS OUR LABORATORY

CLEMENT OF ALEXANDRIA IS known to have written: "It was not alien to the inspiration of God, who gave the prophecy, also to produce the translation, and make it, as it were, Greek prophecy."[1] The sentiment may well be vintage Clement, but we can also understand how Clement would latch on to the idea. In the context in which the idea occurred, Clement was not seeking to be polemical. Clement was, above all, an evangelist and apologist for the Christian faith, and his concern, here as in all his writings, was to secure a hearing and win the confidence of Greek-speaking educated persons with whom he shared a common intellectual culture. The Greek translation that for Clement had also acquired the authoritative character

---

1. Clement, "Stromateis and Protreptikos," 22, 334, translation mine.

of "Greek prophecy" was, of course, the well-known Greek translation of Hebrew Scripture, the Jewish Bible in the Greek language, otherwise known as the Septuagint.

It is important to appreciate the full impact of the implications for Clement of the existence of this Greek prophecy. For Clement it was no less prophecy for being in Greek. Accordingly, the God who gave the prophecy in Hebrew must be understood to have intended also to communicate in Greek. The Greek prophecy was the evidence that God did, in fact, communicate in Greek!

I consider Clement to be affirming, in fact, the principle of translatability and the central role of Scripture translation for Christian mission. This has been justly recognized as among the most important developments in recent Christian history.[2] In that respect, Clement sounds uncannily modern and contemporary and contributes an important insight into our subject. I also consider that this modern circumstance brings us full circle to the process of mission by translation, which is what we are most immediately conscious of when we consider the initial encounter of the Christian faith with the Hellenistic world outside of the birthplace of the faith in Palestine.

The significance for us of that first encounter with a religiously and culturally plural world lies in the fact that it was that process of mission by translation that produced the very Scriptures with which we are concerned. Scripture as we have it now, in all its multitudinous linguistic forms, is the fruit of translation that has resulted in not only "Greek prophecy" or Spanish prophecy but also Chinese prophecy and Akan prophecy and so on, to extend Clement's illustration. This, I believe, is a helpful way of thinking of Scripture—as essentially vernacular, or mother-tongue narrative.

RELIGIOUS PLURALITY AS A PLURALITY OF RESPONSE

The other related aspect of our subject is religious plurality, under the theme of Christianity and religious plurality. Here, it seems a fair point to make that there exists a widespread tendency among Christians and non-Christians alike to think of religious plurality in terms of religious systems, as belief systems or creeds, in relation to which Christianity also functions as a belief system.

Yet it is doubtful whether Scripture itself lends support to such a view of religious plurality as a plurality of autonomous belief systems. The religious plurality that emerges from the biblical narrative is, distinctively,

---

2. See Stine, *Bible Translation*.

the plurality of persons, seen in the quality of personal response—not to be confused with individualism—to the intimations of the divine impact upon human life and on the plane of human history. Thus, participation in the covenant community of the Old Testament, despite appearances to the contrary, depended on personal obedience or disobedience to the revealed divine will. This quality of religious plurality in the Old Testament as plurality of personal response becomes intensified in the New Testament. Hence one reads the startling saying of Jesus to a Jewish audience in John 8:47: "He who belongs to God hears what God says. The reason you do not hear is that you do not belong to God" (NIV).

The eschatological vision of the great multitude "from every nation, tribe, people and language . . ." (Rev 7:9), is the conclusive picture of the biblical plurality of persons, made into one community on the basis of response from within a plurality of traditions, to the one Lord and Savior of all humankind. This was the understanding Justin Martyr came to in his attempt to establish the grounds for Christian self-consciousness in terms meaningful to the cultural and intellectual tradition he shared with his Hellenistic opponents[3] when he claimed that in Hellenistic tradition, as in the Israelite tradition, there were persons who could be described as "Christians" before the time of Christ because they witnessed to their knowledge, though partial, of the "the presence in them of an implanted seed of the logos."[4] Justin grasped firmly the Pauline insight that the truth of the Christian gospel is the truth of the person rather than of the religious tradition to which one belongs, "so that they who lived with the logos are Christians, even though they have been thought atheists; as, among the Greeks, Socrates and Heraclitus, and people like them; and among the barbarians, Abraham, and Ananias, and Asarias, and Misael, and Elias, and many others."[5]

What was the common thread uniting all these men? Socrates and Heraclitus denounced idolatry—hence the accusation of atheism—and were persecuted and even martyred for their response to the truth. In the Old Testament, Abraham is noted for his willingness to abandon the religious tradition of the past in obedience to the call of God; Ananias, Azarias, and Mishael are mentioned for their refusal to bow to the golden image set up by Nebuchadnezzar, while Elijah's significance lies in the fact that he took a firm stand for Yahweh and suffered persecution for doing so. Richard A. Norris affirms, "Christ as Logos becomes the universal mediator of the

---

3. For more detailed account of Justin and his understanding of Christ in the Hellenistic heritage, see Bediako, *Theology and Identity*, 137–73.

4. Martyr, *First and Second Apologies*, §13, 84.

5. Ibid., *First Apology* §46, 55; cf. *Second Apology* 8, 79.

knowledge of God, and as such the culmination of the history not merely of Israel but of the entire 'inhabited world.'"[6]

Justin, therefore, points us to the helpful realization that it is within the plurality of our human traditions that living religiously acquires its significance. If we have to speak of religions, then we may do so provided we understand them not so much as belief systems as ways of living religiously, being integral to the matrix in which men and women experience and respond to whatever intimations of the Divine, or of the Transcendent, they are made conscious of in their human existence.

Looked at as "a tradition of response" to the reality and disclosure of the Transcendent, therefore, every religion can be probed for the truth of the human response to the divine action within that tradition. As a tradition of response, every religion also displays within it "the same tension between conservatism and development which characterizes all human response to the call of God which comes through the new situation," notes John V. Taylor.[7] In other words, within every religion, there are indicators that point *toward* Christ, and there are indicators that point *away* from Christ. However, our concern is not so much with those indicators per se as with the *human* responses to those indicators.

It becomes possible, then, to speak of a plurality of responses within every religious tradition. Thus, it is possible to understand how one response to Old Testament religious teaching can lead to the Mishnah and the Talmud, and the rejection of the messiahship of our Lord Jesus Christ, while another response can lead to the New Testament and the recognition of the same Jesus Christ as Lord, Messiah, and Savior of the whole world.

SCRIPTURE AND THE THEOLOGICAL SIGNIFICANCE OF LANGUAGE

The importance of recognizing religions—or, as I prefer to say, ways of living religiously—as integral to the matrix within which we come to respond to the intimations of the divine impact on our lives, brings our discussion to the theological significance of language itself. Every language plays this role.

Aloysius Pieris of Sri Lanka has suggested that "language is the experience of reality, religion is its expression."[8] If this is the case, then it makes language, each language, a distinct way of apprehending and experiencing truth. The significance of Scripture translation here is that it enables a

---

6. Norris, *God and World*, 44.
7. Taylor, *Go-Between God*, 183.
8. Pieris, *Asian Theology*, 70.

people's language, and thus their experience of truth, to be connected to the reality and actuality of the living God. It is this that makes language itself into a theological category, conferring upon it "eternal significance . . . and transcendent range," as affirmed by Lamin Sanneh.[9]

Whatever our notions regarding the actual technicalities and processes of translation, the point to be made is that the end product in Scripture in a particular language provides the enabling environment for recognition and response to the living God to take place with enhanced intentionality within that experience of reality. The vital place of mother-tongue Scriptures, therefore, resides in the fact that by enabling us to "hear in our own language[s] the wonderful things of God" (Acts 2:11), they create resonances and reverberations that make other overlapping recognitions occur. Mother-tongue Scriptures, accordingly, come to constitute an irreplaceable element, among others, for "the birth of theology" in that they enable persons to "drink from [their] own wells," to use the title of a book by Gustavo Gutierrez.[10] A sign that this birthing of theology has effectively taken place is the emergence of new idioms and categories of thought derived from the experience of reality in the language but shaped by the encounter with the world of meaning of Scripture.

Clement of Alexandria[11] perceived, as Justin Martyr had, that the truth of the Christian gospel is not that of a religious system over against other systems but rather the truth of the one beneficent and loving God of all humankind who could be understood, however minimally, outside of and prior to the constituted Christian community. But Clement advanced beyond the intuitions of Justin by postulating a tradition in Hellenistic culture that bore witness to an apprehension of the divine truth in the Hellenistic past. He argued:

> Rightly then to Jews belonged the Law, and to the Greeks Philosophy, until the Advent; and after that came the universal calling to be a peculiar people of righteousness through the teaching which flows from faith brought together by one Lord, the only God of both Greeks and Barbarians, or rather of the whole of men.[12]

The reason Clement could say this is not because he believed in separate and autonomous traditions that led to the same end, but because he believed that it was the biblical revelation that illuminated the true significance

---

9. Sanneh, "Horizontal and Vertical in Mission," 165–67, 170–71.
10. Gutierrez, *We Drink*; and see Allmen, "Birth of Theology," 37–52.
11. See Bediako, *Theology and Identity*, ch. 5.
12. Clement, "Stromateis," 6, 17, 517–18, translation mine.

and meaning of Hellenic thought and speculation: "The declaration of Hellenic thought is illuminated all round by the truth, bestowed on us in the Scriptures."[13] And the route to that conviction is through the Scriptures in the Greek language: "Greek prophecy." Only in this way could the Christian gospel be seen as the "true philosophy," and the discovery of the truth come through the Son, to the extent that "philosophers are children unless they have been made men by Christ."[14] Clement found new and creative ways from within Hellenic culture to describe the gospel, such as the "New Song of salvation,"[15] and to envision Christ as the unifying principle of all knowledge, such as the "new Minstrel: The Lord fashioned man a beautiful, breathing instrument after His own image; and assuredly He Himself is an all-harmonious instrument of God, melodious and holy, the wisdom that is above this world, and the heavenly Word."[16]

In this regard, one of the most interesting developments in African academic theology in the decade of the 1990s was the emergence, not to say profusion, of new images for discussing the African apprehension of Christ; all of which are derived from African pre-Christian experience of reality, yet were clearly intended to serve Christian ends.[17] Images of Christ as Ancestor, Elder Brother, Healer, and Master of Initiation, initially give the impression that biblical vocabulary and concepts are much less the currency of African Christology. However, only when one has explored what these categories relate to in the languages from which they are derived does it then become apparent that they are, in fact, new expressions of biblical truth. In my experience in Ghana, while hardly anyone will pray in English to "Ancestor Jesus" or "Chief Jesus," many will readily pray in Twi and Mfantse to "*Nana Yesu*." *Nana* means "ancestor" and is the title for ancestors (and chiefs).

This simple illustration shows us how subtle and nuanced the discussion needs to be in this area, for it means that the valences of "biblical concepts" and "biblical vocabulary" are not established simply by word equivalents. For example, in considering the two terms "Word" (*Logos*) and "Son," when applied to Jesus, can we say the second is more biblical in view of the prehistory of the first in Greek philosophy? Indeed, is that the important question? Is *Nana Yesu* therefore less biblical because *Nana* translates

---

13. Ibid., 6,2, 481.
14. Ibid., 1,22; 53,2.
15. Ibid., 7,16; 102,3.
16. Clement, "Protreptikos," 1:5,4, translation mine.
17. For a convenient sampling, see Schreiter, *Faces of Jesus*. See also my commentary on the prayers of Afua Kuma in Bediako, "Cry Jesus!," 7–25.

"ancestor" in English? Is not the question whether the experience of the reality and actuality of Jesus, as intended in Christian affirmation, inhabit the world of *Nana* in the same way that it could inhabit the Greek world of Logos?

In this specific case, even though *Nana* recalls the category of "ancestor," and so in that sense translates the term, in actual fact it is not adequate to leave it as such. For whereas "ancestor" is a generic term in English, *Nana* is both a title and a personal name, in the same way, incidentally, that *Christos* (Christ) was both a title and a personal name in early Christian usage. All this means that, in fact, *Nana* is a more satisfactory term for speaking of the actuality of Christ than "ancestor." It should therefore be clear that the real theological problem here has to do with the English word "ancestor" and not with *Nana*.

Indeed, the matter should not be about words and their equivalents at all. It is rather about discerning and recognizing what is happening creatively in the context as people encounter, live out, and attempt to express their experience of the reality and actuality of Jesus Christ. This example from contemporary African Christianity recalls parallel developments within the New Testament itself. As Andrew Walls notes, when the early preachers "started to speak of Kyrios Jesus, parallel to Kyrios Serapis . . . [that] act of metaphysical translation . . . [was inevitably followed by] explanation, qualification, supplementation, and definition as the identity of Jesus was explored in terms of Hellenistic language and thought." It is as though "the full stature of Christ becomes attainable" as the Gentiles enter the community, "as though Christ himself grows as he penetrates Gentile thought and society in the persons of his people," as though "the full stature of Christ is revealed only as a fresh cultural entity is incorporated into the Church which is his body."[18] The situation is that of a dynamic two-way process, in which a "translatable" faith finds ways of establishing its valences, its equivalents, within the thought world and amid the spiritual realities that the receptor inhabits. Underlying the whole process is the view that religious ideas and images are more interpenetrable than we sometimes assume. But the logic of the process implies also that as the development continues, we may expect new idioms to emerge, to fill out the hopefully growing understanding that becomes established in much the same way that a meaningful conversation can take new and occasionally unanticipated turns.

---

18. Walls, "Old Athens and New Jerusalem," 148.

TRANSLATABILITY AND SCRIPTURE AS CONTEXT

I have referred to the difficulties of translation. John Sawyer, referring to Jacques Derrida, states the prevalent view "that 'true' translation from one language into another is impossible. Something is lost in translation: it is essential to study a text in the original."[19] However, might it be that the postulate of translatability allows us to think of Scripture as more than merely text? I suggest that we think of Scripture also as context; a context into which the reader or hearer may enter, and so actually participate in its world of meaning and experience.

This is how Justin apprehended Jesus Christ as the divine Word (*Logos*) and Redeemer of [hu]mankind. For him there was an identity of content between the knowledge derived from the Scriptures and the inward participation in the Word. Indeed, it has been argued that the term "the seed of the Word" is understood better when rendered as "the Word who sows," in which case Justin was describing an activity of the Word who sows his seed in an actual religious and moral illumination, most probably based on Jesus's parable of the sower who sows the Word (Matt 13:3ff.).[20] In this understanding, the text has become a context through which Jesus Christ is identified as the true Logos, a living person, known and loved.

I believe that it is upon this basis that the Scriptures can make sense to us who are many centuries removed from their initial composition. It is not only text, which we may appropriate through the requisite skills and techniques of exegesis and hermeneutics; I believe it is also a context in which we can share as illuminating of our own human experience. This is what lies behind the apostle Paul's recalling of the declaration in Ps 116:10, relating the words to himself in 2 Cor 4:13: "The scripture says, 'I spoke because I believed.'" In the same spirit of faith, we also speak because we believe. It seems to me that this must form part of what is meant in the Christian affirmation of belief in the Holy Spirit and in the communion of saints, which, as Kenneth Cragg has suggested, could be interpreted as "participation in holy things."[21]

In this sense Scripture comes to function sacramentally, so to speak, enabling the reader or hearer to gain access to the world of experience intended for all those to whom Scripture is addressed. All Christians share in an "Abrahamic link"; all Christians worship the God of Israel.

---

19. Sawyer, *Sacred Languages*, 79.
20. For a fuller discussion of this see Bediako, *Theology and Identity*, 148.
21. Cragg, *Christianity in World*, 71.

But translatability and the impact of translated Scripture also ensure that the "world of experience" can be expanded in the other direction, leading occasionally to startling and novel ways of participating in the context of Scripture shaped, in these instances, by the cultural world of experience of the reader or hearer. This was again true of Justin's Logos/Word theology. The Logos philosophy in the Hellenistic context provided the launch pad in Justin's quest for a way to give account of the witness of the Living God in the Hellenistic pre-Christian past. This was not merely for the sake of devising a satisfactory theory at the level of head knowledge. Justin was seeking to provide a Christ-centered interpretation of Hellenistic tradition and experience, which would yield new ways of participating in the Scriptures and an answer to the need among Christians to integrate their Hellenistic self-consciousness and their commitment as Christians.

Something analogous happened in the ministry of the twentieth-century West African Christian prophet William Wadé Harris. Harris experienced trance-visitations in which, according to his own testimony, he saw Moses, Elijah, the Angel Gabriel and Jesus, and he alone would speak with them.[22] In other words, Harris, who evidently underwent a deep Christian conversion experience, appeared also able to function in a spiritual universe that was akin to his African world of ancestors, the living-dead, and operated on the assumption that the spiritual universe of the African primal world did offer valid perspectives for participating in the biblical world.[23]

For our present purposes, what is important is how this outlook affects Harris's relation to the Bible. It is interesting that in David A. Shank's illuminating study of Harris's career, it was the concept of participation, "vital participation," generally associated with Africa's primal cultures, that Shank, himself a non-African, came to settle on as the most adequate explanation for Harris's understanding of his direct involvement with Moses, Elijah, the Angel Gabriel, and Jesus Christ.

Harris, through vital participation had been "grafted in" to the "holy root" of Israel's life and faith to such an extent as to "partake of the root and fatness of the olive tree," to use the apostle Paul's expression (Rom 11:16–24). In so doing he was indeed participating in the life of the living dead and their God, of whom Jesus said, "He is not a God of the dead but of the living, for all live unto him" (Luke 20:33ff and parallels). Harris had earlier cut himself off from his Glebo life and family in a radical conversion; yet he was not now without living ancestors. He had simply changed family connections, now based on faith in Christ as known through the Scriptures

22. Shank, *Prophet Harris*.
23. Bediako, *Christianity in Africa*, ch. 6.

but by means of a spirituality of vital participation totally indigenous to his African way of being.²⁴

Shank's description of Harris's appropriation of the truth of the Bible is revealing:

> [It] was in ways that were no longer simple patterns of "belief in" the truth as he had known previously, but an African pattern of "participation in" the truth. It was no longer a question of what Moses saw, or what Elijah did, or the words and works of Jesus as reported in the Bible. It became a question of involvement as with the ancestors, the living-dead, with Moses, with Elijah, with the Archangel Gabriel, and supremely with Jesus Christ.²⁵

SCRIPTURE AS CONTEXT AND THE EMERGENCE OF MOTHER-TONGUE THEOLOGIES: SOME UNEXPECTED OUTCOMES

If there is any merit in the concept of Scripture not only as text but also as context into which persons of varied cultural backgrounds can enter and participate, bringing their own cultural worlds of meaning with them, then I would suggest that the exegesis of biblical words and texts may not be taken as completed when one has established meanings in Hebrew, Aramaic, and Greek. Instead, the process needs to continue into all possible languages in which biblical faith is received, mediated, and expressed. If this makes the task infinitely more difficult than any one person or group of persons can achieve, then it shows all the more how tentative, provisional, and contextual all our theological efforts are. This becomes even more important with the increasing significance of non-Western Christianity and the fact that it is posing all sorts of questions and producing a whole range of problems for which our theological knowledge, gained through the study of Christianity as shaped by the intellectual experience of the modern West, may not have prepared us.

I began by recalling Clement of Alexandria and his observation that the church's Bible in Greek amounted to Greek prophecy. I would like to suggest, based on reflections from my own context, that Clement's intuition was not intended to end with him.

Nsɛm nyinaa ne Nyame is a well-known and well-used proverbial saying among the Akan people of Ghana, of whom I am one. Perhaps a simple

---

24. Shank, "Prophet of Modern Times," 467.
25. Ibid., 466.

translation is: "All wisdom is from God."²⁶ It may also be rendered, "God is the source of all wisdom."²⁷ There are two important indicative words here—the opening and the closing, *Nsɛm* and *Nyame*. *Nsɛm* is the plural of *asɛm*, which has become in the Akan Scriptures the common rendering for *logos* in Greek, or *dabar* in Hebrew. But *asɛm* has a range of meanings, from an item of speech to a matter for public discussion or even disputation. It can also connote the essential characteristic of reality as experienced or observed and therefore can be used to denote a self-evident truth, held and received as such by and in the community. Indeed, it is with a view to affirming and reinforcing such self-evident truth that proverbs are formulated in the first place: *Asɛm ba a, na n'abebu aba* ("When a matter comes up, that is to be settled; then comes the making of proverbs: the appropriate proverb comes"). *Asɛm* is used for "Word" in John 1:1 Because, to the Akan mind that is exposed to Christ, Christ appears to signify precisely such a self-evident reality, Akan Christian thought has moved the discussion on, taking a direction almost akin to the development in Hellenistic Christian thought in its oscillation between *logos* and *sophia*.

But there is a second important indicative word in our Akan proverb, "*Nyame*," the name for the Creator God, equivalent of Yahweh. *Nsɛm nyinaa ne Nyame* cannot be claimed as the fruit of Christian proclamation among the Akan, since it existed prior to Christian proclamation. Yet the situation whereby the God whose name has been hallowed in pre-Christian religious tradition, born along by indigenous language, has now turned out to be the God of the Bible, cannot be without significance. The Akan case is in no sense exceptional. In virtually every Christian community in Africa, the Christian name for God is usually a divine name for the Supreme God inherited from the pre-Christian tradition. This process of the identification of the biblical God with the African God has occurred with so little hiatus, if any at all, in the majority of instances, that the absence of questions relating to possible theological repercussions from it can only be ascribed to a delayed reaction. That the African God has been found to be the biblical God in a way that none of the old European gods could be—whether Zeus, Jupiter, or Odin—is a fact that appears not to have struck many African

---

26. It features as the concluding saying in what are probably the two most important published collections of Akan proverbs; namely, Christaller, *Twi Mmebusem Mpensa-Ahansia Mmoaano: Three Thousand Six Hundred Ghanaian Proverbs*, and Akrofi, *Twi Mmebusem: Twi Proverbs*.

27. Akrofi, *Twi Mmebusem*, 169. Akrofi annotated his collection of one thousand proverbs and gave this rendering. The two publications are separated by nearly a century; the fact that this particular saying is identified as, in some sense, the summary of all Akan wisdom is significant.

Christians as rather exceptional. This is to say nothing of early Western missionaries, who by their prior outlook and formation were not predisposed to find God in Africa, being concerned, instead, to teach Africans about God.

If, as it turns out, Scripture is the revelation of Olorun, Chineke, Ngai, Muungu, Nkosi, Unkulunkulu, Nyame (or Nyankopon, a more intense form of Nyame)—all African divine names—what might be the implications for Christian presence and witness in the midst of religious plurality? Almost all the early missionary encounters with African pre-Christian religious practice presumed a widespread African polytheism. As a consequence, in translating the Bible the early missionaries felt bound to devise a plural form, *anyame* (gods), of Nyame, the Akan personal name for God. And so when we read the Akan version of Exod 15:11: "Who among the gods [*anyame*] is like you, O Lord? Who is like you—majestic in holiness, awesome in glory, working wonders?" (NIV); or Ps 86:8: "Among the gods [*anyame*] there is none like you, O Lord; no deeds can compare with yours" (NIV);[28] or Exod 20:1–3: "And God spoke all these words: I am the Lord your God, who brought you out of Egypt, out of the hand of slavery. You shall have no other gods [*anyame*] before [or besides] me" (NIV);[29] in each case, the word *anyame* is semantic nonsense—it sticks in the throat and obscures the meaning. Akan people do not know *anyame*, for only Nyame is Nyame, just as Yahweh alone is Yahweh. Yet the greatest Bible translator among them, Johannes Christaller, came to realize that "the heathen negroes [sic] are, at least to a great extent, rather monotheists, as they apply the term for God only to one Supreme Being."[30]

Indeed, Patrick Ryan has argued more recently that "the Yoruba and the Akan are better equipped linguistically than are Semites, Greeks, Romans and their inheritors to express the absolute uniqueness of God."[31] While Lamin Sanneh notes that "God was a hospitable deity who was approached through the mediation of lesser deities,"[32] Africans knew who God was—with the various entities designated in academic literature as "lesser deities, divinities, gods" not being God. In the Akan world of transcendent power—made up essentially of Onyame (Nyame) or Onyankop<u>o</u>n (God), *Nananom Nsamanfo* ("ancestors" or "spirit fathers"), *Abosom* ("divinities" or

---

28. *Obiara nte sɛ wo, anyame mu, Awurade; na biribiara nte sɛ wo nnwuma* (ibid.).

29. Na Onyankop<u>o</u>n kaa nsɛm yi nyinaa sɛ: Mene Awurade wo Nyankop<u>o</u>n a miyii wo Misraim asase so nkoafi mu no. Nnya anyame foforo nka me ho (ibid.).

30. Christaller, *Dictionary*, 342–43.

31. Ryan, "Arise O God!," 160–71.

32. Sanneh, *Translating the Message*, 160.

"lesser deities") and *Asuman* ("material repositories of impersonal power"), in that descending order of preeminence—there are no "gods" beside God; *abosom* not being "gods."

Here are indigenous religious and theological categories that can have far-reaching consequences for biblical understanding in our African context. Yet their full implications have not yet been realized. Nor have we taken the full measure of the significance of the assimilation of Onyame (Onyankopon) into Yahweh of the Old Testament and the God and Father of our Lord Jesus Christ of the New Testament.

However, if one were to use authentic Akan religious categories in the texts cited above—replacing *anyame* with *abosom*, for example—the way would be open for recognizing that the dire warning implied in the first commandment given in Exodus 20 has to do with the inward disposition of the worshiper much more than with any external or material objects of rival worship—this latter concern is adequately addressed in the second commandment—and with exalting the living God over and above all the other entities believed to populate the spiritual realm. This appreciation of Akan religious categories enhances the meaning of the text in context. In other words, African linguistic medium may permit a fresh and possibly more nuanced sense of the received biblical narrative and help us come to grips with the issues arising from a religiously plural world.

CONCLUSION

So we come full circle and hopefully can affirm, along with Justin and Clement and a great cloud of witnesses down the ages and from many parts of the world, that the exegesis of Scripture is not completed with the establishment of meanings in Hebrew and Greek in the first century context. Indeed, the task continues into all possible languages and contexts in which Scripture is read, heard, and lived, including all the "prophecies" produced by the same Spirit, and so leading to an enhanced dialogue within the biblical narrative itself, from the perspectives of our religious plurality, a plurality of persons.

The point of such an exercise in dialogue between Scripture in various languages is that it illustrates the different capacities of different languages and hence the need for us to hear and perceive the meanings that each has to offer. Here we anticipate the eschatological vision of redeemed humanity: the crowd from every nation, tribe, people, and language standing before the throne of God and singing, in their varied languages, the one new song of praise and adoration to the one Savior of all the redeemed, the Lamb of God, Jesus Christ the Lord (Rev 7:9–12).

BIBLIOGRAPHY

Akrofi, Clement Anderson. *Twi Mmebusem: Twi Proverbs with English Translation and Comments.* Accra, Ghana: Waterville, n.d.

Bediako, Kwame. *Christianity in Africa: The Renewal of a Non-Western Religion.* Edinburgh: Edinburgh University Press, 1995.

———. "Cry Jesus! Christian Theology and Presence in Modern Africa." *Vox Evangelica* 23 (1993) 7–25.

———. *Jesus and the Gospel in Africa: History and Experience.* Maryknoll, NY: Orbis, 2004.

———. *Jesus in Africa: The Christian Gospel in African History and Experience.* Akropong, Ghana: Regnum Africa, 2000.

———. *Theology and Identity: The Impact of Culture upon Christian Thought in the Second Century and in Modern Africa.* 1992. Reprint, Oxford: Regnum, 1999.

Christaller, Johannes Gottlieb. *Dictionary of the Asante and Fante Language called Tshi (Chwee, Twi).* Basel: Basel Evangelical Missionary Society, 1881.

———, comp. *Three Thousand Six Hundred Ghanaian Proverbs (from the Asante and Fante language).* Translated by Kofi Ron Lange. Lewiston: Mellon, 2000.

———. *Twi Mmebusem Mpensa-Ahansia Mmoaano: A Collection of Three Thousand and Six Hundred Tshi Proverbs in Use among the Negroes of the Gold Coast Speaking the Asante and Fante Language, Collected, Together with their Variations, and Alphabetically Arranged.* Basel: Basel Evangelical Missionary Society, 1879.

Clement of Alexandria. "Stromateis and Protreptikos." In *The Ante-Nicene Fathers*, edited by Alexander Roberts and James Donaldson. Edinburgh: T. & T. Clark, 1989.

Cragg, Kenneth. *Christianity in World Perspective.* London: Oxford University Press, 1968.

Gutiérrez, Gustavo. *We Drink from Our Own Wells: The Spiritual Journey of a People.* Translated by Matthew J. O'Connell. London: SCM, 1984.

Martyr, Justin. *The First and Second Apologies.* Translated by Leslie William Barnard. Mahwah, NJ: Paulist, 1997.

Norris, Richard A., Jr. *God and World in Early Christian Theology: A Study in Justin Martyr, Irenaeus, Tertullian, and Origen.* London: Black, 1965.

Pieris, Aloysius. *An Asian Theology of Liberation.* Edinburgh: T. & T. Clark, 1988.

Ryan, Patrick J. " 'Arise O God!' The Problem of 'Gods' in West Africa." *Journal of Religion in Africa* 11 (1980) 161–71.

Sanneh, Lamin O. "The Horizontal and the Vertical in Mission: An African Perspective." *International Bulletin of Missionary Research* 7.4 (1983) 165–67, 170–71.

———. *Translating the Message: The Missionary Impact on Culture.* Maryknoll, NY: Orbis, 1989.

Sawyer, John F. A. *Sacred Languages and Sacred Texts.* New York: Routledge, 1999.

Schreiter, Robert J., ed. *Faces of Jesus in Africa.* London: SCM, 1992.

Shank, David A. *Prophet Harris: The 'Black Elijah' of West Africa.* Abridged by Jocelyn Murray. Leiden: Brill, 1994.

———. *A Prophet of Modern Times: The Thought of William Wadé Harris, West African Precursor of the Reign of Christ.* PhD diss., University of Aberdeen, 1980.

Stine, Philip C., ed. *Bible Translation and the Spread of the Church: The Last 200 Years.* Leiden: Brill, 1990.

Taylor, John V. *The Go-Between God: The Holy Spirit and the Christian Mission*. London: SCM, 1972.
von Allmen, Daniel. "The Birth of Theology: Contextualization as the Dynamic Element in the Formation of New Testament Theology." *International Review of Mission* 64 (1975) 37–52.
Walls, Andrew F. "Old Athens and New Jerusalem: Some Signposts for Christian Scholarship in the Early History of Mission Studies." *International Bulletin of Missionary Research* 21.4 (1997) 146–50, 152–53.

Part 2

The Consequences of Christendom before 1800

Chapter 3

Christians, Social Location, and Religious Plurality

Wilbert R. Shenk

INTRODUCTION

THE RELATIONSHIP BETWEEN CHRISTIANS and people of other faiths has long been regarded as a contested issue. The Hebraic-Christian Scriptures recognize the fact of religious plurality without offering comprehensive or systematic critique. Religion has been integral to all human experience, with every people group having its own gods and religious practices. The identity of a people group was determined in profound ways by its particular religious views and practices. Christian scholars have relied on theories developed by theologians and philosophers to guide them in thinking about and relating to people of other religious traditions. But how do we explain the long history of fraught relations between Christians and adherents of other faith traditions?

In this essay it is argued that sociopolitical location—although by no means the sole cause—has been highly consequential in all societies in shaping attitudes toward other peoples, including religious groups. Here we will consider the role that sociopolitical location has played in determining Christian understandings and attitudes toward people of other faith traditions in three historical periods: a) 33–312 CE; b) 312–1700; and c) since 1700.

The monotheism associated with Judaism emerged in a world of countless gods. The Old Testament depicts a continuous struggle between Yhwh and the gods. The Jewish scriptures convey a double message concerning the gods. On the one hand, it is taken for granted that each people group has its own gods; on the other, the prophets characterize these so-called gods as impotent human contrivances. Instinctively, humans sense their own vulnerability, finitude, and dependence, so from time immemorial humankind has been in quest of power that will enable it to cope with life-threatening enemies. Human experience has been defined by this primal need to relate to an ultimate reality beyond the temporal that will insure good health, well-being, and salvation. Across time and in every culture humans have engaged in making and worshiping the gods of their devising.

In response to the human condition, the first word of the Decalogue is a call to the Israelites to embrace radical monotheism: "You shall have no other gods before me" (Exod 20:3). The gods and the religions they engendered were everywhere. And in spite of the repeated warnings of their prophets, the Israelites succumbed to the temptation to join in the worship of the gods of their non-Israelite neighbors—thereby abrogating their covenant with Yhwh.

For each of the three periods since the beginning of Christianity, the question of *agency* will be considered. Did the individuals who became members of the Christian church do so of their own volition or were they coerced into joining—whether by legal requirement, threat of lethal force, or enforced social isolation? And, as corollary, how did changing sociopolitical location affect the attitude of Christians toward people of other religious persuasions?

33–312 CE: EMERGENCE OF THE JESUS MOVEMENT

The Incarnation took place around 5 BCE during the reign of Roman Emperor Augustus in a society in crisis. The Jewish people chafed under this empire they regarded as both idolatrous and oppressive. Ever-present anger and resentment lay just beneath the surface. From the beginning of his public ministry, Jesus was widely acclaimed as a prophet. Indeed, some hailed him as the long-awaited messiah who would rescue Israel from the resented Roman occupation and establish a new order. The prophet John the Baptist signaled that a turning point had been reached; something momentous was imminent.

The Jesus Movement exhibited characteristics that have been observed across history and in diverse cultures. These have been identified as millennial and prophetic phenomena. Based on extensive knowledge of such activities, Kenelm Burridge hypothesized that "millenary activities predicate a new culture or social order coming into being." Such movements represent "new cultures-in-the-making, or . . . attempts to make a new kind of society or moral community . . . a new religion in the making. New assumptions are being ordered into what may become a new orthodoxy."[1] People respond to these movements because they posit a new truth, which promises a creative new beginning. They are persuaded that a way of escaping the tyranny of "Egypt" is assured.

Public Ministry and Calling of Disciples

Jesus launched his public ministry in Galilee, the region where he grew up. Galilee was the religious and cultural hinterland of Jewish society. Within Jewish society, Galilean Jews were relegated to an inferior social and political status. Various kinds of Gentiles were intermingled with the Jewish population in this region. As Jesus began his public ministry, he signaled that he was no solitary prophet; he called out a group of twelve men whom he designated to be his disciples. These men represented all that the Jewish establishment disdained about the Galileans. Jesus included in his inner circle several fishermen, a tax collector, a political radical, a traitor, and several other men whose only mark on history is that they were named as disciples of Jesus.

With his choice of disciples Jesus was making a bold statement. He was setting out to constitute a new Israel—laying a foundation for a new kind of peoplehood.[2] He began evangelizing in the villages and towns of Galilee. The Gospels report that throngs of people flocked to hear this wonder-working prophet and compelling preacher. The central theme of his proclamation was that "the time is fulfilled, and the kingdom of God has come near; repent, and believe in the good news" (Mark 1:15). Jesus

1. Burridge, *New Heaven, New Earth*, 9. Some scholars are reluctant to accord contemporary relevance to the terms and concepts associated with "messiah" and messianism. Such fastidiousness obscures both biblical history and contemporary religious reality. Kenneth Cragg critiques this attitude (*Christianity in World Perspectives*, 56–58). For the foundational importance of Jesus the Messiah for understanding the New Testament and mission theology, see Shank, "Jesus the Messiah," 37–82. John Gager, *Kingdom and Community*, uses millenarian theory as the analytical framework for his study of the emergence of the Christian movement.

2. Lohfink, *Jesus and Community*, 31–35.

declared that the old order was under divine judgment. He performed acts of healing and deliverance that pointed to God's creative and redemptive power. He urged his listeners to embrace this new order; that is, God's reign. This would entail new ways of behaving, including the radical actions of forgiving one's enemies and giving primary loyalty to God—not to religion, clan, or nation. A hallmark of Jesus's ministry was the considerable time he devoted to teaching his audiences about kingdom ethics that marked the new order being introduced.[3]

The Gospels emphasize that Jesus's mission was to "the house of Israel." But, inevitably, Gentiles were also drawn to this Jewish prophet. On various occasions Jesus encountered these seekers. Without exception he accorded them respect and compassion—ranging from the stigmatized woman in Samaria (John 4:1–42) to the Syrophoenician woman whose daughter was demon possessed (Mark 7:24–30) and the Roman centurion whose slave was ill (Luke 7:1–10). Jesus's actions stirred consternation in the Jews, including his own disciples. His freedom to meet and engage with people of other ethnicities and religions challenged the traditional rules and mores of Jewish society and religion. Jesus boldly broke rules that he insisted inhibited people from experiencing God's compassion.

The Mediterranean World

The pagan philosopher Maximus of Tyre (c. 125–185) estimated that eastern Mediterranean peoples worshiped some three thousand gods.[4] Thus, the Christian movement emerged in a situation of dynamic religious plurality. The Jesus people were viewed as an aberrant Jewish sect. Their Gentile neighbors practiced various traditional religions. As people under the control of the Roman Empire, all inhabitants were required to worship the emperor. One of the ways the Jewish religious leaders tried to entrap Jesus was to show that he was improperly deferential toward the emperor, thus demonstrating his disloyalty to Judaism (Matt 22:15–22).

For several centuries the Jewish people had been scattering across the Mediterranean world as traders, moneylenders, scholars, and craftsmen. The crowds of pilgrims that came each year to Jerusalem to celebrate Passover were increasingly made up of people speaking a wide variety of languages (Acts 2:5–13), thus reflecting a growing degree of cultural and linguistic adaptation. Clearly, diaspora Judaism represented a cosmopolitan cross section. The dominant figure in the Jesus Movement during the three

3. Stassen and Gushee, *Kingdom Ethics*, xi–54.
4. Norris, *Christianity*, 16.

decades following Pentecost, Saul of Tarsus, was the quintessential diaspora Jew. He was aware of the significance of social location and claimed the rights to which he was entitled by virtue of his Roman citizenship and acculturation to Roman culture; but he also possessed impeccable credentials as a Pharisee, having been trained under the esteemed rabbi Gamaliel. Saul quickly became the pivotal figure in convincing the first Christians that Jesus intended the liberating message of the Kingdom of God to be shared with all people, not only the Jews. Saul, who soon took the name Paul, believed himself to be specially commissioned as apostle to the Gentiles. In a showdown with Peter and the Council in Jerusalem, Paul prevailed (Acts 15; cf. Gal 1–2).

Following his "turning" Christ-ward, the apostle Paul devoted the remainder of his life to evangelizing Jews and Gentiles. On one of his journeys, he stopped in Athens, a city "full of idols" (Acts 17:16). "Epicurean and Stoic philosophers debated with him" (17:18). He went to the Areopagus on Mars Hill and addressed the crowd: "I see how extremely religious you are in every way" (17:22). He remarked that he had observed among their sacred objects an altar dedicated to the worship of "an unknown god." Paul respectfully engaged with them, testifying to the God who created "the world and everything in it" (17:24). This God, declared Paul, had communicated with humankind through various witnesses. Paul's testimony was forthright, respectful, and contextually appropriate.

While the New Testament writers do not address other religions in terms of their teachings and practices, the apostolic witness was marked by focus, flexibility, and openness in responding to particular situations as modeled by Paul (1 Cor 9:22b–23).

Early Christian Attitudes toward Other Religions

Following the destruction of the temple in Jerusalem in 70 CE, the Christian movement no longer looked to Jerusalem as its symbolic spiritual center. Various influential schools led by eminent teachers emerged in metropolitan centers around the Mediterranean region. They worked at shaping the theology of the Christian movement as it engaged with the philosophies and religions in their particular contexts.

One of the earliest Christian thinkers to develop an apologetic response to contemporary philosophies and religions was Justin Martyr. Gradually, other apologists took up the theme of the religious other. It is instructive to correlate Christian responses to the religious other with their social location in particular historical periods. Within 350 years of its founding, the church's relationship vis-à-vis its sociopolitical status had evolved from a marginal and illegal religious group to become the officially sanctioned religion of the Roman Empire. This had decisive and long-lasting implications for the way Christians viewed and related to people of other religious persuasions. The church's new sociopolitical location made it increasingly less tolerant of religious differences.

As a religious minority, Christians did not escape persecution and obloquy during the first several generations. Nonetheless, they accepted that they had to compete in the marketplace of ideas and religions even though they had neither ecclesiastical nor political power to shield them against opponents. By the beginning of the second century, Christian theologians were developing an apologetic approach to presenting the claims of the Christian faith to the Greco-Roman intellectual world. Justin Martyr (d. 165), considered to be the most important apologist of this period, wrote his *Apology* and *Dialogue with Trypho* after 151 CE. Justin attempted to engage both the Greek philosophical world and Judaism in terms of the superior truth of the Christian faith. He promoted the idea that Christ was the *Logos spermatikos* that informed all true philosophy. Before the incarnation, Christ had been present to the Greek philosophers, enabling them to discover and propound philosophical truth. Tertullian (d. 212) is regarded as the last of the "Greek" apologists, because of his writings on the "rule of faith." His concern was to maintain the doctrinal correctness of Christian faith.

During this period, the status of Christians went from that of a persecuted to a tolerated minority. This evolving status conferred no special rights or protection, but the pressure on Christians began to lessen. The persuasiveness of their witness depended on the integrity of their lives and compassion toward their neighbors.

The documents that comprise the New Testament canon were written during this early phase of the Christian movement. The New Testament reflects the marginal social location of the early church and the vulnerability Christians felt in this early phase. Willaim R. Farmer argues persuasively that in view of the threat of persecution, the church fathers put priority on strengthening "the faith and discipline of its members."[5] In considering which documents belonged in the canon, a test was used: does this document help prepare a disciple to face persecution?

Throughout this period, the *agency* by which individuals joined the Christian movement was personal decision. It took courage for an individual to leave one's inherited religio-cultural role. Only those individuals who felt strongly attracted to Jesus Christ and were committed to following him

---

5. Farmer and Farkasfalvy, *Formation*, 8–9; Farmer, *Jesus*, 206–21.

in discipleship dared affiliate with the church. Those who desired to become members were required to undergo rigorous examination and catechism to insure their profession of faith was genuine.[6] Recent studies of conversion have emphasized its multiple dimensions, summarized in terms of *believing*, *behaving*, and *belonging*. Conversion was understood to be the gateway to a new "world" that presented a clear contrast to the old world in terms of these three dimensions. One dared not enter this new sphere lightly or without thorough preparation. "Converts" had to willingly undergo preparation to cope with the official, religious, and social strictures imposed on this new religious group. In spite of such rigor, the movement continued to attract new members. Christians accepted their marginal status as normal. They were called to "love your enemies and pray for those who persecute you" (Matt 5:44b). Under the lordship of Jesus Christ, all fellow humans were potential brothers and sisters.

312–1700 CE: THE IMPERIAL CHURCH

By the closing years of the third century, the relationship of the church to the civil order was changing.[7] The Christian population was growing, and persecution of Christians began to slacken. The Christian movement still lacked official approval, but Christians were no longer regarded as an imminent threat to public order. Indeed, early in the fourth century, a paradigmatic change was introduced that would fundamentally alter the character of the Christian church.

Essential to this incipient new identity was the changing sociopolitical location of Christians. A growing number of Christians were beginning to move from the periphery toward the mainstream of society. For them, this meant increasing access to political, social, and economic power. As Christian social location changed, the elites of society began to regard church membership as advantageous. By the end of the fourth century, the church's identity was fundamentally altered: it was now the official church of the empire. Embracing all the symbols of power and privilege, the imperial church had superseded the primitive apostolic church.

The leading actor in the first phase of this unfolding drama was Roman Emperor Constantine (d. 339 CE). Like other emperors, Constantine understood the importance of religion for the stability of the empire. He saw that Christianity could become a "pillar of the state."[8] Our interest here is

6. Kreider, *Worship and Evangelism*, 5–23.
7. Norris, *Christianity*, 28.
8. Ibid., 36.

not in the considerable controversy that surrounds Constantine, including his motives and actions. What is beyond dispute is that by the early years of the fourth century CE, the trajectory of the Christian church was re-set as the result of the emperor's interventions. From this point forward, the church increasingly became aligned with the state. A generation after Constantine, in 379 CE, the first Roman emperor who was a confessing Christian was crowned as Theodosius. He sponsored a series of laws that insured Christianity would have a privileged position in the Roman Empire. When Theodosius I died in 395 CE, the basic elements that would subsequently determine the relationship between church and state were in place. Christianity was now the official religion of the empire.

These fourth-century developments included trends that would have long-term consequences. The earlier concern to provide biblical and moral instruction to new Christians was replaced with preoccupation with doctrinal and liturgical teaching. "Being a Christian was now defined primarily in terms of doctrine and not in terms of behavior."[9] The modeling of lived Christian faithfulness was left to monks. Inevitably, these trends resulted in what Paul Bradshaw aptly terms "half-converted laity."[10] Christian leaders felt they had to allow pagan practices to be incorporated in Christian practice to make it easier for new adherents to feel at home. Indeed, "liturgical developments were often part of the process of disintegration,"[11] contributing to the undermining of Christian worship. On the one hand, it was becoming socially desirable to be identified with the church; on the other, increasing numbers of half-converted—or even unconverted—people were seeking membership in the church. They wanted the benefits of being identified with the church without committing themselves wholeheartedly. Thus, they chose to defer baptism as long as possible. Fearing that such people might die unbaptized, the clergy lowered the bar and encouraged them to receive baptism without undue delay.[12] It is hardly surprising that such people did not live their daily lives according to Christian precepts and practices. Nominality was becoming common, and membership in the Body of Christ was undergoing fundamental redefinition.

Aiding and abetting the development of this new model of church was Augustine (b. 354), Bishop of Hippo (396–430 CE). He, of course, was only one of many church leaders who took these changes in stride. Augustine is noteworthy for two important contributions. The first concerns the

---

9. Ferguson, "Catechesis and Initiation," 268.
10. Bradshaw, "Effects," 269.
11. Ibid., 275.
12. Ibid., 276.

evolving meaning of conversion and baptism. As the church grew, the radical demands of conversion associated with the Jesus Movement in the apostolic era underwent decisive modification. The rigorous catechetical process required during the first two centuries was gradually replaced by a ritualized incorporation into the socioreligious system of "Constantinian" Christianity.[13] Early in the fifth century, Bishop Augustine wrestled with a critical contradiction, which he felt existentially. Augustine had come to faith as an adult after an intense struggle. His conversion experience remains, perhaps, the best known in Christian history. In his eloquent account of his own conversion in *Confessions*, Augustine makes clear what he believed ought to characterize conversion: a personal decision to submit all of life to Jesus Christ as Savior and Lord. He strongly affirmed that the individual ought to enter into conversion and baptism voluntarily and with full self-awareness. He embraced what has been called "conversion-baptism."[14] As a pastor, Augustine was convinced that *coerced* belief does not produce genuine faith. But increasingly, other agendas demanded attention.

Bishop Augustine became embroiled in theological debates with such groups as the Manicheans, Donatists, and Pelagians. During this time, Augustine's view of baptism evolved. To counter Pelagius's criticism, he argued that newborn children ought to be baptized so that they would be healed of the effects of Adam's sin—original sin. Augustine carried on a polemic against Manicheanism, the Jewish-Christian sect he had been associated with prior to his own conversion. As he wrestled with Manicheanism, Pelagianism, and other deviations, Augustine contributed to a hardening of attitude toward all such adversaries charged with heresy. As his interpretation of baptism shifted, Augustine became an advocate for infant baptism as normative.[15] The goal was for the entire community to embrace the Christian faith, and baptizing all newborn children would aid in achieving this goal.

In 429 CE, Emperor Theodosius II (d. 450) commissioned the compilation of what became known as the Theodotian Code, a comprehensive compendium of imperial laws enacted between 312 and 430 CE. The emperor enacted this Code in 438 CE, which included regulations outlawing the ancient Greco-Roman religions. Now, "Christian persecution of pagan believers put coercion into conversion, pressure in place of persuasion."[16] The Roman Empire now had a comprehensive religiopolitical system that

---

13. Kreider, *Change of Conversion*, 43–70.
14. Wright, "Augustine and the Transformation," 290–94.
15. Ibid., 296–307.
16. Norris, *Christianity*, 43.

secured the legal position of Christianity as its official religion. The church worked hand-in-hand with the state.

By 500 CE the western half of the Roman Empire no longer existed. Barbarian tribes had invaded and seized this territory, holding it until it was recouped by the Byzantines in the middle of the sixth century. But this incursion from the north opened the way for the faith to be carried north into Europe and the eventual "Christianization" of that region.[17] In spite of theological disputes that led to divisions among Christians—for example, Monophysites, Nestorians, and Jacobites— missionaries continued to carry the faith eastward to regions beyond the empire.

"Constantinian" Christianity fundamentally changed the *agency* by which people became "Christians." No longer was affiliation a matter of personal decision and volition. The imperial law required the parents of every child born in the Roman Empire to have their newborn baptized soon after birth. Neither the child nor the parents were allowed a choice in the matter: church membership was mandated by law. The church was a full partner in a coercive system that regulated the lives of all citizens. The radically changed social location of the "church" resulted in its transformation, and it took on an identity quite different from what it had been in the time of the apostles. Deviation from the state religion—that is, Christianity—was dealt with harshly. People of other faiths were soon labeled pagans or infidels.

The Rise of Islam in the Seventh Century

In 610 CE, a man named Muhammad (b. 570) from the Arabian Peninsula reported he had received visitations from the Angel Gabriel, who brought messages to him from God.[18] Muhammad began to preach a message of radical monotheism that clashed with the traditional religion of the local people. At first his message was not well received by many people. In 622, Muhammad, and those who had accepted him as God's messenger, carried out a strategic retreat from Mecca. They went to Medina 280 miles north, where Muhammad was invited to introduce religious and political reforms. Here he quickly consolidated his leadership over a growing group of followers. He died in 632. However, he had imbued his followers with a sense of mission, and within a year after the prophet's death, most of the Arabian tribes had been brought under Islamic control.

Islam shared with Judaism and Christianity a commitment to monotheism but presented itself as a corrective, especially with regard to crucial

---

17. Fletcher, *Barbarian Conversion*, 97.
18. Armour, *Islam, Christianity*, 5–9.

Christian teachings. Muslims had a strong sense they were to bring people everywhere under Islamic influence, establishing societies that obeyed God's law fully. Within a century Islam had displaced Christianity, starting in Syria and continuing southward and westward along the Mediterranean, all the way to Morocco and across the Straits of Gibraltar to the Iberian Peninsula. Eventually, Muslims would gain control of Turkey, including Constantinople, seat of the Orthodox Church. Later Islam would extend its influence into the Balkans. While Jewish and Christian enclaves survived in areas under Muslim control, they lived with religious, social, and political restrictions. Generally, Muslim military prowess proved unstoppable during its first several centuries. Measured in terms both of population and territory brought under Muslim control, the rise of Islam in the seventh century resulted in the greatest losses suffered by Christianity up to the twentieth century.

Since the seventh century, relations between Islam and Christianity have been the source of continual tensions, periodic armed conflict, and persistent misunderstanding. The martial disposition of Imperial Christianity clashed with an expansionary Islam from the beginning. Mistrust and ill will continued to define relations across the centuries.

"Infidels" and Enmity

In August 1571, a great public display was staged in Naples. An enormous banner was paraded through the streets. Commissioned by the pope, this banner was to be flown atop the largest ship of Christendom's Holy League fleet as it sailed into battle against the "Infidels." But first it was carried to the Cathedral of Santa Clara for a service of dedication. On the banner was a large figure of Christ impaled on the cross. The focus of this great assembly was Don John of Austria, admiral of the Holy League, resplendent in his ceremonial attire, who knelt at the altar to receive the pope's blessing and commission through the hands of Cardinal Graneville. Don John was charged to lead the forces of Christendom into battle against the Muslim infidels. The Cardinal handed him his staff of office and pointed to the great banner behind him: "Take these emblems of the Word made flesh . . . and may they give thee a glorious victory over our impious enemy and by thy hand may his pride be laid low."[19]

This was the prelude to the naval battle of Lepanto in 1571 between the pope's flotilla and the Muslim armada. Nearly one thousand years after the rise of Islam, the combined military forces of Christendom commanded by

19. Wheatcroft, *Infidels*, 3.

Don John, under the authority of Pope Pius V and Philip II, king of Spain, went into battle with the Muslim army led by Ali Pasha in the Gulf of Lepanto off the coast of Greece.

What are the means by which deep and enduring enmity is engendered and kept virile over such a long period of time? The battle between Christians and Muslims at Lepanto in 1571 was sustained by an "extended skein of fear and hatred."[20] This skein was the product of *maledicta* pronounced by Christians and Muslims against each other from the seventh century on. Andrew Wheatcroft argues that "Maledicta are the most volatile and dangerous elements in any language. . . . [Enemies are] portrayed as subhuman or not even human at all."[21] The history of Christian-Muslim relations shows how aggressively, persistently, and with effect this kind of language has been used down through the centuries. Here we trace briefly some of the influential developments.

Islam proved to be a new kind of challenge. Like Judaism and Christianity, Islam sprang from the radical monotheism associated with Abrahamic faith; but the followers of Islam believed this faith offered a vision more sublime than any before it. The Prophet Muhammad announced that he had received new revelations from God that superseded those of Judaism and Christianity. Islam projected the blueprint for a theocratic society in which every individual was a member of the *Umma*, the community governed by Islamic law. Those who rejected Islam were *infidels*.

Islam's meteoric rise, followed by the rapid and efficient conquest of lands where the Christian movement was born and became established, was unnerving. These armies from the desert did not wage war like the Byzantines. They were nimble and flexible in adapting to new terrain and foiling the tactics of their opponents. Soon Muslims had become the focal point of Christian fear and suspicion. Over time they constructed an image of Islam as the ultimate enemy. This has been documented in terms of the epithets, slurs, and stereotypes that Europeans used, drawing on disparaging images of Muslims. In the sixteenth century, Protestants insulted Catholic priests as "Jesuits and mamelukes." William Tyndale said English Catholics were "the Antichriste of Rome's mamelukes."[22] Succeeding generations added new terms of reproach against Muslims. Although Muslims were neither the first nor the only enemies of Western Christendom, Islam "quickly became its prime focus for fear and hatred."[23] It has been observed that Muslims

---

20. Ibid., 52.
21. Ibid., 296.
22. Wheatcroft, *Infidels*, 36.
23. Ibid.

showed little interest in the *dhimmis*, the Jews and Christians living among them.[24]

As noted above, from earliest days Christians were conscious of the presence of people around them who adhered to other religions. With the rise of Islam, and the antipathy that soon developed between Christians and Muslims, Christian theologians felt compelled to instruct the faithful how to think about Islam as a rival religion. Earlier in life, John of Damascus, like his father, had served in the Caliph's government. He knew Muslims, their culture, and religion well. Around 725, John entered the Mar Saba monastery near Jerusalem. He soon was recognized as the leading Christian writer on Islam. John proclaimed: "He who does not believe according to the tradition of the universal church is an infidel."[25] In spite of John's critical stance toward Islam, some fellow Christian clerics regard him as too moderate, and five years after he died in 754 John was condemned as "Saracen-minded." From the seventh century on, Christians named Muslims their mortal enemy. Nonetheless, John's critique of Islam had long-lasting influence in shaping the way Christians viewed Islam.

In the pre-Constantine period, the *martyr* played an important role in defining Christian idealism. In the post-Constantine era, Islam emerged as Christians' most potent threat, and Christians responded by anathematizing Muslims as *infidels*. The Muslim conquest of al-Andalusa in 711 opened another front in the struggle between Christians and Muslims that would continue until the end of the fifteenth century. In Spain, Christian writers characterized Muslims as the "quintessence of evil" and the "antichrist." However, some Christian writers were more measured. They interpreted the successful Muslim invasion of Christian territory as God's judgment on the unfaithfulness of those who claimed to be Christians.

An interesting counterpoint is the Muslim outlook during the ninth to twelfth centuries. Muslim scholarship was developing in multiple directions. Several Muslim scholars produced scholarly studies of other faiths. Tabarī (838–923) wrote about Persian religion; Mas'udī (d. 956) studied Judaism, Christianity, and Indian religions; Alberūnī (973–c. 1050) researched and wrote about the religions of India and Persia. Abū Muhammad ibn Hazim (994–1064), theologian and literary figure, produced a five-volume study of religious beliefs among Skeptics, Peripatetics, Brahamins, Zoroastrians, Christians, and Jews. Shahrastānī (d. 1153) published a study of religion in world literature titled *Religious Parties and Schools of Philosophy*. This is a

---

24. Ibid., 361n3, citing Jacques Waardenburg.
25. Ibid., 44.

systematic account of religions in the then known world.[26] This flowering of Islamic scholarship in Spain in the twelfth and thirteenth centuries, especially in philosophy, is credited with stimulating a renaissance in Europe.[27]

A few Christian scholars did address the role of lethal force in relation to Muslims. Peter the Venerable, Roger Bacon, and Thomas Aquinas all acknowledged that use of force in evangelizing Muslims was problematic and to be avoided as much as possible. But none of them hesitated to endorse the call to armed crusade against Muslims in defense of Christendom. The missionary orders also struggled with this issue but did not arrive at a position that was theologically and missiologically satisfactory.[28]

The Crusades

In 1095, Pope Urban II preached a sermon calling the faithful to a holy war against the Muslims who had conquered and controlled the Holy Land for several centuries. The pope gave two reasons that justified such a war. First, this would be a response to the pleas from fellow Christians living under Muslim control in that region. Second, Christians, like Jews, regarded this to be the "holy land" that had been wrongfully seized and occupied by the Muslims. Those joining in this crusade were granted plenary indulgence and promised that the Holy Land would be reclaimed and farmland acquired. Fired by apocalyptic visions and unrealistic promises, thousands of men and women joined the crusade. This movement turned into a major disaster. Inevitably, the crusading mentality bred a virulent spirit of bellicosity that led to multiple crusades over several centuries.[29] But the complete failure of the Crusades left a long-lasting stain on Christian history.

It is striking, as Richard Fletcher points out, that Medieval Islam had quite a different view of the Crusades: "There is no Islamic historiography of the Crusades as such."[30] From the Muslim viewpoint, the Crusades were small-scale skirmishes that they successfully thwarted. In Christian history, encounters with Islam have cast a long, dark shadow compounded of memories of conquest and stereotypes, ignorance, and misunderstanding of their opponent. With no other religion has Christianity had such a contentious relationship as with Islam over much of the past fourteen centuries.

26. Sharpe, *Comparative Religion*, 11.
27. Goddard, *History of Christian-Muslim*, 96–104.
28. Ibid., 92–96; Mastnak, *Crusading Peace*, 208–16; Siberry, "Missionaries and Crusaders," 103–10.
29. Goddard, *History*, 64–71.
30. Fletcher, *Cross and the Crescent*, 84.

The Crusades between 1095 and 1270 did not occur in a vacuum. Christendom had—albeit unwittingly—been preparing for this tragic misadventure for many centuries. The seeds of radical and violent movements—Christian and Muslim—in the twenty-first century were sown long ago. Steven Runciman's pungent summary is worth pondering:

> The Crusades were launched to save Eastern Christendom from the Moslems. When they ended the whole of Eastern Christendom was under Moslem rule. When Pope Urban preached his great sermon at Clermont, the Turks seemed about to threaten the Bosphorus. When Pope Pius II preached the last Crusade, the Turks were crossing the Danube.[31]

Geographical Exploration and Exploitation

The year 1492 marks two major historical events. That year Spain expelled from its territory all remaining Jews and Muslims who declined to "convert" to Christianity. And in 1492, Queen Isabella, Spanish monarch known for her piety, sponsored the exploratory voyage by Christopher Columbus that led to his landing on the island of Hispaniola and establishing the first European colony in the Americas. Carried out under the authority of the pope, this marked the start of the missionary movement from Christendom to the rest of the world. After 1500, the pace of European exploration and settlement in the Americas quickened. Wherever the explorer went, he was accompanied by the priest.[32] Imperial Christianity knew only one mission method: conquest. Within the first generation, the indigenous peoples were staging periodic rebellions against the constant brutality they suffered at the hands of the Europeans.

An eighteen-year-old Spaniard, Bartolomé de las Casas (1484–1566), arrived in Hispaniola as an *encomendero* in 1502. He was assigned to collect taxes levied on the indigenous people. At first, las Casas participated uncritically in the system by which the Spanish ruthlessly subjugated and exploited the indigenous people. But hearing the Dominicans sharply criticize other Spaniards for their abuse of the Indians, his conscience began to be awakened. In 1507, las Casas entered the priesthood; and in 1514, he experienced a deep conversion, a pivotal moment and process that changed the direction

---

31. Runciman, *History of Crusades*, 469.

32. Goodpasture, *Cross and Sword*, 5–27, provides an overview of the temper of the times and Queen Isabella's instructions to the governor of the new settlement in Hispaniola.

of his life.³³ From that point on, he focused on reforming colonial policy and practices toward the indigenous peoples. Las Casas made repeated trips to Spain in order to make representation to the Spanish government concerning the inhuman treatment of the indigenous people by the colonial governments and settlers. He tirelessly wrote reports documenting the abusive practices he witnessed.

In 1534 las Casas produced a pamphlet, *The Only Method of Attracting All Peoples to the True Faith*, in which he argued that only peaceful means should be used to evangelize people. He attacked the widely held prejudice among "civilized people"—namely, the Europeans—that the indigenous peoples being encountered in other continents were subhuman. In response, Pope Paul III issued a decree in 1537 affirming that, indeed, the indigenous peoples of the Americas were rational beings, created in the image of God and deserving of the same respect and rights as Europeans. Predictably, las Casas incurred the wrath of the colonial governments. While his writings helped moderate some of the colonial policies on paper, these governments did not reform their practices and continued to employ inhumane methods in governing the peoples throughout Iberian America for several centuries. With good reason, twentieth-century theologians of liberation regarded las Casas as their patron saint.³⁴

Reformation and Struggle for Religious Freedom

The trigger for the Protestant Reformation was the nailing of Martin Luther's ninety-five theses to a church door in Wittenberg in 1517, in protest against Roman Catholic pastoral practices. But this occurred in a context of mounting social and political unrest. Although Renaissance humanism had not directly criticized church or society, the new ideals that it advanced engendered ferment that contributed to the undermining of the old system. Its emphasis on personal agency and individual expression inevitably reflected negatively on the authoritarianism of the church-state system that had long controlled all aspects of life. Luther's protest was heard by many as a call for relief from this systemic oppression—but within limits.

In 1524 Balthasar Hubmaier, evangelical pastor at Waldshut, submitted a four-page statement, "On Heretics and Those Who Burn Them," to the vicar of Constance. This has been cited as "the first Protestant declaration for religious freedom."³⁵ Hubmaier boldly asserted that those who kill heretics

33. Vickery, *Bartolomé de las Casas*, 57–74.
34. Gutiérrez, foreword to *Witness*, xi–xxii.
35. Bender, *Anabaptists and Religious Liberty*, 9.

> are the greatest heretics of all, because counter to the teaching and example of Jesus they condemn heretics to fire.... Christ did not come to slaughter, kill, burn, but so that those who live should live yet more abundantly.... Yea, we should pray and hope for repentance as long as a person lives in this misery. But a Turk or a heretic cannot be overcome by our doing, neither by sword nor by fire, but alone with patience and supplication, whereby we patiently await divine judgment.[36]

The following April, Hubmaier was baptized and joined the Anabaptist movement, becoming pastor of a large congregation at Nikolsburg, Moravia. For his convictions and witness, in 1528 he was burned at the stake in Vienna, and his wife was drowned in the Danube.

A major and sustained theme of the sixteenth-century Radical Reformation was the belief that every human is endowed by the Creator with a conscience and this must be respected as such. To be human was to have the most basic freedom; that is, to choose the path of faith one felt called to embrace. Neither church nor state had the right to control this decision. It is noteworthy that across the sixteenth century, advocates of religious liberty emphasized the universality of this human right by referring to "the Turk"—namely, the Muslim—and the "heretic," the foremost foes of Christendom, as being equally entitled to freedom of conscience. Hubmaier argued that coerced belief does not produce genuine faith but is counterproductive. This criticism was threatening to both church and state. Consequently, a great many of the first generation of sixteenth-century advocates of religious plurality paid with their lives for the stand they took. Ultimately, their witness would bear fruit. Indeed, in the next century the Free Church tradition, drawing directly on Radical Reformation thought, led by John Smyth, Thomas Helwys, and others, gradually gained acceptance.[37] This movement influenced the formulation of modern political theory.

1700–2000 CE: ENLIGHTENMENT, MARGINALIZATION, RELIGIOUS PLURALITY

In unanticipated ways, the sixteenth-century Protestant Reformation and Catholic Counter-Reformation contributed to the breakup of Christendom and the secularization of European society. The thousand-year symbiotic relationship between church and state was steadily undermined by intellectual and cultural developments stemming from the Renaissance. The

36. Pipkin, *Balthasar Hubmaier*, 62.
37. Ibid., 17; Payne, *Anabaptists*, 18–21.

introduction of the printing press, the flowering of humanism and development of new perspectives on what it means to be human and the modern human rights movement, the steady development of science, and Descartes's philosophy all played roles in promoting radical changes. But the church rejected new theories emerging, for example, from the work of astronomers Copernicus (1473-1543) and Galileo (1564-1642), which collided with traditional church teaching. Copernicus was censured for proposing unorthodox ideas, but in 1633 the Inquisition charged Galileo with heresy and forced him to recant. The state churches were caught on the wrong side of history.

The Thirty Years War (1618-48) was fueled by continuing religious controversy. The Peace of Westphalia, which ended this protracted war, was achieved through a series of treaties signed among European powers the spring of 1648. These agreements laid the basis for the modern nation state. Throughout this period, the leading change agents were not churchmen—statesmen and intellectuals led the way.

Mathematician and philosopher René Descartes (1596-1650) propounded a new epistemology that was based on the rational, thinking self. Sir Isaac Newton, a mathematician, offered a new theoretical framework for understanding the universe. The Enlightenment called for a rethinking of all areas of knowledge. Tradition that had dominated society and religion was now viewed as a drag on human progress. Scientific knowledge rapidly assumed the role of ultimate arbiter of truth. Religion was regarded as little more than superstition. Increasingly, organized religion was on the defensive.

In the seventeenth century, new ways of understanding religion began to be explored. Herbert of Cherbury (1583-1648), father of Deism, approached the role of religion in terms of rationality and nature. The more scientists learned about the physical universe, he argued, the more they discovered the "laws of nature," and the more evident it was there must be an Author. All religions were human attempts down through history to make contact with this Author through the mental faculties bestowed on all; namely, natural instinct, internal apprehension, external apprehension, and discursive thought or reason.[38] Religious plurality was an intellectual option that began to gain a foothold.

John Locke, a philosopher, played a leading role in reconceptualizing the relationship of government to the individual citizen. He argued that secular government has no authority over the individual conscience. A century later Thomas Jefferson took the lead in incorporating this principle—the

---

38. Thomas, *Attitudes toward Other Religions*, 30.

separation of church and state—into the founding documents of the fledgling United States. He was influential in the drafting of a key statement of the French Revolution, the Declaration of the Rights of Man and of the Citizen (1789). The French Revolution targeted both the monarchy and the Roman Catholic Church as the main sources of oppression that must be overthrown. In 1791 Jefferson participated in writing the United States Bill of Rights.

The Enlightenment was one of the great revolutions in human history. All that is called *modern* originated from impulses set in motion by the Enlightenment, which has left no dimension of human existence untouched, including all fields of knowledge, political theory, and human rights. This movement was essentially a Western development, but the Enlightenment philosophes were imbued with the sense they had a universal message that ought to be propagated worldwide. Over time Enlightenment ideas and influence have been carried to all parts of the world; nonetheless, cultures in Asia, Africa, and Latin America have not embraced the Enlightenment wholesale.

Under the impact of powerful Enlightenment influences on Western culture, religion has been progressively marginalized. It was relegated to the category of subjective belief and superstition because it had no scientific validity. To be sure, an individual had the right to entertain whatever beliefs one chose, but this was a personal choice to be practiced in private space. Over several centuries, religion has been progressively eliminated from the public square. During this time Christendom as a territorially based religiopolitical system has been effectively dismantled. Remaining vestiges are valued and retained primarily for their symbolic historical meaning.

Secularization theory had a ready explanation for these developments: religion was irreconcilable with modern scientific knowledge. As such, religion was fated to disappear. This dogma was virtually undisputed in intellectual circles until the late 1960s. Suddenly, respected sociologists began to report important new observations. Far from being headed for extinction, religions the world over were alive and well. Even in advanced technological societies in Europe, North America, and Japan religion per se showed no signs of impending extinction. It was true that some traditional religious groups were in decline. Churches that failed to adjust to the changing culture were under challenge. But the empirical evidence left no doubt as to new growth and vitality.

A singularly important development since 1945 has been the dynamic globalization process. Apart from the globalization of scientific knowledge, communications, transportation, commerce, and popular culture, there have been massive movements of people from one part of the world to other regions and countries for study, work, political asylum, and pleasure. Of course, as people moved, they brought their cultures and religions with them. And as the fact of religious plurality was on display worldwide, the task of understanding religious plurality, both conceptually and empirically, took on greater urgency.

CONCLUSION

Religion has been a constant element in human experience in every age. The empirical fact of religious plurality—that is, the "many-ness" of religious expression—is amply documented in the history of religions and cultures. The thesis argued in this essay is that sociopolitical location has been a key determinant in the way members of a religious group view adherents of other religions. The experience of Christians over the past two millennia has served as a case study. Christians have made substantial adjustments as their sociopolitical location has changed repeatedly. Christianity went from being a marginal Jewish sect to the official religion of state. This change in status was followed by increasing intolerance of dissent within the church accompanied by hostility toward other religions. The *imperial* church did not hesitate to use lethal force when conflicts with heretics and members of other religious groups arose. Religious plurality was ruled out. That hegemonic position, however, was bound to come to an end.

In post-Christendom, Christians have the opportunity to reclaim their integrity in a vastly new environment. With adherents now located all over the globe, Christians necessarily must adapt to varied social, religious, and political realities. Christian faith and history furnish important resources for meeting these new demands. The Christian vocation remains unchanged: to witness to the God of limitless compassion, revealed to us in the work of Jesus Christ, whose love comes to us without coercion or imposition.

BIBLIOGRAPHY

Armour, Rollin S. *Islam, Christianity and the West*. Maryknoll, NY: Orbis, 2002.
Bender, Harold S. *The Anabaptists and Religious Liberty in the 16th Century*. Philadelphia: Fortress, 1970.
Bradshaw, Paul F. "The Effects of the Coming of Christendom on Early Christian Worship." In *The Origins of Christendom in the West*, edited by Alan Kreider, 269–86. New York: T. & T. Clark, 2001.
Burridge, Kenelm. *New Heaven, New Earth: A Study of Millenarian Activities*. New York: Schocken, 1969.

Cragg, Kenneth. *Christianity in World Perspective*. New York: Oxford University Press, 1968.
de las Casas, Bartolomé. *Witness: Writings of Bartolomé de las Casas*. Edited by George William Sanderlin. Maryknoll, NY: Orbis, 1992.
Farmer, William R. *Jesus and the Gospel: Tradition, Scripture, and Canon*. Philadelphia: Fortress, 1982.
Farmer, William R., and Denis M. Farkasfalvy. *The Formation of the New Testament Canon: An Ecumenical Approach*. New York: Paulist, 1983.
Ferguson, Everett. "Catechesis and Initiation." In *The Origins of Christendom in the West*, edited by Alan Kreider, 229–68. New York: T. & T. Clark, 2001.
Fletcher, Richard A. *The Barbarian Conversion: From Paganism to Christianity*. Berkeley, CA: University of California Press, 1999.
———. *The Cross and the Crescent: Christianity and Islam from Muhammed to the Reformation*. New York: Viking, 2003.
Gager, John G. *Kingdom and Community: The Social World of Early Christianity*. Englewood Cliffs, NJ: Prentice-Hall, 1975.
Goddard, Hugh. *A History of Christian-Muslim Relations*. Chicago: New Amsterdam, 2000.
Goodpasture, H. McKennie, ed. *Cross and Sword: An Eyewitness History of Christianity in Latin America*. Maryknoll, NY: Orbis, 1989.
Kreider, Alan. *The Change of Conversion and the Origin of Christendom*. Harrisburg, PA: Trinity, 1999.
———. *Worship and Evangelism in Pre-christendom*. Cambridge: Grove, 1995.
———, ed. *The Origins of Christendom in the West*. Edinburgh: T. & T. Clark, 2001.
Lohfink, Gerhard. *Jesus and Community: The Social Dimension of Christian Faith*. Philadelphia: Fortress, 1984.
Mastnak, Tomaž. *Crusading Peace: Christendom, the Muslim World, and Western Political Order*. Berkeley, CA: University of California Press, 2002.
Norris, Frederick W. *Christianity: A Short Global History*. Oxford: Oneworld, 2002.
Payne, Ernest A. *The Anabaptists of the 16th Century and Their Influence in the Modern World*. London: Carey Kingsgate, 1949.
Pipkin, H. Wayne, and John Howard Yoder, eds. and trans. *Balthasar Hubmaier: Theologian of Anabaptism*. Scottdale, PA: Herald, 1989.
Runciman, Steven. *A History of the Crusades*. Vol. 3, *The Kingdom of Acre and the Later Crusades*. Cambridge: Cambridge University Press, 1954.
Shank, David A. "Jesus the Messiah: Messianic Foundation of Mission." In *The Transfiguration of Mission: Biblical, Theological and Historical Foundations*, edited by Wilbert R. Shenk, 37–82. Scottdale, PA: Herald, 1993.
Sharpe, Eric J. *Comparative Religion: A History*. 2nd ed. LaSalle, IL: Open Court, 1986.
Siberry, Elizabeth. "Missionaries and Crusaders, 1095–1274: Opponents or Allies?" In *The Church and War*, edited by W. J. Shiels, 103–10. Oxford: Basil Blackwell, 1983.
Stassen, Glen H., and David P. Gushee. *Kingdom Ethics: Following Jesus in Contemporary Context*. Downers Grove, IL: InterVarsity, 2003.
Thomas, Owen C., ed. *Attitudes toward Other Religions: Some Christian Interpretations*. New York: Harper & Row, 1969.
Vickery, Paul S. *Bartolomé de las Casas: Great Prophet of the Americas*. Mahwah, NJ: Paulist, 2006.

Wheatcroft, Andrew. *Infidels: A History of the Conflict between Christendom and Islam.* New York: Random, 2005.

Wright, David F. "Augustine and the Transformation of Baptism." In *The Origins of Christendom in the West*, edited by Alan Kreider, 287–310. New York: T. & T. Clark, 2001.

Chapter 4

Diversity and the Challenge of Difference
Historical Perspective on the Muslim World and Western Impact

Lamin Sanneh

EUROPE HAUNTED

AT A CRUCIAL CROSSROAD in relations with Islam, the West has been weighing its options on the future of interfaith understanding, as Pope Benedict XVI's Regensburg comments on September 12, 2006 show.[1] In the address, which was on a completely different subject, the pope digressed to cite the uncomplimentary remarks of a medieval Byzantine emperor about how Islam originated in holy war, adding that, unlike Christianity, Islam has failed to embrace reason. The ensuing violent Muslim reaction surprised the pope and the world but mobilized Muslim moderates and radicals alike, from allies in Morocco, Turkey, and Afghanistan to opponents in Iran,

---

1. The pope cited a remark made by a fourteenth-century Byzantine emperor to the effect that Muhammad used violence in *jihád* to spread Islam. The remark provoked a worldwide Muslim uproar, forcing the pope to backtrack and to call instead for support for Turkey's entry into Europe, and for dialogue.

Lebanon, and Gaza. It was as if the spirit of Islam had once again and for a poignant moment eluded an uncomprehending West. The pope's offense was his perceived personal attack on Muhammad as the perpetrator of *jihád* and on Islam as a religion of violence. The pope was also faulted for overlooking Islam's facilitating role in the European Enlightenment. His sidetrack remark soon assumed center stage.

Yet the violent reaction shows how cultural estrangement makes it easy to telescope the polemical sentiments of a fourteenth century Byzantine potentate about Muhammad and *jihád* to ignite a raging global protest movement that took lives and destroyed churches. It left people wondering how much work religions still need to do to promote a culture of peace and reasonableness, and to make violent reaction to perceived insult unworthy of religion and of the goal of respect between and among religions. Mutual flattery cannot compensate for self-criticism.

This incident prompts several questions: How should ecumenical statesmanship rise to the unresolved challenge of Islam and the West? Can religious people disagree—even when they are being wrongheaded—without resort to physical violence and intimidation? However uncomfortable, should difference condemn people to recrimination and fear instead of challenging them to self-criticism and restraint? Should *Shariah* trump the primacy of peaceful persuasion? How fair is the view that the West has used 9/11 as a pretext for its "war on terror" because the West is captive to the Crusades and thus hostile to Islam? Is it also plausible that Muslims invoke the Crusades as a diversionary ploy in the face of 9/11 and as a foil for Islam's anti-Western sentiments? Haunted by the ghost of the past, what is the rightful responsibility of Europe for the Crusades—or for radical Islam?

THE BOOMERANG

The Crusades, we should recall, were a double-edged sword: they were far more damaging for the Christian world than for the Muslim world, which may explain why contemporary Muslim historians—Ibn Khaldún preeminent among them—paid them little attention. Of far greater strategic consequence for the Islamic world was the Mongol invasion that reduced the caliphate to ruins: told that if he spilled the blood of the caliph the world would be darkened and an earthquake would engulf the Mongols, Hulagu, the grandson of Chingis Khan (1167–1227), placed the caliph and his sons in sacks and ordered his horsemen to trample them to death. Thus ended, in effect, the Abbasid empire that claimed credit for the ascendancy of the Orthodox cause.

In the West, however, the Crusades dominated society and scholarship, and for good reason. In November 1095, when Pope Urban II announced the idea of the Crusades it was primarily to try to establish his authority against secular forces in Germany, France, and England that were challenging papal supremacy in the church, rather than because of an anti-Muslim hysteria. The pope's offer of plenary indulgence for the Crusades was part of his strategy to mobilize the popular will against obstructive rulers like Henry IV and Philip of France. In that regard, Peter the Hermit embodied the triumph of the popular imagination over the political challenge to papal authority—a challenge that ultimately undermined the goal of recovery of the holy land. The crusade of King Louis of France in 1270 to Tunis, for example, was a split drive against the Byzantines in one direction and the Muslims in another. It ended in disaster. When in 1390 the Duke of Bourbon led a crusade that attacked Mahdia, the Tunisian capital, he was bogged down in a fruitless siege, extricating his forces only under a truce negotiated by the Genoese. For reward, the Genoese used the occasion to bolster their trading influence in the Mediterranean, showing how the notion of holy war hatched secular ambition.

The career of Frederick II of Sicily illustrates further the ambiguities of the Crusades. He undertook the crusade but largely in order to secure respect and recognition from Sultan al-Kamil, a respected rival, who had asked for Frederick's help against his estranged brother, al-Mu'azzam. Frederick's alliance with the sultan opened a cultural corridor of deepening Islamic influence upon Sicily. The Dome of the Rock in Jerusalem served as a prototype for his pleasure palace in Sicily, the Castel del Monte. The Dome of the Rock became a prominent motif in Renaissance art, such as in Perusino's work and in Raphael's *The Marriage of the Virgin*. The women of Frederick's palace traveled in covered palanquins attended by eunuchs in the style of Muslim ladies. Frederick adopted the art of falconry he had learned from Fakhr al-Dín bin al-Shaykh, the sultan's ambassador to his court. In fact, among Frederick's crusaders were a number of Muslim soldiers—just to show how undogmatic was his idea of the Crusades.

There was the additional fact that Frederick II turned his weapons against the forces of the pope, who was compelled to rescind his order of excommunication against Frederick. Accused even by otherwise amenable Muslim scholars of making a sport of Christianity, Frederick II wagered liberally with Muslim powers of the Mediterranean world, including sending embassies to the Assassin headquarters in northern Persia and gifts for the head of the Ismá'ílís at Alamut, who were allied with Richard the Lionhearted. It was at Richard's behest that the Assassins murdered Conrad of Montferrat. All that gave Frederick's crusade a deserving eclectic reputation rather than the stigma of interfaith bigotry. Indeed, Frederick II was far more a problem for the cohesion of the Christian world than he was for Muslim hegemony. Accordingly, he incurred for the second time the penalty of excommunication from Pope Gregory II, and for the second time to little effect. The Muslim reality made excommunication a feeble instrument of policy. It is thus implausible to view the Crusades as an anti-Islamic vendetta.

The Crusaders in Syria, for example, were a motley crowd of adventurers whose roots were in peasant society. Appropriately, they were quartered in castles and barracks where their contacts were with local peasant farmers and artisans rather than with the educated classes. Scarcely seeing them as a threat, Muslims derided these Christian crusaders for their inferior cultural standards and preserved their memory, not in elevated prose but in condescending humdrum anecdotes. One such anecdote mocks the crusaders' ideas of justice, noting how the crusaders employed the crude procedure of trial by duel and by water. The intended contrast with existing magisterial Islamic works on law and jurisprudence could not be more stark. There was only one known scholarly work that the crusaders brought with them out of Syria, and that was the medical treatise of al-Majúsi of Antioch.

By contrast, the Crusades in Europe were more consequential. When in 1207 Innocent III declared a crusade against fellow Christians in France, the result was the repeated devastation of the productive agricultural provinces of the South of France, accompanied by staged burnings of heretics. This Christian *fitnah* lasted for more than a century, with new outbreaks of persecution being reported between the years 1304 and 1312. The sack and capture of Byzantium in 1204 belonged with this intra-Christian conflict and had little in it of an anti-Islamic spirit.

Then beginning in 1347 the Black Plague struck Europe. In the few years between 1347 and 1352, the plague carried off some 60 percent of the adult population aged between twenty and sixty. A vast pool of orphan poor flooded the cities now turned into ghost towns. It created what historians have called the chimney effect. Europe's population in 1402 was a third what it was a century earlier. The spiritual heirs of Saladin in the Ottoman Empire may be forgiven for thinking this was as good a time as any to pick on Europe. It is not hard to imagine how bewildering Islam's growing confidence appeared to the leaders of Austria and Hungary on one side, and of Spain and Portugal on the other. The best Europe could do was to decline contest and to choose to bypass the Muslim world, and thus to postpone issues of intercultural encounter.

While Constantinople was under siege by the forces of Sultan Bajazet, the Western leaders undertook a foolhardy campaign to take all the lands of the Turks up to Persia. Such victory would "deliver Jerusalem out of the hands of the Sultan and the enemies of God," the leaders claimed.[2] Crossing the Danube, the crusaders encountered the Muslims at Nicopolis, where the Christian army was destroyed and large numbers of prisoners, including most of the Western leaders, taken captive. The most important prisoners were held for ransom, while the mass of the remaining captives were massacred.

The flame of the Crusades was virtually extinguished, leaving the sultan free to resume the siege of Constantinople. Only the ironic intervention of Tamarlane saved the city. In 1402 he defeated and captured the Ottoman sultan. But the Turks never abandoned their goal of taking Constantinople. In the circumstances, the Christians decided in a foolhardy move to break the truce they signed with Sultan Murad in 1443 and crossed the Danube once more to engage the Muslims. They met with ignominious defeat. In November 1444, King Ladislas of Hungary and the cardinal-legate were killed, and with them any remaining hopes of success.

Nothing in the experience of medieval Europeans came anywhere close to what Islam represented. Here was a religion that disappointed all the devout expectations of the church and yet had the adherence of men and women whom the West learned genuinely to admire—scholars, philosophers, and scientists like al-Farábí, Avicenna, Averroës, al-Ghazálí, al-Jabr (whence "algebra"), the physician al-Rází, al-Birúní, chivalric heroes like Saladin, the genius of Rúmí, and even the cult of Fatima. The contrast was repeated at the level of society and culture. Medieval Europe was mainly agrarian, feudal, monastic, and largely restricted in literacy at a time when the power of Islam lay in its great cities and entrepôts, its wealthy courts and centers of culture, its universal system of pilgrimage and Qur'án schools, and its long, unbroken lines of communication that controlled all major inland channels of trade and commerce. From the perspective of Western ideals—essentially celibate, ascetic, reflective, heroic, sacerdotal, and hierarchical—Islam opposed the outlook of a laity who were frankly indulgent, lax, sensual, extrovert, and worldly. In principle and by consensus, Islam was egalitarian; in practice and observance, exoteric and uniform yet enjoying a remarkable spirit of freedom of speculation, with no priests and no monasteries built into the basic structure of society as they were in the West.

The paths of development of the two societies based on very contrary principles and experiences were also wholly dissimilar. The West arrived at its position through a long stretch of stagnation in the Dark Ages to acquire in the later Middle Ages a social and economic impetus that propelled it

2. Froissart, *Sir John Froissart's Chronicles*, 230.

forward; while, by contrast, Islam achieved status, power, wealth, and fulfillment almost in one bound, with the turban and the throne the convergent points of an accelerating global urban momentum, from Baghdád, Cordoba, and Qayrawán to Cairo, Delhi, and Timbuktu. Islam's military successes helped to extend its range over a vast empire of Arabs and non-Arabs alike and to infuse its religious vocation with undiminished ardor and vitality. At centers of Islamic power and culture, the intellectual pillars of Muslim religious thought were erected, carved out of Greek thought and Byzantine ideas and carried into the wider world. Medieval Timbuktu scholars, for example, studied Greek science and mathematics from Arabic sources. Greek thought made its enormous impact felt again in the later Western Enlightenment but only because Islam had conserved much of what survived of Hellenic learning.

The astonishing fact about Islam becoming such a fertile setting for Greek thought is that barely a couple of hundred years earlier Islam was the religion of acephalous untutored Bedouin tribes, those whom Justin Martyr described as dwellers in tents, scattered in unmapped desert camps, and who thought camphor was salt and finely wrought rugs mere trophies to be torn up and carried off in strips as souvenirs. For these tribes, Mecca with its commercial and cosmopolitan ethos and Medina with its thriving agricultural economy were belated acquisitions whose ethos changed little of the spare habits and tough reflexes of a weather-worn, nomadic people. A rallying Islamic faith changed all that, as Ibn Khaldún noted, saying the desert was Islam's natural advantage.

By the mid-fifteenth century, Latin Christendom had lost its cohesion at a time when Ottoman power was on the rise. The Feast of the Pheasant, held at Lille in 1454, served as an official statement of Europe's exhausted cultural impulse. The Knights of the Golden Fleece attended a tourney in which a spectacle was enacted to show the plight of Christian Europe before rising Islam. A huge man dressed as a Saracen of Granada led an elephant on whose back was installed a lady in a little castellated palanquin. The lady represented the church in captivity to the Muslims. She addressed the noble and gallant company, declaiming in verse the plight of the church since the fall of Constantinople, and appealing to knightly honor to defend the faith. After an interval of more elaborate rituals followed by hearty applause, the knights took an oath to undertake a crusade once more against Islam.

The oath was only for theatrical effect, however, for nothing came of it. At the time, England was worn down by the Wars of the Roses; Frederick III's grip on the Empire was precarious at best; under Louis XI, France was still recovering from its long struggle with England; the kingdoms of the Iberian peninsula had unfinished business to attend to in North Africa;

and the Italian powers were preoccupied with the struggle between Venice and Milan. Repeated papal attempts to unite and galvanize Europe in the circumstances failed. The Venetians broke ranks with the Christian West to broker in 1464 an alliance with the Ottoman Empire to preserve their interests as a Levantine power. At the threat of French invasion in 1494, Alexander VI corresponded with Bayazid II (ruled 1481–1512) to seek a pact that would protect Naples and ultimately Turkey. At various times, Hungary, France, Genoa, Naples, and the empire had negotiated or concluded treaties with the Ottomans. It led Charles VIII to distrust his fellow European leaders and to open direct negotiations with Bayazid II.[3]

By the time Pope Calixitus ascended the throne of St. Peter in 1455, only the tattered shreds of the girdle of the Crusades were left. Calixitus's successor was Pius II, who tried to patch up the cause and for that convened an ambitious council in June 1459. When he appeared in person on June 1, 1459, at Mantua, however, the pope found not a single European prince or envoy present. His address was eloquent and stirring though his audience remained incredulous and silent. He was reduced to bemoaning the fact of who was not present rather than acknowledging who was. Competing with St. Louis for the title of the "Last Crusader," the pope went on at St. Peter's in June 1464 to declare a crusade and to offer himself personally to lead it. Those who subsequently assembled at Ancona had begun to disperse by the time the pope arrived, and within a month he died. It was at this stage that Prince Henry the Navigator of Portugal launched the maritime explorations to take the Crusades in a new direction and out of its Mediterranean crucible. The Crusades ended where they began—in European self-assertion.

A study of the period in question concluded that in spite of numerous discussions, with the papacy pressing European governments to undertake anew the Crusades, the project of a common European stand against the Turks was never a credible option. The powers of Christendom were too rent by conflicting views and interests to agree on a concerted policy toward the Muslim world. Consequently, fear of an alien religion and an alien culture sat awkwardly with "a policy of accommodation and appeasement that, ultimately, had the effect of admitting the Turkish Empire as one of the components of the European state system."[4]

---

3. Babinger, *Mehmed the Conqueror*, 411.
4. Gilmore, *World of Humanism*, 18.

THE FUTURE IN RETROSPECT

Down the centuries the stalemate has persisted, although today the challenge is cultural rather than political or military. As the Iraq debacle has shown, the cost of estrangement is far greater than the fate of armies or the weight of Western coalitions. Relevant to the current standoff is the fact that a declining and weakened church in the West as the most recent Christian heartland does not augur well for the West's cultural coherence and security, or for its encounter with an awakened Islam.

To begin with, except as converts, Islam rebuffed outsiders, including Europeans. A boundary was drawn between Muslim and non-Muslim, supported with legal instruments. Where they were successful, the Muslim victors preached conversion but only to Islam, not out of it. Christian and Jewish subjects, considered *ahl dhimma* under the *Shariah* code, were granted protection or *dhimmí* status as long as they adhered to the rule of not converting Muslims and in other ways not threatening Muslim authority. With legal backing, submission and compliance were rewarded, difference stigmatized, backsliding and defiance punished, dissent and resistance crushed, and power sequestered. The entire Mediterranean basin began to overheat with the sudden pressure of Muslim forces buoyed by steed and sword as they stormed the strongholds of Byzantine power. Europe was saved, but not spared, as the Muslim Arabs took Spain in the early eighth century and threatened elsewhere. With the exception of lands to the north, Islam completely encircled the Mediterranean, with Baghdad as the new gravitational center. As Ibn Khaldún put it in an arresting phrase, "The Christians [of the Mediterranean basin] can no longer float a plank upon the sea."[5]

Yet, despite mixed reviews from travelers there, Constantinople as the seat of Byzantine power continued to enjoy unquestioned respect and admiration even in the Muslim world. In Baghdad, the capital of the Abbasid Islamic empire, Greek diplomatic missions were welcomed by the caliphs in the name of the superiority of Greek learning. The caliphs of Baghdad had recently embarked on an energetic project of promoting the Greek enlightenment with the collection, preservation, and translation of Greek philosophical and scientific works into Arabic, using Greek-speaking citizens of the caliphate for the purpose—a story Franz Rosenthal has documented in painstaking detail.[6]

---

5. Pirenne, *Mohammed and Charlemagne*, 166.
6. Rosenthal, *Classical Heritage in Islam*.

For their turn, Muslim sultans and emirs presided over diverse populations and nationalities, with the process reaching its culmination in the great cities. Ibn Hawqal, for instance, said he found in Islamic Sicily some three hundred mosques and three hundred schoolteachers of whom he had a rather poor opinion in respect of what he called their mental deficiency and light brains, though Sicilians themselves had a high regard for the teachers. Palermo was one of the most affluent Muslim cities as a crossroad between Christian Europe and Muslim Africa. Reflecting on trade as an avenue of virtue, al-Ghazálí writes that "the markets are God's tables and whoever visits them will receive [generously] from them."[7] The character of the people is formed by the conduct of business, and without trade the community will perish. That describes the urban ethos of Islam.

The introduction of Arabic numerals, including the zero (*sifr*) introduced to the West by Leonardo Fibonacci of Pisa first as "*cephirum*," then "*zefiro*," brought about an intellectual revolution on account of the speed and accuracy in calculations that had been impeded by reliance on unwieldy Roman numerals and the abacus. Leonardo was a student under Arab masters. In China, where the first written evidence of it appears in a thirteenth-century source, the zero was represented by a blank space.

IDENTITY AND BOUNDARY

Cultural stereotypes in the Islamic world were often mitigated by questions of religious faith, and so Africa, like Asia and Europe, was conceived in the Arab mind by the exigencies of religious practice, not by the immutability of racial difference. The Islamic religious sensibility avoided the hardcore prejudice of racial stigmatization, as Olaudah Equiano discovered. On a visit to Ottoman Smyrna in 1768, the Nigerian Equiano saw white slaves kept by Turks just as black slaves were kept by whites in the Christian world.[8] Far more potent than social labels such as, for example, *musta'rab* (referring to Muslim Spanish of non-Arab origin), *muwallad* (adopted), and *mamlúk* (referring to slaves of Turkish origin), was religious stigmatization: *káfir* (infidel), *dhimmí*, *munáfiq* (hypocrite, traitor), *murtadid* (apostate), and so on. With some exceptions, Muslim Arabs refrained from viewing sub-Saharan Africa as only a remote and exotic region of amusing tales and self-indulgent moral stereotypes. For the Arabs, blacks could be and were enslaved, but more importantly, they could be and were saved, and as such they might not be enslaved according to the *Shariah* canon. That golden

7. Al-Ghazálí cited in Grunebaum, *Medieval Islam*, 215.
8. Duffield and Edwards, "Equiano's Turks and Christians," 433–44.

rule of immunity by salvation was breached time and again, admittedly, but it was never expunged from the code. As the jurists of Islam contend, the original state of the race of Adam is freedom (*asl huwa al-hurriyah*), and so the offer and cultivation of Islam assume freedom as a corollary.

It struck Ibn Battúta that the Muslim Africans he saw were more averse to committing injustices than any people he had come across in his wide travels in Africa and Asia. Even the sultan did not spare any of his officials guilty of such acts. Ibn Battúta also commented on the admirable state of public security. The continent was a reality in Arab historical consciousness centuries before it became a plank of fantasy and plunder in the eyes of Westerners. In those intervening centuries, Muslims controlled all the strategic overland routes that carried the bulk of the global trade of the time, leaving Western Europeans feeling isolated, fearful, and hemmed in. The Christian movement, meanwhile, was surging in eastern Europe and Russia.[9]

Unlike Islam, Christianity was banished for good from its birthplace in the Holy Land, and the subsequent attempt in the centuries of the Crusades (1096–1271) to correct the anomaly by recovering a piece of that birthright ended in ignominy, with the shame of it erected as justification for excluding Christian missions in the Muslim world. It left the encircled Christian communities and footloose client families with a crippling dilemma: the Christian religion in their hands survived as a private, orphaned religion, subversive if it avowed its Palestinian roots publicly, and belittled if it abjured those roots openly.

In deference to Islam, the claim of a Christian promised land was abandoned as ruinous folly, though if Christianity wished to maintain its right to be considered a world religion and the equal of Islam, it could not forsake its origins entirely, if only as historical memory. Instead of promoting a culture of plurality, with Jewish and Greek ideas melding with Egyptian, Ethiopian, and Arab materials, the Hellenization of Christianity formally foreclosed on Christianity's debt to its Palestinian origins and exposed it as an upstart faith before Islam, adrift in the tide of cultural assimilation against which the church abandoned any credible resistance or defense. Muslims concluded it was because loyalty to culture supplanted loyalty to truth.

STRATEGY OF DIVERSION

Few contemporary European leaders understood more deeply and expressed more eloquently the sense of frustration brought about by Islam's

---

9. Mauny, *Tableau géographique*; Bovill, *Moors*.

suffocating grip on the world's economic lifeline than Portugal's Prince Henry (1394–1460), called "the Navigator" in respect of his role as the principal architect of early modern maritime expansion. Prince Henry was determined to break the Islamic blockade of Africa. Maritime exploration offered a viable alternative to the seemingly impregnable Muslim land routes. Europe's power and its faith, Prince Henry felt, were at stake in such a project. Islam was the dark shadow of Europe's intellectual preoccupations.

The challenge of Islam shows how perspicacious were the views of Prince Henry. His assumptions about the Near East, Egypt, and North Africa as impregnable Muslim lands lying directly in the path of Europe's southward and eastward expansion were proved right. Islam would not suffer any major territorial recession that would cause it to retreat from its central geopolitical position the way Christianity had, and it was sensible, therefore, to concede that world to Islam and to shift to another theatre of operation. That was Henry's insight, understandable in light of nascent Ottoman power but remarkable for its confident, cogent clarity against what Southern[10] has described as the loosening of the intellectual cohesion of the Western world. That rallying vision helped to inspire a distracted world.

Henry inherited from his medieval Christian predecessors a view well expressed by Ramón Lull (c. 1235–1316) to the effect that the gains of Islam, especially with the recent strategic conversion of the Mongols, diminished all hope of a Christian breakthrough and of the chances of securing dependable external allies for Europe. Taking stock of relations with Islam through the Crusades, Ramón Lull challenged the church to embrace a different path: "It is my belief, O Christ! That the conquest of the Holy Land should be attempted in no other way than as Thou and Thy apostles undertook to accomplish it—by love and prayer, by the shedding of tears and blood."[11]

When he reflected on the fortunes of the Western world, Edward Gibbon admitted to a deep sense of frustration with Islam. He indulged the highly speculative thought that had the Christian Ethiopians succeeded in maintaining their power in Arabia before the Persians toppled them, they would have been able to crush Islam in its cradle and thus have prevented a religious revolution that changed the world.[12] It is an admission that nothing of the intellectual confidence of Europe in its Christian heritage seemed to make an iota of difference to the Islamic world's disconcerting resistance to the church, and as it turned out, even Spain's vast empire in the New World was not enough to make people forget the unyielding Moors and Turks.

10. Southern, *Western Views of Islam*, 77.
11. Neander, *History of the Christian Religion*, 191.
12. Gibbon, *Roman Empire*, 2:626.

Fear of Islam was a major motivation in New World exploration. On his voyage to the New World in 1492, Columbus took time to reflect on why he was commissioned for his enterprise. He recalled how earlier in that year the Spanish monarchs had achieved the surrender of the Almoravids in Granada, and the triumph of hoisting the royal banners over the towers of the Alhambra palace. He remembered seeing the subdued sultan come out of his gates and kiss the hands of the king and queen. He continued:

> Your Highnesses, as good Christian and Catholic princes, devout and propagators of the Christian faith, as well as enemies of the sect of Mahomet . . . conceived the plan of sending me, Christopher Columbus, to this country of the Indies, there to see the princes, the peoples, the territory, their disposition and all things else, and the way in which one might proceed to convert these regions to our holy faith.[13]

According to Bahá al-Dín ibn Shaddád (d. 1234), his able biographer, Saladin (1137–93) in his time had a related maritime ambition, drawing up a will and saying after he finished off the Christian Crusaders in Palestine, he would "set sail on this sea for their far off lands and pursue the Franks there, so as to free the earth of anyone who does not believe in God, or die in the attempt."[14] It taxed the credulity of his biographer that Saladin's sincere love of religion—and deep antipathy to the Christians—should be great enough to overcome the prevailing phobia of the sea among Muslims. As it happened, it was on the sea that Muslims would forfeit their power to the Europeans.

The European powers that might take the lessons of Prince Henry to heart had brooded long and hard on how to gain a foothold in Mediterranean lands by planting Christian settlements there. Well into the nineteenth century, converts entered, or were made to enter, Islam from Christianity, a pattern reinforced by an interdiction on conversion to Christianity that in effect drained the religion of any vitality or confidence in its future.

The fate that overtook a community of Christian captives in the holy city of Qayrawán in Tunisia, founded by Arab warriors in the seventh century, became more general. Traders of Sardinia established the Christian captives as a colony in the city where eventually they adopted the language and religion of their Muslim hosts and became absorbed into the religion. In other ways, the death penalty was instituted for apostasy from Islam, and such restrictions turned Christians inward for their own safety and survival. The value of the preservation of Christian communal identity counted more

---

13. Goodpasture, *Cross and Sword*, 6–7.
14. Gabrieli, *Arab Historians*, 101.

than the promotion of distinctive Christian teachings, and local clergy became minders to their own people who were forced into a religious *cul-de-sac*. There were few theological schools to offer education and training, and little by way of viable Christian support to maintain them. A deep sense of inferiority corroded the will and eroded the imagination to challenge the terms of capture and stigma placed on Christians who now lived on sufferance under Muslim rule, alike under the Mongols and the Ottomans.[15]

BEYOND CULTURAL IMPASSE

Whatever the case, it is relevant here to recall the work of a contemporary scholar, John of Segovia, who wrote in 1453 about the danger and futility of confronting Islam in a military contest in the otherwise wholly defensible effort to assert Christianity's credentials as a world religion. Islam was equipped with a tradition of Holy War, while it manifestly was the case that Christianity was not, he contended. Calling attention to the Crusades, John of Segovia said that a military and territorial contest with Islam revealed Christianity's weakness and left Islam entrenched in its strongholds. Missions to Islam, he argued, were futile: whether as proclamation or as silent witness, missions were in conflict with Islam's intrinsic political reflex of *cuius regio eius religio*. Furthermore, Islam's territorial claims offered little room for Christian missions. Missions would be allowed only on territory reconquered from Islam, and since John of Segovia rejected war, he excluded reconquest. The remaining option was dialogue, what John of Segovia called "conference." With that call he let it stand that Islam and Christianity were valid religions, however much they understood themselves in radically different terms. It is flawed logic as much to blame a cat for not barking like a dog as it is to blame Christianity for not behaving like militant Islam, and vice versa.

It is pertinent to John of Segovia's arguments to point out that a century earlier Humbert of Romans spoke of the general abhorrence of the idea of the Crusades among lay Europeans, including their reasoning that the shedding of blood is not compatible with the Christian religion. In the fourteenth century, enthusiasm for crusading had evaporated decisively and lacked any basis in popular appeal.[16] Weaned on the bitter aftertaste of the Crusades, scholars and educated clergy might continue to flirt with the notion but now only as a lost cause. Where it existed and however inflammatory, literary

15. Volney, *Travels through Egypt and Syria*; Courbage and Fargues, *Christians and Jews under Islam*, 52–90; Abu Husayn, "Duwayhi."

16. Daniel, "Impact of Islam," 116–17.

polemic became just a diversionary vehicle of Europe's stalemate with Islam. John of Segovia stepped into that intellectual vacuum to offer a systematic defense of repudiation of the Crusades. The issue had been settled by the time of Thomas Carlyle, for whom rhetoric was an ornament worth more than its weight in words. Carlyle offered in his *Heroes, Hero-Worship and the Heroic in History* (1841) an inventive evocation of Islam and of the Prophet that was a long way from the blood and guts of the Crusades.[17]

Nicholas of Cusa (1401–64), the German cardinal very much at the center of reconciliation efforts with the Greek Church, echoed John of Segovia's views. He believed that the destructive wars between Christians and Muslims were a challenge the Christian world could afford to do without and could not now ignore. He promoted the idea that Christians were more likely to have an influence on Islam from the inkpot than from the barrel of a gun. At the request of Pius II, he wrote in 1461 a study on dialogue with Islam called *Cribratio Alchoran (Scrutiny of the Qur'ān)*, to which he brought an admirable spirit of generosity, showing where the Gospels and the Qur'ān were in agreement. He proposed "one religion in a plurality of religious rites."[18]

Nicholas was perceptive in his view that it was similarity and common ground rather than difference and variety that explained why Muslims and Christians felt so intolerant of each other. His novel approach drew attention to the issue of the one and the many, of one God and the many practices by which religious people sought a path to God. Truth is one, and Muslims and Christians demonstrated that by the practices they observed separately. In Nicholas's formulation, acknowledgment of difference should be by virtue of the truth that God is one, not by evading that truth or denying diverse practices on account of it. Difference should not be a denial of oneness but an asset in diversity, and by the same token, diversity should not mean the suppression of difference lest diversity beget the intolerance it set out to remedy. In either case, difference and diversity offer a standing caution that culture can escalate into a truth claim unless a truth claim exists to restrain it. Without the check, cultural vanity becomes its own and only authority. That was one implication of the theological work of Nicholas of Cusa.

In that light, Christian truth claims and their heritage in the West can be affirmed without denying other religions and cultures. According to Nicholas of Cusa, there is one salvation history even though by their diversity religions orient their fallible followers to salvation with varying

---

17. For a study of the treatment of Islam in European historical scholarship, see Fück, "Islam as an Historical Problem."
18. Nicholas of Cusa, *Nicholas of Cusa's De Pace Fidei*, 5.

success. Thus, Christ's perfection is the model God holds before us without dispensing with the demands of daily discipleship. Nicholas says that the fundamental operations of the religious life are perfectly manifested in Christ, and in affirming their faith in Christ, Christians also share a deep and inviolable bond with all religions.

RELIGION AND GEOPOLITICAL INTERESTS

While unwittingly opening the West to the treasures of Greek learning, the fall of Constantinople in 1453 was a central part of the process that checked the worldwide Christian movement by sucking in portions of southern Europe and otherwise containing Christian energies elsewhere. Reduced to a sputtering stalemate in the Aegean and Eastern Mediterranean, the Christian flame spread elsewhere in pockets of provincial social unrest, to unite momentously in the 1517 German Reformation within earshot, as it were, of Charlemagne's long defunct imperial center at Aachen.

The Reformation was the sort of radical *jihád* that made unbelief no respecter of persons. Turning on itself, a shaken Europe withdrew from any sustained engagement with the world of Islam. Luther, for example, though concerned with the conquest of much of Hungary in 1526 by Suleiman I (1495–1566) and with the unsuccessful siege of Vienna in 1529, was still ignoring Islam. Instead, he called for a crusade within Christianity against the pope. Luther argued that Islam was, indeed, valuable as a rallying point in that intramural feud, for Islam shows how moribund are works without faith, the Reformers' battleground. For Luther, the Qur'án was like the decretals of the pope, and the Muslim threat was of a piece with the call to action against Rome.[19]

Conscious of a major religious schism having rocked an image-encumbered church, with Luther an inspired iconoclast assuming the mantle of Muhammad, Ottoman officials sought to exploit the Reformation for strategic gains against the West, acting on the principle that controversy found Christianity a sect and made it a faction. A letter by Selim II (1524–74) to the Protestant leaders of the Spanish Netherlands speaks of their anti-Catholicism as something that might benefit a Muslim power:

> You do not worship idols and declared your faith by stating that God Almighty is One and Holy Jesus is His Prophet and Servant, and now, with heart and soul, are seeking and desirous of the true faith; but the faithless one they call Papa does not

---

19. Henrich and Boyce, "Martin Luther," 250–66.

recognize his Creator as One, ascribing divinity to Holy Jesus (upon whom be peace!), and worshipping idols and pictures which he has made with his own hands, thus casting doubt upon the Oneness of God and instigating how many servants to that path of error.[20]

Perhaps Selim II sensed that the paradox of the century in which Europe became most Christian would be the century also in which Europe started to become less so. Centuries later, a united Europe found itself repudiating its Christian heritage just as it was preparing to welcome Turkey into its ranks. The scandals of the papacy under Innocent VIII (1484–92) must have seemed to the Ottomans at the time a harbinger of the intellectual unraveling of Europe. Committed to riding a new wave of imperial expansion, the Sublime Porte was not predisposed to indulge an exaggerated opinion of the pope, symbol of Europe's imagined cultural decline. In fact, Europe meanwhile was stirring itself to new heights of greatness, the feuds of Christianity notwithstanding. Religion would not be a reliable gauge of Europe's new global role, and that possibility would dawn on Ottoman officials only after the fact. Ancient codes must of necessity be reimagined in the new idiom of power to survive.

CULTURAL WATERSHED

The loss of Muslim Spain on the outer rim of the Islamic heartlands arguably dealt Muslims a setback, including the setback of having new alien influences thrust upon them. The fallout, however, from the fall of Spain was marginal for Islam. Furthermore, the defeat in Spain had ostensibly less to do with European reasons than with internal forces, such as the devastating twelfth-century Almohad invasion from North Africa and its legacy of division and instability. Yet, to adopt an observation in a different connection, Muslims may be blamed but not shamed for losing Spain. It had been someone else's country after all.

The point was underscored in one Muslim's intellectual assessment of relations with the West in the context of the loss of Spain. One of the last Spanish Muslims to be expelled with his fellow Moriscoes challenged the new Christian rulers on the sovereign principle of religion, and in that light offered his opinion about how the two civilizations compared. He said the bitter fate of Muslims at the hands of the Christian Spaniards contrasted unfavorably with the situation bequeathed by his victorious Muslim ancestors

20. Lewis, *Emergence of Modern Turkey*, 177.

who never attempted to extirpate Spanish Christianity when it was in their power to do so. He said forced conversion of Christians was forbidden by official policy as being contrary to the public ordinances of Islam and to sound Muslim sentiment. He noted that the Christian policy of suppressing Islam violated the very heart of what made a person religious; namely, a free and unfettered conscience. Islam adhered to that rule by limiting itself only to tinkering with the ordinary habits of outward appearance rather than having the inquisitor thrust his hand into people's conscience with the force of penal sanction.[21]

The Morisco might have given the example of the great Jewish scholar Moses Maimonides (1135–1204) who, under the intolerant Almohads in Spain, feigned conversion to Islam and then fled to Muslim Egypt where he promptly declared himself to be a Jew. A Muslim jurist from Spain denounced him for his apostasy and demanded his execution as a renegade. The case was quashed by al-Qádí al-Fadl 'Abd al-Rahím b. 'Alí, one of the most famous Muslim judges and a prime minister of Saladin (1137–93), the sultan of Egypt. Al-Rahím issued an authoritative legal opinion to the effect that a person who had been converted to Islam by force could not rightly be considered a Muslim, thus voiding the sentence.[22] The story has been vigorously contested by some Jewish writers, although it is relevant to point out that the first writer to mention the story, Ibn al-Qiftí, was himself a contemporary of Maimonides.[23]

At any rate, with pointed reference to the Inquisition, the Morisco witness probes the principle of toleration based on the primacy of conscience as a defining issue in relations between Islam and the West. Muslims, he admits, do not have clean hands in the matter, as witness their treatment of the Jews. Yet even there, Muslims dealt with Jews only "according to justice and equity; but we cannot legally touch their consciences" even when the Jews persisted in their antinomian defiance about being "God's Favourite and Elected People."[24]

The Morisco challenged the new Spanish Christian powers, saying Muslims were careful not to establish the Inquisition when they could have done so. Without question, he stressed, Muslims were eager to welcome converts and to accept them fully and without reservation as members of the Muslim *ummah*, allowing them to marry Muslims and to hold positions of wealth and influence. And without question, he continued, Muslims

21. Rabadan, *Mahometism*, II, 297–98.
22. Badger, *Nestorians*, 1:133f.
23. Berliner, "Zur Ehrenrettung des Maimonides," 103ff.
24. Rabadan, *Mahometism*, II, 345f.

punished those who reviled Islam and in other ways brought the religion into disrepute, on the grounds that converts were such by their own choice and so should be held responsible for actions that contradicted their profession.

Yet for all their desire and eagerness to welcome converts, the writer persists, Muslims refrained from mounting an Inquisition to reduce Christians to victims of repression and terror. How different were the methods of the Christian Inquisition, he lamented. Not content merely to employ the weapons of terror to force people to convert, Christian authorities conducted a background check of converts, tracing pedigrees up to the tenth generation to try to find even a drop of new Christian blood, as if that evidence proved insincerity and made converts guilty of moral infamy. The writer continued: Christians pleaded a zeal for God's church, but if that was God's work, which, then, was the Devil's? God is all justice, mercy, and bounty, and the Christians who had the presumption to call themselves God's ministers showed by their actions how far short they came of those standards.[25] In the event, Spain was lost, though Muslims never lost their sense of moral superiority. It was just that in one bad dream, history had dealt them a mean hand.

ISLAM OUTFLANKED

On a different front, Islam was poised for encounter of a different kind, one that would involve a radical overhaul of its medieval imperial superstructure. In the Ottoman Empire, the Turks effaced themselves in Islam to confront a rising Europe that was freeing itself from religion—the situation is little different today. The Muslim powers of the Mediterranean world were only too aware of Europe's cultural split following the earthquake of the Reformation. The British, for instance, were quick to denounce Irish and Italian Catholics for their idolatry, knowing that would impress the Muslim sultans they were trying to cultivate. Elizabeth I sold armaments to the Moroccans in their campaign against Spain in the 1620s. From 1704 Britain relied on Algiers and Morocco to defend Gibraltar and Minorca against Catholic Spain. Each side looked for Muslim allies.

At a personal level, Islam was invoked as a riposte to Catholicism. Islam banned images from the mosque, treated marriage not as a sacrament but as a civil contract, repudiated the idea of a sacerdotal clergy, banned monasteries, and abolished rank at worship. In its differences with Catholicism, Protestantism looked for a natural ally in Islam. Joseph Pitts, for example, an autodidact Presbyterian, wrote in 1704 an appreciative account of

25. Ibid., 297–98, 345–46.

Muslim devotion, drawing particular attention to how, unlike Catholicism or even the Church of England, Muslims gave primacy to the word of God, he argued. Pitts was convinced that Islam was utterly unlike, and far superior to, the religion of cradle Catholics who "live and die in an implicit faith of what they are taught by their priests."[26] Just to show the extent of Islam's appeal, that opinion was shared by many Catholic witnesses in the Muslim world. For these Europeans, Islam had the intellectual edge.

When in 1747 the Ironmongers' Company of London—which had been set up with a rich endowment to redeem British captives in North Africa—received a request from British ministers to rescue Britons held captive, the Ironmongers rejected the request on the grounds that the captives in question were Irish Catholics whose Britishness was, therefore, unacceptable.[27] As if to return the compliment, the Butlers—a powerful dynasty of Irish Catholic merchants who had established a commanding position in Morocco by the mid-eighteenth century—used their leverage to help Continental European traders beat their British Protestant competitors. The Butlers aided and abetted Spanish intrigues to retake Gibraltar.[28] It is testimony to Muslim dominance of the Mediterranean, and especially of the North African part, that even Britain's jingoist Prime Minister, William Pitt, opted to leave unchallenged Moroccan assertions of superiority and apologized to Sidi Mohammed for Capt. Hyde Parker's insult and insubordination in 1756. As restitution, Britain paid a ransom of 200,000 Spanish dollars for the hundreds of British captives held on that account in Morocco. Pitt's consul in Morocco was treated with deliberate slight until the sultan was satisfied that the consul had "observed the courtesies incumbent on him."[29] In a letter to George II in 1760, the sultan taunted the elderly king. "It will not be unknown to you that you were the servants of our noble ancestors and it was your obligation to gladden us before any other nation."[30] The reference to "our noble ancestors" was an allusion to the Sa'did Sharífian dynasty that, beginning in the sixteenth century, conducted raids against the southern English coast and took hundreds of local captives. After the 1760s, Britain's maritime power was expanding, to the ultimate disadvantage of Muslim power, but even then, Britain had no stomach to take on Muslim North Africa. Writing in 1801, army officer Major Lowe gave vent to a sense of frustration with respect to Britain's ineffectiveness in the Medi-

26. Pitts, *Religion and Manners*.
27. Colley, *Captives*, 120.
28. Ibid., 121.
29. Ibid., 131.
30. Ibid., 132..

terranean when he wrote that the Muslims were "invariably men of large stature who appeared to look down on us."³¹ Even as late as 1816, when the Royal Navy bombarded the city of Algiers in retaliation for corsairing and white slavery, the impression persisted that armed confrontation with Islam was foolhardy. In that attack, British casualties were proportionately heavier than at the Battle of Trafalgar. Islam was a boundary the West was careful not to cross. "In the Mediterranean, at the start of the nineteenth century, the Crescent and its powerful rays could still seem far from eclipsed to a people even now conscious of their own modest, indigenous size."³²

Yet there was an ominous tide bearing the forces of Western secular ascendancy. Divesting itself of the debilitating distractions of Christendom to pursue the Crusades, Europe expanded abroad to amass wealth and acquire territory. The contest with Islam took a dramatic turn, and it altered permanently the strategic balance of power with the Ottomans. An astute Ottoman witness in 1625 tried to rally the Muslim world, saying it was still possible to pursue an economically successful but overextended Europe to its commercial strongholds in the east by first regaining control of the Suez and the coasts of Yemen, Europe's economic lifeline.

In the era before the rounding of the Cape of Good Hope, the goods of India, Sind, and China used to come to Suez and to the Red Sea ports, and from there were distributed by Muslims to the rest of the world. Now these goods were carried on Portuguese, Dutch, and English ships to Europe and were spread all over the world from there. "What they do not need themselves they bring to Istanbul and [to] other Islamic lands, and sell it for five times the price, thus earning much money."³³ The writer offered a plan to reverse the course of European hegemony, which was that the Ottoman Empire should seize control of the Suez and the Yemeni coastline in order to dominate the trade passing through those ports. Maritime preeminence and commercial advantage were indivisible, a fact which the Ottomans must perforce recognize. If that was not done, he predicted, it would not be long before Europeans would rule over the lands of Islam.

It was a prophetic warning. In spite of progressive decline of the fortunes of the empire, compounded by reckless military adventures, the Ottomans maintained a posture of belligerency toward their European enemies. In 1682 they undertook one more major military offensive against Austria only to fail disastrously outside the walls of Vienna in 1683. The defeat had a domino effect. In the Austrian counterattack, previous Ottoman gains in

---

31. Ibid., 133.
32. Ibid.
33. Ibid.

Hungary, Greece, and the Black Sea coast were rolled up. In January 1699 the Ottoman rulers signed a peace treaty as a defeated power. It was the first time they had done so, and their humiliation was sealed with the giving up of extensive territories to the infidel. These territories had long been under Ottoman rule and thus regarded as part of the Islamic heritage. The territorial retrenchment continued, however. European powers lined up in a land-grab frenzy to dispossess the Ottomans, and by 1774 even the heartland of Anatolia was vulnerable. Crimea was lost in the process, lighting a fuse that would engulf Europe a century and a half later. Napoleonic upheavals intervened to afford the Ottomans a period of reprieve, and Selim III took advantage of that to modernize the army, the navy, and other parts of the state infrastructure.

Faced with Islam's view of religion as its preeminent domain, European nations retreated and responded with a secular program. It created the contrasting situation of Europe as the champion of worldly means and the Muslim world as the champion of religion. Thus, European nations opted, *faute de mieux*, to sponsor and support their communities in Muslim lands as transient national groups rather than as bona fide faith communities.

The brilliant salvage operation of Max Weber in restoring rationality to religion, or to Puritan forms of religion, saved rationality but not necessarily religion, except that, tellingly, Islam survived his method. Or did it? According to a recent assessment, "Weber sees Islam as transforming itself more and more into a legalistic religion oriented toward feudal property."[34] Weber claimed that Islam was really never a religion of salvation.[35] Weber exempted Islam because he considered Islam anti-capitalist without conceding Islam's truth claims. Marx, perhaps, had the last word: class dialectics, if not the imperatives of a well-ordered society, displaced revealed ethics.

While taking stock of the revolutionary ideas of the French Revolution, Ottoman observers were alarmed by the movement's anti-religious campaign. They endorsed a statement that called on Muslims to beware:

> O you who believe in the unity of God, community of Muslims, know that the French nation (may God devastate their dwellings and abase their banners, for they are tyrannical infidels and dissident evildoers) do not believe in the unity of the Lord of Heaven and Earth, nor in the mission of the intercessor on the Day of Judgment, but have abandoned all religions, and denied the after-world and its penalties . . . so that they have pillaged

---

34. Harrison et al., *Greek Religion*, 487.

35. Weber, *Economy and Society*, 1:625, and 2:1076, 1096–97, 1183; Turner, *Weber and Islam*.

their churches and the adornments of their crucifixes and attacked their priests and monks.[36]

The combative secularism of the French Revolution scandalized the Muslim world, and that scandal beset the modern nation state as it took hold in the Muslim world. The revolutionary ideology that targeted Christianity in France was unlikely to spare Islam, Muslims concluded, and the cult of reason must be combated for the dangerous idolatry it was. The encounter with Greek science and philosophy of earlier centuries gave the Muslims a psychological advantage: al-Ghazálí, for instance, had drawn the sting of Averroëism and received thereby the accolade that was the envy of his opponents in philosophy—"the proof of Islam." At any rate, at the level of *raison d'état*, Ottoman rulers felt constrained to recognize a confident Napoleon as emperor, while, at that of society, the *'ulamá* spawned a festering anti-Western opposition. The formal structures of the national state increasingly took on the administrative proportions of its European prototype while popular social institutions gained ground as moral strongholds of Islam. In spite of Western backing, Muslim political elites were only half credible.

Nineteenth-century Ottoman history was dominated by the era of reforms known as the Tanzimat. The reforms were a response to Europe's supremacy as well as to accumulated strains in the sprawling Ottoman imperial system, which at the time included Albania, Bosnia, Bulgaria, Crete, Iraq, Jordan, northern and eastern Greece, Rumania, Saudi Arabia, Syria, Egypt, and Libya, with ties to Tunisia. In the reforms, authority was decentralized, new schools established, new institutions of the executive and judiciary created with separate jurisdiction, and bureaucratic reorganization implemented. From this ferment rose the Young Ottomans who campaigned for constitutionalism and parliamentary government. A vigorous culture of journalism grew to canvas these ideas and to act as an intellectual clearinghouse for arguments of continued Westernization and modernization.

But these reforms provoked determined opposition among the members of the old guard such as the *'ulamá*, who mobilized their ranks to drive the Young Ottomans into exile and underground. Yet the Tanzimat reforms had built such a strong head of steam that it was impossible to dissipate it entirely. In 1876 a new Ottoman constitution was crafted featuring the establishment of consultative and judicial bodies and the codification of civil law, modernization of education, and a code on the administration of the provinces—many of these reforms were inspired by the French constitution. Facing the double crisis of war with Russia and a massive foreign debt,

---

36. Lewis, *Emergence*, 67.

Turkey was unable to stem the tide of imperial decline. By 1878 the architects of the new constitution had become the targets of charges of failure and incompetence, and pursued into exile or prison, they were defeated. The rumbles of reform subsided in an atmosphere of national weariness as the sultan tried to gather what remained of his disintegrating empire. Yet, as the era of the Young Turks (1908–18) would show, the impulse for reform had not wilted and would revive in a later age when Turkey, drained to its core from its bloated imperial pretensions, transformed itself into a modern nation state.

Nevertheless, for all the talk about Europe's secular ascendancy with the sixteenth-century maritime penetration of distant lands and the establishment in the nineteenth century of the colonial empires in Muslim countries, Islam suffered no fatal territorial loss. "The raping of the west," testified Akbar Husayn Allahabadi, "did not penetrate to the head. At least there was this strong point in favor of the turban."[37] Mecca and Medina offered an effective barrier against infidel intrusion. Consequently, Islamic theology declined the chance to develop a tradition of critical historical consciousness with respect to its Scripture.

THE BALANCE SHEET

Almost everywhere, the encounter with the modern West left Islam's moral core virtually untouched, and having left the dubious honor of empire building to others, the Muslim world was much stronger than before in spite of its being territorially dispersed: Muslim numbers grew at an unprecedented rate, thanks to the decline in the death rate and the rise in the birth rate; neighboring communities were incorporated into Muslim ranks; law and order and improved communication facilitated trade and travel, and Islam spread with them; the pilgrimage to Mecca grew by being better organized and funded; Arabic works and manuscripts were collected, catalogued, and housed in archives and libraries constructed for the purpose; literacy rates rose; women were educated and mobilized in sufficient numbers to alter the social balance and to weaken the *Shariah*-inspired distinction between the public and private; the export of Western technology allowed the successful exploitation of natural resources such as oil and minerals to create a bonanza for hitherto remote and peripheral societies; and international financial institutions furnished the mechanism and legal framework for investment and development in Muslim countries.

37. Cited in Cragg, *Alive to God*, 9.

The French empire in North Africa collapsed to reveal a scarcely diminished Islamic adherence in rural centers, while the retreating British Empire in India enabled new Muslim elites to ensconce Islam in the nation state system in Pakistan while leaving their fellow Indian Muslims to draw on the advantages of citizenship there to promote Islam in its old imperial stronghold. Islam shed the illusion of caliphal grandeur only to acquire the cumulative advantage of the modern nation state. The achievements were more than any *jihád* movement had obtained for Islam since the conquests (*futúh al-buldán*) al-Baladhuri describes of the early caliphate.

These vast historic changes were mounted on a foundation laid by Western colonial rule. In a study on the subject, J. Spencer Trimingham notes that regulations adopted in 1933 excluded missions from any part of the Sudan recognized by the government as Muslim.[38] Furthermore, in Christian schools established elsewhere, Muslim children were forbidden from receiving Christian instruction without authorization by their parents. Lord Cromer came within a whisker of banning the distribution of Bibles when he forbade publicity promoting their sale. The government published regulations concerning conversion, taking due care to ensure Muslim involvement in the decision-making process.[39] It amounted to an officially sanctioned restriction on conversion from Islam. The publicity alone exposed the convert to public opprobrium, and the elaborate procedure of verification discouraged all but the most persistent and foolhardy.

The other matter is that Muslim leaders were inclined to regard the colonial administration itself as invalid on account of its infidel status, and so administrative ordinances touching on religion carried little weight unless they had been anticipated by Muslim demands. At the outbreak of the First World War, the governor-general, for example, summed up the policy of patronage of Islam in an address to the *'ulama*. He said the government had facilitated the pilgrimage to Mecca, subsidized and assisted the men of religion, built and encouraged the construction of new mosques, modernized Islamic law, and trained Muslim magistrates to preside over Islamic courts.[40] Disheartened by the prospects of a Western breakthrough in this state of affairs, W. H. T. Gairdner, a senior Anglican missionary, observed that colonial rule remained an offense to the Muslim conscience regardless of appeasement and other forms of blandishment. The principle "of being governed by a non-Muslim power [will] be unappeasably resented by Muslims. European Powers holding territory in Africa may as well make up their

---

38. Trimingham, *Christian Approach to Islam*, 29–30.
39. Ibid., 34.
40. Ibid., 26.

minds on this score. No amount of placency can alter the principle that has been formative of Islam since its very rise, and that underlies Islam still today."[41] Colonial rule continued to be perceived by Muslims as an objectionable instrument of Christianity, which compounded the issue of colonial restriction of missions. Secularism and Christianity both suffer from the unified offense of infidel guilt in the Muslim mind. Colonial government is "Christian" government by reason of its not being an Islamic government. This has been at the root of Christianity's credibility in Muslim eyes, making the religion a double target of colonial suppression and Muslim opposition. Sudan was among the clearest examples of that fact.

Lord Cromer was not himself immune to the taint of infidel stigma. When on behalf of the administration he donated £30 to the shaykh of the Omdurman mosque, the shaykh declined to acknowledge the gift. When asked why, he replied with scorn, "Do you think I would say 'thank you' to a *káfir*?"[42] The shaykh was apparently unmoved by the threat to bring his remark to Lord Cromer's ear. Trimingham says that missionaries are not justified in blaming colonial administrations for the failure of Christianity to make gains among Muslims. He puts that to Islam's intrinsic resistance and to the foreignness of Christianity. Trimingham could have added that Islam's natural political proclivity enabled it to secure the collaboration of colonial rule, whatever the complex nature of that alliance, while, without that political favor, Christianity came under a cloud. The differential outcome was that under colonial rule Islam prospered while Christianity faltered, leaving privatization as Christianity's natural fallback.

The changes show how in its proximity to the modern West the Muslim world inherited a bifurcated legacy of the nation state as the inheritor of the fruits of secular advance on the one hand, and on the other, of an educated modern *'ulamá* as the keepers of the conscience of Islam. The nation state broke up the *ummah* into separate, competing national jurisdictions, but it also contributed to the duplication of Islam's moral influence within the family of nations. Thanks to the system of international institutions and protocols, Muslims acquired global respect and access. Islam did not retreat anywhere, even in the Soviet Union.

Accordingly, Europe's nineteenth-century colonial ascendancy created the right mix of factors necessary to pitch a revitalized Islam that set out to contest the normative claims of the national secular order. The Súfí orders, for example, crumbling in isolated pockets of waning practice, were resuscitated and rearmed by a reaction to colonial rule to become the backbone

---

41. Ibid., 26–27.
42. Ibid., 28.

of popular anti-colonial resistance in many places. The orders fused with the spine of other radical movements, such as the Deobandi, Salafí, and Wahhabí movements, to foment national grievances and to contend against Western political domination.

While nation states in the Muslim world have achieved a degree of equality and mutual recognition with their counterparts in the West, they have been less successful in disentangling themselves from their roots in Islam's normative sources. With a 98 percent Muslim population, for example, even a secular Turkey has not been able to bypass or to suppress that fact. Europe's revolutionary secular ideology—along with the machinery of the nation state—failed to impose the rule of cultural domestication it had successfully applied to Christianity and thus to subdue Islam. As colonial subjects, Muslims forfeited little of their religious heritage, including the potent appeal of a public role for Islam. Now as newly settled immigrant communities they have challenged Europe in its own backyard. By demanding structural integration, the Muslim diaspora has superseded the ghetto as a marginal and leftover social institution. What went round as unilateral colonial overrule abroad has come round as multicultural challenge at home. Separate identities for masters and subjects under the imperial dispensation have been replaced by critical mutual self-appraisal under the new multiculturalism. The boundaries have shifted.

FRONTLINE AND FAULTLINE

Even in earlier centuries the old cultural assumptions about an exotic and remote Islam had undergone radical change on some fronts. When in the 1740s Frederick the Great of Prussia formed the first lancer unit from Tartar Muslim deserters from the Russian army, leading eventually to some one thousand Muslim soldiers serving in Prussia, he did so from his commitment to Enlightenment ideals of religious toleration. Frederick the Great allocated a prayer room for the use of Muslim troops, but on Sundays!

Frederick's attempt to conciliate Islam left him unwittingly extending the uncomplimentary left hand to his Muslim troops. By construing worship as a Sunday affair the king failed to understand the elementary rule of Islam's five daily prayers and of Friday simply as "the Day of Assembly," which did not tie the hands in giving and taking in commerce and traffic.[43] More appropriately, Frederick later had a Muslim cemetery built in Berlin.

---

43. The Qur'án urges the faithful to hasten to worship on the Day of Assembly leaving trafficking aside, but when the worship is ended to return to their normal business "and seek God's bounty." *Qur'an* 62:9–11.

Through ups and downs, the Muslim community survived in Germany, and after 1951 the community created the organization *Geistliche Verwaltung der Muslimflüchtlinge in der Bundesrepublik Deutschland* to administer the affairs of Muslim refugees in Germany.

For all his Enlightenment inclinations, Frederick the Great and his successors stopped short of instituting *Shariah* law. That happened in the Austro-Hungarian Empire. Following the absorption of large Muslim populations of Ottoman Bosnia-Herzegovina in 1878, the government in Vienna in 1909 incorporated the region into the central imperial system, and in 1912 it passed an act granting recognition to the Hanafite branch of *Shariah* law. This was extended to all Muslim communities of the empire, not just to those in Bosnia-Herzegovina. The way was paved by the translation into German of the Hanafí code of Muslim family law, published in Vienna in 1883. In 1979 that legal framework was renewed, and Austrian law applied Islamic family law in its courts in Bosnia-Herzegovina.[44]

Many in the West have looked forward to Turkey's likely entry into the European Union for the consoling thought that a secularized Islam will emerge to act as a moderate counterbalance to radical Islam and thus help advance the prospects of intercultural understanding. Expressing remorse for his Regensburg speech, for example, Pope Benedict XVI reversed himself and expressed support for Turkey's bid to join Europe. Yet the hope for a rapprochement is not well founded. Despite the guarantee given to the Greek Orthodox community in Turkey under the terms of the Treaty of Lausanne in 1923, and subsequently confirmed in article 37 of the Turkish Constitution, there has, for example, been a steady diminution of Christian numbers. Riots that broke out in Istanbul and Izmir in 1955 led to a mass exodus of Greek Orthodox Christians. Turkey moved to place the jurisdiction of the Ecumenical Patriarchate under state control with the provision that only Turkish citizens qualified for the Patriarchate and as members of the Holy Synod. In 1971 the government closed the Theological School of Halki, the only institution existing for the training of clergy in Turkey.

That action is compounded by the fact that since 1936 the Greek Orthodox Church has been prohibited from acquiring property in Turkey. Of the original estimated 110,000 Greek Orthodox Christians at the time of the Lausanne Treaty in 1923, there are now only about 2,000 left, and they are said to be subject to numerous restrictions, such as inability to replace officers on community boards.[45] The general Christian population has dwindled from several million at the time of the fall of the Ottoman

---

44. Nielsen, *Muslims in Western Europe*.
45. Prodromou, "Turkey Between," 149–54.

Empire to about 70,000 in 2006.⁴⁶ A report in the 1970s by the European Commission on Migrant Labor documented numerous cases of discrimination and persecution among Turkey's Christian minorities.

Abroad, Turkish military intervention in Cyprus in 1974 led to partition of the island and to the installation under Rauf Denktash of a satellite government that in 1983 adopted the name of the Turkish Republic of Northern Cyprus, with its capital in Nicosia. It has left Europe with a bitter legacy on its doorstep. The ensuing widespread destruction of churches in partitioned Cyprus has combined with other truculent issues to make it hard to think that Turkey will trace a path for Europe "from anathema to dialogue," or from partisan confrontation to shared commitment. Internal Islamist forces are unlikely to be constrained by membership of Europe and its guarantee of religious toleration, which leaves Turkey's role as a promoter of dialogue an open question. The festering Armenian issue within Turkey and abroad has remained a difficult obstacle.

Thanks to the standoff in Cyprus, the Mediterranean has remained an unstable theatre of intercultural encounter. Deadlock has complicated its destiny. Elsewhere Christianity was conflated with Western imperialism, making the religion a lightning rod.⁴⁷ On one reading of the region's tangled history, it is conceivable that the smoldering embers of anti-Ottoman resentment in the Balkans and elsewhere, such as Austria, combined with festering Armenian resentment, could be rekindled in an enlarged Europe, making Europe a frontline of the clash of civilizations. Such a denouement would strain the resources of traditional diplomacy; it would not be too early to start preparing for that future now.

In Britain, for example, with its 1.6 million Muslims, there have been calls for Muslim representation in Parliament to be greater than the present number of four Members of Parliament (MPs). According to Tarique Ghaffur, assistant commissioner of the Metropolitan Police and Britain's most senior Muslim police officer, Muslims are entitled to twenty MPs to reflect their number in the country.⁴⁸ In the meantime, while acknowledging that tolerance and respect for Muslims in post-7/7 Britain⁴⁹ have remained higher than elsewhere in Europe, Ghaffur nevertheless noted that "British Muslims still feel more resentful, more alienated and more suspicious

---

46. Hirst, "Pushed to the Periphery." Hirst is news editor of the London-based Catholic weekly, *The Tablet*.

47. Sharkey, "Arabic Antimissionary Treatises," 98–105.

48. Ghaffur, "Muslim Britain in Denial."

49. The July 7, 2005, bombing in the London Underground, carried out by homegrown terrorists, killed fifty-two people.

than Muslims polled in Germany, France and Spain."⁵⁰ Sir Iqbal Sacranie, secretary-general of the Muslim Council of Britain and a self-declared supporter of Khumaynī's *fatwa* against the writer Salman Rushdie, has blamed the Zionist conspiracy for anti-Muslim prejudice in Britain. In his naiveté, Sir Ian Blair, London's police commissioner, declared before the London bombings: "There is nothing wrong with being an Islamic fundamentalist. . . . Bridges will be built."⁵¹ Bridgebuilding, however, acquired a challenging meaning in the aftermath of 7/7 and the Madrid bombings of March 11, 2004. Europe seems defensive, with many Euro-secularists resolved to deploy the European Union as a barrier against the return of religion, while, somewhat maladroitly, backing multiculturalism. The bandwagon of cultural pluralism seems lost for direction.

Other forces are wearing down Europe's moral stamina, such as declining fertility rates of 1.2 each for Italy and Spain, 1.3 for Germany, 1.5 for Sweden, according to a report by the World Economic Forum.⁵² Such low birthrates threaten major social and economic disarray whose demographic consequences will not take long to manifest themselves. It is as if a strange moon has appeared in the firmament like a circulating anti-aphrodisiac compounded of moral apathy and is lulling Europe into self-negation. Religion today is all about crossing borders, physical as well as spiritual. Few faith traditions are container-proof and none is credible in isolation.

Europeans persisted in speaking of religions as denominations and as an appendage to the imperial agenda. Christianity was regarded as a national dividend, and that promoted the religion's fragmentation abroad and complicated immensely perceptions of its status as a world religion. The "plurality" of national expressions of Christianity diminished the chances of Muslims recognizing its religious merit. National expressions acquired a religious status and vice versa. Nearly everywhere in the colonial empires, Muslim communities, whatever their size, regarded the presence of Christian missions as secular foreign intrusion that was to be resisted as such. Like the Romans before them, Muslims felt little inclination to treat Christianity as a true religion; only as provocation in the politics of colonial hegemony. That perception has survived in historical accounts of the Western empire,

---

50. Ghaffur. "Muslim Britain in Denial." In spite of the siege mentality, there has been a steady trickle of British converts to Islam, including white British women. See Dixie, "Allah's Daughters," 33. A prominent Muslim convert is Joe Ahmed-Dobson, a youth worker and the son of Frank Dobson, a former Health Secretary in the Cabinet of Tony Blair. Ahmed-Dobson expressed impatience with the dilatory response of the government to Muslim demands ("Britain's Plans," 54).

51. Phillips, *Londonistan*, 54.

52. World Economic Forum, *Living Happily Ever After*, Table VI–9.

though Islam is spared in accounts of the Muslim empires. In fact, empire is understood as a synonym for Europe's colonial system even though Muslim empires were as widespread and longer lasting.

CONCLUSION: STYLE AND SUBSTANCE

Without difference and particularity to give it substance, diversity is a hollow trophy. It is hard to see how the world can be genuinely diverse without also being genuinely different, and it is impossible to be either without the ability to differentiate and to evaluate. No culture thrives simply by being whimsical and arbitrary. Tolerance is only the spirit of common acceptance with a commitment to variety and difference, Christian or other. Nothing conflicts with diversity more than the refusal to acknowledge difference, and nothing makes diversity more meaningful than the affirmation of difference. Violence and intimidation can in the short run be appeased; in principle, however, they discount self-criticism and dialogue as pointless. Ecumenical leadership faces a unique opportunity to show how in the face of difference commitment can nurture tolerance and plurality divested of threats and intimidation. Bearing witness has never been the issue. The issue is commitment that can challenge easy assumptions and inspire action.

BIBLIOGRAPHY

Abu Husayn, Abdul-Rahim. "Duwayhi as a Historian of Ottoman Syria." *Bulletin of the Royal Institute for Inter-Faith Studies* 1 (1999) 1–13.

Babinger, Franz. *Mehmed the Conqueror and His Time.* Edited by William C. Hickman and translated from German by Ralph Manheim. Bolingen Series 96. Princeton: Princeton University Press, 1978.

Badger, George Percy. *The Nestorians and Their Rituals.* 2 vols. London: J. Masters, 1852.

Berliner, A. "Zur Ehrenrettung des Maimonides." In *Moses ben Maimon: Sein Leben, seine Werke und sein Einfluss Zur Errinerung an den siebenhundersten Todestag des Maimonides,* edited by Wilhelm Bacher et al., 103–30. 2 vols. Leipzig: G. Fock. 1914.

Bovill, Edwin William. *The Golden Trade of the Moors.* London: Oxford University Press, 1968.

Colley, Linda. *Captives, Britain, Empire and the World, 1600–1850.* New York: Anchor, 2002.

Courbage, Youssef, and Philippe Fargues. *Christians and Jews under Islam.* New York: Tauris, 1997.

Cragg, Kenneth. *Alive to God: Muslim and Christian Prayer.* New York: Oxford University Press, 1970.

Daniel, Norman. "The Impact of Islam on the Laity in Europe from Charlemagne to Charles the Bold." In *Islam: Past Influences and Present Challenge,* edited by Alford

T. Welch and Pierre Cachia, 105–25. Edinburgh: Edinburgh University Press, 1979.
Dixie, Anne. "Allah's Daughters: Muslim Converts." *The Times Magazine* (July 1, 2006) 33.
Duffield, Ian, and Paul Edwards. "Equiano's Turks and Christians: An Eighteenth Century African View of Islam." *Journal of African Studies* 2 (1976) 433–44.
Froissart, Jean, Saint-Palaye et al. *Sir John Froissart's Chronicles of England, France, Spain and the Adjoining Countries: From the Latter Part of the Reign of Edward II to the Coronation of Henry IV*, vol. 11. London: Longman, Hurt, Rees, and Orme, 1806.
Fück, Johann W. "Islam as an Historical Problem in European Historiography since 1800." In *Historians of the Middle East*, edited by Bernard Lewis and Peter Malcom Holt, 303–14. London: Oxford University Press, 1962.
Gabrieli, Francesco, ed. *Arab Historians of the Crusades*. Translated by E. J. Costello. 1969. Reprint, Berkeley and Los Angeles, CA: University of California Press, 1984.
Ghaffur, Tarique. "Sections of Muslim Britain in Denial about Extremism." *Sunday Times*, July 2, 2006.
Gibbon, Edward. *The Decline and Fall of the Roman Empire*. 3 vols. New York: Modern Library, n.d.
Gilmore, Myron Piper. *The World of Humanism: 1453–1517*. New York: Harper Torchbooks, 1962.
Goodpasture, H. McKennie, ed. *Cross and Sword: An Eyewitness History of Christianity in Latin America*. Maryknoll, NY: Orbis, 1989.
Harrison, Jane Ellen, et al. *Themis: A Study of the Social Origins of Greek Religion*. Cambridge, MA: Cambridge University Press, 1912.
Henrich, Sarah, and James L. Boyce, eds. "Martin Luther—Translations of Two Prefaces on Islam: Preface to *Libellus de ritu et moribus Tucorum (1530)*, and Preface to Bibliander's Edition of the Qur'an (1543)." *Word and World: Theology for Christian Ministry: Islam* 16 (1996) 250–66.
Hirst, Michael. "Pushed to the Periphery." *America* (June 2006) 10–13.
Lewis, Bernard. *The Emergence of Modern Turkey*. 2nd ed. London: Oxford University Press, 1968.
Lyall, Sarah. "Britain's Plans for Addressing Its Muslims' Concerns Lag." *New York Times*, August 19, 2006, A3.
Mauny, Raymond. *Tableau géographique de l'Ouest Africain au Moyen Age, d'après les sources écrites, la tradition et l'archéologie*. Dakar: IFAN, 1961.
Neander, Augustus. *General History of the Christian Religion and Church: From the German of Doctor Augustus Neander*. Translated by Joseph Torrey. Boston, MA: Crocker & Brewster, 1854.
Nicholas of Cusa. *Nicholas of Cusa's De Pace Fidei and Cribratio Alkorani*. Edited and translated by Jasper Hopkins. Minneapolis: Arthur J. Banning, 1994.
Nielsen, Jørgen S. *Muslims in Western Europe*. Edinburgh: Edinburgh University Press, 1992.
Phillips, Melanie. *Londonistan: How Britain is Creating a Terror State Within*. New York: Encounter, 2006.
Pirenne, Henri. *Mohammed and Charlemagne*. New York: Dover, 2001.
Pitts, Joseph. *A Faithful Account of the Religion and Manners of the Mahometans. In Which is a Particular Relation of Their Pilgrimage to Mecca, . . . By Joseph Pitts,*

... *The Third Edition, corrected, with additions. To this Edition is Added a Map* ... London: Printed for J. Osborn, T. Longman, and R. Hett, 1731.

Prodromou, Elizabeth H. "Turkey between Secularism and Fundamentalism?: The 'Muslimhood Model' and the Greek Orthodox Minority." *The Brandywine Review of Faith and International Affairs* 3 (2005) 149–54.

Rabadan, Muhammad. *Mahometism Fully Explained Etc: Written in Spanish and Arabic in the Year 1603 for the Instruction of the Moriscoes in Spain*. Translated and edited by J. Morgan. 2 vols. London: E. Curll, W. Mears, and T. Payne, 1723–25.

Rosenthal, Franz. *The Classical Heritage in Islam*. Translated by Emile and Jenny Marmostein. London: Routledge & Kegan Paul, 1975.

Sharkey, Heather J. "Arabic Antimissionary Treatises: Muslim Responses to Christian Evangelism in the Modern Middle East." *International Bulletin of Missionary Research* 28 (2004) 98–105.

Southern, R. W. *Western Views of Islam in the Middle Ages*. Cambridge, MA: Harvard University Press, 1962.

Trimingham, J. Spencer. *The Christian Approach to Islam in the Sudan*. London: Oxford University Press, 1948.

Turner, Bryan S. *Weber and Islam: A Critical Study*. Boston, MA: Routledge & Kegan Paul, 1974.

Volney, Constantin-François. *Travels through Egypt and Syria in the Years 1783, 1784 and 1785: Containing the Present Natural and Political State of Those Countries; Their Productions, Arts, Manufactures & Commerce; With Observations on the Manners, Customs and Government of the Turks and Arabs*. New York: J. Tieboiut for E. Duyckinck, 1798.

von Grunebaum, Gustave E. *Medieval Islam: A Study in Cultural Orientation*. Chicago, IL: University of Chicago Press, 1966.

Weber, Max. *Economy and Society: An Outline of Interpretive Sociology*. Edited by Guenther Roth and Claus Wittich. 2 vols. Berkeley, CA: University of California Press, 1978.

World Economic Forum. *Living Happily Ever After: The Economic Implications for Aging Societies*. Table VI–9, January 2004.

Chapter 5

Religious Plurality in South Africa
Some Historical Perspectives

Gerald J. Pillay

IN THIS VOLUME WE are concerned to understand religious plurality in the context of our globalized situation and to deal with the question of how people from diverse religious backgrounds can meaningfully relate to each other. It is commonly assumed that religious plurality is a post-World War II global issue. But this view must be modified. The formation of Christendom was completed just as the fifteenth century was ending, and it began unraveling almost immediately. The prerequisite for its perpetuation was uniformity that was largely territorially determined; its biggest threats and its eventual undoing were diversity and plurality.

In 1505 René II, Duke of Lorraine, brought together a group led by the German cartographer Martin Waldseemuller at the monastery near Strasbourg to draw a new map of the world. Waldseemuller produced the earliest map we have of the New World. The world was for the first time portrayed as a globe: North and South America appear in it, and the Pacific Ocean was depicted for the first time.

While the Thirty Years War (1618–48) over a hundred years later was still a battle for denominational dominance over territory, the course of world travel and colonialism that were well on the way were fueled by this new view of the globe and the new lands to "own." The same motivation for territorial domination in the context of the globe brought an unimagined contact with the world's cultures and peoples, which laid down the road to plurality and, in turn, to what we today label "globalization."

This case study is a snapshot of how the upheavals of Europe shaped the colonies and in turn was shaped by them. The South African case is instructive for our reflection about religious plurality. To begin with, it reminds us to take a long historical view and not to focus only on the recent period of rapid global interaction even though the speed of travel, communication, and social intercourse between cultures and individuals has increased on a scale unimaginable just a few decades ago.

The longer view, as far as South African church history is concerned, covers over 350 years during which Christianity took root and spread throughout the country. Today it is the religion of the majority of the indigenous population of the country. Cultural and religious plurality underwent several mutations determined largely by the changes in colonial control, the demise of colonial governments, and the political arrangements that followed colonialism.

We will consider the changing relations between church and state during the period of Dutch colonization, the brief period of Batavian rule, British rule, the period of apartheid, and the emergent period of democracy. Each period increased ethno-cultural diversity and in turn fostered a deeper tolerance of religious plurality, with the apartheid period being the time of retrogression.

RELIGIONS IN THE PERIOD OF DUTCH COLONIALISM

From the Dutch settlement of the Cape in 1652 to the period of the first British occupation of the Cape (1795–1803), church-state relations were determined by the principle *cuius regio eius religio* (the emperor's religion was the people's religion), which was widely accepted in Europe at the time. The unity of the state was confirmed in the unity of religious belief, which for Europe has meant "denominational" affiliation. But this did not guarantee social and political tranquility. The consequent dissatisfaction of the disenfranchised groups within the state contributed to numerous wars for religious liberty in the late sixteenth, seventeenth, and eighteenth centuries. When these discontented groups were numerically significant, struggles on the scale of the devastating Thirty Years War resulted. Vulnerable religious minority groups left Europe to seek safety elsewhere. The Thirty Years War achieved an uneasy truce; but the Peace of Westphalia (1647) did not annul the principle of *cuius regio eius religio*. It merely settled or renegotiated national and denominational boundaries. Neither the Catholic nor Protestant sides liked the peace settlement.

The first European settlement at the Cape—and with it the seeds for the first Christian church—was established merely four years after the Peace of Westphalia, and only thirty-two years after the first settlement of the English Pilgrims and Puritans in New England. The principle of *cuius regio eius religio* prevailed at the Cape in a way that it could not in North America. A possible explanation lies in the way both regions were colonized. What became the United States achieved unprecedented denominational plurality and from the start was set on a course fundamentally different from Europe. The acceptance of denominationalism in the United States was the most effective bulwark against the possibility of a State Church. Any form of territorial definition of Christianity became impossible since the acceptance of all Christian denominations extended to other traditions as well.

In the nonestablishment clause in the Constitution of the United States, over and above its liberal philosophical underpinnings, the historical awareness of religious plurality was validated and entrenched.[1] The political rationale for a state church that had existed for centuries wherever nationalism fed on the religious persuasions of a people had become untenable in the United States.

In spite of the possibilities for similar denominational plurality at the Cape, a different course was followed for at least the first 150 years. The Cape, colonized by the Dutch, established an official Church—the Reformed Church. Other Christian denominations and Muslims, who had come as exiles and slaves to the Cape, were not recognized. There was also little appreciation of traditional African religions among the colonizers. Almost the entire period of Dutch colonization was marked by a general lack of interest in the evangelization of the indigenous people. The popular theory about collusion between the Christian mission and the colonial project is contradicted by the absence of any serious support for mission or any significant missionary success until well into the nineteenth century, by which time the colonization of the Cape and the establishment of the two Boer Republics were completed.

The leaders and ministers of the Dutch Reformed Church (DRC) were generally skeptical about any possibility of evangelizing the local people.[2] The successful propaganda against George Schmidt's work, the first mis-

---

1. The first Amendment to the US Constitution states: "Congress shall make no law respecting an establishment of religion, or prohibiting the free exercise thereof; or abridging the freedom of speech, or the press; or the right of the people peaceably to assemble, and to petition the Government for a redress of grievances."

2. Shaw, *Memorials of South Africa*, 9–10.

sionary to the Cape who arrived in 1737, eighty-five years after the first white settlement, symbolizes the skepticism of the Dutch toward mission.[3]

The Cape government recognized only the DRC, and only members of this Church could hold public office.[4] A statement dating back to 1785 explains the predicament of Catholics at the time:

> There is no toleration for Catholics at the Cape. The public exercise of the religion was prohibited. Catholic children are baptized in the Reformed Church and apparently instructed in this religion. In view of the great significance that is attached by Catholics to the ceremonial, it is impossible for them to live in a country where sacred rites of religion like the celebration of the mass were prohibited. They have no means of obtaining an indulgence or of having extreme unction administered.[5]

About 28 percent of the white population at the Cape during the first one hundred years of white settlement was German and almost all of them were Lutheran. They, like Catholics and other Christians, were not permitted to hold public worship services. In 1742, ninety years after van Riebeeck's landing, a group of sixty-nine Lutherans unsuccessfully petitioned the Council of Policy (as the Cape government was still known) for permission to hold services. Only in 1778 was this permission granted. The period of Dutch colonization was characterized by an effective suppression of religious and, more particularly, Christian plurality.

Furthermore, there were ongoing tensions within the colony between the Cape government and the white settlers. For instance, the free burgers, a motley group that included the God-fearing and those devoid of any religious sentiment, were suspicious of the Cape colonial government. They often openly challenged the authority of the Dutch East India Company by evading the payment of taxes. The further the free burgers moved away from the Cape, the more independent of the Company they became. It was in their joint reaction to the Company, which was under the jurisdiction of the Dutch government, that the permanent white settlers developed a common local identity. This local solidarity formed the nucleus of what was to become "the Afrikaner identity" vis-à-vis the Dutch colonial government; it bonded together Dutch, French Huguenots, Germans, and other Europeans around a common religion and a common language.

The Dutch East India Company maintained control of the Council of Policy and its membership. By 1795, when the British first occupied the

3. Bredenkamp and Hatting, *Dagboek en briewe*; Kruger, *Pear Tree*.
4. Valentyn, *Description of the Cape*.
5. Hofmeyr and Pillay, *History of Christianity*, 10–11.

Cape, the free burgers, by now identifiable as "Afrikaners," still had not been able to obtain a single seat on the Council. They were relatively poor farmers, alienated from their European roots, almost entirely dependent on their farms for survival, and now speaking a new language—Afrikaans. They were in no financial position to challenge or compete with the more entrepreneurial settler who arrived in the wake of British colonization of the Cape.

THE BRIEF PERIOD OF BATAVIAN RULE

Under the Peace of Amiens, the Cape Colony was returned to the Dutch and ruled by the Batavian Republic for a brief period of three years (1803–06) before the British again occupied the Cape in January 1807. This short period is significant for the theme of religious plurality because of the constitutional reforms that took place under the Dutch commissioner General J. A. de Mist, and the new governor, J. W. Janssens. It heralded the first of three important constitutional moments in South African history since white settlement. The second formative moment was the establishment of South Africa as we know it today, when four colonies were brought together in 1910; and the third was the establishment of the first democratic South African state in 1994. The first and third of these "moments" dealt with the entrenchment and affirmation of religious freedom, and the right to establish places of worship and conduct public services.

The Batavian rule did not last long enough to see the implementation of all the reforms of Janssens and de Mist. Among the most important changes that were made was the introduction of the Church Ordinance of 1804. It established religious tolerance in South Africa for the first time, granting protection to "all religious associations which for the furtherance of virtue and good conduct respect a Supreme Being."[6] The Catholics and Muslims were among the first to establish their places of worship under this ordinance. By virtue of the DRC's size and entrenched influence among a large section of the white settlers, by the end of the eighteenth century it still maintained its position of dominance; but other denominations and, in terms of the wording of the ordinance, other religions as well, were now entitled to state support.[7]

---

6. See de Mist's "Die Kerk Orde," 55–58.
7. Shaw, *Story of My Mission*, 25–26.

UNDER THE BRITISH

With the arrival of the British garrisons, followed by the planned introduction of larger numbers of British settlers, came numerous Christian denominations from the UK. The Irish garrisons were almost entirely Catholic and the Scottish almost entirely Presbyterian. The principle of *cuius regio eius religio* was by definition now unsustainable.

A religiously plural society along the lines of the United States, though hitherto artificially restrained, was now possible. Governor Janssens formalized the terms by which missionaries could move outside the Cape Colony on February 20, 1805.[8] After the first wave of British settlers in 1820, missionary work took on unprecedented importance partly as a result of denominational diversity itself. New Christian groups and mission societies from Britain arrived with the aim of taking the gospel to the indigenous peoples. Also, South Africa together with the whole African continent became the focus of European interests. In a number of ways, those with a deep concern for proclaiming the gospel to the whole world could not achieve their global mission ("the Great Commission") until the world became accessible, as unfolded for the first time during this period.

At the same time as this religiously plural situation was evolving, the political map of the country was also fundamentally changing. The British annexed and consolidated their power bases in two provinces—the Cape Province and Natal. The Boer trek into the interior led to the establishment of two Afrikaner republics—the Orange Free State and the Transvaal. Then with the discovery of gold and diamonds within the republics came renewed rivalry between Boer and Briton. Anglo-Boer tensions led, finally, to the South African War at the turn of the twentieth century.

The nineteenth-century white hegemonies had a direct influence on the churches. There were now three Reformed Churches: the DRC at the Cape and two further Reformed Churches established by the *trekboers* (pioneer farmers). The rivalry between British and Boer divided the churches themselves along the lines of their political sympathies and support. Very few remained untouched by this white factional struggle.[9] The period of the Anglo-Boer conflict culminated in the consolidation of white control of the country as a whole, leading to the Union of South Africa in 1910. The few black citizens who had qualified for franchise in the British colonies were removed from the voter's roll. This period, therefore, coincided with the emergence of the first concerted black political efforts—predominantly

---

8. See full text of this proclamation in Hofmeyr et al., *History of the Church*, 55–68.

9. Cuthbertson, "Christianity, Imperialism."

Christian leaders: Tile, Plaatjies, and Soga, for example—and the emergence of the Ethiopian movement. The Ethiopian churches were to be the precursors of the fastest growing group of churches in the twentieth century, the *Amazioni*.

The white governments discerned early the political significance of the Ethiopian churches.[10] The African Zionist churches that followed in the wake of Pentecostalism in South Africa adopted a low political profile—ostensibly an apolitical position[11]—but the Ethiopian leaders openly affirmed African leadership and control over their own religious organizations against the continuance of white dominance within the "mission churches." Many Ethiopian leaders themselves played down the fact that their churches were the result of open rejection of white control and the affirmation of African leadership of African churches. Understandably, in the politically charged atmosphere between 1880 and 1910, they did not wish to be regarded primarily as a politically motivated movement.

Despite the principle of *cuius regio eius religio*, the country had in fact always been religiously heterogeneous. Only in 1910 with the formation of the Union of South Africa was there a single government for the whole country as we know it today. The South African map itself is a relatively recent colonial creation.

As a direct reaction to the deliberate exclusion of black citizens in the 1910 constitution of the Union, the South African National Native Congress—later renamed the African National Congress (ANC)—was established in 1912. It is significant that the nucleus of the group that formed the ANC comprised mainly African church leaders.

THE PERIOD OF APARTHEID

Apartheid lasted almost fifty years—from the period just before the National Party won the 1948 elections to the first democratic elections of 1994. Following the elections, the National Party immediately set about implementing a policy for the whole society that established an infrastructure and legal framework that would ensure that the white minority maintained political

---

10. As early as the turn of the century, the Native Affairs Commission of 1903–05 recorded in its investigations the reaction to the emergence of these churches. See Millard, *Perceived Causes*, for citations from the Minutes of Evidence of this Commission, esp. vols. 2, 3, and 4. One of the earliest studies of these churches, which also deals with the 1903 Commission, was Lea, *Native Separatist*. Even Lea understood the Ethiopian Churches to be a quasi-religious and quasi-political body. He claimed that in its extreme form, it stood for "Africa for the Africans," 19.

11. Pillay, "Church and Society."

control and would not in any way be threatened by the majority black and other racial minority groups. Based on the seemingly sublime rationale to give the various racial groups self-determination in their own areas, it crafted a vicious system of domination that separated the races in public, prohibited normal interaction between peoples as equals, and confined those who were not white to a life of subservience and disenfranchisement.

What is important for our deliberations is the fact that the apartheid government was ostensibly a "Christian" government whose philosophical reasoning was sanctioned by the Dutch Reformed churches. The theology of apartheid established an ideology of racial supremacy on "biblical grounds." The few courageous individuals who dared to question these self-justifications bore the anger not just of the church authorities but also of the Afrikaner people themselves; they were seen as traitors of the *volk* (people).

The racialism of the apartheid system, however, had precedents in the experiments with race laws that the British colonial government undertook in the latter decades of the nineteenth century in the colony of Natal. Indian immigrants were brought there at the request of the colonial government to help its ailing economy. They were promised either free passage back to India after the period of their indentured labor or a piece of land on which to settle if they wished to remain in South Africa. Between 1860 and 1911, 110,000 immigrants arrived in Durban, Natal, at which time all Indian immigration was finally ended. Not only were the original promises not kept, these immigrants and their descendants also lived under the threat of repatriation for the first one hundred years of their stay in the country. The xenophobia of our time concerning immigrants was certainly felt by the immigrants to Natal within a short time of their arrival in the colony, notwithstanding their acknowledged economic benefit to the colony. Though the immigrants comprised a minority, 85 percent of whom were laborers, they were perceived to be a threat to white businesses.

Only 2 percent of the Indian immigrants came as Christians. Sixty-nine percent were Hindu and about 18 percent were Muslim. The British did not restrict these people in their freedom of worship or the right to establish their own places of worship. The main concern of the British was that they should not constitute a threat to white businesses and established social life. Elsewhere the British had maintained a strict social hierarchy toward indigenous peoples. In India, the nineteenth-century colonial government ensured the superiority of its officers over their subjects by observing strict conventions about social mixing, even among those subjects who had made headway in the army or civic life. In Natal, the colonial government experimented with legislation to ensure racial separation by introducing the Anti-Asiatic clause to control the purchase of land. The Pegging Act, too, was an early British experiment in apartheid-type legislation. The young Mohandas Gandhi, who came to Natal in 1894 en route to the Transvaal, fell afoul of the rule excluding Indians from first class compartments on trains. That momentous event when he was thrown off the train started him on his spiritual journey and his experiment with *satyagraha*—nonviolent political struggle.

The ideological underpinnings of apartheid were no doubt influenced by the fact that the architects of apartheid had gone abroad to study in Germany and the Netherlands in particular. In Europe, they came under the influence of the theories of Social Darwinism that reinforced the policies they implemented in South Africa on their return in the 1940s and 1950s. They, too, did not prohibit the different religious groups from expressing their faith and worshiping "in their own areas," but there was a general fear about the negative influence of other religions on "Christian society," of which they were the self-appointed guardians. Afrikaner leaders were no less forthright about their faith and mission in the world to protect "Christian civilization" than the kind of rhetoric we hear about the mission to protect Christianity and democracy in the twenty-first century. The apartheid government became the custodian of what was termed "Christian National education" which privileged biblical studies in state schools.

It is noteworthy that the theological mood of apartheid was messianic and its thinking based on a particular reading of the Old Testament. The Afrikaners' Great Trek and their sufferings were interpreted in relation to the freedom struggle of the Israelites as a *volk* with a providential destiny and identity. In that identity, their faith and understanding of divine intervention is interpreted. This is not the place to explore the nature of ideological formation, but what is apparent in this case is that a contextual reading in and of itself does not furnish adequate safeguards against a reading that is self-serving. Stephanus J. du Toit, a Dutch Reformed minister, was among the first to articulate a contextual reading of Afrikaner history as early as 1877 in a book titled *Die Geskiedenis van ons land in die Taal van ons Volk* (A History of Our Land in the Language of Our People). The need for a vernacular translation or contextual reading is necessary but not sufficient to avoid ideological distortion. The "contextual" reading must always be in critical and creative synergy with a "catholic" legitimacy. The inverse from a hermeneutical perspective is equally true and necessary.

Adherents to the religiopolitical creed of apartheid were strategically placed to manage the educational system. By changing the law, the state took over church schools and colleges that were perceived to be the hotbeds of "liberalism." The antidote to liberalism, in Dr. Verwoerd's terms, was an educational system that did not give Africans the false expectation that they could be educated to be competitors in society with whites. "Christian nationalism" was coupled with segregationist laws whereby each race had their own schools and religious institutions in their own areas.

In order to enforce its ideology of race-based separation, the government attempted to subsume all institutions, including the churches, under its program of restructuring South African society. Section 9 (7) of Act 25 of 1945 forbade black South Africans from worshiping "outside a Bantu residential area." The "Church clause" of the Native Laws Amendment Act of 1957 gave the minister authority to prohibit Africans from attending church services in a white area. The Group Act made it physically impossible for Christians from different races to have any real fellowship. Only white people could vote, and the apartheid government fashioned an unworkable system of trying to give each tribe its self-determination in its own self-governed state. Each step toward that grand plan was marked with protest until fifty years later apartheid became unmanageable and unaffordable. Under international and internal pressure it imploded, and democracy, aided by the inspirational leadership of Nelson Mandela and others, became inevitable.

While it lasted, though, apartheid seemed impregnable, and many suffered and died in the struggle. Contrary to our concerns about religious plurality and peaceful coexistence, the reasoning under apartheid was that any peaceful coexistence depended on the legal and physical separation of people. The religious vision informing it was narrow and ideologically determined. The DRC alienated itself from other Christians and other religions. The view that peace could only be had through separation not only contributed to the demise of the unjust system but also robbed all sides in the struggle of any real understanding of the different religious groupings, their faith, or their aspirations.

The church struggles during the fifty years under apartheid have received prolonged and serious scrutiny and have been widely documented.[12] It is unnecessary to repeat those findings here except to point out that the government and the churches that supported its ideology of separation of the races denied other Christians and other religions the rights and freedoms they themselves enjoyed. The confrontation between some churches and the government is perhaps best illustrated in the march on Parliament by twenty-five church leaders on February 29, 1988. In their letter to President P. W. Botha, they objected to the government's unlawful restriction of individuals and some churches.[13] Botha's reply to Anglican Archbishop

12. See De Gruchy, *Church Struggle*; Villa-Vicencio, *Trapped*; Serfontein, *Apartheid*; Cochrane, *Servants of Power*; Paton, *Apartheid*; Klinghorn, *Die NG Kerk*; Worship, *Between*; Gerhart, *Black Power*; and Roux, *Time Longer*.

13. This was widely covered in the press at the time that the "Letter of twenty-five

Desmond Tutu, who led the march, is instructive in how the apartheid government understood the relation between the state and the churches. Accusing the church leaders of furthering Marxist ideals for the country, Botha defined the spheres of jurisdiction of the church and the government thus: "Is it not true that the Christian Church knows no other power than love and faith and no other message than the true message of Christ; and if it brings its spiritual power into secular power play, and the message of Christ into disrepute, then it becomes a secular instead of a sacred spiritual subject, thereby relinquishing its claim to be Church?"[14] In other words, if the churches did not support the "Christian" government or the Christian ideals of the apartheid government, it supported the Marxists. In Botha's mind, the apartheid government's program and Christian ideals were one and the same.

From the perspective of progress toward religious plurality and tolerance that began one hundred years earlier, apartheid was a fifty-year interruption of the process. No church, for example, has enjoyed any preferential treatment in the courts in South Africa since 1889.[15] This did not preclude "excessive entanglement" between some churches, especially the DRC and the Nationalist Party government in the promotion of a certain form of Christian social ideal, nor did it provide mutual patronage for its so-called Christian Nationalism and its race ideology.

Religious plurality in a democratic South Africa has been taken forward together with wide-ranging constitutional changes that followed after the collapse of the apartheid system. With the introduction of democracy in 1994, for the first time South Africa introduced a Bill of Rights and established a Constitutional Court that would have preeminence over the legislature. The new constitution is a secular constitution enshrining the values of a liberal democracy. It bears all the strengths and weaknesses of liberal democratic constitutions anywhere. Among the first rights to be enshrined in the constitution was the freedom of religion. Naturally, although Christianity was the largest of the religious groups in South Africa, it was no longer privileged. While they remain a strong majority, Christians have had to learn to coexist and even collaborate with people of other faiths with whom they arguably have a greater affinity based on common religious values than with many secular humanists.

---

leaders to the State President and Parliament" dated February 29, 1988, was also publicized. See Botha, *Archives Yearbook*, vol. 1, part 2. In it, they wrote: "We regard your restrictions not only an attack on democratic activity in South Africa but as a blow directed at the heart of the Church mission in South Africa."

14. P. W. Botha, South Africa national television, n.d.
15. This issue is discussed more fully in Pillay, "Church and State."

CONCLUDING REMARKS

The argument put forward in this essay can be summarized in eight observations. First, colonialism promoted an irreversible trend of cultural heterogeneity in South Africa. With the arrival of European peoples into South Africa from the early seventeenth century, a growing white minority gained political domination that opened the way for more European settlements. The colonial period set the foundations for globalization, the pace of which has accelerated as the result of growing intercontinental travel and contact.

Second, South Africa was always a heterogeneous community of tribes who traded with each other or sometimes competed for more land. Colonial rule not only reduced all of them to a level of subservience but also contrived a territorially based notion of nationhood, shaped almost entirely in European terms. The Khoisan in the Southwest had far less to do with the Nguni on the East coast than, for example, Slavic people have to do with Anglo-Saxons within the European Union. These tribal territories had been molded into colonies that were then forced into a union that in 1910 became South Africa as we know it, and all their populations were heralded as "one nation." The formation of the United States is not dissimilar, as is the present attempt to create a European Union identity—a complex process still in its infancy.

In the third place, minority religions were tolerated but little understood. Muslims, Jews, and Chinese with their own religions were present from the early days of white settlement in South Africa. They enjoyed no more recognition than did Christians for the first 150 years until the "giant leap" taken by the Janssen-de Mist Ordinance.

Fourth, under the British there was general tolerance of other religions and other peoples as the abolitionist position gained momentum at home and, especially, after the abolition of slavery in 1833. British settlers arrived in South Africa in much greater numbers from 1820 onwards, and with them came more Protestant denominations giving way to a period of an unprecedented denominationalism. The Afrikaner groups found this liberalism manifested in the abolition of slavery and this new denominationalism threatening. The Great Trek into the interior away from the Cape Colony created two Boer republics, and three Dutch Reformed churches emerged as the result. These became bastions against the changes occurring in the Cape, and the protectors of Afrikaner culture, language, and religion. It was little wonder then that the Dutch Reformed churches became the chief protagonists of the apartheid ideology to ensure the identity of the Afrikaner.

The fifth point is that religious tolerance was neither complete nor widespread in the United Kingdom for much of the nineteenth century and colonial governments could hardly be expected to do in the colonies what could not be achieved at home. The Roman Catholic Relief Act, for example, which introduced Catholic emancipation in England and Ireland, was only promulgated in 1829. For the first time, in principle Catholics had the same civil standing as Protestants in England. This Act opened the way for the establishment of the Catholic hierarchy of bishops, which only took place in 1850. While it is true that the colonial governments did little to help educate the indentured Indians in Natal when they arrived in 1860, or to help maintain their traditional religious life in a foreign land, which the churches first intervened to do, it was only in the 1830s that English society itself awoke to the realization that the children of working class English citizens should also be educated. These two advances enabled Catholics to establish their own schools and colleges for the first time in the 1830s and 1840s.

Sixth, apartheid was created by Afrikaners, themselves victims of the Anglo-Boer war. They created a system to protect their *volk* and religion out of fear of being overwhelmed by the majority. The victim became the victimizer. Indians with their different religions were especially treated with suspicion. There was little or no understanding of the difference between the religions of these Eastern settlers—Islam, Hinduism, and Buddhism. The fact that these were the religions of the people from a different culture seemed more important for an ideology based on the self-determination of other peoples in their own areas. Hence, the apartheid government did not undo the rights of other religions to worship and organize their religious life publicly, provided it was done in their own areas and was part of their cultural expression. Culture and racial differences superseded religious identity. This social plan did not readily admit any interest in the missionary endeavor.

Seventh, the struggle against apartheid was enriched by the participation of those from the different religions. Though the struggle was mainly led by Christians, there were always prominent Jewish, Hindu, and Muslim voices among them, even though these religions constituted small minorities. The new constitution, born out of systematic racial separation, was consciously inclusive. It attempted to ensure that Christianity, although the religion of the majority, was not privileged. For the sake of equity, reconciliation, and "leveling the playing field"—a term repeated in the constitutional debates—the minority religions obtained equal status and representation. The strength of a viable democracy is dependent on its capacity to accommodate religious and cultural minorities both constitutionally and in civic life.

The eighth point is that the South African case demonstrates the ways in which the different religious groupings made a fundamental contribution to the reconciliation process after apartheid, even though a form of ideologically driven Christianity had bolstered apartheid itself.

The interaction between the religions in South Africa has been neither the same nor uniform for any period of time. Besides the obvious factor of changing governmental formation, the chief reason for any lack of uniformity has been the context of ambiguity that accompanies their "being in the world but not of the world." Only where the Christian witness is completely subsumed, as is the case under tyrannical, ideological regimes or where it dominates, as in a form of Christendom, is this ambiguity diminished. It never actually disappears. Both these options were never real possibilities in South African history.

The 350 years of Christian history in South Africa may be divided, as far as religious plurality is concerned, into two periods lasting about 150 years each. In the first 150 years, in spite of the presence of other Christian denominations and other religions, there was a state church, and only this church had full religious freedom and official status. The next 150 years saw a slow move toward a situation of religious plurality. Religious toleration and denominationalism only very gradually became accepted ideas. The apartheid era was an interruption of this process. One of the first achievements after the demise of apartheid was the restoration of the progress toward religious plurality as religious freedom became one of the first rights to be protected in the new constitution.

BIBLIOGRAPHY

Botha, C. G., et al, eds., *Archives Yearbook for South African History*, vol. 1, part 2. Cape Town: Cape Times, 1938.

Bredenkamp, B., and J. L. Hatting, eds. *Dagboek en briewe van George Schmidt, eerste sendeling in Suid Afrika (1737-1747)*. Cape Town: Belville Wes Kaapslandse Instituut vir Historiese Navorsing Publikasie reeks BI, 1981.

Cochrane, James R. *Servants of Power: The Role of English-Speaking Churches in South Africa, 1903-1930*. Johannesburg: Ravan, 1987.

Cuthbertson, G. "Christianity, Imperialism and Colonial Warfare." In *A History of Christianity in South Africa*, vol. 1, by J. W. Hofmeyr and G. J. Pillay, 150-71. Pretoria: Kagiso, 1994.

De Gruchy, J. W. *The Church Struggle in South Africa*. Cape Town: David Philip, 1979.

de Mist, J. A. "Die Kerk Orde," July 24, 1804. Quoted in *History of the Church in South Africa: A Document and Source Book*, edited by J. W. Hofmeyr et al., 55-58. Pretoria: University of South Africa, 1991.

du Toit, Stephanus J. *Die Geskiedenis van ons land in die Taal van ons Volk*. Paarl: Du Toit, 1895.

Gerhart, Gail M. *Black Power in South Africa: The Evolution of an Ideology*. Berkeley, CA: University of California Press, 1978.

Hofmeyr, J. W., et al., eds. *History of the Church in South Africa: A Document and Source Book*. Pretoria: University of South Africa, 1991.
Hofmeyr, J., and G. Pillay. *A History of Christianity in South Africa*, vol. 1. Pretoria: Kagiso, 1994.
Kinghorn, Johann, ed. *Die NG Kerk en Apartheid*. Johannesburg: Macmillan, 1986.
Kruger, B. *The Pear Tree Blossoms: The History of the Moravian Church in South Africa, 1737-1869*. Genadendal: Moravian Book Depot, 1966.
Lea, Allen. *The Native Separatist Church Movement in South Africa*. Cape Town: Juta, 1928.
Millard, Joan Anne. *A Study of the Perceived Causes of Schism in Some Ethiopian-Type Churches in the Cape and Transvaal, 1884-1925*. ThD Thesis, University of South Africa, 1995.
Paton, Alan. *Apartheid and the Archbishop: The Life and Times of Geoffrey Clayton, Archbishop of Cape Town*. Cape Town: David Philip, 1973.
Pillay, Gerald J. "Church and Society: Some Historical Perceptions." In *Sociopolitical Changes and the Challenge to Christianity in South Africa*, edited by C. W. du Toit, 19-33. Pretoria: University of South Africa, 1994.
Pillay, Nirmala. "Church and State: Some Legal and Constitutional Perspectives." In *Sociopolitical Changes and the Challenge to Christianity in South Africa*, edited by C. W. du Toit, 34-47. Pretoria: University of South Africa, 1994.
Roux, Edward R. *Time Longer than Rope: A History of the Black Man's Struggle for Freedom in South Africa*. London: University of Wisconsin Press, 1948.
Serfontein, J. H. P. *Apartheid, Change and the NG Kerk*. Johannesburg: Taurus, 1982.
Shaw, Barnabas. *Memorials of South Africa*. Cape Town: Struik, 1860.
Shaw, William. *The Story of My Mission in South-Eastern Africa: Comprising Some Account of the European Colonists with Extended Notices of the Kaffir and Other Native Tribes*. London: Hamilton, Adam and Co., 1860.
Valentyn, F. *Description of the Cape of Good Hope with the Matters Concerning It, Amsterdam 1726*. 2 vols. Cape Town: Van Riebeeck Society of Collection, 1972.
Villa-Vicencio, Charles. *Trapped in Apartheid: A Socio-Theological History of the English-Speaking Churches*. Cape Town: David Philip, 1988.
Worsnip, Michael E. *Between the Two Fires: The Anglican Church and Apartheid 1948-1957*. Pietermaritzburg: University of KwaZulu-Natal Press, 1991.

Chapter 6

Religious Plurality in East Asia before 1800
The Encounter between Christianity and Asian Religions

Peter C. Phan

THE TITLE OF THIS essay contains several terms that require preliminary clarification both to circumscribe its scope and to indicate its limitations. "Religious plurality" here means not only the mere fact that there are many and diverse religions existing side-by-side in East Asia but also, and primarily, the challenges that such plurality poses to Christianity's self-understanding, its mission, and its theology ("religious pluralism"). Generally speaking, "East Asia" includes both Northeast Asia (China, Hong Kong, Japan, Korea, Macau, and Taiwan) and Southeast Asia (Myanmar, Thailand, Cambodia, Laos, Vietnam, The Philippines, Malaysia, Singapore, and Indonesia). This essay will concentrate on one northeastern and one southeastern country—namely, China and Vietnam respectively—countries that share a relatively common cultural and religious heritage and a long history of mutual interaction, both friendly and hostile. It is hoped, however, that this focus will not unduly narrow the parameters of the discussion but rather will serve as a paradigm for understanding the encounter between Christianity and East

Asian religions in general.[1] The emphasis will be on how *Christians*, both Asian and expatriate, viewed Asian religions, along with a few examples of how Asian non-Christians reacted to Christianity.[2] "Before 1800" indicates the *terminus ad quem* of my historical survey.[3] There will unfortunately be no discussion of East Asian religions themselves, and given limited space, only a highly selective treatment of key moments in the encounter between them and Christianity can be offered.

In what follows, I will first survey religious plurality and the encounter between Christianity and religions in China. The second part will discuss three significant writings that exemplify the interaction between Christians and the followers of other religions in Vietnam. The essay will conclude by highlighting the theological challenges that religious pluralism poses to Asian Christianity today.[4]

CHRISTIANITY AND RELIGIOUS PLURALITY IN CHINA

Church historians have recently grown much more aware that Christianity is an "eastern" rather than "western" religion. It is a religious movement that in its earliest stages spread from the Middle East not only into the western parts of the Roman empire but also into Asia, in particular Syria,

---

1. A study of the encounter between Christianity and Asian religions in Japan and Korea would be necessary for a more adequate understanding of this theme.

2. Recently there has been a great interest in discovering how Asian natives themselves, both Christian and non-Christian, reacted to Christianity rather than how expatriate missionaries attempted to inculturate Christianity into Asia. This essay will offer examples of how both groups viewed the relation between Christianity and Asian religions. It will discuss both how missionaries presented Christianity to Asia and how natives—mainly Christians—reacted to Christianity.

3. The choice of this *terminus ad quem* is well justified since the beginning of the nineteenth century marked several important events: the death of Emperor Qianlong (1799), the suppression of the Society of Jesus in China (1773), the persecution of Christians (1785), the Beijing persecution (1805/1811), and the arrival of Protestant missionaries on the mainland (between 1805 and 1810). See Standaert, *Handbook*, 1:xi. This monumental work (964 pages) with multilingual and extensive bibliographies is an indispensable resource for our study.

4. The literature is vast. Fortunately, a three-volume bibliography on Asian Christian theologies is available: England et al., *Asian Christian Theologies*. For general histories of Christianity in Asia until 1800, see in addition to the volume edited by Standaert, Moule, *Christians in China*; Latourette, *History of Christian Missions*; Laurentin, *Chine et Christianisme*; Gernet, *Chine et christianisme*; Charbonier, *Histoire des Chrétiens*; Gillman and Klimkeit, *Christians in Asia*; England, *Hidden History*; and Moffett, *History of Christianity*.

Mesopotamia, Persia, Armenia, and India.⁵ Furthermore, what was brought to these lands is not a monolithic Christianity but rather a variety of Christianities with different languages, liturgies, spiritualities, theologies, modes of organization, and cultures; a dazzling multiplicity and variety that is unfortunately concealed by the reality of Christendom that emerged in the West since the Middle Ages and was subsequently brought to the other parts of the globe. This diversity was further increased by the varied ways in which the Christian faith was received or, to use a neologism, inculturated, in these countries. Inculturation refers to the two-way process whereby the Christian faith, or more concretely, a particular form of Christianity—usually the Western one, and not some pure, a-cultural Christianity that of course does not exist—encounters a particular group of people, assumes their language and culture as its mode of self-realization and expression, transforming, and when necessary, correcting them with Christian beliefs and values, and at the same time is enriched in turn by them. And among the many factors that played a key role in this process of inculturation in Asia are its many and diverse religions.⁶

For our purposes, we will not refer to the so-called ancient religion of East Asia as such, with its belief in the supreme deity (Shangdi/Tian), nature deities, mother goddesses, mythological figures (especially ancestral spirits, the Three Sovereigns, and the Five Emperors), its practices of shamanism and divination, and the ancestor cult.⁷ These elements will be touched upon only insofar as they are found in the three religions of East Asia; namely, Confucianism, Daoism, and Buddhism, often referred to in Sino-Vietnamese as *tam giao* (the "Three Religions"). It is the history of how Christianity interacted with these religions in China that concerns us here.

Christians Encountering Other Religions in T'ang China (635–907)

There is little doubt that the Silk Road, which stretched westward from the Great Wall of China across numerous kingdoms of Central Asia and through the Persian empire into Armenia and Syria brought constant

---

5. See Irvin and Sunquist, *History of the World*, 1.

6. Of myriad introductions to East Asian religions, see the brief and helpful one by Ching, "East Asian Religions," 347–467. On Buddhism as an East Asian religion, see also Ching, "Mahayana," 284–320. For a more comprehensive presentation of Chinese religions, see Ching, *Chinese Religions*.

7. On these elements of Chinese "ancient religion," see Ching, *Chinese Religions*, 15–50.

contacts between Chinese traders and the peoples of the West, even as far as Alexandria, Carthage, and Rome, many centuries before the birth of Christianity. Christian merchants and monks (particularly of the Nestorian Church), too, followed this trade route and it is highly likely that through them Christianity from its earliest days reached the Middle Kingdom through Central Asia.

There is a tradition that before his martyrdom, the apostle Thomas left India and set sail for China, but Thomas's voyage is extremely unlikely.[8] One of the most extensive and unequivocal evidences of Christian presence in China is the large black stone stele discovered in 1623 or 1625 near Xi'an (the site of the ancient imperial capital of Ch'ang-an).[9] Erected in 781, the stele contains a text of 1,800 Chinese characters and about seventy Syriac words together with a long list of names of Persian or Syrian missionaries. The author of the text is a Persian priest named Adam, whose Chinese name is recorded as Jing-jing. The text is entitled "Lapidary Eulogy on the Propagation of the Luminous Religion (i.e., Nestorian Christianity) in China" and the frontispiece on the top of the stele reads: "Stele on the propagation on the Luminous Religion of Da Qin (i.e., the Byzantine empire) in China." The text opens with an exposition of the Christian faith and then presents a history of Nestorianism in China from 635—when the monk Aluoben (A-lo-pen) is supposed to have entered into China—to 781, when the stele

---

8. This tradition seems to be based on information gleaned from a breviary of the Syrian Malabar Church composed in the thirteenth century. According to Gillman and Klimkeit, the South Indian Christians might have had contacts with fellow Christians in China in the T'ang period and very likely projected their origin back to the time of St. Thomas. Of this Christian presence in pre-T'ang China, they write: "Thus direct or indirect Christian influence on pre-T'ang China remains a matter of conjecture. There are, however, traces of Manichaean and Zoroastrian activities in the China of that period. Since Manichaeans often followed the Christians in their eastern mission, a Christian presence in China in the 6th century cannot be completely ruled out." See their *Christians in Asia*, 267. See also Tubach, "Der Apostel Thomas," 58–79.

9. On Christian mission under T'ang China, see in particular Moffett, *History of Christianity*, vol. 1, 288–323; Gillman and Klimkeit, *Christians in Asia*, 267–82; and Standaert, *Handbook*, vol. 1, 1–42. For the Nestorian documents, see Saeki, *Nestorian Documents* and Pelliot, *L'inscription*. The monument, often referred to as the "Xi'an stele" or "Nestorian monument," was erected in 781. Prior to this date, there are other, brief indications of the presence of Christians in China: the decree of 683, issued by the T'ang emperor Taizong (T'ai-tsung), which refers to "the Persian monk Aluoben [A-lo-pen] bringing scriptures and teaching from afar"; a historical note for the year 731 affirming that "the king of Persia sent the chief P'an-na-mi with the monk of great virtue, Chi-lieh, as ambassadors with tribute"; and the decree of 745, issued under Emperor Xuanzong (Hsüan-tsang), mentioning the spread of Nestorian Christianity. See Gillman and Klimkeit, *Christians in Asia*, 269–70. For a helpful history of China under the T'ang, see Roberts, *Concise History*, 51–78.

was erected. It continues with an encomium to the donor Yisi (I-ssu) and a versified composition in praise of the Luminous Religion under the T'ang dynasty, and concludes with a colophon stating the date of the erection of the stele and a list in Syriac of bishops and monks of the Da Qin monasteries.

In addition to this stele, there are other Chinese written sources on Christianity of the T'ang period often referred to as the "Dunhuang Documents" found in the library of the Dunhuang grottoes.[10] Several of these documents are of great interest for our purposes since they offer concrete examples of how Christianity encountered Chinese religions. Some of these documents were older than the Xi'an stele, such as the *Xu ting Mi shi suo jing* (Book of Jesus-Messiah), probably written by Aluoben after his arrival to China and before 638, and the *Yi shen lun* (Discourse on Monotheism), written perhaps in 638 or 641 and composed of three parts: *Yu di er* (The Parable, part two), *Yi tan lun di yi* (Discourse on the Oneness of the Ruler of the Universe, part one), and *Shi zun bu shi lun di san* (The Lord of the Universe's Discourse on Alms-giving, part three).[11] Indeed, it has been rightly noted that both the Xi'an stele and the Dunhuang Documents represent a very early example of fruitful interreligious collaboration in Asia.

This first encounter between Christianity and Chinese religions was friendly and enriching for both sides. First, this section will focus on the part of the Chinese. The powerful T'ang dynasty maintained diplomatic relations, trade, and cultural contacts with most countries of Central Asia and adopted a policy of high tolerance for religions of Western Asia, such as Zoroastrianism, Judaism, Manichaeism, Islam, and of course Christianity.[12] It was under the rule of Emperor Taizong (627-49) that according to the Xi'an stele, the monk Aluoben arrived in China in 635 and was given a grand reception. The Sacred Scriptures he brought with him were translated into Chinese, and their content was examined and approved by the emperor himself, who judged it to be in conformity with "the Way," and ordered it to be preached and transmitted. A monastery with twenty-one monks was founded in the I-ning quarter of the capital.

---

10. For an English translation of these texts, see the volumes by Saeki and Moule cited above.

11. See Standaert, *Handbook*, vol. 1, 4-5. For analysis of these texts, see Gillman and Klimkeit, *Christians in Asia*, 275-82.

12. It was only later, in 845, that an edict was issued, ordering the secularization of foreign religious establishments. This imperial edict seems to target Buddhism, for economic rather than religious reasons, since Buddhist monks, reported to number 700,000 at the time, did not pay taxes. While Buddhism quickly recovered from this persecution, other religions, including Nestorian Christianity, seem to have suffered a fatal decline. Islam was an exception.

The inscription goes on to report that many more monasteries were established, one in each city, especially under the third T'ang emperor Gaozong (650–83). Aluoben himself was bestowed many honors, being elevated to the rank of a "Great Spiritual Lord, Protector of the Empire." Another Christian monk by the name of Yisi also found much favor with the T'ang and served as a general under three emperors, including Suzong (756–62), Daizong (763–79), and Dezong (780–804).[13]

Secondly, early Christians in China entered into a fruitful collaboration with the followers of the Chinese religions; in particular, Buddhism. Jing-jing is said to have assisted the Buddhist monk Prajñ~ in translating the Buddhist *Đatp~ramit~ Sutra* in 786. Indeed, in composing his own text, Jing-jing perhaps adopted the literary model of inscription from the famous Buddhist inscription of *Tuotuo si bei* (Stele Inscription of the Dhûta Monastery) composed by Wang Jin (d. 505). More importantly, from the point of view of the inculturation of the Christian faith into China, both the Xi'an stele and the Dunhuang Documents exhibit a large amount of Christian borrowing of Buddhist, Confucianist, and Daoist terminology and concepts to convey the Christian beliefs into Chinese. Space does not permit a detailed listing and analysis of such terms and concepts, but clearly such borrowing—short of transliteration—was unavoidable to make Christianity understandable to the Chinese.[14] A few observations, however, would be useful to understand the encounter of Christianity with the Chinese religions in 635–846.[15]

As mentioned above, the stele contains a lengthy exposition of the Christian faith in prose and a shorter summary in verse. The first exposition—the more important of the two—refers to the Trinity, the creation of the world, the original fall of humanity, Satan's rule, the incarnation, salvation, the Bible, baptism, evangelization, ministry, Christian morality, fasting, the liturgy of the hours, and the Eucharist. Needless to say, this is not a complete presentation of the Christian faith but rather of what the author, Jing-jing, considered to be the essentials of the Christian beliefs and practice that could be chiseled down on the very limited space of a stone

13. It is likely that the positive attitude of the T'ang emperors toward Christianity, which is presented in rosy colors by the stele, was motivated not only by religious sentiments but also by a desire for advantageous political and economic relations with the countries of Central Asia. At any rate, clearly the fortunes of Nestorian Christianity were closely bound up with the T'ang emperors, and no doubt one of the reasons why it disappeared so quickly was the fall of the T'ang dynasty in 907.

14. For the Xi'an stele, Moffett reproduces the translation by Saeki and helpfully puts in italics words and concepts possibly borrowed from Chinese religions. See his *History of Christianity*, vol. 1, 514–17.

15. See Chiu, "Historical Study."

stele. Furthermore, the exposition reflects Nestorian Christianity, especially its monastic tradition and practices.[16]

Jing-jing's borrowing of the concepts and terminology of Chinese religions was by no means slavish. Rather, his purpose was to make Christianity understandable to the Chinese, and as we will see, his approach was quite creative. He made ample use of Daoist expressions to describe God such as "unchanging in perfect repose," a formula used by the *Daode jing* to describe the Dao ("Way"). God is said to have produced "the four cardinal points" (a basic concept of Chinese geomancy) and "the two principles of nature," or the "yin and yang" of Daoist and Confucian cosmology. He speaks of some people mistakenly identifying "non-existence" (the Daoist "nameless nothingness") with "existence." He refers to Christianity as the ever-true and unchanging Dao itself. Jesus is said to have established his "new teaching of non-assertion," the key Daoist notion of *wu wei* (non-action). Jing-jing also adopted Confucian expressions. The Messiah is said to teach "how to rule both families and kingdoms"—a Confucian phrase in the book of *Great Learning*. Buddhist concepts and images are also pressed into service. Jesus is said to have "hung up the bright sun" (i.e., crucifixion), taken an oar in "the vessel of mercy" (the boddhisattva or the Kuan-yin), and "ascended to the Palace of Light."

Borrowing from the Chinese religions is also evident in the earlier Dunhuang Documents. Two of these are attributed to Aluoben; namely, *Book of Jesus-Messiah* and *Discourse on Monotheism*. *Book of Jesus-Messiah*, which contains an explication of God's qualities and commandments and a narrative of Jesus's life from the incarnation to the crucifixion, reflects a conscious effort to make Christianity comprehensible to the Chinese. It emphasizes Chinese virtues such as filial piety, ancestor worship, and loyalty to the emperor, who is acknowledged as the "Son of Heaven." Its exposition of the commandments is given with the use of Buddhist and Confucian terms. *The Parable, part two* of the *Discourse on Monotheism* emphasizes God's quality of *wu-wei* (non-action), and gives examples of it by means of short parables. *The Discourse on the Oneness of the Ruler of the Universe, part one* speaks of the "five qualities" of the body, a concept that recalls the Buddhist notion of the *skandhas*. In its exposition on the consequences of evil deeds, it incorporates the Buddhist notion of reincarnation in a lowly state as a punishment for bad actions. *The Lord of the Universe's Discourse on*

---

16. I do not claim that the text explicitly presents "Nestorian" teachings as opposed to the "orthodox" faith. As Moffett points out: "There is virtually nothing in the documents that can be conclusively labeled 'Nestorianism' even by the standards of the Chalcedonian orthodoxy of Constantinople and Rome," *History of Christianity*, vol. 1, 306. As far as Christology is concerned, see the five-volume series edited by Malek, *Chinese Face*. Thus far, volumes 1 and 2 have appeared, which are of interest for our theme.

Alms-giving, part three extols the virtue much praised in Buddhism; namely, almsgiving to monks.

Among other Dunhuang Documents, some are attributed to Jing-jing. Of these, the one that most resembles a Buddhist text is *Zhi xuan an le jing* (The Book of Mysterious Rest and Joy). Here, Jesus—called "the peerless and unique Lord of Eternity"—gives a sermon, elicited by his disciple Peter, as the Buddha was by his disciple Ananda. The Master is asked by Peter about the means for obtaining salvation, and responds in words that are redolent of Buddhist and Daoist teachings. The means consist, we are told, in preparing for the "Victorious Way" by getting rid of "motion" and "desire." Through "non-motion" and "non-desire," one arrives at "non-solicitation," "non-assertion," and "non-action" leading to "all-illumining" and "all-pervading," which are "the state of Rest and Joy."

The foregoing account of the encounter between Christianity and the Chinese religions should not be taken to mean that the encounter was always harmonious. A text by Yuan-chao dating to 800, referring to the collaboration between Jing-jing and Prajñ~ in the translation of the *Šatp~ramit~ Sātra*, decries such a common endeavor:

> Since a Buddhist convent (*ch'ieh-lan*) and a monastery of Ta-ch'in monks differ in customs and are wholly opposed to one another in their religious practices, Ching-Ching must preach the teaching of Messiah (*Mi-shih-he*) and the Buddhist monk (*sha-mên*) make known the *sutra* of Buddha. We wish to have religious teaching well defined that men may have no uncertainty. Truth and error are not the same; the Ching and the Wei [rivers] are not alike.[17]

Clearly, by the end of the eighth century, there was local opposition to the new religion that was regarded as propagating error; as opposed to Buddhism, which was affirmed to teach truth. Collaboration between the two religions was deemed harmful to the purity of the true religion. With the decree of 845, Nestorian Christianity was irremediably reduced, and there is little evidence that it survived this persecution. In sum, with reference to its encounter with Chinese culture and religions, Nestorian Christianity "was a case of a marginal religion in Chinese society. In the history of its reception, one observes aspects characteristic of the reception of other foreign religions in Chinese society. The important, albeit limited, collection of documents in Chinese shows how quickly Christianity had taken a Chinese form."[18]

---

17. Gillman and Klimkeit, *Christianity in Asia*, 283.
18. Standaert, *Handbook*, vol. 1, 38. For an overall view of Chinese Christianity in

Christians under the Mongol/Yuan Dynasty (1279–1368)

After the collapse of the T'ang dynasty in 907, China itself went through half a century of disunity. The extreme northeast of China was ruled by the Qidan Liao dynasty, whereas the northern section was governed by a succession of five dynasties, and the southern section fragmented into ten kingdoms. This disunity was brought to an end in 960 by Zhao Kuangyin, who established the Song dynasty. The (Northern) Song dynasty itself (960–1127) was conquered by the Jurchen Jin in 1127 and was forced to move to the South. The Southern Song dynasty (1127–1270) in turn was conquered by the Mongols, one of whose leaders, Khubilai, established the Yuan dynasty.

At the end of the T'ang dynasty, Nestorian Christianity virtually disappeared from China. A Nestorian monk sent from Baghdad to China at the end of the tenth century returned with the report that Christianity in China was extinct. There is evidence, however, that Nestorian Christians entered China again when—as members of the Central Asian tribes, who had been influenced by the more advanced Uighur culture—they moved to the northern parts of China. Many of them were employed as administrators by the Qidan Liao (1125–1201) and the Jin (1115–1234) dynasties. Indeed, when the Mongols conquered Northern China in the first half of the thirteenth century, they continued to employ these Nestorian tribesmen as administrators.[19] These Nestorian Christians in Mongol China have left behind important artifacts such as crosses (known as the "Ordos crosses"—found in the Ordos region and resembling the Maltese cross), stone slabs, tablets, tombstones, headstones, and a Syriac prayer book.[20]

During Khubilai's reign (1260–94), Roman Catholics entered China for the first time. These included Italian merchants (the best known are the Polo brothers—Niccolo and Maffeo—and their more famous son and nephew, Marco), a small number of slaves deported after the Mongol invasion of Eastern Europe, Franciscan missionaries and papal legates (the best known

---

the seventh and eighth centuries, see Raguin, "China's First Evangelization," vol. 1, 159–79. For an exposition of Chinese Nestorian Christology, see Eskildsen, "Christology," 181–218. In terms of their Christology, Eskildsen says: "The texts of the first category expound a Christology and a soteriology that are quintessentially Christian, while the later texts virtually ignore the crucifixion in favor of a Christology and soteriology that could be more aptly described as Daoist and Manichaean" (208).

19. Regarding these Nestorian Christians of Kerait and Цngьt (Öngüt) origin and of other tribes, and in particular Nestorian Christians in Zhenjiang, see Standaert, *Handbook*, vol. 1, 63–68.

20. On these archaeological finds of Nestorian origin, see Standaert, *Handbook*, vol. 1, 52–59. For a list of Nestorian settlements in Mongol China, see 109–11.

are Giovanni da Montecorvino and Odoric da Pordenone), and Chinese and non-Chinese converts.[21]

As far as the reception of Christianity by Mongol China is concerned, it is interesting to note that in the Chinese sources of the Yuan dynasty there is no specific indigenous Chinese word for Christianity in general, Nestorianism, Roman Catholicism, or any other form of Christianity. Rather, Christians were referred to as *Yekilewen*—the transliteration of the non-Chinese word, *erke'ʋn*, of doubtful origin. *Yekilewen* connotes either the Christian clergy living in monasteries who enjoyed tax exemption, or the lay Christian non-Chinese people, one of the four groups of Chinese into which Khubilai divided the inhabitants of China.[22] *Yekilewen* is sometimes described as a *jiao* (teaching, way of learning, religion), as found in Liang Xiang's *Zhishun Zhenjiang zhi* (The Annals of Zhenjiang of the Zhishun Period), where Liang Xiang emphasized the foreign origin of Christianity and its practice of worship toward the East.

As was the case during the T'ang dynasty, Christianity during the Yuan dynasty had also to confront Chinese religions, in particular Buddhism and Daoism. Willem van Rubroek, the Flemish Franciscan who set out on a mission to the Mongols in 1253, related in his *Itinerarium ad partes orientales* that he was summoned by Möngke Khan to Qaraqorum on May 30, 1254, to side with the Nestorians in a debate with the Buddhist abbot Fuyu, representing the Muslims and Buddhists. Van Rubroek defended Christian monotheism against what he took to be Buddhist atheism. Later, in 1304, the Nestorians who had settled in Jiangnan attempted to proselytize the common people and the Daoist clergy. The latter accused the Nestorians of usurping the authority of the indigenous Buddhist and Daoist clergy, especially at public worship. The Board of Rites ordered that the ritual order by which the Buddhist and Daoist clergy stood above the Nestorian clergy be respected and that the Nestorians were no longer allowed to register the common people as belonging to their *jiao*. Again, in 1311, an imperial edict ordered two Nestorian monasteries that had been built on land legally belonging to a Buddhist monastery on nearby Mount Jin be restored to the Buddhists. On this occasion, an inscription composed by Zhao Mengfu and Pan Angxiao referred to Nestorianism as *waidao* (off the straight path) and proclaimed Buddhism as the only true law.[23]

21. On these early Roman Catholics in Mongol China, see ibid., 68–78.

22. Khublai divided the Chinese population into four groups in descending order of dignity: the Mongols (*mengguren*), the miscellaneous aliens such as Central Asians and Westerners, among whom were Christians (*semuren*), the Northern Chinese (*hanren*), and the Southern Chinese (*nanren*). See Roberts, *Concise History*, 108–9.

23. See Standaert, *Handbook*, vol. 1, 92–94. For primary and secondary sources on

With the death of Kublai Khan in 1294, protector of Christianity, and the eventual dissolution of the Yuan dynasty in 1368, Christianity experienced its second disappearance in China. What Samuel Hugh Moffett writes with poignant sadness about Chinese Christianity under the Mongolian rule speaks volumes about the encounter of Christianity with China and its religions:

> It is no surprise that the church fell with the old dynasty. This was the pattern of past Chinese history. But the Christians of the Yuan dynasty compounded the errors of their forerunners under the T'ang who had disappeared with their imperial patrons four hundred years before. That earlier Christianity had at least been unitedly Nestorian. The China of the fourteenth century, however, could not fail to note the enmity between Nestorians and their newly arrived rivals, the Catholics, and both were considered foreign by the Chinese. Compounding the handicap this imposed on the church, the Mongol dynasty itself was foreign. So to the Chinese, Christianity appeared as a foreign religion protected and supported by a foreign government. Catholic missions gave the impression of being even more foreign than the Nestorians, who were almost entirely Mongol, for they received far more visible support from outside China than ever was true of the Nestorians either in the ninth or fourteenth century.[24]

Christianity in the Ming and the Early Qing (1368–1800)

Such disappearance of Christianity was so undramatic and extensive that when the next wave of Western missionaries, all Roman Catholic, came to China two centuries later, they did not seem to be aware that there had been Christians there before them. This third coming of Christianity to China and its encounter with the Chinese religions during the later years of the Ming dynasty (1368–1644) and the early period of the Qing (Manchu) dynasty (1644–1911) are much better documented than its first two comings and have been extensively investigated.[25] The main actors in this

---

Christianity during the Yuan dynasty, consult ibid., 99–108. Of particular importance are the writings by Chinese scholars, notably Cai Meibiao, Chen Yuan, Fang Hao, Liu Xutang, Wu Youxiong, Xia Nai, Xu Pinfang, Yang Qinzhang, Zhang Xinglang, Zhou Liangxiao, and Zhuang Weiji.

24. Moffett, *History of Christianity*, vol. 1, 474.

25. For a brief overview of Chinese Christianity under these two dynasties, see ibid., vol. 2, 105–42. For Chinese Christianity under the Ming and Qing dynasties, see Standaert, *Handbook*, vol. 1, esp. 592–688, and Malek, *Chinese Face*, vol. 2.

encounter were mostly Jesuits and their earlier Chinese converts, though the later presence of Dominicans, Franciscans, Augustinians, members of the *Missions Etrangeres de Paris* (Paris Foreign Missions), and Lazarists also played a key role.[26]

THE EARLY JESUITS AND THEIR CONVERTS

Christianity's encounter with Chinese religions from the last two decades of the sixteenth to the end of the eighteenth century was deeply shaped by the Jesuit policy of accommodation (*il modo suave*) espoused by Alessandro Valignano (1538–1606), who attempted to wean Christian mission from dependence on the Portuguese *padroado* and insisted on the learning of Chinese language and culture. This policy was implemented by Michael Ruggieri (1543–1607), and above all by Matteo Ricci (1552–1610).[27] From Macao, Ruggieri was able to penetrate into mainland China (Guangzhou) in 1581, and with Ricci he built the first Jesuit residence in Zhaoqing in 1583. At first, in an attempt to win religious acceptance, both Ruggieri and Ricci dressed in the gray robes of Buddhist monks. However, when they realized that Buddhism was despised by the Chinese literati as superstitious and uncouth, they adopted, with Valignano's approval, the Confucian scholars' garb in 1595. In 1598, Ricci reached Beijing but could not meet with the Emperor Wanli (who reigned 1573–1620) face-to-face. He had better luck in his second attempt in 1600 when he was able to present, though not in person, several gifts to the emperor, who was much impressed with the striking clock and the harpsichord. As a result, Ricci was allowed to establish residence in the capital.

In terms of interreligious encounter, clearly the early Jesuits, like most Confucian scholars, had a low opinion of Buddhism and Daoism. In general, their general policy was summarized in the slogan: *qin ru pai fo* (draw close to Confucianism and repudiate Buddhism). We will examine below how they "drew close" to Confucianism. With regard to Buddhism, Ricci's most celebrated encounter with it took place in 1599 in Nanjing, where he had a disputation with the famous Buddhist Huang Hungen, better known as San Huai. Though neither disputant was declared a winner, Ricci later incorporated his rebuttal of Buddhist teachings in his masterpiece *Tianzhu shiyi*

---

26. On the missionary activities of Dominicans, Franciscans, Augustinians, *Missions Etrangeres de Paris*, and the Lazarists, see Standaert, *Handbook*, vol. 1, 322–54.

27. On Valignano and how his missionary policy was implemented in China and Japan, see Ross, *Vision Betrayed*.

(The True Meaning of the Lord of Heaven), published in 1603.[28] Among the many Buddhist doctrines Ricci refuted, the most important are those concerning "Voidness" (Chapter 2), which Ricci took to be an absurd description of God; the teaching that "Heaven, Earth, and all things form one body" (Chapter 4); reincarnation (Chapter 5); and the prohibition against killing animals (Chapter 5). What Ricci thought of the Buddha as a person is revealed in the following passage:

> The Buddha failed to understand himself, so how could he understand the Lord of Heaven? He, in his small body, was illumined by the light of the Lord of Heaven; but, happening to be possessed of some talent, and having been given a task to perform, he became boastful and arrogant, and recklessly, and with no inhibitions whatsoever, considered himself to be as worthy of honor as the Lord of Heaven. Can such behavior be regarded as raising our value or as honoring our virtue? Rather is it to cheapen man and to cause him to lose his virtue! Arrogance is the enemy of all virtues.

There is no worse condemnation of the Buddha, from the Confucian perspective, than accusing him of being a *xiaoren* (small-minded person), as opposed to being a *junzi* (superior person), who is characterized by the cultivation of virtues. Because of his antipathy toward the Buddha, Ricci failed to engage Buddhism seriously as a religious system, and his negative attitude toward, as well as his gross misinterpretations of certain Buddhist doctrines, would later provoke a fierce attack of Christianity by Buddhist authors.[29]

As for Daoism, Ricci's attitude toward it was no less negative, reflecting that of Confucian literati, who regarded Daoism, especially its popular manifestations, as rank superstition. As the "Chinese Scholar" informs the "Western Scholar": "The superior men of my country too are vehement in their dismissal of Buddhism and Taoism and have a deep hatred of them."[30] Philosophically, Ricci objected to the Daoist concept of *wu* ("nothing") as a

---

28. For an English translation with the Chinese text, see Ricci, *True Meaning*.

29. See the collection of writings by more than forty authors published in 1640 by Xu, *Shengchao*. See also Lancashire, "Anti-Christian Polemics" and "Buddhist Reaction"; and Zürcher, "First Anti-Christian Movement." Ricci has been rightly criticized for not understanding and/or misinterpreting both Buddhism and Daoism. For instance, translators Lancashire and Hu Kuo-chen write: "Ricci did not really grasp the central ideas of the various Chinese schools of thought of his day, or their historical background.... Ricci seems not to have understood correctly the Taoist *Wu*, the Buddhist *K'ung*, and the Neo-Confucianist *T'ai-chi*, *Li*, and *Ch'i*" (Ricci, *True Meaning*, 47).

30. Ricci, *True Meaning*, §68 (99).

designation for God and for the creator, taking it to mean "nothingness."[31] Ricci also attacked the Daoist theory that one should act without "motivation," which he regarded immoral, since, according to him, "good and evil, virtue and vice all stem from right or corrupt motives. If there are no motives there can be no good or evil or any distinction between superior or inferior men."[32]

It is interesting to note that this opposition to both Buddhism and Daoism is found also in early Chinese converts, in particular in the so-called Three Pillars of Christianity in China. Xu Guangqi (1562–1633), baptized as Paul in 1603, proposed to use Christianity "to supplement Confucianism and replace Buddhism" (*pu ru yi fo*).[33] For him, both Buddhism and Daoism promote the abandonment of public responsibilities to the society and focus instead on the private realm. That is why, he pointed out, although Buddhism had been in China for almost two thousand years, it was unable to change people's hearts and the way of the world. On the contrary, morality had deteriorated. He also attacked the Buddhist doctrine of reincarnation and the practice of *p'o-yu*; that is, of attempting to save other souls by means of burning paper money and making offerings to monasteries. Finally, Xu rejected Zen Buddhism for its insistence on meditation as a means of salvation and its cultural elitism. Li Zhizao (1565–1630), baptized as Leo in 1610, had been a prominent Buddhist. He was convinced by Ricci of the Buddhist errors and was received into the church after he had agreed to monogamy.[34] Yang Tingyun (1562–1627), baptized as Michel in 1611, had a longstanding and extensive interest in Buddhism. After his conversion, he wrote many treatises against Buddhism, the most important of which is *Tianshi mingbian* (Clear Discussion on Heaven and Buddhism), in which he outlined in thirty chapters the apparent similarities and essential differences between Christianity and Buddhism.[35]

31. See ibid., §72,§85, §87 (103–13).

32. Ibid., §324 (287).

33. For a discussion of Xu Guangqi, see Young, *Confucianism*, 41–58, and Jami et al., *Statecraft*.

34. On Li Zhizao, see Liang, "Towards a Hyphenated Identity."

35. On Yang Tingyun, see Standaert, *Yang Tingyun*. Standaert neatly summarizes Yang's attitude to Buddhism: "There was no evidence for the formal membership of Buddhism, but it seems that he received a Buddhist religious education at home. . . . The degree to which Yang Tingyun identified himself with Buddhism and the extent to which he was accepted by the Buddhist community could not be ascertained, but indications of his self-identification or acceptance can be found in his Buddhist-inspired actions: he practiced *fangsheng*, he received Buddhist monks at home, sponsored the building of temples and wrote religious poems. However, these criteria no longer were valuable after he had become a Christian. Not only did he break with Buddhism,

Ironically, in spite of his rejection of Buddhism and Daoism, in his exposition of Christian doctrines, Ricci made extensive use of Buddhist and Daoist concepts and terminology. For instance, the word *tianzhu* ("master of heaven"), which the Jesuits coined to refer to God—in addition to *tian* ("heaven") and *shangdi* ("sovereign-on-high")—is found in Buddhist canonical writings as a term for a deity. Similarly, words for heaven (*tiantang*), hell (*diyu*), the intellective soul (*linghun*), and holy (*sheng*), all have Buddhist roots.[36]

It is commonplace that while rejecting Buddhism and Daoism as the "sects of idolaters and sorcerers" and "false religions," the early Jesuits and their converts welcomed Confucianism (the "sect of the *literati*"), or more precisely, "original Confucianism" (*xian ru*) as a worthy dialogue partner with Christianity. Their positive attitude is shown particularly for monotheism—which they claimed is taught in Confucian classics, as opposed to nontheistic Neo-Confucianism—and for Confucian moral teachings. The early Jesuits' positive reception of Confucianism was made possible by their strongly humanistic formation in Europe, which focused on the human being as the center of reflection, and their interest in the Confucian classics was in accord with their appreciation for Greek and Latin classics. This enthusiasm for Confucianism is abundantly evident not only in Ricci's *Tianzhu shiyi* and in the works of later Jesuits such as Giulio Aleni (1582–1649)[37] but also in the writings of the "Three Pillars of Christianity in China" mentioned above. Indeed, it is the resemblances between Christianity and Confucianism (and of course the superiority of the former over the latter) that facilitated the conversion of these *literati*.

In his encounter with the Confucianism of his time, Ricci was convinced that it had gone astray in forgetting the belief of early or original Confucianism in the one God the Creator (*tian* or *shangdi*) and that the Neo-Confucian concepts of *li* ("principle"), *qi* ("ether"), and *taiji* ("supreme ultimate") cannot be regarded as divine. As for the Confucian moral ideals, in particular the notion of *ren* and the cultivation of virtues, Ricci had nothing but the deepest respect. While fully aware of significant differences between Confucian and Christian morality, Ricci and the early Chinese

---

the formal expression of which was shown by the destruction of gilded boddhisattva statues, but took a polemical position of rejection in his writings. Furthermore, the Buddhist community no longer recognized him as a Buddhist follower, as was clearly shown in the anti-Christian writings" (211).

36. For a discussion of the Buddhist origin of these terms, see Ricci, *True Meaning*, 33–38.

37. On Giulio Aleni, see Criveller, *Preaching Christ*. Aleni's most important work is *Wanwu Zhenyuan* (The True Origin of All Things), published in 1628.

converts perceived a deep and extensive consonance between the two moralities. It is at this practical level that, according to them, Christianity can encounter Confucianism most fruitfully.[38]

FRENCH JESUITS AND FIGURISM

Another significant attempt to bring Christianity into dialogue with the Chinese religions was carried out later by the French Jesuits who came to China after 1688. Initiated by Joachim Bouvet (1656–1730) and developed by his collaborators, notably Jean-François Foucquet (1665–1741) and Joseph de Prémare (1666–1736), the movement, dubbed *Figurism* by its critic Nicolas Fréret (1688–1749), proposed a new method of interpreting the Chinese classics. Inspired by patristic typological exegesis, the *prisca theologia* ("ancient theology"), which recognized divine revelation outside of the Jewish-Christian history, and the Jewish kabbala, the Figurists tried to show how the classical Chinese texts, in particular the *Yijing* ("The Book of Changes"), contain in them *figurae* ("signs") referring to Christian realities. In particular, the Figurists held that the *Yijing* espouses the ancient scheme of the three ages of the world; namely, the *tiandao* ("the time of paradise"), the *didao* ("the time of the rebellion of angels and humans"), and the *rendao* ("the time of Jesus Christ"). They also argued that the *Daode jing* teaches not only monotheism (the *Dao*) but also the doctrines of the Trinity (especially in Chapter 42) and of divine Wisdom or *sophia*, which is called *wanwu zhi mu* ("mother of all beings"). Finally, the Figurists also regarded Confucius as a forerunner, like John the Baptist, of the redeemer, and Hou Di, mentioned in *Shijing* Ode 245, as a figure for the Messiah, since he was mysteriously conceived by his mother during her sacrifice to *Shangdi* ("the Lord-on-high").[39]

Though Figurism had its support among the Emperor Kangxi and the German philosopher Leibniz, it aroused suspicion among the Jesuit superiors, especially when its proponents claimed they could compute the date of

---

38. On how the early Jesuits and their converts perceive the consonance between Christian and Confucian morality, see Standaert, *Handbook*, vol. 1, 653–62. Two dividing issues, however, remain: namely, celibacy and polygamy. There is of course a fundamental question of whether Ricci and the early Jesuits have correctly interpreted what Ricci calls "Original Confucianism" and whether they have "manufactured" Confucianism, as a recent study has suggested; see Jensen, *Manufacturing Confucianism*. Rule rejects Jensen's charge in his review of Jensen's book in *Journal of Chinese Religions*, 105–11 and in "Jesus of the 'Confucian Christians,'" vol. 2, 499–516.

39. On Figurism, see the many writings of von Collani, in particular *Die Figuristen*; and Standaert, *Handbook*, vol. 1, 668–79.

the end of the world. Furthermore, since Figurism asserted that the ancient Chinese had already known about the Christian mysteries, it was feared that it would furnish a powerful weapon to the opponents of the Jesuit position in the Chinese Rites Controversy (see below). As a result, the Figurists were dispersed to various areas and their studies interrupted.

CHRISTIANITY AND THE CHINESE RITES

The third important aspect of the encounter of Christianity with the Chinese religions refers to what is known as the Rites Controversy. The issues and the main protagonists involved in this long and painful controversy are well known, and only the briefest outline of it is given here.[40] The Rites Controversy, which lasted for three hundred years (1643–1941), may be said to originate in Ricci's accommodationist policy toward the ceremonies in honor of Confucius, performed by the literati in temples and halls dedicated to him and the cult of ancestors that forms the core of Chinese religious life. Ricci believed that such practices would be permissible to Christians since, in his view, they were essentially "civil" and "political" acts, and not superstition. Though not all Jesuits (e.g., Ricci's successor, Niccolò Longobardo) shared the same positive attitude toward these rites, and though not all non-Jesuits condemned them, the opposition to the Jesuit policy was sparked by the "Seventeen Questions" which the Dominican Juan Bautista de Morales (1597–1664) submitted to the Propaganda Fide in 1643, attacking the Jesuits' practices. The controversy reached its peak in 1693 when Charles Maigrot, a member of the Paris Foreign Mission Society and Vicar Apostolic of Fujian, issued a mandate forbidding participation in the rituals being practiced in honor of Confucius and the ancestors. There followed a series of papal condemnations of the Chinese Rites, from Clement XI (*Ex illa die*, 1705) to Benedict XIV (*Ex quo singulari*, 1742), with two intervening visits to the Emperor Kangxi by papal legates, Carlo Tommaso Maillard de Tournon (1706) and Carlo Ambrogio Mezzabarba (1720). The resolution of the controversy came in 1939 when, in response to the events in Tokyo and Manchukuo, the Propaganda Fide issued the decree, *Plane compertum est*, permitting the practices of venerating Confucius and the ancestors insofar as they "merely preserve civil expression of devotion toward ancestors, or of patriotism, or of respect for fellow countrymen."[41]

---

40. On the Chinese Rites Controversy, see Minamiki, *Chinese Rites*; Mungello, *Chinese Rites*; and Noll, *100 Roman Documents*.

41. Noll, *100 Roman Documents*, 87.

In significant ways, the Rites Controversy contains in a nutshell the complex history of the encounter between Christianity and Chinese religions. Various types of Christianities (humanistic Renaissance Christianity vs. the conservative post-Tridentine church) and opposing evaluations of the Chinese culture and religions (good or at least neutral human creation vs. superstition) collided with each other. The potentially peaceful and mutually enriching encounter between Christianity and Chinese religions turned into a disastrous and protracted conflict, exacerbated by rivalries among religious orders (Jesuit, Dominican, Franciscan, Augustinian, and the Paris Foreign Mission Society), competing interests of colonial powers (Spanish, Portuguese, and French), and claims of independence of two world establishments (Catholic Rome and Imperial China). There are of course profound theological and missiological issues underlying the Rites Controversy, and these still remain unresolved even after the conditional acceptance of the rites by Rome.[42]

Christianity, Catholic and Protestant, in Taiwan

While Christian mission to China until 1800 concentrated heavily on the mainland, the little island one hundred miles off China's southeast coast known today as Taiwan was not neglected.[43] The Spanish Dominican province of the Most Holy Rosary of the Philippines was founded in 1582 with the explicit intention of missionary work in China. After several attempts to enter Fujian directly from Manila proved fruitless, the Dominicans thought of entering mainland China by way of Taiwan (then called Formosa). They came and settled at the northern tip of the island, in Jilong in 1626 and in Danshui in 1629. They were soon followed by Franciscans and Augustinians. The missionaries were active in Taiwan until their expulsion by the Dutch in 1642.[44]

Formosa was seized by the Dutch East India Company (Verenigde Oostindische Compagnie (VOC) [1602–1798]) from the Spaniards in 1626 with the purpose of developing trade with mainland China. The island did not come under the full control of the Dutch until 1642. The VOC's primary

---

42. For a discussion of these theological and missiological issues, see Phan, *In Our Own Tongues*, 109–29.

43. The island was named Taiwan by the Chinese in 1612 and came under China's firm control only under the Manchu dynasty after 1683. Discovered by the Portuguese in the sixteenth century, it was called Formosa (beautiful island).

44. On early Catholic mission in Taiwan, see Alvarez, *Formosa geográfica*, and Fernández, *Dominicos*.

purpose was trade, not evangelization. However, with the Dutch came Protestant missionaries. These were not sent by their own churches to do mission; rather they were hired by the VOC to minister to its personnel. At first, Dutch Protestant ministers restricted themselves to serving their fellow countrymen. From 1634, however, there were contacts with the indigenous people as the missionaries moved inland from their base fort in Zeelandia on the inshore islet of Tayouan. They began learning the native languages and translating the Bible, completing the gospels of Matthew and John.

Between 1626 and 1662, some thirty ministers worked on the island. The most famous of them included Georgius Candidius and Robertus Junius, who both came in 1627; and Antonius Hambroek, who came in 1648 and was killed in 1661. Their mission proved highly successful. Most of the converts were non-Chinese tribal people. Before his departure from Formosa in 1647, Junius reported that there were 17,000 Christian Formosans, of whom he baptized over 5,400 in twenty-nine villages. The rapid growth of conversions required the formation of two presbyteries, one in Zeelandia and the other in Soulang.

Religious instruction was given pride of place. Junius organized a little school for seventy boys and sixty girls. Junius himself translated two *Catechisms* and a *Formulary of Christianity* into Sinkan, one of the five major Formosan dialects, writing the words in a Romanized alphabet. In 1636, in an effort to develop the native clergy, Junius requested permission to bring four to six boys to Holland for ministerial training, and when this was denied, he planned to found a seminary on the island. Unfortunately, by the time permission for a seminary was granted in 1650, Junius had already left the country. Antonius Hambroek was appointed principal of the seminary, which was never opened, however, because the Dutch rule over the island, and with it Christian mission, was brought to an end in 1661 by Koxinga (Zheng Chenggong)—a Ming naval commander who had been driven by the Manchus to Formosa along with 25,000 soldiers and who had had Hambroek and several other missionaries decapitated. After the death of Koxinga's son in 1682, Formosa was annexed to China, and Protestant Christianity virtually disappeared from the island until the late nineteenth century when another wave of missionaries, this time English, came to evangelize.[45]

---

45. On Protestant mission in Taiwan, see Blussé van Oud-Alblas, "Dutch Protestant Missionaries," 155–84; Campbell, *Formosa*; Covell, *Pentecost*; and Ginsel, "Gereformeerde Kerk." For brief surveys, see Standaert, *Handbook*, 1:376–79 and Moffett, *History of Christianity*, 2:218–22.

Russian Orthodox Christianity in Asia

Until the second half of the seventeenth century, the Russian Orthodox Church was mainly concerned with the evangelization of nations within the Russian Empire. It was only with Tsar Peter the Great (r. 1682–1725) that Christian mission proper began to be undertaken in China. Diplomatic contacts with China had been made in 1618, 1656, and 1676 but without great success.

Meanwhile, entry of the Russian Orthodox Church into China occurred by happenstance. Siberian Cossacks had built settlements near the Chinese border, one of which was the garrison Albazin at the Armur River, founded in 1651, with a church built in 1671. Emperor Kangxi considered the location of the garrison to be Chinese territory, and in 1685 ordered an attack on Albazin. Thirty-one Cossacks and some deserters joined the Chinese army. Among the Cossacks was their priest Maksim Leont'ev who took with him sacred books and icons for divine service. Kangxi gave them a building in the northern part of Beijing and supported them with land and salary. In 1696, a former Buddhist temple was consecrated as the church of "Heavenly Wisdom" (Sophia), also called "Saint Nicholas" because of the icon brought from Albazin (the Chinese called it *Luochamiao*). Leont'ev, who functioned as the head of the Russian Orthodox community until his death in 1712, obtained official acknowledgment in 1695 from the Metropolitan Ignatij of Tobolsk.

In 1700 Peter the Great ordered the Metropolitan Varlaam (Jasinskij) of Kiev to send a priest as missionary to China with two or three monks who should learn Chinese. In 1702 the Metropolitan Filofej Lesinskij of Tobolsk sent priests in the company of trade caravans to China. Beijing did not allow a Russian parish to be established, but the merchant Oskolkov obtained permission to have Russian clerics stay there permanently. In 1716, however, a permanent Russian ecclesiastical mission was established in Beijing, and the Archimandrite Illarion Lezhaiskij arrived with money to build a church. Lezhaiskij was made a mandarin of the fifth order, and his priests and deacons mandarins of the seventh order. Each month, the parish made a report to Emperor Kangxi.

The Treatise of Kiakhta (1727) further expanded the Russian ecclesiastical mission: the Russian mission was legalized; the Albazins were allowed to build a new church with a cloister in the ambassador's residence and to establish a school; the archimandrite would function as Russian ambassador, with two or three priests allowed to live with him; and five or six laymen would join the mission to learn Chinese and Manchu. This Russian ecclesiastical and diplomatic mission would last until 1860.

By 1731, nine Chinese had been baptized. At the end of the eighteenth century, the Orthodox community in Beijing numbered four women and thirteen men, including five Chinese and twenty-five Albazins. They used Chinese words for God, church, and priest. In general, the Russian Orthodox Church engaged little in evangelization among the Chinese, partly because the archimandrites functioned mostly as ambassadors and would return home after a decade of service, partly because the mission focused more on diplomatic, commercial, and scientific activities. As a result, the Russian Orthodox Church remained a small community, with very few Chinese converts.

On the other hand, the Russian mission has made significant contributions to sinology. As mentioned above, Peter the Great mandated the study of Chinese. Illarion Rossochin (1717-61), who had been attached to the Russian mission as interpreter, translated *Zizhi tongjian gangmu* (Comprehensive Mirror to Aid in Government). Aleksej Leont'ev (1716-81), who also went to Beijing on a diplomatic mission, opened a college to teach Chinese in St. Petersburg and published twenty-one original works and translations, including *Daxue* (Great Learning), *Zhongyong* (Doctrine of the Mean), and Chinese law codes.[46]

CHRISTIANITY IN DIALOGUE WITH OTHER RELIGIONS IN VIETNAM

Christianity seems to have made its first appearance in Vietnam in the first decades of the sixteenth century, but it was only with the arrival of the Jesuits in Cochinchina (i.e., the southern part of the country, then known as Annam) in 1615 that Christianity began to take root. In 1626, two Jesuits arrived in Tonkin, the northern part of Vietnam. Most of the Jesuits were Portuguese, some Italian, a few Japanese; all, however, worked under the authority of the Portuguese *padroado*. Most famous among them and widely regarded as the most influential missionary in Vietnam was a Frenchman by the name of Alexandre de Rhodes, who came to Cochinchina in 1624 and then in 1627 was sent to Tonkin. When de Rhodes was expelled from Vietnam in 1645, he was sent to Rome to recruit more missionaries. As a result of his efforts, Propaganda Fide dispatched two bishops—François Pallu (1626-84) and Pierre Lambert de la Motte (1624-79), both French—as apostolic vicars for Tonkin and Cochinchina respectively, directly responsible to Propaganda Fide and independent of the Portuguese *padroado*. With

---

46. For a brief presentation of the Russian Orthodox mission in China before 1800, see Standaert, *Handbook*, vol. 1, 378-75, with an ample bibliography.

them came members of the Paris Foreign Mission Society. Eventually, other religious orders such as the Augustinians, Dominicans, and Franciscans joined in the missionary enterprise.

As in China, Christianity in Vietnam had to face the same three religions; namely, Buddhism, Confucianism, and Daoism. Known in Vietnamese collectively as *tam giao* (Three Religions or Triple Religion), these three religious traditions are regarded as "imported" religions, in distinction from the indigenous cult of Heaven and spirits. Buddhism entered Vietnam first from India and then from China, especially toward the second century of the Common Era, but it was only in the sixth century that Buddhism began to take root. Between the eleventh and the fourteenth centuries, Buddhism reached its apogee. Thereafter it suffered a long decline, and during the Ming domination of Vietnam (1407–28), the Ming rulers confiscated Buddhist books, closed pagodas, and imposed Confucian doctrines and practices on the country.

Daoism as a religious practice came to Vietnam from China in the first century of the Common Era and brought not only a philosophical worldview regarding the "Way" (i.e., the non-contriving [*wu wei*] creative force) but also a complex of cultic, dietary, and hygienic practices to achieve longevity and immortality. Additionally, it introduced to Vietnam a host of deities and spirits that were added to the already well-populated pantheon of the Vietnamese indigenous religion. Along with Daoism, Confucianism entered Vietnam in the first century of the Common Era. But more than Buddhism and Daoism, thanks to China's ten-century-long domination over Vietnam and its imposition of its culture and educational organization, Confucianism, particularly as an ethico-political system, exercised a long-lasting and pervasive influence on the Vietnamese society. Finally, there is the native Vietnamese religion in which the cult of *Ong Troi* (Mr. Heaven)—the personal, transcendent, benevolent, and just God—and the cult of ancestors play a key role.[47]

Our survey of the encounter between Christianity and Vietnamese religions in the seventeenth and eighteenth centuries will be done by examining three key works. These works are largely unknown to Western readers and contain rich information on how Christians in Vietnam regarded non-Christian religions.

---

47. For an exposition of Vietnamese religions, see Phan, *Mission and Catechesis*.

Alexandre de Rhodes (1593–1660) and the Cathechismus (1651)

How Christianity encountered Vietnamese religions in the seventeenth century has been well documented in the historical writings of Alexandre de Rhodes, one of the pioneers of Christian mission in Vietnam.[48] In addition to these historical memoirs, de Rhodes wrote a catechism, the first theological work printed in *chu quoc ngu* (the national script; i.e., the alphabets), in which he discussed in great detail the Vietnamese religions.[49] De Rhodes divided his catechetical course into eight days, the first four days devoted to teaching truths that are accessible to reason and the remaining four days to teaching the truths of faith. It is important to note that de Rhodes suggests that methodologically the critique of Vietnamese religions be undertaken only on day four, and not before in other words, only after it had been shown in the first three days by reasonable arguments that there is but one God and that God is the creator of all things, including spirits. By this time, de Rhodes believed, the Vietnamese listeners would have been convinced of the truths of Christianity and would be psychologically disposed to perceive the errors of their religions. Only at this stage, then, would an attack against the Vietnamese religions be pastorally opportune and effective. De Rhodes argued that one should not begin an exposition of the Christian truths with an attack against the Vietnamese religions, thus risking alienating the audience. Rather, the rejection of the Vietnamese religions should follow as a natural consequence of accepting the truth of Christianity.

---

48. De Rhodes's first work is *Histoire du Royaume*. We possess a manuscript of this two-volume history written in Latin in *Archivium Romanum Societatis Jesu, Jap-Sin* (henceforth: *ARSI, JS*), 83 and 84, f. 1–62v. It was composed in 1639. It was published first in Italian in Rome in 1650 under the title *Relazione de' felici successi della Santa Fede Predicata da Padri della Compagnia di Giesu nel regno di Tunchino, alla santita di N.S.PP. Innocenzio decimo. Di Alessandro de Rhodes avignonese* in 326 pages. The Latin original was published last in Lyon in 1652 under the title *Tunchinensis historiae libri duo, quorum altero status temporalis hujus Regni, altero mirabiles evangelicae praedicationsi progressus referuntur. Coeptas per Patres Societatis Jesu, ab anno 1627, ad Annum 1646. Authore P. Alexandro de Rhodes, Avenionensi, eiusdem Societatis Presbytero, Eorum quae hic narrantur teste oculato*. The second work is entitled *Divers voyages et missions du P. Alexandre de Rhodes en la Chine, & autres Royaumes de l'Orient. Avec son retour en Europe par la Perse & l'Armŭnie. Le tout divisŭ en trois parties* (henceforth *Divers voyages*). It was first published in Paris in 1653 and republished in 1666, 1681, 1683, 1854, and 1884. This Latin manuscript forms the second part of *Divers voyages*, though the French printed text differs considerably from the Latin manuscript.

49. The catechism is entitled *Cathechismus pro iis*. On the history, structure, and method of *Cathechismus*, see Phan, *Mission and Catechesis*, 107–54. In addition, de Rhodes published the first *Dictionarium anamiticum, lusitanum et latinum*, with a discussion of the grammar of the Vietnamese language (1651).

With regard to the three imported religions, de Rhodes wished that when Vietnam threw off the yoke of the Chinese domination it would also have rejected the religions and "superstitions" imported from China. De Rhodes regretted that these religions continued to flourish, in particular Buddhism, which enjoyed, he noted, a greater prestige in Vietnam than in China. He remarked that

> there are today in the kingdom of Tonkin innumerable pagodas and idols. There is not a small village that does not have a pagoda with idols where people come to practice their superstitious devotion. However, these pagodas are filthy and badly kept; the bonzes who serve there are greedy, appropriating all the offerings for their own use and for their wives and children, and not taking care of the decorations of the pagoda and the statues of their gods.[50]

While he had little esteem for the Buddhist monks, de Rhodes greatly admired the devotion of the Buddhist faithful. Twice a month, he notes, they would come to the pagodas to make their prayers and offerings: "They perform these practices with great piety; there is hardly anyone among them, however financially deprived, who would not bring offerings on those occasions and place them reverently at the feet of these dusty statues."[51]

For Buddhist teachings, however, de Rhodes had nothing but condemnation. Buddhism, according to him, teaches two pernicious errors. The first, which he calls the "external way," promotes the worship of idols; and the second, which is worse, and which he calls the "internal way," teaches atheism, that is, the teaching that "nothingness is the origin of all things, and that at death all things return to nothingness as to their ultimate end."[52]

To rebut the errors of Buddhism, de Rhodes begins by discrediting the Buddha as a morally corrupt person. The Buddha, he says, is "one who had a violent and evil temper; from his tender age he gave himself up to magic and had two demons as friends from whom he learned both his conduct and his teaching."[53] The Buddha was also, says de Rhodes, a deceiver. To the common people he taught the worship of idols (the "external way"), since they could not be dissuaded from the innate belief that God exists and that there would be recompense for the good and punishment for the wicked. To

50. De Rhodes, *Histoire du Royaume*, 69.

51. Ibid., 70.

52. De Rhodes, *Cathechismus*, 107. Like Ricci, de Rhodes takes *nirvana* and *sunyata* to mean nothingness.

53. De Rhodes, *Histoire du Royaume*, 66. Like Ricci, de Rhodes uses the *argumentum ad hominem* against the Buddha.

his clever disciples he taught atheism (the "internal way"), saying privately that his teaching on idols was merely designed to amuse the simpleminded folk.[54] Against the Buddhist teaching on the transmigration of the soul, de Rhodes advanced a host of arguments to show the absurdity of such teachings and to demonstrate the immortality of the human soul.[55]

While he was adamantly opposed to what he took to be Buddhist doctrines, de Rhodes took great pains to convert Buddhists because, given their deep religious devotion, once converted to the Christian faith, they would be the most ardent believers and zealous missionaries. In particular, he sought to engage Buddhist monks in public disputations because when any one of them became a Christian, he usually brought with him many of their followers. Indeed, among de Rhodes's converts, both in Tonkin and Cochinchina, many had been Buddhist monks and became his most effective collaborators.

Of the "Three Religions" in Vietnam, de Rhodes considered Daoism the crassest and the most pernicious because "it is the most widespread and the most devoted to the service of the devil."[56] As far as Daoist teaching is concerned, de Rhodes regarded it as nothing short of a meaningless conundrum. The famous statement of the *Daode jing* that "Dao produced the One. The One produced the two. The two produced the three. And the three produced the ten thousand things" (Chapter 42), for de Rhodes meant nothing but pure nonsense.[57] However, the most harmful thing about Daoism, in de Rhodes's view, was its worship of demons and its practice of sorcery, especially for the purposes of divination and healing. He noted that Daoism was extremely attractive for both high and low born, for whom magic and witchcraft were powerful weapons against sickness and death.

De Rhodes's strategy against Daoism was a mixture of the natural and the supernatural. On the one hand, he would simply show by his actions that such practices as divining chicken feet and consulting the horoscope were totally useless and could sometimes hinder the prosecution of a worthy project. For example, once, when twenty merchant ships were preparing to sail and the chicken feet were interpreted to be a bad omen, their captains decided to postpone the trip, whereas de Rhodes persuaded the captain of his boat to set sail. His boat had a peaceful voyage and arrived on time,

---

54. Ibid., 66–67 and *Cathechismus*, 106–7.
55. Ibid., 72 and ibid., 118–20, respectively.
56. De Rhodes, Histoire *du Royaume*, 72.
57. Note that for the Figurists, this cryptic statement of the *Daode jing* intimates that the early Chinese knew the doctrine of the Trinity.

while the others had to wait for fifteen or twenty days and even then sailed in foul weather.[58]

On the other hand, de Rhodes sought to demonstrate that Christian sacred objects such as the crucifix and holy water and rituals were much more powerful and effective than those of Daoism, even for the healing of diseases and the resuscitation of the dead. He himself was not loath to performing healing. At least twice he performed exorcism on female mediums who later became Christian.[59] Once, a pagan chief with a Christian wife asked de Rhodes to send some Christians to his town to cure many of his subjects who had fallen sick. De Rhodes dispatched six catechists whose miraculous healing would put any Daoist sorcerer to shame:

> They started out, weapons in hand to make war on the devil, who was held to be the cause of these ailments. The weapons were the crucifix, holy water, blessed palms, holy candles, and pictures of the Virgin that I had given them at baptism. They went, planted crosses at the entrance, the middle, and the end of the town, and visited the sick, saying a prayer, and giving them a few drops of holy water to drink. In less than a week's time they cured 272 sick people. News of it spread throughout the kingdom. The chief of the town came to thank me with many tears. This heartened the Christians greatly, and many pagans were thereby convinced of their errors.[60]

Like other Jesuits, de Rhodes held Confucianism in the highest esteem. In evaluating Confucianism he carefully distinguishes between the teaching of Confucius and the cult rendered to him. With regard to Confucius's teaching, de Rhodes recognizes that "Confucius, in the books we have received from him, gives proper instructions to form good morals."[61] In Confucius's teachings on law, politics, and the administration of justice, "there is nothing contrary to the principles of the Christian religion that should be rejected or condemned by those who follow them."[62] On the other hand, de Rhodes faulted Confucius for not teaching explicitly the existence of "the supreme creator and Lord of all things, source and origin of all holiness and goodness."[63] He argued that either Confucius knew or did not know that this divine creator exists. If he did not, then he could not

---

58. Ibid., 76.
59. De Rhodes, *Divers voyages*, 142–43.
60. Ibid., 97–98. See also de Rhodes, *Histoire du Royaume*, 185–86.
61. De Rhodes, Histoire *du Royaume*, 62.
62. Ibid., 63.
63. De Rhodes, Cathechismus, 113.

be good and holy. If he did but did not teach this truth to others, he would not be worthy to be called good and holy either.[64] Furthermore, even when Confucius spoke of "the first principle of all things," he made it out to be "bodily, insensible, lacking in knowledge, deprived of reason and soul, and incapable and unworthy of worship and adoration."[65] Finally, de Rhodes reproached Confucius for never mentioning eternal life and the immortality of the soul, thus opening the door for atheism and immorality of all sorts.[66] For all these reasons, Confucius did not deserve, in de Rhodes's judgment, to be called and revered as a "saint."

Thus, de Rhodes, contrary to most Jesuits of his time, was opposed to the cult of Confucius, of which he gave a detailed description.[67] First of all, he was careful to correct the false rumors that the Jesuits condoned it: "We have trouble persuading converted Christians not to genuflect before his statues, which almost all have in their houses; and those who started the rumor that the Jesuits permit their neophytes this idolatry are very badly informed."[68] Secondly, de Rhodes recognized the legitimacy of rendering Confucius the kind of reverence and honor due to other teachers, such as kowtowing to the ground, which did not exceed "a purely political cult."[69] Thirdly, de Rhodes demanded that if there were pagans present at the cult of Confucius, in order to avoid misleading them and giving scandal, Christians must explain beforehand that such reverence "is not done to Confucius as to a god but only as a teacher from whom one has received writings and political guidance."[70] Fourthly, since very few Christians would have the courage to make such a public protestation, de Rhodes urged most vigorously that "such reverence to Confucius be omitted, lest it becomes a trap to someone."[71]

---

64. De Rhodes reports that he once used this line of argument in a sermon in a church in Tonkin where there were, besides Christians, a group of Confucianists. The Christians "listened to [him] with great satisfaction, whereas the Confucianists . . . were very saddened and confused, though they remained obstinate in their old error" (*Histoire du Royaume*, 62).

65. Ibid., 63.

66. Ibid., 63–64.

67. Ibid., 64–65.

68. De Rhodes, *Divers voyages*, 54.

69. De Rhodes, *Cathechismus*, 114. The Latin text uses the well-known phrase *cultum publicum*, whereas the Vietnamese text simply says that the cult of Confucius should not go beyond the norms of politeness.

70. Ibid., 115–16.

71. Ibid., 116.

De Rhodes's attitude toward the cult of ancestors was likewise negative. While admiring the sentiment of filial piety that this cult expressed, de Rhodes firmly rejected certain rituals and beliefs associated with it. He mentioned the anniversary banquet offered to the dead and the practice of making wooden houses and paper clothes for them. He attacked the notion that the dead need food, shelter, and clothing. While insisting that Vietnamese Christians show as much filial piety as their fellow nationals, de Rhodes proscribed these customs and suggested alternative practices such as offering prayers and votive masses for the souls in purgatory and works of charity.

In addition to the cult of ancestors, de Rhodes also mentioned the cult to Heaven that the king, in the capacity as the Son of Heaven, performed on New Year's Day in the name of all his subjects. The sacrifice, called *Te Nam Giao* (sacrifice at the South Gate), was offered in honor of Heaven and Earth and in honor of the king's ancestors according to an elaborate ritual prescribed in minutest details.[72]

In establishing a restrictive policy for Vietnamese Christians in matters of both the cult of Confucius and the cult of ancestors, de Rhodes differed from his confreres in China who took a pastorally more lenient position. The reason is that his confreres in China were scholars who believed they could prove, on the basis of the Chinese classics and with the help of rationalist Neo-Confucian philosophers, that such a cult, strictly speaking, had no religious meaning. By contrast, de Rhodes was no scholar of Confucianism; his knowledge of the Confucian classics was minimal. But he was deeply in touch with the common people for whom many of the gestures and objects in the Confucian rites, whatever their original symbolism, were susceptible to superstitious interpretation. Therefore, he thought it wise pastorally to forbid them altogether. Such a strategy was unduly narrow and did prevent at least two influential mandarins from accepting Christianity.[73] For the majority of Vietnamese Christians, however, it offered at the time useful guidelines in dealing with such a confusing issue, which as we have seen above, bedeviled the Asian churches for three hundred years.[74]

72. For a detailed description of this ceremony, see de Rhodes, *Histoire du Royaume*, 11–13.

73. De Rhodes, *Divers voyages*, 182–85.

74. For a detailed discussion of de Rhodes's attitude toward Buddhism, Daoism, and Confucianism, see Phan, *Mission and Catechesis*, 82–96.

Adriano di St. Thecla (1667–1765) and the Opusculum de Sectis apud Sinensis et Tunkinensis (1750)

The second author who offers a rare view into how Christians viewed Vietnamese religions is Adriano di St. Thecla, an Italian of the Order of the Discalced Augustinians, or Augustinian Recollects. Between 1701 and 1761, thirteen Italian Augustinians were working in the Eastern Tonkin diocese. In 1735, one of them, Ilario Costa di Gesù (1694–1754), was chosen as bishop. In 1749, he made one of his confreres, Adriano di St. Thecla, who had arrived in Tonkin in 1738, vicar general. In 1761 the Dominicans were granted total control of the Eastern Diocese, and the Augustinians were ordered to leave. Adriano, then ninety-four years of age, refused to abandon the missionary field in which his order had been laboring for sixty years, and went on working until his death in 1765.

Of Adriano's three works, the most important is his *Opusculum de Sectis apud Sinenses et Tunkinenses*.[75] It has six chapters: "Introduction," "Confucianism," "Spirits," "The Sect of Magicians" (i.e., Daoism), "Fortune-Tellers," "Buddhism," and "Christianity." The last chapter on Christianity was left unfinished. Even though the treatise's title includes the Chinese, the information it provides deals basically with religions in North Vietnam.

As to the order of the discussion of the Vietnamese religions, Adriano explains in the introduction that he adopts the order set by Zhou Wudi, an emperor ruling in Northern China from 561 to 578, who proceeded first with Confucianism because it was an imperial ideology, second with Daoism because it was an indigenous doctrine, and third with Buddhism because it was a foreign religion. The order may reflect another interest of Adriano who, according to translator Olga Dror's suggestion, arranges his discussion of the Vietnamese religions according to the ascending degree of their spiritual harmfulness to the Christian faith. Thus, Confucianism would be the least, and Buddhism the most deleterious religion from the Christian point of view. This also explains why Adriano adds a chapter on spirits—the longest chapter with thirty-six pages, compared with nineteen pages for Confucianism, twelve for Daoism, and twenty-four for Buddhism—immediately after the chapter on Confucianism; and a chapter on fortune-tellers before the one on Buddhism. Presumably, for Adriano, the cult of spirits among the Vietnamese was not as harmful as the widespread practice of fortune-telling, an evil practice second only to Buddhism, compared with

---

75. Adriano's other two works include *Chronologia Sinensis* and *Compendium Vitae*. The *Opusculum* has been translated into English by Olga Dror, with collaboration of Mariya Berezovska.

which the cult of spirits would be far more acceptable since it at least opens up the transcendent dimension of life.

It is not possible to review in detail what Adriano says about each of the Vietnamese religions here.[76] Of Confucianism, or as Adriano calls it, the "Sect of the Literati," five topics are treated: the life of Confucius, the books and teachings of Confucianism, the religion of the literati (in particular, the *Te Nam Giao* and the cult of ancestors), the cult of Confucius, and a description of the preparation for and the solemn sacrifice to Confucius.

On spirits, Adriano describes the spirits of Heaven and Earth, the legendary sage-kings of Chinese antiquity, military heroes, tutelary deities, and miscellaneous personages who became objects of worship. In particular, he describes some ceremonies hitherto unknown; namely, the ceremony of welcoming the god of spring named Cau Mang, the *Te Ky Dao* (The Ceremony of the Leader's Banner), the ceremony of taking the Oath of Loyalty, and the ceremony of raking tutelary genies. On these, Adriano is a unique source of information.

On Daoism, or the "Sect of Magicians," Adriano discusses the life of Laozi, the growth of Daoism, its practice of magic and sorcery, its worship of spirits, and its worship of Emperor Jade. In connection with Daoism, Adriano also briefly discusses fortune-tellers and diviners.

Finally, on Buddhism, or the "Sect of Worshipers of Buddha," Adriano discusses the life of "The Founder of This Sect among Indians," the spread of Buddhism in China, its teachings, and its worship of idols. Like other missionaries, Adriano was more opposed to Buddhism than to other religious traditions. Dror suggests two reasons for this pronounced hostility. First, doctrinally, the Buddha was believed to have derived his alleged teaching on the transmigration of souls and vegetarianism from Pythagoras who was also considered responsible for the theory of heliocentrism espoused by Nicolas Copernicus and Galileo Galilei, and condemned by the church. Second, and more importantly, it was thought that Buddhism is a kind of counterfeit Christianity. Missionaries—Ricci, de Rhodes, and Adriano among them—had been telling the story that Emperor Ming of the Han dynasty saw in a dream a man with a golden body sixteen cubits tall who told the emperor that he was from the Western region. Informed by his interpreters that he had seen a wise and holy man who could bring him prosperity and happiness, the emperor sent messengers to the West to search for the holy man. When the messengers arrived in India, they were discouraged by the pains of further travel. So, the story goes, they took the books and the statue of the Buddha home and deceived the emperor, telling him that the books

---

76. For a summary, see Dror's analysis in Adriano, *Opusculum*, 39–60.

and the statue were of the man of the West. Thus mistaken, the emperor ordered his subjects to follow the teaching of the Buddha and to worship him. The point of the story for Christian missionaries is that people naturally believed in the one God, or in other words, the Christian God, and that it was only through deception that Buddhism was accepted as the true religion.[77]

Hoi Dong Tu Giao Danh Su (Conference of Scholars of Four Religions)

The third important witness to the encounter of Christianity and Vietnamese religions is the anonymous *Hoi Dong Tu Giao Danh Su*, often referred to as *Hoi Dong Tu Giao* (Conference of Four Religions). The origin of this text is wrapped in mystery. It exists in three scripts: *chu nho* ("Chinese script"), *chu nom* ("demotic script"), and *chu quoc ngu* ("national script").[78] In sum, it is fairly likely that *Hoi Dong Tu Giao* was first composed in *chu nom* ("year unknown") before 1887, then transliterated into *chu quoc ngu* before 1887, and then finally translated into *chu nho* in 1887/1888.

The reason this text is discussed here in our account of the encounter between Christianity and the Vietnamese religions *before* 1800 is that the *event* it purports to narrate is said to take place in 1773. The preface to the *chu quoc ngu* text, which is absent in the *chu nom* text, states that in the reign of Kinh Canh Hung of the Le dynasty, Lord Tinh Do Vuong—that is, Trinh Sam, who ruled in 1767-82—arrested two Catholic priests: Jacinto

---

77. In addition to the *Opusculum*, there exists another manuscript titled *Tam Giao Chu Vong* (The Errors of the Three Religions). It is located at the Archives des Missions Etrangères de Paris (AMEP), number V-1098. It was composed in 1752, most probably by Bishop Ilario Costa di Gesu, who wrote fourteen books in Vietnamese (and not by Adriano who wrote only in Latin). One of these books, *Di Doan Chi Giao* (The Superstitious Doctrine) is a critique of Buddhist teachings, which Adriano used as one of his sources for his *Opusculum*. *Tam Giao Chu Vong* is written in the form of dialogue between a Western religious scholar and an Eastern religious scholar and is divided in three parts corresponding to the Three Religions, in the following order: Confucianism, Daoism, and Buddhism. In terms of both content and style, there are marked similarities, with identical citations from the classical sources, between Adriano's *Opusculum* and *Tam Giao Chu Vong*. The former, written in Latin, was addressed to foreign missionaries to inform them of Vietnamese religions; the latter, written in Vietnamese national script, was addressed to the Vietnamese Christians themselves to help them differentiate their own beliefs from those of other religions.

78. Until the beginning of the twentieth century, Chinese characters were used for official documents in Vietnam. *Chu quoc ngu* was devised by Catholic missionaries in the seventeenth century (esp. Alexandre de Rhodes) by using Roman alphabets and various diacritical marks to transcribe phonetically the Vietnamese tonal language. In 1917, an imperial decree made this alphabetized script the national script.

Castañeda, a European, and Vincent Liem, a native. Both were decapitated on November 11, 1773. The lord's uncle was an important mandarin whose mother, by the name of Thuong Tram, was a Christian. She earnestly urged her son to join the Catholic faith. Out of love for his mother, the mandarin was disposed to acquiesce to her wish, but before doing so, he wanted to find out which of the four religions was the true one. So he called for a conference at his palace during which a Christian scholar, a Confucian master, a Buddhist monk, and a Taoist bonze would present the teachings of their respective religions and debate with each other, the mandarin himself serving as moderator.

However, given that this mandarin was reported to have died in 1763 after his baptism, it is impossible that such a conference, at which he was said to preside, took place some ten years after his death. Very likely then, the conference of the representatives of the four religions did not take place as it is presented by *Hoi Dong Tu Giao*.[79] Rather, the text is a literary composition written shortly before or after 1800 in the apologetic genre in which a Christian writer, well versed in the doctrines and practices of the Three Religions and of Christianity and fluent in Vietnamese—likely an expatriate—presents the truths of the Christian faith and rebuts the alleged errors of other religions.[80]

The *Conference of Four Religions* is framed as a three-day meeting, each day with its own theme for debate. The Christian/Western scholar (*tsy si*) begins by denying that Christianity is the religion of the Portuguese, as it was called in Vietnamese in the seventeenth century.[81] Rather, he says, it must be called "religion of God" because it teaches the worship of the one God.[82] As for the themes for debate, he suggests three—one for each day. The first refers to the past: What is the origin of the world and humanity? The second refers to the present: What must one do morally? The third refers to the future: Where will one go after death?

To these three questions each religious representative gives answer, mostly by appealing to the canonical texts of his religion. Needless to say,

---

79. Castañeda is reported to have recited during the interrogations a few prayers and especially the Creed, which he explained to his captors. But this hardly qualified as a debate as reported by *Hoi Dong Tu Giao*.

80. A text of *Hoi Dong Tu Giao* is published privately, with the *chu nho* and *chu quoc ngu* texts face-to-face, by Tran Kim Vinh, Nguyen Huy Hung, and Nguyen Duc Quy.

81. Christianity was called *dao Hoa Lang* (religion of Portugal). For more on this misunderstanding, see Phan, *Mission and Catechesis*, xv.

82. Even today Christianity is known in Vietnamese as *dao Thien Chua* (religion of God).

the Christian scholar has the lion's share of the conversation, since he has not only to present the Christian teaching but also to challenge the explanations of the other three partners. Naturally, he is presented as the undoubted winner in the debate, and the mandarin declares as much at the end of each day. However, the author does not attempt to short-circuit the discussion; on the contrary, each discussant has the opportunity to present the teachings of his religion and the supporting reasons. The Christian scholar is willing to grant validity to the teachings of other religions when they are in accord with reason and are morally useful, and objects to them only to the extent they contradict the Christian teachings. Generally, the tone of the conversation is civilized and respectful, even when there is unequivocal disagreement.

One significant feature of *Hoi Dong Tu Giao*, in contrast to the works examined above—such as Ricci's *Tianzhu shiyi*, de Rhodes's *Cathechismus*, and Adriano's *Opusculum*—is that it makes a full presentation of the Christian faith, even of truths that are divinely revealed and not accessible to unaided reason; such as the fall, the Trinity, the incarnation, and redemption (Day Two) and hell, heaven, the last judgment, and the general resurrection (Day Three). In this sense, the work is a true catechism in an interreligious context. It not only explains to Christians what they should believe but also informs them of the beliefs of non-Christian religions, and in this way the Christian distinctiveness can easily be grasped. At the same time, it justifies Christian beliefs to non-Christians and clarifies possible misunderstandings. It is most interesting to note the various objections that Confucianists, Daoists, and Buddhists have raised against Christian teachings and the replies given by the Christian scholar. These objections-and-answers represent the concrete doctrinal encounter between Christianity and the Three Religions in Vietnam in the eighteenth and nineteenth centuries.

ENCOUNTER, CONFLICT, APOLOGETICS, DIALOGUE

The presence of Christianity as the "Fourth Religion" in China and Vietnam—from the seventh in the former, and the seventeenth in the latter—created a new dynamic in the nineteenth century among the Asian "Three Religions"; namely, Buddhism, Confucianism, and Daoism. For various reasons, in both countries Christianity has found an ideological ally in Confucianism—at least the "Original Confucianism." From Ricci to the author of *Hoi Dong Tu Giao*, Confucianism was held in high regard, especially for its alleged monotheism and its moral teachings. Even Alexandre de Rhodes, while critical of Confucius himself, acknowledged the beneficial impact of his teachings on the moral and political order. Among Chinese converts, many defended the possibility of being a Christian and a Confucianist at the same time.

With regard to Buddhism, however, as a whole, missionaries were hostile to it, partly because many Buddhist teachings—as the missionaries understood them and, some would argue, misunderstood them—stand opposed to the Christian faith, and partly because by the sixteenth century Buddhism had suffered a decline in both China and Vietnam and was held in contempt by the literati. As for Daoism, its philosophical doctrine was not taken seriously, or was seriously misunderstood by missionaries, since its categories and thought forms were so alien to the Western mind. On the other hand, such practices as divination, magic, and sorcery popularly associated with Daoism were roundly condemned as immoral.

As to the character of the encounter between Christianity and Asian religions, both in China and Vietnam, history shows that it was far from uniform. At one extreme of the spectrum, represented by the Figurists, there was a totally positive, even naive, attitude toward the native religions and cultures, so much so that an attempt was made via a study of the Chinese classics and ideograms to show that the Chinese had already known many of the Christian mysteries. At the other end, represented by most, though not all Dominicans, Franciscans, and the members of the Society of Foreign Mission of Paris, there was a pervasive and deep suspicion of Asian religions as fundamentally idolatry and superstition. Between these two ends of the spectrum was an affirmative yet critical appreciation for Asian cultural and religious traditions, represented by those schooled in humanism, such as Valignano, Ricci, de Rhodes, the author of *Hoi Dong Tu Giao*, and even Adriano. These missionaries made a conscious and prolonged effort to learn the local languages and acquainted themselves with the beliefs and practices of Asian religions. In fact, their descriptions of these religions (e.g., those of de Rhodes and Adriano) remain the best sources available for an understanding of them. In addition, their lexicographical, grammatical, and literary compositions constitute a permanent contribution to the native cultures.

These opposing attitudes toward Asian religions and cultures transformed the peaceful and fruitful encounter between Christianity and Asian religions into a conflict in the case of the Chinese Rites. Whatever one thinks of the impact of the Rites Controversy on Christian mission in China and Vietnam, there is no doubt that it is one of the saddest chapters of the history of Asian Christianity. As mentioned above, more than theology was at stake in this dispute: rivalries among religious orders; personal pride and arrogance; political interests; and cultural and religious chauvinism. Apart from the fact that ancestor veneration or worship still remains a contentious issue in contemporary Asian Christianity, the Rites Controversy constitutes a useful cautionary tale about the challenges and dangers of the inculturation of Christianity into Asia.[83]

Fortunately, the encounter between Christianity and Asian religions was not always marred by conflict. It was also punctuated by several attempts at understanding the other religions. In keeping with the literary conventions of the time, the preferred genre was apologetics. Ricci's *Tianzhu shiyi*, Adriano's *Opusculum*, and the two anonymous works *Tam Giao Chu Vong* and *Hoi Dong Tu Giao* are distinguished examples. In general, their tone is not hostile or aggressive; rather, there is a sincere attempt to recognize the truth of the teachings and practices of other religions whenever warranted and to find a common ground if and when it exists.

Today, with the urgent need for interreligious dialogue and inculturation, past strategies such as encounter, apologetics, and a fortiori suspicion would no longer be adequate and appropriate. Rather, there must be a humble and grateful acknowledgment of the active presence of the divine Spirit at work in Asian religions and cultures with which Christianity enters into a dialogue in which there is *mutual* learning, correction, and enrichment.[84]

BIBLIOGRAPHY

Alvarez, José María. *Formosa geográfica e históricamente considerada*. 2 vols. Barcelona: Luis Gili, 1930.

Blussé van Oud-Alblas, J. Leonard. "Dutch Protestant Missionaries as Protagonists of the Territorial Expansion of the VOC on Formosa." In *Conversion, Competition, and Conflict: Essays on the Role of Religion in Asia*, edited by Dick Kooim, 155–84. Amsterdam: Free University Press, 1984.

Campbell, William. *Formosa under the Dutch, Described from Contemporary Records with Explanation Notes and a Bibliography of the Land*. London: Kegan Paul, Trench, Trubner, 1903. Reprint, Taipei: SMC, 1992.

Charbonnier, Jean. *Histoire des Chrétiens de Chine*. Paris: Les Indes Savantes, 2002.

Ching, Julia. *Chinese Religions*. Maryknoll, NY: Orbis, 1993.

---

83. One aspect of the encounter between Christianity and Asian religions that needs further exploration is the missionaries' dependence on the goodwill of local political power. This is true of Nestorian Christians during the T'ang dynasty, of Catholic missionaries during the Mongolian and Manchu dynasties in China, and of Catholic missionaries in Vietnam under the Trinh and Nguyen lords in Tonkin and Cochinchina, respectively. The fortunes of Christianity waxed and waned depending on the favors of the local government.

84. On this dialogue, see Phan's works: *Christianity*; *In Our Own Tongues*; and *Being Religious Interreligiously*.

———. "East Asian Religions." In *World Religions: Eastern Traditions*, edited by Willard Gurdon Oxtoby, 347–67. New York: Oxford University Press, 1996.

———. "Mahayana in East Asia." In *World Religions: Eastern Traditions*, edited by Willard Gurdon Oxtoby, 284–320. New York: Oxford University Press, 1996.

Chiu, Peter Chung-hang. "An Historical Study of Nestorian Christianity in the T'ang Dynasty between A.D. 636–845." PhD diss., Southwestern Baptist Theological Seminary, 1987.

Covell, Ralph R. *Pentecost of the Hills in Taiwan: The Christian Faith among the Original Inhabitants*. Pasadena, CA: Hope, 1998.

Criveller, Gianni. *Preaching Christ in Late Ming China: The Jesuits' Presentation of Christ from Matteo Ricci to Giulio Aleni*. Taipei: Ricci Institute, 1997.

di St. Thecla, Adriano. *Chronologia Sinensis et Tunkinensis*, Pre-1750.

———. *Compendium Vitae D. ni P. Hilarii a Jesu. Episcopi Coriensis*, 1756.

———. *Opusculum de Sectis apud Sinenses et Tunkinenses*. [A Small Treatise on the Sects among the Chinese and Tonkinese: A Study of Religion in China and North Vietnam in the Eighteenth Century]. English translation by Olga Dror, with Mariya Berezovska. Ithaca, NY: Cornell University, (1750) 2002.

England, John C. *The Hidden History of Christianity in Asia: The Churches of the East before the Year 1500*. Hong Kong: CCA, 1998.

England, John C., et al., eds. *Asian Christian Theologies: A Research Guide to Authors, Movements, Sources*. Vols. 1–3, Asian Region 7th–20th Centuries. Maryknoll, NY: Orbis, 2002, 2003, 2004.

Eskildsen, Stephen. "Christology and Soteriology in the Chinese Nestorian Texts." In *The Chinese Face of Jesus Christ*, vols. 1 and 2, edited by Roman Malek, 181–218. Nettetal: Steyler Verlag, 2002.

Fernández, Pablo. *Dominicos donde nace el sol: Historia de la provincia del santísimo rosario de Filipinas de la orden de predicadores*. Barcelona: Yuste, 1958.

Gernet, Jacques. *Chine et Christianisme: Action et réaction*. Paris: Gallimard, 1982.

Gillman, Ian, and Hans-Joachim Klimkeit. *Christians in Asia before 1500*. Ann Arbor: University of Michigan Press, 1999.

Ginsel, Willy Abraham. *De Gereformeerde Kerk op Formosa of de lotgevallen eener handelskerk onder de Oost-Indische Compagnie, 1627–1662*. PhD diss., The Hague: University of Leiden, 1931.

Hoi Dong Tu Giao. Published privately (with the *chu nho* and *chu quoc ngu* texts face-to-face) by Tran Kim Vinh, Nguyen Huy Hung, and Nguyen Duc Quy. Houston, La Vang Tung Thu, 2000.

Irvin, Dale T., and Scott W. Sunquist. *History of the World Christian Movement*. Vol. 1 of Earliest Christianity to 1453. Maryknoll, NY: Orbis, 2001.

Jami, Catherine, et al., eds. *Statecraft and Intellectual Renewal in Late Ming China: The Cross-Cultural Synthesis of Xu Guangqi (1562–1633)*. Leiden: Brill, 2000.

Jensen, Lionel M. *Manufacturing Confucianism: Chinese Tradition and Universal Civilization*. Durham, NC: Duke University Press, 1997.

Kooyman, Dick, ed. *Conversion, Competition, and Conflict: Essays on the Role of Religion in Asia*. Amsterdam: Free University Press, 1984.

Lancashire, Douglas. "Anti-Christian Polemics in Seventeenth-Century China." *Church History* 38 (1969) 218–41.

———. "Buddhist Reactions to Christianity in Late Ming China." *Journal of the Oriental Society of Australia* 6 (1968–69) 82–103.

Latourette, Kenneth Scott. *A History of Christian Missions in China*. London: SPCK, 1929.

Laurentin, René. *Chine et christianisme: Après les occasion manquées*. Paris: Desclise de Brouwer, 1977.

Liang, Yuansheng. "Towards a Hyphenated Identity: Li Zhizao's Search for a Confucian-Christian Synthesis." *Monumenta Serica* 39 (1990-91) 115-30.

Malek, Roman, ed. *The Chinese Face of Jesus Christ*. Vols. 1 and 2. Nettetal: Steyler Verlag, 2002.

Minamiki, George. *The Chinese Rites Controversy: From Its Beginning to Modern Times*. Chicago: Loyola University Press, 1985.

Moffett, Samuel Hugh. *A History of Christianity in Asia*, vol. 1 and 2. Maryknoll, NY: Orbis, 1998, 2005.

Moule, Arthur. C. *Christians in China before the Year 1550*. London: Society for Promoting Christian Knowledge, 1930.

Mungello, David E., ed. *The Chinese Rites Controversy: Its History and Meaning*. Nettetal: Steyler Verlag, 1994.

Noll, Ray R., ed. *100 Roman Documents Concerning the Chinese Rites Controversy (1645-1941)*. San Francisco: Ricci Institute, 1992.

Oxtoby, Willard G., ed. *World Religions: Eastern Traditions*. New York: Oxford University Press, 1996.

Pelliot, Paul. *L'inscription nestorienne de Si-ngan-fou*. Edited with Supplements by Antonio Forte. Kyoto: Scuola di Studi sull'Asia Orientale, 1996.

Phan, Peter C. *Being Religious Interreligiously: Asian Perspectives on Interfaith Dialogue*. Maryknoll, NY: Orbis, 2004.

———. *Christianity with an Asian Face:Asian American Theology in the Making*. Maryknoll, NY: Orbis, 2003.

———. *In Our Own Tongues: Perspectives from Asia on Mission and Inculturation*. Maryknoll, NY: Orbis, 2003.

———. *Mission and Catechesis: Alexandre de Rhodes and Inculturation in Seventeenth-Century Vietnam*. Maryknoll, NY: Orbis, 1998.

Raguin, Yves. "China's First Evangelization by the 7th and 8th Century Eastern Syrian Monks: Some Problems Posed by the First Chinese Expressions of the Christian Traditions." In *The Chinese Face of Jesus Christ*, vol. 1, edited by Roman Malek, 159-79. Nettetal: Steyler Verlag, 2002.

Rhodes, Alexandre de. *Catechismus pro iis, qui volunt suscipere Baptismum, in Octo dies divisus: Ope sacrae Congregationis de Propaganda Fide in lucem editus. Ab Alexandro de Rhodes u Societate Jesu, ejusdemque Sacrae Congregationis Missionario Apostolico*. Rome, 1651.

———. *Dictionarium annamiticum lusitanum, et latinum ope sacrae congregationis de propaganda fide in lucem editum*. Rome, 1651.

———. *Divers voyages et missions du P. Alexandre de Rhodes en la Chine, & autres Royaumes de l'Orient, avec son retour en Europe par la Perse & l'Arménie: Le tout divisé en trois parties*. Henceforth: *Divers voyages*. Paris: Samuel & Grabriel Cramoisy, 1653, repub. 1666, 1681, 1683, 1854, and 1884.

———. *Histoire du Royaume de Tunquin, et des grands progrez que la predication de l'Evangeile y a faits en la conversion des infidèlles: Depuis l'année 1627 jusques a l'Année 1646. Composée en latin par le R. P. Alexandre de Rhodes, de la Compagnie* de Jésus. Et traduite en françois par le R.P. Henry Albi, de la mesme Compagnie. Lyon, 1651.

Ricci, Matteo S. *The True Meaning of the Lord of Heaven*. Translated by Douglas Lancashire and Peter Hu Kuo-chen. Taipei: Ricci Institute, 1985.

Roberts, J. A. G. *A Concise History of China*. Cambridge: Harvard University Press, 1999.

Ross, Andrew. *A Vision Betrayed: The Jesuits in Japan and China, 1542–1742*. Maryknoll, NY: Orbis, 1994.

Rule, Paul. "The Jesus of the 'Confucian Christians' of the Seventeenth Century." In *The Chinese Face of Jesus Christ*, vol. 2, edited by Roman Malek, 499–516. Nettetal: Steyler Verlag, 2002.

———. "Review of *Manufacturing Confucianism*." *Journal of Chinese Religions* 27 (1999) 105–11.

Saeki, P. Yoshiro. *The Nestorian Documents and Relics in China*. Tokyo: The Naruzen, 1951.

Standaert, Nicolas, ed. *Handbook of Christianity in China*, vol. 1. Leiden: Brill, 2001.

———. *Yang Tingyun, Confucian and Christian in Late Ming China: His Life and Thought*. Leiden: Brill, 1988.

Tubach, Jürgen. "Der Apostel Thomas in China: Die Herkunft einer Tradition." *Zeitschrift für Kirchengeschichte* 108 (1997) 58–74.

von Collani, Claudia. *Die Figuristen in der Chinamission*. Frankfurt: Lang, 1981.

Xu, Changzhi. *Shengchao Poxie ji*. Collection of Writings of the Sacred Dynasty for the Countering of Heterodoxy. N.p.: N.p.

Young, John D. *Confucianism and Christianity: The First Encounter*. Hong Kong: Hong Kong University Press, 1983.

Zürcher, Erik. "The First Anti-Christian Movement in China (Nanking, 1616–21)." In *Acta Orientala Neerlandica*, edited by P. W. Pestman, 188–95. Leiden: Brill, 1971.

Part 3

Contemporary and Global Perspectives

Chapter 7

Religious Plurality and the Christian Mission in the People's Republic of China

Kim-Kwong Chan and Daniel H. Bays

INTRODUCTION

As PETER PHAN'S ESSAY indicates,[1] after the early 1700s and the proscription of Christianity by the Qing government, Christianity—including the European church hierarchy, a few underground Chinese priests, and perhaps 200,000 converts—existed in a new context of religious plurality. Confucianism, Buddhism, and Daoism enjoyed official favor. Along with a host of other indigenous sects such as the White Lotus, Christianity was categorized as an illegal sect and relegated to the margins of society.[2] It was one of the least important of the multiplicity of religious currents in Chinese society until well after 1800.

Even before the ban on Christianity in the 1720s, the early missionaries to China—Catholics, the few Dutch Protestants in Taiwan, and the handful of Russian Orthodox who did not evangelize actively—had no

---

1. See Ch. 6 of this book.
2. See Bays, "Tradition," 25–39, and Laamaan, *Christian Heretics*.

diplomatic or military support from their home governments. Thus, they had to recognize the primacy of the Chinese state and live within its laws and regulations.[3] This situation changed drastically in the 1840s when the British defeated China in the Opium War and forced the lifting of the legal prohibition of Christianity. The legalization of Christianity was only one element in the new system of Western privilege that was imposed upon China by the Western powers, which is usually called "the treaty system." These treaties also provided for extraterritoriality, tariff limits, coerced trade and investment, and designated autonomous living areas for foreigners in many Chinese cities.

This well-organized system of imperialism that began before 1850 lasted for almost exactly a century—that is, until the 1940s. During this time, China experienced what has been called semi-colonialism. Except for British Hong Kong and Portuguese Macao, no part of China was officially a colony, but many areas of major cities functioned like colonies. This highly unequal system, which made China the prey of Western nations, was the context within which Christianity, both Catholic and Protestant, grew from the first treaties of the 1840s to the establishment of a Communist regime in 1949.

Thus, after 1850 the context of religious plurality within which Christianity operated was highly politicized. In important ways, foreign missionaries because of their privileged legal/political status could give the Chinese church advantages in competition with other groups. Nevertheless, on the whole, the strong link with foreigners was a disadvantage for Chinese Christianity. In the nineteenth century, the growing Christian movement had to face the strong forces of both popular xenophobia and elite fears of ideological heterodoxy. In addition, the Qing state remained deeply suspicious.[4] The latter's instinctive aversion to Christianity as a sectarian religious superstition was greatly compounded by the clear claims of Christian identity on the part of the leaders of the Taiping Rebellion, the mid-century civil war in which over twenty million were killed and the dynasty nearly toppled.[5] The heterodox ideological makeup of Christianity was as much a liability as its association with foreigners. In the decades of the late nineteenth century, Christianity was a minor element in the spectrum of religions in China and struggled simply to survive.

3. Discussed in Bays, ibid.

4. Cohen, *China and Christianity*, remains one of the best analyses of popular anger and elite hostility toward missionaries and Christianity.

5. A large literature base exists covering the Taiping Rebellion. Two works that particularly highlight the religious aspects are Spence, *God's Chinese Son*, and Reilly, *Taiping Heavenly Kingdom*.

In 1900 the greatest of all traditional xenophobic antiforeign paroxysms of violence occurred. The Boxer Rebellion inflicted immense casualties on both foreign missionaries and Chinese converts—Catholic and Protestant—alike.[6] But by this time, the forces of change were pulling China into the modern world, and the post-Boxer years were a time of political, economic, and educational reforms that made Christianity, especially Christian schools, more attractive to many Chinese.[7] Both Catholic and Protestant communities grew rapidly in the early twentieth century. Despite a respectable attempt to ride the wave of reform and adapt to the changing times, the Qing dynasty was doomed and fell in 1912. In its last few years, the central government lost control over religion. The new Republic of China that took over in 1912 had even less control over the country, especially foreigners. As a result, for the next several decades there was a de facto "religious freedom" simply because there was no Chinese government capable of monitoring, much less regulating, religious activity.

For more than two decades in the twentieth century, Christianity took its place as an important participant in the circle of diverse religions constituting China's arena of religious plurality. Perhaps we should say "pluralities" because the diversities that developed among Christians were almost as striking as the great variety of Chinese religions. The latter were themselves highly diverse. With the decline of central authority, many millenarian sects and local cults sprang up and gained many adherents. In addition, there were followers of the established "three teachings." A striking aspect of Christianity in these decades was its proliferation into segments. This was especially true for Protestants whose incorrigible tendency toward division resulted in a world of plurality among themselves: a cacophony of claims and particularistic doctrines associated with some 150 different Christian mission groups seemed to many Chinese both confusing and unnecessary. It is not surprising that many Chinese Christians were so frustrated by the fractious denominationalism inflicted upon them by the missions—deriving from centuries-old doctrinal controversies in Europe—that they welcomed the Communist government's dismantling of denominational structures in the 1950s.

Proliferation of plurality could also be seen among Catholics. French Catholics were reluctant to relinquish the control they had exerted over Catholic missions in China since the mid-1800s, while the Vatican was determined to extend its direct control over Chinese affairs through its own

6. Among numerous sources, see particularly Esherick, *Origins of the Boxer Uprising*. For a concise overview incorporating recent scholarship, see Cohen, *History in Three Keys*, Part 1.

7. See Dunch, *Fuzhou Protestants*.

representatives such as vicars apostolic.[8] Moreover, new national orders, such as Maryknoll from the United States, took on an important role as well.[9] Of course, all maneuvered for influence under the flag of the pope. Overall, then, the religious scene in the first quarter of the twentieth century was chaotic but full of energy and growth that carried on without the restraining hand of a strong central government.

In the mid-1920s this situation changed drastically for Chinese Christianity, especially for Protestants. Those groups still most visibly led by foreign missionaries felt the greatest pressure. A tidal wave of urban nationalism that had been brewing since before World War I exploded in the events of the May 4 Movement of 1919 and spread all through China's cities in the early 1920s. It culminated in the emotional mass movements and urban turmoil that began with the May 30, 1925, incident and went on for more than two years.[10] By this time, students—including many in Christian schools; intellectuals; and patriotic urbanites of all classes—were roundly denouncing Christianity as a vile accomplice of imperialism, which allegedly denationalized and alienated converts from their native culture.[11]

This sudden turn against Christianity and its Sino-foreign institutions was a massive shock to the leaders of the Protestant movement, especially to the foreigners. Whereas it had been assumed by all parties that Christianity was integral to China's modernization, it was now reviled as both foreign and superstitious; or viewed as decidedly "unmodern." The problem, in part, stemmed from the fact that the transfer of real authority and leadership in the churches and Christian schools from foreign missionary to Chinese national had been exceedingly slow. In this suddenly antiforeign age, the church looked distinctly foreign. Revolutionary "modern" nationalists made Christianity their target, and Christians suffered accordingly. Because they had more urban institutions, Protestants were involved in more publicized incidents, but Catholics also had to deal with these forces. Protestant missions were forced to give over formal leadership of many organizations to Chinese colleagues. The pope appointed several Catholic bishops during these years—the first Chinese to be consecrated bishops since the seventeenth century.

8. Hanson, *Catholic Politics*.

9. Wiest, *Maryknoll in China*.

10. A profusion exists of scholarly literature on the May 4 period and the politics of the 1920s. The classic work is still Chow, *May Fourth Movement*. A recent study addressing themes we are emphasizing is Wang, *China's Unequal Treaties*.

11. Both the Guomindang (Nationalist) and Chinese Communist parties shrewdly manipulated these attacks through effective propaganda. A fine study of this period is Lutz, *Chinese Politics*.

Our contention here is that just as in the nineteenth century the close association of Christianity existed with foreign powers and the treaty system of foreign privilege, in the twentieth century the close association of Christianity with foreigners handicapped Christianity in the crucial task of establishing itself as a fully Chinese participant in the pluralist roster of religions and religious movements in China. Not until the 1940s was the Chinese government able to sign treaties with the United States and Great Britain to end the extraterritoriality and other remaining vestiges of the old "unequal treaties."

During the late 1930s and 1940s civil strife, the Japanese invasion, then the Pacific War, and finally a civil war (1946–49) leading to the new Communist regime in Beijing, were certainly not conducive to Christian growth. The exception was a few sectarian native Christian groups, such as the Jesus Family, that addressed the needs of China's poorest and most destitute in rural areas. These groups grew rapidly during these years.[12]

While, in retrospect, the late 1940s would be seen as the end of an age, many missionaries returned to China and were joined by others coming for the first time. Despite the end of the treaty system, some missionaries instinctively tried to reestablish their former positions of authority over Chinese colleagues, and the financial power of foreign mission agencies gave the foreign component of Sino-Western Christianity continuing influence. While this was true for many Protestants, it was especially true for Catholics with their centralized ecclesiastical structure stemming from the Vatican. So no profound change occurred in the status of Christianity until 1949–50 when the Communists took power and the Guomindang fled to Taiwan. In mid-1950 the Korean War broke out, resulting in direct conflict between the Chinese and the United Nations forces led by the United States and Great Britain. The Communist regime cracked down on all Christian groups, often subjecting missionaries to humiliating trials with forced denunciations by Chinese colleagues. They were then expelled from the country.[13] This was traumatic for the missionaries and ominous for Chinese Christians. It was apparent that time had run out for the modern missionary movement to China; a new era was beginning in which Chinese Christians would be on their own.[14]

12. See Tao, *Yesu Jiating*.

13. Works reflecting various points of view on this wrenching experience include Jones, *Church in Communist China*; Bush, *Religion in Communist China*; and Wickeri, *Seeking the Common Ground*.

14. There were recriminations in some mission circles, along with thoughtful reflections in others. One of the latter, a penetrating and brutally frank analysis, appeared in 1953; although less than one hundred pages in length, it is considered a classic: Paton,

The context of religious plurality in which Christianity had existed in China from the early 1950s until about 1980 was one in which all religions were more or less similarly harassed and constrained, although Chinese Christians (both Protestants and Catholics) were treated more harshly than most other religious believers because of the recent close association many had with foreigners, especially with the United States—China's foremost national enemy in the 1950s and 1960s. All religions came under pressure, and foreign resources diminished and eventually dissipated.

Communication with foreigners was almost impossible. Chinese Christians shared the same status as all other recognized religions in China: placed under constant monitoring and having to register all religious venues, personnel, and activities. This is not the place to describe the evolving, generally worsening, fortunes of religions in China for the thirty years until 1980. Briefly stated, a powerful antireligious state applied relentless pressure against *all* religions in an attempt to systematically eliminate all religion. Yet during these decades, Christianity established itself as a legitimate part of the religious spectrum, as a part of Chinese religious plurality.

Dramatic policy shifts came in the 1970s. United States President Richard Nixon visited China in 1972 and set in motion a new alignment between China and the United States. This did not have an immediate effect on religious affairs in China. But Deng Xiaoping's even more dramatic break with past policy and his launching of a far-ranging set of internal economic, social, and cultural reforms after 1978 began a whole new era for religion in China.

The 1980s and 1990s witnessed an astonishing explosion of religious activity and dynamism all across China. No religion has been more impressive in its growth than Christianity, especially in its many forms of Protestantism. Yet, as we will see, religions still must operate in a public arena that is debilitating in many ways. The state has reestablished all the old institutional mechanisms of monitoring, registration, and control that were in place before the mid-1960s: for Protestants that is the Three Self Patriotic Movement (TSPM), and for Catholics the Chinese Catholic Patriotic Association.[15] Even though it took a half-century after the end of the missionary age in China to achieve legitimacy, the Chinese church today seems secure in its Chinese identity. For three decades Christianity has been functioning as one of several Chinese religious expressions, not as a "foreign religion."

Christian Missions.

15. The state also created a new "companion" organization overlapping with the TSPM, the China Christian Council, which had not existed before the Cultural Revolution.

We now turn to an examination of the diverse scene that comprises Chinese religious plurality in the twenty-first century.

RELIGIOUS ENVIRONMENT AND POLICY

The People's Republic of China (PRC) is governed by a single ruling party, the Communist Party of China (CPC) that promotes Socialism as the nation's official ideology and promotes Atheism-Dialectical Materialism in all public domains, such as education. Being the State orthodoxy, atheistic Marxism-Leninism is the privileged state-supported ideology and considered to be the "state religion." Like other religions in China, Christianity is a minority and powerless, existing at the mercy of the civil authority. Currently, the government allows religion to exist openly in society with certain qualifications: religion is a private affair and should not influence the society or challenge the state; and all religious activities operate within sanctioned space, time, personnel, and structures regulated by state agencies. Furthermore, the status, organization, development, and activities of religion are under the control and guidance of the civil authority. All religious groups in China have to register with the government in order to gain their legal status and operate within the government's political guidance. Failure to do so renders them illegal and hence open to various forms of harassment, suppression, and even prosecution.[16]

Within this aforementioned framework, called the Policy of Freedom of Religious Belief, the state recognizes five major religions that exist nationwide; namely, Buddhism, Daoism, Protestantism, Islam, and Roman Catholicism.[17] In addition to these five officially recognized major religions, the government also acknowledges the minor or smaller religious groups, such as Russian Orthodox communities, Judaism, local folk religions such as Mazu worship in Fujian, ethnic religions that are part of the cultural identity of national minority groups such as Shamanism among the Oluncun people, and some New Religious Movements (NRMs) recently developing in China, such as the Church of Jesus Christ of Latter-Day Saints (LDS, or Mormon Church) and the Ba'hai Faith communities.[18] However, the

---

16. For a comprehensive treatment of the Chinese government's religious policy and regulations, see Chan and Carlson, *Religious Freedom in China*.

17. The PRC issued a White Paper in 1996, *Freedom of Religious Belief in China*, in which five religions are recognized.

18. The State Administration of Religious Affairs established a new directorate in 2005 to handle affairs of religious groups not belonging to the five officially recognized religions. Such administrative arrangement suggests that the Chinese authorities are beginning to include religions other than the five recognized as legitimate religious

government bans many NRMs and spiritual movements such as the Falungong or Yiguandao, categorizing them as Evil Cults, and suppresses as illegal those religious groups that have not registered with the authorities, such as underground Catholic and Protestant communities. Both of these categories are subject to legal prosecution.

The official figure on religious believers in China is estimated to be more than one hundred million, which is a minority of roughly 10 percent within the Chinese population of 1.3 billion. The 90 percent are supposedly either non-religious or atheist. This figure of religious believers is a rough estimate at best; it includes all those who are affiliated with religious organizations or who attend religious activities in mosques, temples, or churches.[19] It does not include those who may join these activities during festival days or practice ancestral worship at home. Further, no particular religious group is dominant among the five major religions. China is a multireligious society, and religious groups are always a minority. The government's policy on religion is to keep these religious groups coexisting in order to maintain a harmonious sociopolitical environment. The government does not encourage the growth of any particular religious group, for such growth may be at the expense of other religious groups and upset the delicate socioreligious dynamics.[20] Consequently, the reported phenomenal growth of Christianity in China has caused alarm among the national leadership more for sociopolitical than for religious reasons. The following is a current profile of various religious groups, among which Christianity is situated.

Buddhism and Daoism

Although Daoism is indigenous to China, it carries little influence, for it has low membership and no formal structure. Daoism centers on temples and occasional liturgies. Few claim themselves as pure Daoist. Mahayana Buddhism is popular among the Han and Tibetan Chinese and has a large number of followers called the *sangha*, but there is no effective organizational structure—except in Tibet and Inner Mongolia, where almost all Tibetans and most Mongolians are Tibetan Buddhists and Tibetan Buddhism is regarded as part of Tibetan cultural identity. Mahayana Buddhism owns

---

groups in China.

19. Because of the methodological issues of defining a religious believer, as well as the feasibility of doing such a headcount in China, no clear figures accounting for numbers of religious believers exists. The government uses "more than 100 million" in official publications. See People's Republic of China, "Religious Belief."

20. For more details, see Xiaowen, "China's Religions."

numerous temples and monasteries and has many religious schools to train their monks and nuns.

Theravada Buddhism is popular among some of the ethnic minority groups such as Dai and Hani in Southwestern China. Among these people, Theravada Buddhism becomes their cultural identity. It is difficult to obtain a reliable statistical figure on Buddhists and Daoists in China because there is no clear membership other than the *sangha* among the Han and those who have taken Buddhism as their ethnic identity such as the Tibetan, Hani, and Dai. Because of the prolonged cultural influence of these two religions in Chinese society, the influence of Daoism and Buddhism in China goes far beyond their institutional strength. The government has not exercised strong measures against these two groups.

Islam

Muslims in China are mostly concentrated in the Northwestern part of the country and are predominantly Hui Chinese, along with more than a dozen other minority ethnic groups, such as the Uygurs and Kazaks. Often Islam is the only religion, as well as the cultural identity, of these ethnic groups. The numerical strength of Muslims in China is identical to the number of ethnic groups that embrace Islam and numbers about thirty million.[21] Since Muslims are geographically concentrated, they do have a much stronger socio-political influence, both regional and national, than other religious groups have. Being situated mostly in strategic border areas, Muslims receive concessions from the government in exchange for their support. Furthermore, the apparent militaristic bent of Islam—Jihad, compounded by the 9/11 incident—induces the government to treat Islam with extra caution so as not to provoke the Muslims to social unrest. Muslims in China have often exploited this bargaining power. Usually the government complies with Muslim demands even at the expense of the rights of other groups.

Christianity

Both Catholicism and Protestantism long carried a negative sociopolitical stigma among the Chinese as "foreign religions forcibly brought to China by imperialists." The introduction of Christianity to China was often associated

---

21. Xiaowen gave the figure of eighteen million, whereas the official publication of the Chinese government (People's Republic of China Government, State Council, 58) puts the figure at more than twenty million (*China's Religions*). However, informed sources within the Chinese Muslim community suggest a figure of thirty million.

with national humiliation. Ascertaining the precise membership system for Christian believers is complicated by the unregistered Christian groups that claim some impressive yet unsubstantiated membership numbers. On the other hand, those who opt to register with the government may use a deflated figure for political reasons. The official figure for Catholics is six million; Protestants are estimated to be at least twenty-three million by the China Christian Council, an official body representing registered Protestants, who had printed and distributed more than fifty-five million copies of the Bible by 2010. Although some writers have suggested a higher figure—for example, a combined count of up to eighty million[22]—such a figure is difficult to verify.

We would put the estimate at about ten million Catholics and at least forty million Protestants. If this estimate in is error, it is on the conservative side. This number reflects tremendous growth since 1950 when there were only three million Catholics and one million Protestants. By the early 1980s there were perhaps three million of each. About 25 percent of the Catholics are in Hebei Province, where Beijing is located; the rest are scattered all over the country. As for the Protestants, about half are concentrated in the Central and Eastern provinces; the rest are scattered across the provinces. Russian Orthodoxy has been in China for more than 300 years, but its influence is more historical than social. Current Orthodox membership is around 30,000.[23] Since Christianity, especially Protestantism, is the fastest growing religion, it is often the target of government repression, particularly for those unregistered.

Folk Religion

Many Chinese—but especially the Hans—adhere to Chinese folk religion. It is a syncretistic form of Daoism, Buddhism, and local folk deities. It is not uncommon for a Chinese to claim religious allegiance to several local deities. Such a belief system cannot be classified as Buddhism nor regarded as Daoism. The estimated strength of the followers of Folk Religion can be as high as several hundred million. Furthermore, many of the national minority groups embrace their own forms of traditional religion, most of an animist or primal nature. Folk religion is not included with the five major recognized religions; it once was labeled as "Feudal Superstition" and targeted for suppression. However, for the most part, the Chinese government

---

22. Aikman, *Jesus in Beijing*, 7.

23. Fr. Dionis Pozdnyayev of the Russian Orthodox Parish of St. Paul and St. Peter in Hong Kong provided this rough estimate for me via personal communication.

turns a blind eye to these practices, and local authorities have even encouraged them. Furthermore, these religious systems do not have any major regional or nationwide institutional structure, and hence pose minimal social threat to the authorities. Recently the government has been taking active measures to regulate these practices. By recognizing the practices, the government can rally the support of national minority groups while co-opting believers in folk religions for political gains.

Other Religions

Other religious groups in China, found mostly among foreigners, include the LDS (Mormon Church), Ba'hai Faith, Judaism, and Hinduism. These religions currently have minimal influence among the Chinese population and are not yet a major concern to the government. However, some NRMs and spiritual movements, especially those that have developed in China in recent years, such as Falungong, have attracted the attention of the government. Official policy toward these NRMs and spiritual movements is suppression, because the government regards these groups as evil cults. The followers of these suppressed religious movements are rather popular among the population and number from tens of thousands to over one million. Many NRMs owe their origin to Christianity and developed their distinctive characteristics by incorporating local religious elements. Currently, there are at least thirty of these pseudo-Christian groups numbering at least three million members.[24] These groups, such as Eastern Lightning (*Dongfang shandian*), have competed with Christian groups for followers.

Atheism

Another ideological group embraces Marxism-Leninism. As the state orthodoxy, Marxism-Leninism and atheism have been publicly promoted for half a century as the only accepted worldview of the government. The eighty million plus members of the CPC—the largest political party in the world[25]—and at least forty million members of the Communist Youth League (CYL) comprise the largest organized ideological bloc in China. This bloc, enjoying full state support, vigorously promotes atheism and is quite antagonistic to religion. The presence of this bloc holds serious implications

---

24. See Kupfer, "Christian Inspired."

25. As of December 2010, there were 80.2 million CPC members (*China Today*, "China Information").

for the development of religion in China, especially the massive antireligious propaganda that the party promotes through the entire education system and in all secular spheres.

PATTERN OF CHRISTIAN DEVELOPMENT

In this section, we will consider the main patterns of development of the Christian movement in China since 1950. The analysis includes both rural and urban elements.

Biological Growth

Especially among Catholics, the Christian faith is transmitted through families as tradition and heritage, particularly in rural communities. As the population has grown, the Catholic church has also grown. The Chinese population has tripled since 1950, and the Catholic communities have also tripled in number. If one is born into a Catholic family, typically one inherits the Catholic faith. The likelihood of children born into Catholic families remaining in the church is even greater if the family has been Catholic for several generations. Such biological growth in membership does not usually cause any major social tension other than from local educational (state) authorities who uphold a mandate to prevent children from being exposed to worldviews and influences other than atheism, including Christianity. There are also records of inter-Christian membership transfer, such as transfer from Protestantism to Catholicism, or vice versa. However, such inter-confessional dynamics has not caused any major discourse between the two Christian traditions in China since the small number of these cases is too insignificant to cause any major concern.

Growth among the Urban Population

The urban population is usually more educated than the rural population and is more controlled, ideologically speaking, than their rural counterparts. Christianity's new converts among the urban population are usually people who have transferred their allegiance from Marxism-Leninism; in other words, from atheism to Christianity. These transfers cause sociopolitical tension, for it is a gain for Christianity and a loss for other ideological blocs. The bulk of the new urban Christian converts are professional-intellectuals, business people, and workers; this is especially true in the past ten years in all major urban centers.[26] The main rival parties are the CPC and the CYL. One can easily understand that the government may not be pleased to see many educated urban dwellers convert to Christianity since such conversion challenges the claim of the government that atheism is the absolute truth upon which the CPC is built. University campuses and state-owned enterprises take measures to prohibit the spread of Christianity and curb Christian activities. Therefore, the growth of Christianity in urban areas is regarded as a direct sociopolitical threat to the ruling regime, generating resentment among the government leadership that often results in administrative measures to limit the growth of Christianity. These measures include refusal to grant permits to Christian groups to operate legally, denial of applications to hold more religious services or activities, and limiting foreign travel for these groups.

Growth among the Rural Han Population

From 1980 to 2000, the majority of Christianity's numerical growth, especially by Protestant Christianity, resulted from winning converts among the rural Han Chinese with no Christian background. These were mostly adult conversions. Almost all of them were from folk religion background, with a majority of them being female with low educational background—illiterate to primary school level. Signs and wonders such as faith healing, exorcism, and miracles often became the pivotal point for conversion. The Mount Carmel type of power encounter recorded in the Old Testament is common in this context.[27]

Those who convert to the Christian faith usually abandon their former traditional religious practices and join a well-organized Christian group—church or family gathering points—that often has a regional network much more powerful than the local folk religious temple activities. There is little resistance from folk religious groups to the advance of Christianity simply because of the lack of any organized effort on behalf of these temples of local deities. Another attracting factor is the post-conversion positive character exhibited in these Christian converts. Pragmatic-minded Chinese peasants with high moral ideals shaped by the Confucian tradition find this attractive.

Upon joining a Christian group, the new adherent is immediately aware of belonging to a large network of believers—even international—who share similar aspirations. Such networks offer virtually unlimited opportunity for an individual to pursue personal development, be it psychological,

26. See "Crossing the Communists."
27. For example, see the case study by Yamamori and Chan, *Witnesses*, 42–48.

religious, or social—a factor especially appealing to a rural population that is traditionally socially and politically deprived.[28] Recently, this social factor has become more evident as rural Christian networks connect with international human traffic networks as well as global activities of Chinese merchants. Thus the global missiological development reaches beyond the geopolitical boundary of China through these Christian networks, especially the rural ones.[29]

The major factors prohibiting Christian missiological advancement in rural China include, first, resistance from local government, which is the only social structure authorized to provide for the whole spectrum of social needs of the people but most often fails to do so. Christian groups often become an alternative means of providing social identity, caring, physical support, and meaning of life for their members. These groups can easily become a threat to the local civil authority, and their growth often triggers repression from the local authority—even with brutal force. The second prohibiting factor, ironically, comes from the success of such Christian advance. With the rapid increase of membership often taking place among people of folk religions background, in the absence of adequate Christian formation, the level of the average member's understanding of Christian faith and practices declines as the membership increases. The rapid increase in the number of Christians puts a strain on the leadership, and new believers often assume important leadership positions without formal training. Such conditions give rise to severe internal leadership crises leading to infighting, tension, and splitting. Furthermore, it also contributes to the development of numerous extreme sects and cults that continue to claim the name of Christianity and compete with the more orthodox Christian groups for members. Thus, the rapid growth of Christianity in rural areas often develops elements that ironically weaken the Christian community.

Growth among National Minority Groups

Ethnic groups in China that do not embrace Tibetan Buddhism or Islam usually have their own religious tradition—often a form of animism with multiple deities. As Christianity extends into these groups, it elicits two general

---

28. The government attempts to explain such growth as a phenomenon resulting from foreign infiltration, a low level of agricultural population, corruption, simplicity of Christian doctrine, and lack of proper implementation of the government's religious policy. See Lambert, "Growth of the Gospel."

29 For example, see information regarding the Back to Jerusalem Movement at www.backtoJerusalem.com.

responses: For groups that have already embraced Christianity for a long time—the Lisu, Miao, Lahu, Wa, and Jinpo—the reception is rather positive, and in some cases, such as the Lisu where the majority are already Christian, it appears that Christianity will become their group's cultural identity as well.[30] These groups may have a substantial number of their people who already have embraced the Christian faith and have Bibles and hymnody in their languages. In certain instances, the local government even encourages these people to embrace Christian faith, because they believe that if these people become Christians, they are likely to become better citizens, hence making it easier for the government to administer civil affairs. There are also cadres who feel that converting these people to Christianity is in fact an advancement from polytheism to monotheism, a necessary step toward the ultimate goal of social evolution—atheism. Therefore, they anticipate that Christianity will pave the way for these polytheistic national minorities to eventually embrace Communism.[31] In these situations, the local government does not discourage the growth of Christianity among these groups, and we have seen, in fact, rather rapid Christian progress among some of them.

Toward other groups that have long embraced the official religions such as Buddhism, the Dai, and Hani, there is strong resistance from the predominantly Buddhist ethnic minorities to Christian advancement, for they feel that it is a threat to their cultural-religious identity. Frequently, a minority of their members are Christian. Gaining a Christian means a loss for the majority group. Often the local authority composed of ethnic minority leaders undertakes measures to curb the growth of Christianity. It is not uncommon to hear that Christian churches and Christian households are burned to the ground by their Buddhist neighbors while the local authorities stand by and watch, in some cases even initiating such aggressions, as in the case experienced by newly converted Hani Christians living in Honghe County in Yunnan Province.[32]

---

30. See Yamamori and Chan, "Missiological Ramifications."

31. See Chan, "Gospel and Opium."

32. This was revealed in the course of personal communications with Christians in Honghe 1997 to 2005. The first Hani household in Honghe County to embrace the Christian faith did so in about 1995, and they spread this faith to other Hani relatives and friends. This tiny company—currently about 200 believers spread over several villages—experienced harsh suppression from the local authority despite intervention from the provincial authority. Up to May 2005, the local authority still refused to recognize the legal existence of Christians in this county—not an uncommon situation in many parts of China.

RELIGION-DOMINATED AREAS: TIBETAN BUDDHIST REGIONS (TIBET, QINGHAI) AND ISLAMIC REGIONS (XINJIANG, NINGXIA)

In Tibet, Qinghai, Xinjiang, and Ningxia, the predominant religions are Tibetan Buddhism and Islam. Ethnic minority groups embrace one of these two religions. Often there are multiple ethnic minority groups that inhabit the same region. These two religious groups fiercely defend the status quo in order to secure political concessions. Christians in these regions, almost all of whom are Hans, have virtually no say and are at the mercy of the Muslims or Tibetan Buddhists, who dominate the local government's key posts. A member of these minority groups who embraces another faith, such as Christianity, faces the danger of being cut off from the community. To pacify these minority groups, the government has ordered Christians not to convert Muslims or Tibetan Buddhists to the Christian faith because such conversion may trigger social unrest and upset the delicate balance of ethnic harmony.[33] Gaining a Christian convert from one of these groups may result in bloody riots, for these groups may claim that the government is trying to diminish their cultural heritage by allowing Christians to sinicize their people. Christianity makes the least progress in these regions, and new converts from these religious backgrounds often practice their new faith in secret. Even normal Christian activities, guaranteed by the constitution, can be disrupted by the authorities should the local Muslim or Tibetan Buddhist leaders want to take action. Social and political stability overrides the rights of minority groups.

DIVERSE EXPERIENCES

China itself is a diverse country—from the rich coastal provinces and metropolitan areas such as Shanghai, to extremely poor mountainous areas where there is no running water or even electricity. There are at least fifty-six distinct ethnic groups in China, using a range of languages. Even the majority Han speak hundreds of dialects that may be mutually unintelligible. Such social and linguistic diversity is compounded by vastly different regional and cultural patterns. Religious plurality is but one of the many facets of social plurality in China, which has at least three times the population of the European Union and almost five times the population of the United States.

33. Such a government order is not communicated in printed form; instead, government officials announce such standing orders orally to religious leaders (reported in personal communication with Christian leaders in Xinjiang in 2002–2003).

Therefore, the missiological experiences of the people of God in China are extremely varied.

For those living in the urban areas, faith issues are often intellectual in nature. The existence of God becomes the central concern as one encounters the gospel. The relationship of science and faith is often a hotly debated topic among new believers and seekers. For many, conversion to Christian faith requires the abandonment of atheism; and this logically leads to the denial of Communism and the state orthodoxy. The political risk this decision involves cannot be ignored. It is no surprise that this decision is frequently preceded by inner struggle and search for truth. Choosing Christian faith can come at a high cost, including the loss of one's sociopolitical advantages if one renounces the state orthodoxy. It is a costly religion for urban intellectuals, so costly that many—like Nicodemus—choose to remain as hidden Christians; especially those in civil service.

For the rural Han Christians, Christianity represents a powerful God that intervenes in one's daily life through supernatural means—so powerful that this God has overshadowed the local deities that have been worshiped for generations. For them, this God is the true and merciful one that can be depended upon in times of need, especially because many of the rural social welfare and medical systems have virtually collapsed since the mid-1980s. Therefore, a change in religious allegiance is natural, as the people have found a better or more competent god to depend on. Many of them can echo the Prophet Elijah's experience on Mount Carmel, or the Samaritan woman at the well. Once they experience this new religious reality, they immediately introduce their relatives and friends to it. Such natural sharing of religious experience is the primary means of faith transmission and explains the reason for rapid growth of the Christian population in China. Often, this new religious reality will lead to dramatic transformation of character, further enhancing the credibility of Christian faith.

As for the non-Han Christians among those ethnic minority groups that welcome Christianity, they feel they are the chosen ones. Certainly the Israelites' experience in the Old Testament as God's chosen people can be a key theme among these people, especially the Lisus. The Lisus have felt so grateful to be God's chosen ones that they have believed it is their honor and privilege to send missionaries to evangelize other minority groups. During the past several years, they have successfully reached and won converts among the Tibetans, the Pumis, the Musous, and the Dulongs. The possibility of substantial numbers of some of these groups becoming Christian is not an unrealistic goal. Certain groups are deliberately embracing Christian faith as the religion of their ethnic group and Christianity as their cultural identity, an identity that may elevate their social status.

Many non-Han Christians are minorities within their community. Currently, one can document Christian population among virtually every national minority group in China. In some cases, they may be only a handful. For example, in 2004 there were just six Mali Masha Christians among this tiny group of 1,200 people classified under the Naxi ethnic minority group.[34] Most of these newly converted expressed the sentiment that because they are the first batch of believers, naturally they are eager to follow the mandate to bring the gospel to their own people. In spite of severe rejection and even persecution they may experience, these people are still making headway among their groups. The number is still growing steadily among some of these groups, such as the Dulongs.[35] One of their most favored parts of the biblical text is the book of Acts.

Those who live in areas dominated by Islam and Tibetan Buddhism feel suppressed and discriminated against. In spite of the negative religious environment for Christianity, many of these Christians are strongly motivated to share the gospel with these people. The eschatological motive has been especially critical to the Christians in Northwestern China. They have endured decades of hardship as they have sought opportunity to share the gospel with their Muslim or Tibetan Buddhist neighbors. This has triggered the controversial "Back to Jerusalem Movement" among some of the evangelical mission organizations. They envisage preaching the gospel all the way back to Jerusalem through the Muslim regions of Central Asia and the Middle East as a precondition to the second coming of Jesus Christ. Driven by this missional vision, these Christians regard themselves as having the honor to be the forerunners, carrying the last baton in this missional marathon that will climax in the Eschaton.[36]

COMMON THEMES

The more China links with the global market, the more China seems to assert its unique Chinese nationalism within the international community. On the one hand, globalization brings uniformity as a result of international

---

34. Information gathered in a personal visit to Mali Masha people in Wexi County, Yunnan Province, April 2004.

35. Information gathered on a personal visit to the Christian communities in Dulong Valley, Yunnan Province, October 2002. In 1990 there were just a few dozen Dulong Christians; but by the end of 2002 there were close to 1,000 Christians among the population of 4,000 people in Dulong Valley.

36. This mission desire by Chinese missionaries during the 1940s has become the theological basis for the current "Back to Jerusalem" (www.backtoJerusalem.com) mission movement.

networking; on the other, it triggers the consciousness of local uniqueness and personal identity that globalization seems to threaten. Although there are many diverse faith journeys among Christians in China, Chinese Christians do have some common experiences that transcend their diversity.

Virtually every Christian community in China senses its powerlessness. It has little social recognition, virtually no political power, few financial and material resources, limited international connections, and no rich cultural heritage within the context of China's long history. In spite of its seeming powerlessness, ironically it has grown at least tenfold during the past two decades. Even a mission agency with every resource it desired—including the latest church growth theories and methods—would have difficulty matching these results. The Chinese Christian community, characterized by powerlessness and living amid a multireligious environment under a government officially opposed to religion and exerting control over religious affairs, may have learned the secret of the kind of power that brings spiritual success.

Theologically, a majority of Chinese Protestants embrace some form of Christian Fundamentalism, dating back to the pre-1949 era. Having been cut off from world Christian trends for more than half a century, only since the 1980s have Chinese Protestants had access to the more irenic evangelicalism that has arisen in the West since the 1950s. While some may criticize the tendency toward legalism in the Chinese Protestants' firm grip on Fundamentalist doctrines, few would question that Chinese Christians are Pentecostal. Chinese Christians stress the baptism of the Holy Spirit and the gifts of the Spirit, such as speaking in tongues, healing, and prophecy. They tend to emphasize evangelism to the extent that there is little development of theologies of ecclesiology, Christian formation, or social concern. It is precisely this strong missional impetus that keeps the Chinese Christian community on the edge of expansion regardless of where their members live—be it urban Han or rural Uygur. There is also virtually no discussion of interfaith dialogue, for such dialogue is regarded as "liberal" theological thinking that dampens evangelistic zeal.

Almost all Christian communities, even those opting not to register with the government, tend to be law-abiding and model citizens in a moral sense. This loyalty to nation and high moral standards, perhaps a reaction to the unpatriotic or foreign image Chinese Christianity once held, has become a unique social stance that Christians in China uphold. Christians gladly contribute their time and money to charity and social welfare; often they become exemplary models that make the authorities embarrassed, because Christians' voluntarism outpaces the Communists'. It is precisely this good social behavior that becomes a silent witness to the religious claims of Christianity that Christians cannot openly defend in word.

Since all religious groups are minorities within China, faith communities—at least those that are sanctioned by the government—tend to have a subtle alliance because all of them are facing a common civil authority that is officially atheist. Instead of fighting among themselves, religious groups in China are learning to work together for their rights and social space. After all, they can easily attract new members among the 90 percent non-religious population rather than struggle to win converts among other religious believers. Consequently, we are observing the growth of various religious groups without a corresponding increase in interreligious tension—a phenomenon seemingly unique in China.

Perhaps the biblical imagery of the yeast and the dough can illustrate the Christian mission in the multireligious Chinese society. Almost invisible and insignificant in weight, the yeast acts silently, yet effectively, transforming the flour into rising dough. Similarly, the Chinese Christian community, an apparently powerless community armed only with strong evangelical desire, steadily brings neighbors and friends into a new religious reality and silently shapes the very fabric of the society.

BIBLIOGRAPHY

Aikman, David. *Jesus in Beijing: How Christianity is Transforming China and Changing the Global Balance of Power*. New York: Regnery, 2003.

Bays, Daniel H. "A Tradition of State Dominance." In *God and Caesar in China: Policy Implications of Church-State Tensions*, edited by Jason Kindopp and Carol Lee Hamrin, 25–39. Washington, DC: Brookings Institution, 2004.

Bush, Richard C., Jr. *Religion in Communist China*. New York: Abingdon, 1970.

Chan, Kim-Kwong. "Gospel and Opium: A Case Study in China." *Protestant Church Development in China: How Did It Happen and Where Is It Leading?*, edited by Chun Lam, 57–72. Geneva: Lutheran World Federation, 2003.

Chan, Kim-Kwong, and Eric R. Carlson. *Religious Freedom in China: Policy, Administration, and Regulations; A Research Handbook*. Santa Barbara, CA: Institute for the Study of American Religion, 2005.

China Today. "China Information and Sources: The Communist Party of China (CPC, CCP)." Online: http://www.chinatoday.com/org/cpc/.

Chow, Tse-tsung. *The May Fourth Movement: Intellectual Revolution in Modern China*. Cambridge, MA: Harvard University Press, 1960.

Cohen, Paul A. *China and Christianity: The Missionary Movement and the Growth of Chinese Anti-foreignism, 1860–1870*. Cambridge, MA: Harvard University Press, 1963.

———. *History in Three Keys: The Boxers as Event, Experience, and Myth*. New York: Columbia University Press, 1997.

Dunch, Ryan. *Fuzhou Protestants and the Making of a Modern China, 1857–1927*. New Haven, CT: Yale University Press, 2001.

"Crossing the Communists: Christianity Is Becoming Popular with China's Urban Elite." *The Economist*, April 21, 2005. Online: www.economist.com/displaystory.cfm?story_id=3896585.

Epoch Times. "United Nations Envoy Condemned Chinese Community Party Who Had Persecuted Falungong." Hong edition, May 10, 2005.

Esherick, Joseph. *The Origins of the Boxer Uprising*. Berkeley, CA: University of California Press, 1987.

Hanson, Eric O. *Catholic Politics in China and Korea*. Maryknoll, NY: Orbis, 1980.

Jones, Francis P. *The Church in Communist China: A Protestant Appraisal*. New York: Friendship, 1962.

Kupfer, Kristin. "Christian-Inspired, Spiritual-Religious Groups in the People's Republic of China Since 1978." Presentation to 18th IAHR Congress, Tokyo, March 25, 2005.

Laamaan, Lars. *Christian Heretics in Late Imperial China: The Inculturation of Christianity in 18th and Early 19th Century China*. New York: Routledge, 2005.

Lambert, Tony. "The Growth of the Gospel in Northern Anhui." *China Insight Newsletter*, February–March, 2005.

Lutz, Jessie G. *Chinese Politics and Christian Missions: The Anti-Christian Movements of 1920–28*. Notre Dame, IN: Cross-Cultural, 1988.

China Source Team. "New Church Was Dedicated in Hangzhou with 5,000 Seating." *Gospel Post*. Online: http://www.chinasource.org/blog/posts/the-grand-opening-of-chinas-largest-church.

Paton, David M. *Christian Missions and the Judgment of God*. 2nd ed. Grand Rapids: Eerdmans, 1996.

People's Republic of China. *Freedom of Religious Belief in China*. Beijing: Information Office of the State Council, 1996. Online: http://china.org.cn/e-white/Freedom/index.htm

———. "Religious Belief." Online: www.china.org.cn/english/features/38101.htm.

People's Republic of China, State Council. *China Facts*. N.p., n.d.

Pozdnyayev, Fr. Dionis. Personal communication with the author. Russian Orthodox Parish of St. Paul and St. Peter in Hong Kong, January 2004.

Reilly, Thomas H. *The Taiping Heavenly Kingdom: Rebellion and the Blasphemy of Empire*. Seattle: University of Washington Press, 2004.

Spence, Jonathan D. *God's Chinese Son: The Taiping Heavenly Kingdom of Hong Xiuquan*. New York: Norton, 1996.

Tao, Feiya. *Yesu Jiating: Zhongguo de Jidujiao Wutobang 1921–1952* [A Christian Utopia in China: The Jesus Family, 1921–1952]. Hong Kong: Chinese University Press, 2004.

Wang, Dong. *China's Unequal Treaties: Narrating National History*. Lanham, MD: Lexington, 2005.

Wickeri, Philip L. *Seeking the Common Ground: Protestant Christianity, the Three-Self Movement, and China's United Front*. Maryknoll, NY: Orbis, 1988.

Wiest, Jean-Paul. *Maryknoll in China: A History, 1918–1955*. Armonk, NY: Sharpe, 1988.

Yamamori, Tetsunao, and Kim-Kwong Chan. "Missiological Ramifications of the Social Impact of Christianity on the Lisu in China." *Missiology* 26 (October 1998) 403–18.

———. *Witnesses to Power: Stories of God's Quiet Work in a Changing China*. Carlisle, UK: Paternoster, 2000.

Xiaowen, Ye. "China's Religions: Retrospect and Prospect." February 19, 2001. Online: www.china.org.cn/english/features/45466.htm#5.

Chapter 8

Christianity in Interaction with the Primal Religions of the World
A Historical and Global Perspective

Gillian Mary Bediako

PREAMBLE: A PERSONAL TESTIMONY

"THE STRANGER HAS BIG eyes but sees little." The truth of this Akan proverb is constantly being impressed upon me, even though I have lived in Ghana for twenty-eight years as the wife (and now widow) of a Ghanaian. For it conveys in a highly expressive way a fact that many Westerners who encounter and observe African life little realize: Africa defies all the media stereotypes and is different than what it may seem on a cursory acquaintance. African cultures and their religious consciousness have many riches to share, but they are revealed only to those who come with open hearts as respectful learners.

The substance of this essay is a fruit of my own learning, in Africa and from Africans. It will readily be apparent that this learning reaches beyond what may be discovered about the African Christian story as a product of the engagement between primal religions and Christian faith—to look with new eyes at the Christian story and primal past of my own ancestors. For that also is the genius of Africa: to cast a fresh, and in some respects, searching light on an old familiar story and to reveal its hidden treasures.

INTRODUCTION: THE PRIMAL RELIGIONS OF THE WORLD

The term "primal" may be unfamiliar to some, but it has become a term used to describe, in a positive light, the religious traditions of indigenous peoples around the world and down through the ages who were formerly despised in Europe and the West generally as "primitive, superstitious, and even demonic." The rationale behind the designation "primal" is that it does justice to the fact that primal religions existed prior to all other religious traditions and underlie them all. The term also bears witness to the undeniable family likeness among the various primal religious traditions around the world—a likeness that cuts across all the differences. It also situates these religious traditions as truly significant, as the fundamental substratum to all subsequent religious experience and therefore as persisting, to varying degrees, in all consequent religious traditions that thus "represent, as it were, second thoughts," as expressed by Andrew F. Walls. "Primal" describes universal, basic elements of human understanding of the transcendent and the known world, essential and valid religious insights that may be built upon or suppressed but cannot be superseded. Walls adds that "all other believers, and for that matter non-believers, are primalists underneath."[1]

Contemporary primal religions comprise the religions of "circumpolar [Arctic] peoples, of various peoples of Africa, the Indian subcontinent [the so-called tribals], South and North East Asia [particularly Korea], Inner Asia [such as Siberia and Mongolia], North and South America [the "first nation" peoples], Australia [the Aborigines] and the Pacific [Maori of New Zealand, as well as the Micronesian, Melanesian and Polynesian island groups]."[2] Primal religious traditions also have historical depth and include the Semitic religions of the Old Testament period, the religions of Greece and Rome in the early Christian era, the pre-Christian religions of the tribes-people of northern and western Europe, such as the Celts, Franks, Saxons, and Nordic peoples,[3] as well as the religions of the ancient civilizations of Egypt and the Americas, such as the Maya, Aztec, and Inca.

Primal religion is a complex reality, defying the stereotype that it belongs to preliterate and technologically unsophisticated cultures. For Greek

---

1. Walls, *Missionary Movement*, 121.
2. Ibid., 120.
3. Ibid., ch. 6; also see Bediako, "'Be Thou My Vision.'"

primal culture was highly literate; Egyptian, Inca, and Maya cultures were highly technological.[4] It is also an enduring reality within some traditions, such as those of the First Nation peoples in North America, who endured for millennia before they were decimated by European contact. Remarkably, many still persist and are enjoying a revival in recent times.[5] An indication of the scope of primal religions would not be complete without mentioning the vast array of new religious movements that have emerged within primal societies as a result of contact with other religions, and in particular, with Christianity.[6]

For our purposes, the fact that primal religion has constituted the most fertile soil for the reception of the Christian gospel throughout Christian history says something deeply significant, not only about the intrinsic nature of Christian faith but also about the nature of the interaction of Christianity with primal religions.[7] In seeking to provide a new map for understanding the multifaceted Christian interaction with religious plurality with respect to the primal religions of the world, two factors need to be taken into consideration. The first is the long history of negative Western perceptions of primal religion, existing until recent times. The second is the contemporary massive accession to Christian faith among peoples of a primal religious background from around the world. The legacy of the former seriously impedes appreciation of the significance of the latter. This deficiency becomes all the more acute when we consider that the most widespread and fruitful interaction of Christian faith with other religious traditions throughout Christian history has been with the primal religious traditions.

PRIMAL RELIGIONS: A HISTORY OF NEGATIVE PERCEPTION

It was the consensus of Christian Europe at the beginning of the twentieth century that the primal religions of the world, usually designated at that time by the term "animism," were as primitive as the people who practiced them. The term "animism" was coined by the nineteenth-century British

---

4. See a recent account of Maya history and civilization in Johns et al., "Mysteries of the Maya," 112.

5. See Sullivan, *Central and South America* and *North America*.

6. Harold W. Turner was one of the earliest to draw attention to this phenomenon and make it the core focus of research. See his "New Religious Movements."

7. Christian historian Andrew F. Walls has drawn attention to this fact most consistently; see his *Missionary Movement*.

anthropologist E. B. Tylor to denote the religious system of traditional societies, which corresponded to the presumed social, technological, and moral inferiority of "uncivilized" peoples. Tylor built up a picture of a religious system that was "unmoral" and "devoid of that ethical element which to the educated modern mind is the very mainspring of practical religion."[8]

At the World Missionary Conference held in Edinburgh in 1910, the "high-water mark of the missionary movement from the West,"[9] animism was the preferred term to describe "the religious beliefs of more or less backward and degraded peoples all over the world."[10] These religions were held to be the farthest removed from Christianity, at the bottom of a scale of religions that rose through polytheism to monotheism, with Christianity being the highest and most civilized of the monotheistic faiths. This sense of hierarchy among the world's religions had been captured in the third edition of the *Encyclopaedia Britannica*, issued at the end of the eighteenth century, in the following terms:

> When the different systems of religion that have prevailed in the world are comparatively viewed with respect to their influence on the welfare of society, we find reason to prefer the polytheism of the Greeks and Romans to the ruder, wilder religious ideas and ceremonies that have prevailed among savages; Mahometanism, perhaps, in some respects, to the polytheism of the Greeks and Romans; Judaism however to Mahometanism and Christianity to all of them.[11]

Edinburgh 1910 reiterated this perception. Animism was thus "the humblest of all possible teachers . . . and the least sublime of all the five great creeds."[12] Animism was considered by many missionary participants not to provide any preparation for the Christian gospel and even to have "no religious content."[13]

Thus, it was the European Christian consensus that primal religion, as the religion of "savages," was barbaric and crude and lacked a sense of sin. Primal religion was viewed as the very antithesis of Christian faith: simple, not complex, consisting of unconscious unhistorical traditions, as against the revealed historical traditions of Christianity. It was held to be childish, immature, and intellectually inadequate in contrast to the mature, historical,

---

8. Tylor, *Primitive Culture*, 1:426.
9. Walls, *Cross-Cultural Process*, 117.
10. Gairdner, *Edinburgh 1910*, 139.
11. "Religions," *Encyclopaedia Britannica*, 77.
12. Gairdner, *Edinburgh 1910*, 141.
13. World Missionary Conference, *Christian Message*, 52.

and intellectual acuteness of Christian thought. It was considered to be materialistic and concrete, irrational, and incapable of conceptual thinking in contrast to the European Christian ideal of a rational spirituality capable of abstract thought. It was naturalistic religion, as against ethical religion. Christianity was considered to be the most ethical of all religions.[14]

The stark antitheses registered in these views of European Christians of the late nineteenth and early twentieth centuries regarding primal religion and Christian faith would be softened somewhat in the early decades of the twentieth century. Yet the generally negative perception would continue to live on, partly as a result of the general Western sense of cultural superiority and possessiveness of Christian faith.[15] Africa, especially, was held to provide much of the evidence for this Western discourse about primal religions. Until the facts proved otherwise, the dominant view about Africa was the assumption made at Edinburgh 1910 that Islam would prove the more successful missionary faith in Africa and that Christianity would make slow headway. When African theologians began to emerge in the mid-twentieth century, they had a hard time making a case for continuities from the primal past into the Christian present. It was clearly an uphill task to argue for the validity of the primal traditions from a Christian theological perspective and to suggest that there was indeed a preparation for the gospel in the primal pre-Christian religious traditions of Africa.[16] Even the new religious movements and independent churches that arose in response to Christian presence in Africa and elsewhere were studied, with a few exceptions, by scholars of the secular humanities, using intellectual categories other than religious or theological.[17]

The notable attempts to bring the primal religions more to the forefront in areas of academic scholarship and interreligious dialogue where heretofore they were marginal have not, up to the present time, born lasting

---

14. For an extensive expression and outworking of this view in relation to the Semitic (primal) religions of the Old Testament world, see Smith, *Religion of the Semites*, ch. 9.

15. For a contemporary rendering of this outlook, see Sanneh's constructed dialogue with an interlocutor, framed around the solicited criticisms of his own students on the subject of world Christianity in *Whose Religion*, esp. 47–50.

16. For an extensive discussion of twentieth-century African Christian theologians in their varied attempts to rehabilitate African primal traditions as integral to African Christian identity, see Bediako, *Theology and Identity*, esp. ch. 6–10.

17. One of those notable exceptions was, of course, Harold W. Turner, whose seminal study of the phenomenology of primal religion I shall consider shortly. Walls has also drawn attention to this dearth of Western Christian theological awareness of what was happening in the rest of the world, particularly where new Christian forms were emerging in primal contexts. See his *Missionary Movement*, 143–59.

fruit in the Western world. The conference on "Primal World Views—Christian Dialogue with Traditional Thought Forms," held under the auspices of the World Council of Churches Dialogue Programme at Ibadan, Nigeria, in 1973,[18] was not followed through. The pioneer Master of Letters (MLitt) Degree in Religion in Primal Societies, initiated in the Department of Religious Studies in the University of Aberdeen in the early 1970s,[19] did not survive the vision of its founders and was not replicated in any other Western institution.

"Animism" has continued as the preferred term for primal religion in evangelical seminaries and schools of world mission, particularly in the United States, with the result that primal religions continue to be misunderstood and misrepresented. It is somewhat astounding that popular Western mission literature can still depend on the *Encyclopedia Britannica* as the authority on "Animism,"[20] when the *Encyclopedia Britannica* continues to use nineteenth-century definitions and to cite Edward Burnett Tylor as the one who "first competently surveyed" such beliefs.[21] It is as if there has been little Western missionary learning in the two centuries of engagement with primal religions, not to mention learning from Christianity's own primal roots, reaching back to the Old Testament period.

The dominant view in the academic disciplines of anthropology and religious studies has tended to deny the existence of an overarching primal religious consciousness and to insist that one should think in terms of autonomous indigenous traditional religions as the only way to take them seriously in their own right.[22] However, this more recent Western view may perhaps constitute a subtle perpetuation of the marginalization of a worldwide religious phenomenon and also a limiting of the terms of reference for understanding the massive accession to Christian faith among peoples of a primal religious background throughout the world.

---

18. See the published proceedings of the conference: John Burnett Taylor, *Primal World-Views*.

19. For a published announcement of this programme, see ibid., 128–29.

20. See Trans World Radio, "What is Animism?," 10; adapted from *Britannica Student Encyclopedia*, "Animism."

21. *Britannica Concise Encyclopedia*, "Animism," provides the definition: "Belief in the existence of spirits separable from bodies. Such beliefs are traditionally identified with small-scale ('primitive') societies, though they also occur in major world religions. They were first competently surveyed by Edward Burnett Tylor in *Primitive Culture*. Classic Animism, according to Tylor, consists of attributing conscious life to natural objects or phenomena, a practice that eventually gave rise to the notion of a soul."

22. James L. Cox is one exponent of such a view. See his "Classification," 55–76.

PRIMAL RELIGIONS TODAY: A CONTINUATION OF NEGATIVE PERCEPTION

From the vantage point of the beginning of the twenty-first century, it is clear that the scenario envisaged at Edinburgh 1910 was mistaken and that the pessimism regarding the conversion of peoples from a primal background to Christian faith was misplaced. In the past few years, the massive Christian presence among non-Western peoples from a primal background has begun to impinge on the Western consciousness. This is partly because of the increasing presence of vibrant communities of non-Western Christians in the cities of Europe and North America, to the extent that these manifestations become newsworthy for such diverse media outlets as *Time Magazine*, *The New York Times*, *Newsweek*, and *BBC World News* bulletins.

This growing realization may, however, prove to be as undiscerning as the former Western perspectives have been shown to be. As Lamin Sanneh notes, commenting on the Western response to the phenomenon: "We appear unable to cope with the implications of Christian expansion beyond our shores, especially since such a fact rightly suggests that religion is not about to disappear in the rest of the world, as we thought it did with the fall of Christendom."[23] In this regard, it may be significant that Philip Jenkins chose to give as the title of his influential book *The Next Christendom: The Coming of Global Christianity*. It is as though the only way to conceive of the growing vibrant Christian presence in the non-Western world is in terms of the earlier Christendom. Was he expressing his own difficulty with the phenomenon when he spoke of it as "exotic, intriguing, exciting, but a little frightening?"[24]

This would seem to be further suggested by the observation made by Walls that

> Several generations of secularism have blunted the capacity of Western scholars to cope with the sheer quantity, the resilience, and the ebullience of religion in the non-Western world. This is particularly the case when that religion is Christian. It is remarkable that the immense Christian presence in Africa is so little a feature of modern African studies, and how much of the scholarly attention devoted to it is concentrated on manifestations that in Western terms seem most exotic.[25]

---

23. Sanneh, *Encountering the West*, 221.
24. Jenkins, 220.
25. Walls, *Missionary Movement*, 150.

Even after extensively interviewing such informed commentators on the contemporary world Christian scene as Andrew Walls and Kwame Bediako, Ken Woodward, Religions Editor of *Newsweek*, could still draw the conclusion that one should understand the massive movement toward Christianity in the non-Western world as a movement toward "the religion of the world's most successful superpower, the United States."[26]

These are just two examples, but they are indicative of a widespread outlook that is subservient to the perception of Christianity as Western civilized religion and is unaware of what is actually the driving force behind the contemporary massive shifts in Christian allegiance. Kwame Bediako, commenting on Woodward's observation, gives us a more perceptive insight:

> It is not necessary to deny the appeal of the United States as a modern, large economy that seems to offer opportunities often felt to be absent elsewhere in the world, to recognise that this explanation is inadequate. A persisting Eurocentric view of Christian faith, not to mention a residual Western cultural self-flattery, obscures the fact that the world of the Bible itself, and the attraction of the central figure within it, namely Jesus, are largely responsible for the appeal of the faith in the non-Western world.[27]

In other words, what is actually happening in the massive accession to Christian faith among peoples from the non-Western world is a recovery of biblical roots and a vital connection with the person of Jesus. Since this is occurring almost exclusively among persons and communities of primal religious background, it can be argued that the primal worldview or the "primal imagination"[28] has been pivotal in these developments.

If this is so, then the worldwide Church can no longer afford to view the primal religions as marginal to its life, witness, and scholarship, or as having little or nothing to contribute to a fruitful Christian interaction with religious plurality. In order to take in the full weight of what is happening in our time and to reap the benefits of the closer contact among peoples that has come with globalization, there needs to be a deeper appreciation of primal religions and the primal worldview associated with them. Such an appreciation is also needed in order to discern what it is that primal religions bring to contemporary Christian faith, and what it is that their connection with the Christian faith implies about the essential nature of

---

26. Woodward et al., "Changing Face," 52.
27. Bediako, "New Christian World."
28. See Bediako, *Christianity in Africa*, esp. 91–108.

the faith and its outworking in the interface of Christian engagement with people of other faiths.

PRIMAL RELIGIONS: SOME SIGNPOSTS TO A MORE POSITIVE APPRECIATION

One precursor to the few European voices that came to articulate a positive view of primal religion largely as a result of their own experiences and exposure to religious plurality outside the West, was the German theologian of the early twentieth century, Rudolf Otto, in his seminal study *The Idea of the Holy*. This work, in fact, influenced the later work of Harold W. Turner, who wrote a commentary on it.[29] Having been exposed to vital forms of religion and religious fervor in the Middle and Far East, including Middle Eastern Christianity, Otto became dissatisfied with the Christianity of Germany at the time, considering it to be dry and overly rational. He sought to recover an appreciation of religion as religion—that is, in a more fundamental, entirely religious sense. He coined new words: "numen" and "numinous"—terms for divinity that he drew from the primal Roman religion of antiquity, when "the holy" had "an overplus of meaning"[30]—in his attempt to understand and articulate what lay at the heart of religious experience. This was also a way of indicating that religious experience could not be reduced to, or contained by, any other category of experience. He then applied this perspective to the religious experiences described in the Christian scriptures as a route to recovering the nonrational and the suprarational in Christian experience.

Otto thus showed how primal religious intuitions, far from being alien, lie at the heart of the Christian scriptures and Christian faith. In particular, he drew attention to the sense of the numinous, the transcendent mystery that fills human beings with awe and dread and yet attracts in its compelling fascination the sense of "*mysterium tremendum et fascinans.*"[31] Otto's insight into the numinous as the essence of religion throws new light, for example, on Jesus's proclamation of the Kingdom of God. The Kingdom of God is numinous, the wholly other heavenly thing, in contrast to the world of here and now, the mysterious itself in its dual character as "awe-compelling and yet all-attracting."[32] The numinous quality of Jesus's resoluteness in setting out for Jerusalem (Mark 10:32) illuminates the disciples' astonishment and the fear of those who were following him.

29. Turner, *Rudolf Otto*.
30. Otto, *Idea of the Holy*, 6.
31. See ibid., 11–40, for an elaboration of this theme.
32. Ibid., 82.

In the mid-twentieth century, missionary theologians and bishops John V. Taylor and Kenneth Cragg, drawing on their own experiences in engaging with religious plurality in the non-Western world, also explored how the primal vision of the African world could enrich Christian theological understanding and experience.[33] Both Cragg and J. V Taylor insisted that authentic conversion to Christ entailed a turning to Christ of what was already there in the pre-Christian background, and not an obliteration of it, the primal background being no exception. It was not a question of a confrontation of different belief systems as self-contained opposing entities but a question of discerning the traditions in every religion and culture that either tend toward Christ or lead away from him.

Kenneth Cragg called attention, in particular, to the sacramental elements in Christian faith that persons of a primal background recognize immediately and identify with. J. V. Taylor, in his more extensive study of the "Christian presence amid African religion," discerned a number of features of primal religion that resonate with the biblical world. There is the sense that the world is personal and owes its dynamism to personal will, that people are participants in that universe as a responsible presence, affecting and being affected by the environment, society, and the cosmos. Primal religion maintains a holistic outlook of the spiritual unity of the cosmos and allows for no dichotomy between the sacred and the secular. Yet there is also a sense of ambivalence regarding the place of God in primal religion. Christian faith can thus be shown to affirm, purify, clarify, and strengthen that vision through the revelation of Jesus Christ as one who becomes incarnate in that world in order to redeem it. African theologians would subsequently come to similar conclusions in their efforts to vindicate the primal religious past.

Anastasios Yannoulatos, Bishop of the Greek Orthodox Church, in his paper given at the World Council of Churches (WCC) Ibadan Conference on Primal World-Views, called attention to the primal in the Christian heritage from the Orthodox perspective. He noted particularly "vital elements of the religious experience—such as the sense of total devotion, of being cut to the heart, *katanyxis*, of deep symbolism, or of participation of the whole person in worship," and asked whether Christian mission had offered primal peoples the best of the Christian tradition or merely "a dry, moralising type of Christianity."[34] He considered that it was "this profounder and more essential search for the spiritual experience of the whole mankind [sic] that

---

33. See Taylor, *Primal Vision*; Cragg, *Christianity*, ch. 6.
34. Yannoulatos, "Growing," 75–76.

[would] contribute to a more personal and more universal discovery of the 'wholeness of human life.'"[35]

In the 1970s, Turner, drawing on his experiences in West Africa, postulated a phenomenological affinity between primal religions and Christian faith that helped to explain the positive reception of the Christian gospel when it was first proclaimed to people from primal religious backgrounds: "This is what we have been waiting for."[36] He was also a strong advocate of a methodology of research that took religious phenomena seriously in their own right and of the use of terminology that would be acceptable and recognizable to those being studied. He was concerned to move away from pejorative terminology or terminology that did not correspond to people's religious experience.

Turner's analysis of primal religion is worth enumerating as a model that takes seriously the profundity of primal religious experience. It is particularly helpful in identifying the common phenomenological threads woven through the enormously varied tapestries of the primal religions, whose diversities can easily mask their family likeness. It also demonstrates the phenomenological affinity with essential aspects of the biblical and Christian worldview, as a basis for more fruitful engagement.[37]

Turner identified as the starting point "a sense of kinship with nature," in which the environment is used with respect and reverence. Primal religion demonstrates a religious attitude to the natural setting of human beings in the world and finds its outworking in every aspect of daily life. The second feature is a sense of human weakness, of the finiteness, impurity, and sinfulness of humanity and the need for a power beyond one's own. The third feature is a sense that, indeed, human beings are not alone, that there is a world of spiritual powers or beings more powerful and ultimate. The universe is personal; there is a will behind events. These transcendent powers may be ambivalent—malevolent or benevolent—but the benevolent powers are ultimately stronger and provide a means of escape from the terrors of evil forces.

Thus the fourth feature is a belief that it is possible to "enter into a relationship with the benevolent spirit world, to share in its power and blessings and receive protection from evil forces." There is an emphasis on the transcendent source of true life, a longing for a true life not yet achieved. Out of this arises intuition of the need for sacrifice as the way into that quality of life not yet achieved. The fifth feature is an intense belief in the afterlife, as

---

35. Ibid., 78.
36. Turner, "Primal Religions," 27–37.
37. Ibid.

an extension of the belief in the relationship with the spirit world, a belief that one will share spiritual life and power beyond death. Ancestors, as living dead, figure prominently as united in affection and obligation with the "living living," and as having a mediatorial role. Life can be hopeful because of this sense of continuation beyond this life.[38]

The sixth feature is a sense of "living in a sacramental universe where there is no sharp dichotomy between the physical and the spiritual." The physical world is thus patterned on the spiritual. Human life is a microcosm of the macrocosm. An essentially monistic view—"one set of powers, patterns, runs through all things on earth and in the heavens and welds them into a unified cosmic system"—it is nevertheless qualified by "a clear ethical dualism in respect of good and evil."[39]

In the same period, also reflecting on his learning in West Africa, Walls was pointing to the historical fact of close association between the primal religions and Christianity in the twenty centuries of Christian history, which pointed to an affinity between them. The primal religions have constituted the religious background of the majority of Christians of all ages and places, including Christians of European ancestry.[40] Walls has continued to give close attention to the dynamics at work in the reconfiguration of the primal worldview within African Christianity. He notes helpfully how certain features of the primal spirit world gain prominence and take on fuller meaning, such as the apprehension of the Supreme God, while other features recede or change in character under the sharp light of the gospel. He also shows how the primal worldview underlies in significant ways the new forms of African Christianity that have emerged in recent decades.[41]

PRIMAL RELIGIONS: SOME NON-WESTERN CHRISTIAN APPRAISALS

All these nuances have come to the fore among non-Western Christians from a primal context and are being developed further.[42] Christian schol-

38. Ibid., 31–32.
39. Ibid., 32.
40. Walls, *Missionary Movement*, ch. 6.
41. Walls, *Cross-Cultural Process*, ch. 6.
42. It is somewhat unfortunate that the use of the term "primal" to connote the universal significance of indigenous religions and their strategic relationship with Christian faith has been misunderstood by some non-Western Christian scholars. See Jesse Mugambi's Introduction to the second edition of Taylor, *Primal Vision*, xi–xxxv, where he considers the term to express "evolutionist condescendence,"(xii). For this reason, Mugambi takes the liberty of excising *Primal Vision* from the title of the book,

ars from the non-Western world, and especially from Africa, wrestling with the issues of Christian identity, authentic mission, and dialogue, have given a new lease on life to the positive appraisal of the primal religions and worldview, and to the discernment of historical, phenomenological, and theological affinities with Christian faith. They have taken to a new level the exploration of Christian interaction with the primal traditions for the purpose of engaging more fruitfully with them.

Harry Sawyerr of Sierra Leone "may well be the first church theologian of modern Anglophone Africa."[43] Walls makes this assessment by reason of Sawyerr's pioneer work in building upon earlier studies of the patterns of the primal religions in Africa, exploring their "theological implications, the connexions of the old religions with Christian theology, the bridging concepts by which ideas passed in both directions."[44] Sawyerr was particularly concerned with the live issues of ancestors and sacrifice in the African context.[45] In *God: Ancestor or Creator?*, Sawyerr was attempting "to bring the concept [of ancestor] into Christian theological discourse by means of elements already well-rooted in the Christian tradition." With regard to sacrifice, now "evacuated of much of its significance" in the West, "the realities of sacrifice in African life, as well as the motives for sacrifice, offer a starting point for re-examining the biblical imagery."[46]

John Mbiti was another early African exponent of a more positive appraisal of the religious traditions of Africa, seeking to present Jesus Christ as the fulfilment of the pre-Christian religious aspirations, with African

---

elevating the subtitle, *Christian Presence amid African Religion*, as the full title. In my view, Mugambi is thereby undercutting a major thrust of Taylor's work, and, indeed, he plays down the extent of Taylor's use of the term "primal" in the work (see explanatory note to Max Warren's Foreword to the original series, xi). His criticism that "the shift from 'primitive' to 'primal'" was not made sufficiently clear" (xx) is also not fair to the text, as Taylor devotes a significant portion of Chapter 2 to a discussion of the meaning of "primal" over against "primitive." Taylor's understanding of the wider import of the term "primal" is significant: "The title of this book uses the more general term 'primal' in recognition of the fact that so many features of African religion occur elsewhere in the globe and in the history of human belief that we may reasonably claim that we are dealing with the universal, basic elements of man's (sic) understanding of God and of the world. The word 'primitive,' except, oddly enough, when applied to the Church, has taken on too much the sense of backwardness to be applicable in this context" (9). Mugambi acknowledges that Kwame Bediako uses the term "primal" in an "apologetic" sense, yet considers "there is some ambiguity in his usage," (xxi, n2). However, he does not explicate this "ambiguity."

43. Walls, *Cross-Cultural Process*, 171.
44. Ibid., 171–72.
45. Sawyerr, *God*.
46. Walls, *Cross-Cultural Process*, 171.

religion as the soil in which Christian faith took root and flourished. His aim was to encourage creative theological thinking that would draw upon those intuitions, now perceived as authentic preparation for the gospel, thus overturning the verdict of the missionary participants of Edinburgh 1910: "In missiological jargon, these Traditional Religions will have been a real 'praeparatio evangelica' (preparation for the Gospel); it is now up to African theologians to interpret the meaning of that preparation for the Gospel, in the African context of not only the past, but also today and tomorrow."[47]

In another direction, the work of Turner has found affirmation and elaboration in the work of K. Bediako, who revisits the six features of Turner's analysis.[48] In Bediako's view, it is the sixth and final feature that is "the key to the whole structure." While acknowledging that "a starting point for appreciating the primal imagination must be in primal religions themselves," he nonetheless suggests that "it is this abiding presence of the primal world-view" within the whole range of newer forms of Christian presence in Africa that demonstrates "how the primal imagination can transcend primal religions as distinctive systems."[49] He also shows how, among Christians who have not lost their primal perspective in embracing the Christian faith, and who start from a positive rather than a negative perception of the primal worldview, it is possible to explore the relationship between primal and biblical religion in African Christian experience.

K. Bediako draws also on the primal sense of "vital participation," that featured prominently in the work of the Congolese theologian, Mulago,[50] as a helpful way of interpreting the experience of African independent prophets, such as William Wadé Harris, and Emmanuel Milingo.[51]

Lamin Sanneh has taken up the question of the theological significance of African languages as the medium of articulation of the gospel message, emphasizing that the gospel was adequately anticipated in the religious language of African religious traditions: "God was not disdainful of Africans as to be incommunicable in their languages."[52] That this is so derives from the essential nature of the Christian faith itself as a translation movement, revealed in the experience of the earliest church as born witness to in the New Testament. Christian faith is further defined as being particularly at home

---

47. Mbiti, "Future of Christianity," 36.

48. Bediako, *Christianity in Africa*, ch. 6, esp. 93–96.

49. Ibid., 93.

50. See Mulago, *La religion* and *Un visage africain*; also K. Bediako, *Theology and Identity*, ch. 9.

51. Bediako, *Christianity in Africa*, 103–4.

52. Sanneh, "Horizontal and Vertical," 166.

in the vernaculars or mother tongues that are the vehicle for the articulation of primal religious experience and subsequently of the religious experience of Christians from a primal background.[53]

In a more recent work, Sanneh develops the theological ramifications of affinity between primal and Christian by highlighting the continuity of the "ancient religious stock" in Africa through "the adoption of African names for God in Christianity," and its impact. Since

> the name of God is basic to the structure of traditional societies . . . it follows that the adoption of African names for God in Christianity would carry corresponding implications for social and cultural renewal with effects on indigenous ethics and historical consciousness. . . . The name of God contained ideas of personhood, economic life, and social/cultural identity. . . . African religions as conveyors of the names of God were in relevant aspects anticipations of Christianity.[54]

He then draws the conclusion that "theologically God had preceded the missionary in Africa, a fact that Bible translation clinched with decisive authority."[55]

The history and experience of the African Initiated Churches (AIC) are an ample demonstration of the power of the scriptures in indigenous languages to bring about new forms of Christian life that draw inspiration from the primal worldview.[56] The mother-tongue scriptures are also becoming the dynamic behind a new generation of African theologians who are beginning to explore Christian theological concepts in their mother tongue and in relation to traditional ideas. *Yesu, Homowo Nuntso* (Jesus, Lord of Homowo) is a pioneer study by Philip Tete Laryea of Christology in Ga—the language of Accra, Ghana—exploring Jesus as the fulfilment of the aspirations of the most important Ga traditional festival that continues to be widely celebrated.[57]

Looking beyond Africa, the Jesuit Sri Lankan scholar Aloysius Pieris highlights the pattern of continuity from the primal past with respect to

---

53. This is the thrust of Sanneh's monumental study *Translating the Message*.

54. Sanneh, *Whose Religion?*, 31.

55. Ibid., 31–32.

56. See, for example, the writings of Sundkler: *Bantu Prophets* and *Zulu Zion*. Particularly helpful is to note the journey into greater understanding of, and sympathy for, these churches and movements displayed in the modified interpretation of them by the author in the later work, as a result of his association with them in the period spanning these two works.

57. Laryea, *Yesu*.

Asian religions such as Hinduism and Buddhism in his book *An Asian Theology of Liberation*.[58] Primal religions are designated by the term "cosmic," where the highest good is sought among the transcendent and sacramental mysteries of life. These cosmic religions are the inherent and essential basis of all "metacosmic" religions, where salvation is located in the "Beyond."[59] Indeed, far from being "superior," the latter cannot exist without the religiousness of the former, whereas the cosmic—primal—can exist without the metacosmic. "Historically and phenomenologically speaking, there cannot be a metacosmic religiousness having an institutional grip on the people save on the basis of a popular religiousness."[60] This has significance also for Christian faith in an Asian context, where Christianity has been associated with the West and with imperialism. The liberation of Christianity in Asia from its negative associations may come by way of a recovery of the cosmic outlook through the medium of indigenous languages, where language is understood as "the experience of reality."[61] The affinity of Christianity with cosmic—primal—religion needs to be rediscovered in the Asian context through the medium of indigenous languages.

All the features of the primal worldview outlined above relate to religious experience and are present to varying degrees in the diverse contemporary forms of non-Western Christianity. Thus, they help to explain their distinctive focus and can be shown to have much to do with their vitality.

SOME POSITIVE OUTCOMES OF THE PRIMAL RESPONSE TO CHRISTIAN FAITH

Rudolf Otto sensed the need for "a less abstract intuition of the genesis of original and genuine religious communities with the aid of living instances of the thing as it may still be found today." He sensed the need for seeking "places and moments at which even today religion shows itself alive as a naive emotional force with all its primal quality of impulse and instinct."[62] This may now be seen to have been prophetic. Overly cerebral and overly rational forms of worship, the loss of the fervor of religious life and the immediacy of the scriptures, a stance of compromise with a prevailing cul-

---

58. See Pieris, *Asian Theology*, 96–99.

59. Pieris explains that he uses the terms "cosmic" and "metacosmic" as English renderings of vernacular terms that give account of the varied aspects of the Asian religious heritage. See Pieris, *Asian Theology*, 98.

60. Ibid., 99.

61. Ibid., 70.

62. Otto, *Idea of the Holy*, 157.

tural ethos and social ethics that are hostile to the biblical message, and a theological academy that seems to have little relevance for Christian nurture and witness; all these features are even more evident now in the West than they were in Otto's day. They are all signs of a recession from Christianity.

A consistent pattern throughout Christian history has been that primal spirituality, infused with Christian faith, has come to the rescue of tired or imperilled forms of Christianity and has taken Christian mission to a new stage. The "living instances of religion . . . alive with its primal quality of impulse and instinct" that hold the potential for revitalizing the contemporary church are not those of the Islamic or Hindu worlds where Otto had encountered them. They are the forms of Christian life and worship in the primal settings of Latin America, parts of Asia and Oceania, and especially in Africa and the African Christian communities now established in the African diaspora.

What may we identify as some of the positive outcomes among the living forms of non-Western Christianity?[63] We may note, first, a recovery of religious experience and fervent spirituality at the heart of Christian faith. A "rending of the veil" occurs, and the "nature of the whole universe as instinct with divine presence [is] made manifest, as also the divine destiny of [humanity] as an abiding divine-human relationship."[64] The call and careers of Africa's indigenous prophets and the whole range of African initiated churches across the continent bear witness to this phenomenon. The experience of trance-visitations, the "rending of the veil" by which William Wadé Harris met with Moses, Angel Gabriel, Elijah, and Jesus, and was launched into his itinerant evangelistic ministry in the early twentieth century in West Africa, was no isolated event. It also has the conversion of Paul as its biblical paradigm.

Such experiences have been replicated elsewhere in a variety of ways as new traditions of African Christianity have emerged. They are well documented, and it is not necessary to recall them here. What has perhaps not been adequately emphasized is that even the so-called mainline churches are responding to the hunger for vitality in spiritual experience and for the immediacy of God's presence. This began with the emergence of renewal movements within the mainline denominations.[65] Increasingly now, whole congregations are incorporating prayer vigils, healing, and deliverance ser-

63. While this section of the essay focuses mainly on the living forms of African Christianity, the features identified may be seen to be true of the forms of Christianity in Latin America, Oceania, and parts of Asia, where primal religions have been dominant.

64. Bediako, *Christianity in Africa*, 102.

65. For the Ghanaian story, see Omenyo, *Pentecost*.

vices into the mainstream of their activities as well as introducing elements of spontaneity—such as times for "praise and worship" led by a "praise team" rather than the church choir—into the regular liturgy.[66] None of these manifestations are "exotic." They merely constitute a recovery of the spiritual fervor of the church in New Testament times in an African manifestation, the route to them being the primal worldview.

This leads to a second outcome in the recovery of holism and the transcendent at the heart of life: "The divine presence in the community of believers constitutes it into a 'transcendent' community, in which the human components experience and share in the divine life."[67] The evidence for this takes many forms. Perhaps the most visible examples of the acknowledgement of God in the daily lives of Christians in Ghana—found also in other African countries—come in the scripture verses or proverbs expressing a religious outlook on life, written on lorries and public transport in English or in Ghanaian mother tongues: "*Nyame ye*" (God is good), "*Nyame bekyere*" (God will guide). Some may bear the unmistakable bite of social critique with even a hint of eschatological warning: "Heaven's gate no bribe!" A similar acknowledgement of God may also come in the names given to small enterprises, such as "Jesus my Saviour Enterprise," the name of a small retail grocery outlet, or "All to Jesus [I surrender] Communication Centre." "Blood of the Lamb Carpet Cleaners" would probably not appeal to Western sensibilities but must be attractive to prospective Ghanaian customers who have confidence in the cleansing power of the blood of Jesus Christ![68] Some inscriptions may appear enigmatic to an outsider. "No weapon" comes from Isa 54:17: "No weapon fashioned against you shall prosper," and is a statement of faith in Jesus in a world where the presence of evil working through human and spiritual agents is very real. All these

---

66. One notable example in Ghana is the independent, interdenominational English-speaking Ridge Church in Accra, founded in the colonial era initially to provide a home for Anglican expatriates who were not at ease with the "high-church" tradition of Anglicanism in the Gold Coast. Since Ghana's independence, Ridge Church has become popular among Ghana's professional élite and now embraces three denominations: Anglican, Methodist, and Presbyterian. Even such a "Westernized" congregation is now moving in the same direction, with the introduction of prayer vigils, healing services, and times for spontaneous praise and worship in the Sunday morning 10:00 a.m. service, sometimes using choruses in the various Ghanaian mother tongues of the worshipers.

67. Bediako, *Christianity in Africa*, 103.

68. I have not observed this inscription personally; it was culled from what might be considered an unlikely source—the in-flight magazine of South African Airways, *Sawubona*. See Slabbert, "Ghana," 117.

statements have, in fact, a story to tell of God's intervention in the life of the person or persons concerned.

We might be tempted to think that such perceptions are confined to the less educated sectors of African society. This is, in fact, not the case. Christian professionals now address to Jesus Christ "the requests that would formally have been addressed to spiritual powers and their human agents in a primal religious setting."[69] Among these requests one may note: "prayer for fertility, the dedication of a baby at an 'outdooring,' success in an examination, the blessing of a newly built or occupied house, the blessing of a newly purchased motor car to ensure safety for user and vehicle alike." As Kwame Bediako observes: "New knowledge in science and technology has been embraced, but it has not displaced the basic view that the whole universe in which human existence takes place is fundamentally spiritual."[70] In other words, the sense of reality as essentially spiritual, which was a feature of the traditional universe,[71] has a continuing life in the African Christian universe of thought and action. Because this is a comprehensive, all-embracing understanding of reality, such preoccupations do not belong exclusively to the private or personal realm; they can be shown to be operative in social and political spheres.[72]

Third, we may note the recovery of the Bible as a contemporary living witness to the presence and activity of the living God in the world, in which persons and communities of faith may participate. The scriptures become the "road map for our religious itinerary," enabling the reconfiguring of the primal world and both shaping and interpreting Christian experience.[73] This centrality of the Bible as a feature of primal Christian spirituality is not to be understood as independent of the two earlier features outlined. The independent prophets functioned in the biblical realm because they participated in the scriptures. Scriptural inspiration, direct and indirect, informs the popular Christian spirituality that expresses itself in the public sphere, as was noted earlier. Scripture is the integrating centre, "the authoritative, normative deposit given to us of the divine-human encounter that lies at the heart of our faith."[74] This is not simply sound doctrine; it is lived experience,

---

69. Bediako, *Christianity in Africa*, 176.

70. Ibid.

71. Gyekye points this out clearly: "The Akan universe is a spiritual universe, one in which supernatural beings play significant roles in the thought and action of the people. What is primarily real is spiritual" (*Essay*, 69).

72. Bediako, "Christian Witness," 117–32.

73. Bediako, "Scripture," 2–11.

74. Ibid., 2.

born out of the evident affinity of worldview between the Bible and Africa. As Sanneh notes so incisively:

> There is a much greater difference between traditional Africa and the secular West, say, than between Africa and the Bible, a difference that could gravely distort our image of African Christianity were we solely to view Africa, as we have tended to, from our Western vantage point. Traditional Africa, we might say . . . has her hand given in religion, waiting for the written oracle like the Israelites the promised land. Few things, we recall, are as natural to Africans as religious commitment, the written form of which, when it emerged, transcribed the intentions of the inbred variety.[75]

It is central to Sanneh's argument that it is the "native idiom" employed in the vernacular Bible translations that "mobilized African sentiments and commenced a transformation process in society and culture. . . . The Christian Scriptures, cast as a vernacular oracle, gave the native idiom and the aspirations it enshrined a historic cause, allowing Africans to fashion fresh terms for their own advancement and possibility."[76]

The scriptures in the "native idiom" have also unleashed a fervent response of creativity in worship, song, and prayer, drawing out of the wellsprings of primal spirituality a wholehearted adoration of Jesus that is also truly biblical.[77] Yannoulatos tersely expresses the dynamic of primal religion meeting Christian faith in the words: "Primal is not final,"[78] and indeed many who have come to Christian faith from a primal background will testify to the truth of this in their experience. The message of the gospel was something that they had been waiting for. The revelation of Jesus came as the fulfilment of anticipations and as the answer to questions they were already asking within their world of religious experience. As Mbiti notes, the gospel came to "bring the flickering light" of the primal tradition to "full brilliance."[79]

The elements of terror and ambivalence in the "old" also could not be answered from within the tradition. But this is merely an outworking of the

---

75. Sanneh, *Encountering the West*, 92.

76. Ibid., 86.

77. See Kuma, *Jesus of the Deep Forest*. This is one notable expression of mother-tongue worship of Jesus by an unschooled traditional midwife in rural Ghana who draws her imagery from her primal world of religious and cultural experience, interpreted by the scriptures in her mother tongue.

78. Yannoulatos, "Growing," 75.

79. Mbiti, "On the Article," 68.

biblical paradigm of transformation from old covenant to new, from the awesomeness and terror of Sinai to the joy of Zion, the heavenly Jerusalem, so graphically expressed in Heb 12:18–25. Christians from a primal background identify with both of these images. The primal world of numinous presence is the same in both, and its source is the same living God. The difference comes with the change of perception of that world and the change of relationship with that world that Jesus brings. As Christians from a primal background discover who Jesus is in their world of religious experience and what he has done for them in it, so their world undergoes a similar transformation.

RECOVERING THE PRIMAL VISION FOR ENGAGING A PLURALIST WORLD

With the wisdom of hindsight and taking in the due significance of the religious plurality of our time with respect to the constituency and dynamic of the worldwide church, we may now view the past two hundred years of Christian engagement in mission in primal contexts in a different light. In engaging in mission in primal societies, Western Christians were, in the providence of *missio Dei*, being challenged to recover dimensions of the gospel that they were already losing under the influence of the Enlightenment and the advance of secularism. Only a few learned the lesson in their time. In our time, a new day is dawning,[80] which may even be evidence of a "divine irony,"[81] as African and other non-Western Christians make their home in the former "fully missionized lands."[82] As they establish their own vibrant communities of Christian life and witness, their presence may be providing the Western world and the Western church with a fresh opportunity to recover "the one thing needful."

Western Christendom is no more and will not be replicated anywhere else.[83] The church everywhere is now called to bear witness to the gospel

---

80. Reference to the title of a book of essays, presented to Dr. J. J. (Hans) Visser, formerly Director of the Hendrik Kraemer Institute, Utrecht, Netherlands, on his retirement from Christian service—one of those few missionaries who acknowledge their debt to Africa. See Bediako et al., *New Day Dawning*.

81. Expression used by K. Bediako in his address at the Retirement Celebration for Dr. Hans Visser, Mattheuskerk, Utrecht, October 8, 2004, speaking of the presence of African Christians and African churches in the Netherlands.

82. Term used at the World Missionary Conference, Edinburgh 1910, to designate Western countries deemed Christian.

83. Sanneh makes this clear in his illuminating study of the legacy of Christendom in the post-Christendom era, *Encountering the West*, 184–229.

in settings of religious and cultural plurality, as in the days of the earliest church played out in the writings of the New Testament. Yet the legacy of Christendom in coercive and confrontational models of engagement with persons of other faiths constitutes a huge obstacle along the road to fresh and creative patterns of engagement that are faithful to the gospel and suited to the new setting in which the worldwide church finds itself. As Sanneh asks so pertinently: "Can we as believers witness to faith without the coercive recourse implicit in religious territoriality or numerical preponderance? Can we embrace democratic freedoms, including the freedom of religion, as the necessary development of the religious spirit, rather than as a hostile contender with religion?"[84] A new type of Christian mind-set is needed, where the hospitality, generosity, and openness of the primal religious spirit are expressed in witness to Jesus who comes to persons of every culture to be received as the "Alpha and Omega" of their world. This kind of hospitality forms the basis of dialogue, as in the case of traditional prophets and prophetesses in the pre-Christian era, who foretold the coming of a new revelation of the Supreme God and so paved the way for missionary proclamation.[85] Or, as when traditional priests and healers welcomed Christian missionaries, giving them respect as religious specialists like themselves.[86]

A new Christian mind-set is needed that is delivered from nostalgia for a lost Christendom and is thus freed from the residual desire to have "a stem in a pious emperor or ruler from whom official society draws its orthodox sap."[87] New tools for living *Christianly* are needed so that we may be able to bear testimony to the gospel in a pluralistic context without recourse to strategies of domination or confrontation.

A prophetic discernment is needed, akin to that of the great prophets of the Old Testament, a perspective on the world that denies ultimacy to world leaders and expects to see the transcendent kingdom acting in secret to subvert oppressive forces in the current world order, "[bringing] down the mighty from their thrones and [exalting] the humble and meek" (Luke 1:52).

---

84. Ibid., 222–23.

85. An intriguing example of this is documented by Byang Kato in his account of how Christianity came to his own Jaba people in Nigeria. A prophetess, under spirit possession, predicted the arrival of missionaries who would tell them about Gwaza, the Supreme Being, several years before the missionaries arrived. The outcome was a substantial response to the proclamation of the gospel. See Kato, *Theological Pitfalls*, 36.

86. This was the experience of Andreas Riis, the first missionary of the Basel Mission to work in Akropong, in the kingdom of Akuapem, Ghana. See Opoku, *Riis*, 18, 83–4.

87. Sanneh, *Encountering the West*, 187.

A new mind-set is needed where the Enlightenment dichotomies that constrict Western thought—sacred and secular, individual and community, belief and experience, intellect and emotion, reason and faith, theology and discipleship, scholarship and mission—are dissolved and all become integral and interrelated facets of the totality of Christian experience, in which the one cannot exist or be conceived of as existing without the other. A new reverential awe of the living God is needed, along with a new sobriety regarding the human condition, both of which will manifest in intuitive awareness of, and utter dependence upon, the living God in all the circumstances of everyday life. Thus, the first instinct in any situation is to pray and read scripture with humility, allowing its message to interpret our lives and its worldview to critique and transform our own.

The resources required for such a radical reorientation of mind-set have to come from outside, from a primal worldview that does not lie under the shadow of the Enlightenment, and that is skilled in hospitable and generous living amid plurality. For even where Western Christians share some of the religious sensitivities and human sympathies of the primal worldview, there has been such attrition from religious experience, and such a long tradition of interreligious antagonism that these processes and their effects become discernible only through exposure to more vital forms of Christian life in a pluralistic environment. As Sanneh observes: "World Christianity offers a laboratory of pluralism and diversity where instead of faith and trust being missing or compromised, they remain intrinsic. You could not recognize world Christianity without the myriad tongues of praise and hope that also echo humanity's hopes and dreams."[88]

There is often a sense among Western Christians that the primal world is remote from their experience. Some feel this way about the biblical world also. Yet we shall do well to remember that primal religions are the Western pre-Christian heritage, too, and that they inspired creativity in mission and scholarship that made an enduring impact on the development of Western Christianity. A clear example of this is the Celtic Christianity of early Ireland.[89] It is not fortuitous that J. V. Taylor concluded *The Primal Vision: Christian Presence amid African Religion* by quoting in full the quintessential example of early Celtic spirituality known as the "Lorica" or "St. Patrick's Breastplate" as a prayer that he desired to see translated into every language of Africa.[90] The affinities with African Christian spirituality are striking,

88. Sanneh, *Whose Religion*, 75.

89. Among the many books on the subject, see, e.g., Joyce, *Celtic Christianity*; Bradley, *Celtic Way*.

90. Taylor, *Primal Vision*, 196. This early Irish prayer, originally composed in the vernacular, goes back to the eighth century at the latest, and is probably older. For a

particularly when one understands the nature of the Celtic spiritual world that formed the background to the prayer and, indeed, gave it its form, since the "breastplate" was a pre-Christian form of "encircling prayer," calling on the gods for protection. Now it is Christ who encircles and encompasses so that no harm can come, who not merely blesses the individual but is the true sanctifying and binding force of the community. The underlying thought is the same as that expressed in the allusive affirmation on many a Ghanaian taxi to which I referred earlier: "No weapon!"

CONCLUSION

The primal affinities across time and space give cause for hope that it is possible to overcome the seeming remoteness of the Western primal Christian past and the secularizing tendency that reduces such intense expressions of primal Western spirituality to the level of beautiful poetry. Recovery of the primal vision in Christian faith can be mediated to present generations of Western Christians through fellowship with Christians and Christian communities that have not lost their primal vision. In the new agenda for mission in the context of religious plurality, therefore, the modern West cannot be the pacesetter. Almost four decades ago, Bishop Lesslie Newbigin was faced with, and subsequently himself posed, the question: "Can the West be converted?,"[91] thus mooting the idea of a "missiology for the West." Within our present concerns, might there be place to pose another question: "Can Western Christians be learners?"

The process has to be dynamic and ongoing. As Christians from a primal setting grow in the consciousness of their responsibility to reflect upon their primal heritage, to draw from their primal indigenous resources, and to live out and articulate their implications for Christian faith and witness, Western Christians may be helped to discover that "it is not finally some mysterious 'primitive philosophy' that we are exploring but the farther potentialities of our own thought and language."[92] In this process of rediscovering the "farther potentialities" of their own faith, Western Christians will have the opportunity to discover a common humanity with others and new

---

modern translation, see O'Donaghue, "St. Patrick's," 46–49.

91. Newbigin first faced this question when posed by T. B. Simatupang, leader of the Indonesian Council of Churches and lay theologian, at the WCC Bangkok 1973 Assembly, and subsequently used it frequently. See, e.g., Newbigin, "Can the West be Converted?."

92. Godfrey Lienhardt on the study of "primitive society," quoted in Sanneh, *Encountering the West*, 240,

ways of being Christian in the contemporary environment of religious and cultural plurality.

BIBLIOGRAPHY

"Animism." *Britannica Student Encyclopedia*, 2004. Online: http://www.britannica.com/topic/animism.

Bediako, Gillian M. "'Be Thou My Vision': The Lorica and Early Irish Christian Worship in African Perspective." *Journal of African Christian Thought* 8 (2005) 46–52.

Bediako, Kwame. "Christian History and the Kingdom of God: Rescuing Our Memories and Discerning Some Temptations of Our Time." Manuscript. Princeton, NJ.

———. "Christian Witness in the Public Sphere: Some Lessons and Residual Challenges from the Recent Political History of Ghana." In *The Changing Face of Christianity: Africa, the West, and the World*, edited by Lamin Sanneh and Joel A. Carpenter, 117–32. New York: Oxford University Press, 2005.

———. *Christianity in Africa: The Renewal of a Non-Western Religion*. Maryknoll, NY: Orbis, 1995.

———. "A New Christian World: Reading Signs of the Kingdom amid Global Geopolitics." Lecture 1. Princeton Theological Seminary, Stone Lectures, 2003.

———. "Scripture as the Hermeneutic of Culture and Tradition." *Journal of African Christian Thought* 4.1 (2001) 2–11.

———. *Theology and Identity: The Impact of Culture upon Christian Thought in the Second Century and in Modern Africa*. Oxford: Regnum, 1999.

Bediako, Kwame, et al., eds. *A New Day Dawning: African Christians Living the Gospel; Essays in Honor of Dr. J. J. (Hans) Visser*. Zoetermeer: Uitgeverei Boekencentrum, 2004.

Bradley, Ian C. *The Celtic Way*. London: Darton, Longman and Todd, 1993.

Cox, James L. "The Classification 'Primal Religions' as a Non-Empirical Christian Theological Construct." *Studies in World Christianity* 2.1 (1996) 55–76.

Cragg, Kenneth. *Christianity in World Perspective*. London: Lutterworth, 1969.

Gairdner, W. H. T. *"Edinburgh 1910": An Account and Interpretation of the World Missionary Conference*. London: Oliphant, Anderson & Ferrier, 1910.

Gyekye, Kwame. *An Essay on African Philosophical Thought: The Akan Conceptual Scheme*. Rev. ed. Philadelphia: Temple University Press, 1995.

Hayes, Victor C., ed. *Australian Essays in World Religions*. Bedford Park: Australian Association for the Study of Religions, 1997.

Jenkins, Philip. *The Next Christendom: The Coming of Global Christianity*. New York: Oxford University Press, 2003.

Johns, Chris, et al. "Mysteries of the Maya: The Rise, Glory, and Collapse of an Ancient Civilization." *National Geographic* Collector's Edition (2008) 112.

Joyce, Timothy. *Celtic Christianity: A Sacred Tradition, a Vision of Hope*. Maryknoll, NY: Orbis, 1998.

Kato, Byang H. *Theological Pitfalls in Africa*. Kisumu, Kenya: Evangel, 1975.

Kuma, Afua. *Jesus of the Deep Forest: Prayers and Praises of Afua Kuma*. Translated by Jon Kirby from Twi: *Afua Kuma Ayeyi ne Mpaaebo*. Accra: Asempa, 1981.

Laryea, Philip Tete. *Yesu, Hɔmɔwɔ Nuntscɔ, Nikasemɔ ni kɔɔ bɔni Kristofoi naa Yesu yɛ gamɛi Akusumfeemo kɛ blema saji amli*. Akropong: Regnum Africa, 2004.

Lienhardt, Godfrey. "Modes of Thought." In *The Institutions of Primitive Society*, edited by E. E. Evans-Pritchard, 96–97. Oxford: Blackwell, 1961.

Mackey, James P., ed. *An Introduction to Celtic Christianity*. Edinburgh: T. & T. Clark, 1989.

Mbiti, John S. "The Future of Christianity in Africa (1970–2000)." *Communio Viatorum: Theological Quarterly* 13:1–2 (1970) 19–38.

———. "On the Article of John W. Kinney: A Comment." *Occasional Bulletin of Missionary Research* 3.2 (1979) 68.

Mugambi, Jesse. "Introduction." In *Christian Presence amid African Religion*, by John V. Taylor, xi–xxxv. Nairobi: Acton, 2001.

Mulago, Emmanuel. *La religion traditionelle des Bantu et leur vision du monde*. 2nd ed. Kinshasa: Faculté de Théologie Catholique, 1980.

———. *Un visage africain du christianisme: L'union vitale Bantu face à l'unité vitale ecclésiale*. Paris: Présence Africaine, 1965.

Newbigin, Lesslie. "Can the West be Converted?" *International Bulletin of Missionary Research* 11.1 (1987) 2–7.

O'Donaghue, Noel Dermot. "St. Patrick's Breastplate." In *Introduction to Celtic Christianity*, edited by James P. Mackey, 46–49. Edinburgh: T. & T. Clark, 1989.

Omenyo, Cephas Narh. *Pentecost Outside Pentecostalism: A Study of the Development of Charismatic Renewal in the Mainline Churches in Ghana*. Zoetermeer: Uitgeverij Boekencentrum, 2002.

Opoku, A. A. *Riis the Builder*. Legon: Institute of African Studies, University of Ghana, 1978.

Otto, Rudolf. *The Idea of the Holy: An Inquiry into the Non-rational Factor in the Idea of the Divine and Its Relation to the Rational*. 1950, 2nd ed. Reprint, Oxford: Oxford University Press, 1977.

Pieris, Aloysius. *An Asian Theology of Liberation*. Maryknoll, NY: Orbis, 1989.

"Religions." *Encyclopedia Britannica*. 3rd ed., vol. 16. 1797.

Sanneh, Lamin O. *Encountering the West: Christianity and the Global Cultural Process*. Maryknoll, NY: Orbis, 1993.

———. "The Horizontal and the Vertical in Mission: An African Perspective." *International Bulletin of Missionary Research* 7.4 (1983) 165–71.

———. *Translating the Message: The Missionary Impact on Culture*. 2nd ed. Maryknoll, NY: Orbis, 2009.

———. *Whose Religion is Christianity?: The Gospel beyond the West*. Grand Rapids: Eerdmans, 2003.

Sanneh, Lamin, and Joel A. Carpenter, eds. *The Changing Face of Christianity: Africa, the West, and the World*. New York: Oxford University Press, 2005.

Sawyerr, Harry. *God: Ancestor or Creator?: Aspects of Traditional Belief in Ghana, Nigeria & Sierra Leone*. London: Longman, 1970.

Slabbert, Denise. "Ghana: Divine Intervention." *Sawubona* (2005) 116–19.

Smith, William Robertson. *Religion of the Semites: First series; The Fundamental Institutions*. Edinburgh: A & C Black, 1927.

Sullivan, Lawrence E., ed. *Native Religions and Cultures of Central and South America: Anthropology of the Sacred*. New York: Continuum, 2002.

———, ed. *Native Religions and Cultures of North America: Anthropology of the Sacred*. New York: Continuum, 2000.

Sundkler, Bengt. *Bantu Prophets in South Africa*. London: Oxford University Press, 1948.

———. *Zulu Zion and Some Swazi Zionists*. London: Oxford University Press, 1976.

Taylor, John Burnett, ed. *Primal World-Views: Christian Involvement in Dialogue with Traditional Thought Forms*. Ibadan, Nigeria: Daystar, 1976.

Taylor, John V. *The Primal Vision: Christian Presence amid African Religion*. London: SCM, 1965.

Trans World Radio. "What is Animism?" *Africa* 4.3 (2004) 10.

Turner, Harold W. "New Religious Movements in Primal Societies." In *Australian Essays in World Religions*, edited by Victor C. Hayes, 38–49. Bedford Park: Australian Association for the Study of Religions, 1997.

———. "The Primal Religions of the World and their Study." In *Australian Essays in World Religions*, edited by Victor C. Hayes, 27–37. Bedford Park: Australian Association for the Study of Religions, 1997.

———. *Rudolf Otto, The Idea of the Holy: Commentary on a Shortened Version; With Introduction to the Man by Peter R. McKenzie*. Aberdeen: Aberdeen Peoples, 1977.

Tylor, Edward Burnett. *Primitive Culture: Researches into the Development of Mythology, Philosophy, Religion, Art, and Custom*, 3rd ed. 2 vols. London: John Murray, 1891.

Walls, Andrew F. *The Cross-Cultural Process in Christian History*. Edinburgh: T. & T. Clark, 2002.

———. *The Missionary Movement in Christian History: Studies in the Transmission of the Faith*. Edinburgh: T. & T. Clark, 1996.

Woodward, Kenneth, et al. "The Changing Face of the Church: How the Explosion of Christianity in Developing Nations Is Transforming the World's Largest Religion." *Newsweek* 137.16 (2001) 46.

World Missionary Conference. *Report of Commission IV: The Missionary Message in Relation to Non-Christian Religions*. Edinburgh: Oliphant, Anderson & Ferrier, 1910.

Yannoulatos, Anastasios. "Growing into an Awareness of Primal World-Views." In *Primal World Views: Christian Involvement in Dialogue with Traditional Thought Forms*, edited by John Bernard Taylor, 72–78. Ibadan: Daystar, 1976.

Chapter 9

At the Crossroads
Contemporary Indonesian Christianity amid Primal Religions

Martin L. Sinaga

INTRODUCTION

IN THIS ESSAY I will examine the interaction between primal religions and Christianity in Indonesia. Primal religions have been present since the beginning of human habitation in the Indonesian Archipelago. Christianity arrived on the scene with the first Portuguese explorers in the sixteenth century. Consequently, Indonesian Christians have always lived as part of a multireligious community. What can be learned from the Indonesian experience about the challenges of living with respect and civility in multifaith societies?

The Christian narrative in Indonesia presents a contrast to Christianity in the West. In the West, Christianity has been the religio-cultural majority for more than a millennium. Jewish enclaves were the only other religious group. It was claimed that Christianity had long ago displaced Europe's primal religions, although recent scholarly studies have challenged this claim.[1]

---

1. See Wessels, *Europe*.

By contrast, Indonesian Christianity is a relative newcomer, and the interaction between Christian faith and the primal religions is more immediate, lying close to the surface. By listening carefully to these different historical experiences, it is hoped new insights can be gained. The very complexity of the Indonesian experience does not allow for a sharply etched picture; rather, it must be presented as a subtle blending of colors.

The blended colors of Christianity living in the context of Indonesian primal religions are derived from two distinct streams: theological and sociological. The theological stream shows that the interaction has resulted in a dichotomy between formal theology and lived Christian experience; and the sociological stream is the result of the interaction that has formed a new type of community, a *Volkskirche* ("folk church").[2]

LOSS OF THE PRIMAL SPIRIT

The portrait of Christianity in the primal context of the Indonesian Archipelago shows clearly both its religiosocial and theological features; and at once we see that this can be traced to the missionary inheritance. A famous missionary who worked early in the twentieth century in Eastern Indonesia, A. C. Kruyt, saw this issue as a struggle of conversion from heathenism to Christianity. By this he meant, as he said pretentiously, that "becoming a Christian means for him, i.e., the primal man, making his own the ancestors of the Hollanders (the Dutch)."[3] For Kruyt, who used E. B. Tylor's theory of animism, conversion meant—in a Weberian idiom—rationalization of religion. Animistic traditions are not propositional; they are tied to a practical or embodied logic whose sense is related to culturally specific practical activities.[4] Becoming a Christian means, then, accepting a belief system that is relatively coherent, has a universalized doctrine, and offers a superior rationale by which to explain life. And yet, Kruyt expected that there would be a progressive change in the hearts and minds of the primal peoples toward Christianity. As a missionary in Central Celebes, where Kruyt worked with pietistic zeal, he de-emphasized theology—for example, the rationalization of religion—in favor of piety. Thus, Christian orthopraxy—such as atten-

---

2. Van Klinken's comments on *volkskirche* put developments in perspective: "Folk churches offered the opportunity to christianize an entire culture, not merely by reforming social institutions like marriage and labour, but by creating a sense of ethnic identity, greater than the clan but smaller than Netherlands-Indies (colonial state), that previously had not existed at all" (*Minorities, Modernity*, 13).

3. Kruyt quoted in Klinken, *Minorities, Modernity*, 12.

4. Schrauwers, *Colonial 'Reformation,'* 198–99.

dance at worship services—was of greater importance than correct belief. Consequently, the local spirit associated with primal religious experience was left untouched and unchallenged. The people believed the spirit continued to wander about, and in time of trouble they would call on it.

This shows that the Christian theological interaction with the primal Indonesian religions was dualistic. Being a Christian mostly meant adherence to a certain institution where membership was important. Conversion meant enrolling in the modern school, first established for training catechists, and using modern medicine to cure common sicknesses such as cholera. These two institutions—the modern school and hospital—belonged to the church, and participating in those institutions identified a person as a Christian. But when a sickness was not cured and the future seemed uncertain, the person was urged by the community to consult his or her ancestors, communicating with them through a shaman who could channel the spirit.[5]

James Haire's research on Halmahera Island confirms this observation. When the meaning of *gikiri*, the local spirit, was addressed theologically in the context of the Christian God, "there occurred a dichotomy.... This dichotomy, however, was also carried over into Christianity, because while accepting the Christian God the Halmaherans continued in recent years to accept the limited authority and efficacy especially of the *gikiri* and village-spirits within their own sphere."[6] Although Christ is called the Great *Gomanga*, that is the spirit of the living-dead, or the Senior Living Dead—where the dualism is seemingly overcome—what essentially worked in this case was the local "theological notion" of the divine in which the deity incorporates the living and the dead into one family. And the Minister of Word of the Halmaheran Church, who is said to have studied Calvinist-Reformed theology before he was ordained as a minister will, within this family (or *volk*)-church type of Christianity, serve holy communion with a reverent response from the congregation.

Acceptance of the importance of adherence to a church, also seen as formal religion, has in fact created a stable dualism in the popular Christianity of Indonesia. In the case of the Batak Church of North Sumatra, a strategy used to avoid authentic encounter is division of labor: the church acts as a formal religion and thus promotes a cognitive meaning of life, while the primal religious heritage is regarded as mere *adat* (customary law). And *adat* has been secularized as a neutral sphere that is said to be free

---

5. Steedly, *Hanging without a Rope*, is a good study on surviving Shamanism in North Sumatra.

6. Haire, *Character*, 256.

of any religious meaning—although everybody knows that once you break the *adat* a magic curse will come upon you while you sleep. This pattern is said to be found throughout the Indonesian Archipelago.

There is a widespread head-hunting myth in Indonesia. Anthropologically, this myth has to do with sacrifice, and the rumor usually is associated with kidnapping scares. Everybody believes that the head of a child is needed especially when construction of a bridge or school—also a church—is started. But once this rumor is explained, the actual concern and situation of the primal community is revealed. They must give away the "head"—that is, mind and concern—of their children to a new enterprise of the missionaries—that is, Christianity and modernity, while the body remains in its traditional form. The head is "cut off," and that is actually what happened to their primal communal life: the youth left the home village for an urban journey. This happened because the Christian schools taught them to do so. And yet their ancestor will someday free their children from the kidnapper by bringing back the head. In this way, life can be restored.[7]

Although what has been described constitutes theological issues, these are not necessarily free from harsh and tragic realities. In the colonial era when the Dutch Gereformeerd Mission flourished and established significant local Christian communities, a Javanese man called Kiai Sadrach (b. 1835) emerged and promoted a "contextual" Christianity.[8] He was seeking to perfect the spiritual welfare of his people; and at that time the religious climate was filled with a thirst for new spiritual symbols that would be capable of satisfying the inner cry for cosmological gnosis. After studying with local missionaries, Sadrach emerged as a spiritual "guru," a teacher for the soul and a mediator between the self and the divine. Sadrach's spiritual gift was in tune with the primal cry, and in the time of colonial oppression, he gave the Javanese the answer, or, in other words, the means to find one's secure place in the totality of life. His church was characterized by the primal communal solidarity of traditional society, using the *slametan*—that is, celebratory—social gathering and sharing as a way of *koinonia*.

An official investigator, Leon Cachet, came to investigate the Sadrach affair, and the Gereformeerd Church tried to purge Sadrach's community. In 1891, Sadrach had 6,374 followers in Central Java. The Dutch *zending*—that is, mission—replaced local "primal-Christianity" with "proper" religion, which was carried out by a new initiative: purification of the church of all

---

7. Some said that this is the reason why a primal millenarianism (messianism) was so rampant during the era of missionaries. Some even said this is a counter movement from dislocated primal communities and religions. For the Indonesian case, see Hirosue, "Prophets and Followers."

8. Partonadi, *Shadrach's Community*.

traces of Javanese culture. The mission was in a hurry to erect a strong, militant, and modern community that at the same time could counter the growing power of the Islamic anticolonial movement.[9] But this dream took an ironic turn: the remnant of Sadrach's flock that complied with the missionaries' program numbered only about 150 people.

Especially in a time of rapid change and the struggle for democracy that Indonesia is experiencing in the twenty-first century, this sort of "purified" Christian community faces a dangerous hurdle. The theological tools given to the church are inadequate to enable her to cope with the socioreligious conflict common in a pluralist developing country. Due to the way the missions promoted modernity, it is easier for Christian individuals than the wider population to embrace democracy. But the issue lies much deeper. The spread of democracy has encouraged the proliferation of communalism that, in turn, can coalesce with religious intolerance. Unfortunately, the Christian minority in Indonesia is losing its ties to the wider primal cultural web. This traditional cultural web provided mechanisms that could be used to integrate religious rivalry and to dissolve communalism. Given the present situation, it seems that Christianity has no alternative except to build strategic alliances with other religious groups since the culture is marked by primordialism.[10]

This can be seen clearly in the case of communal conflict and violence in the Moluccan Islands (Ambon), which started in 1999 and has resulted in some ten thousand casualties. Outsiders[11] stirred up Muslim-Christian civil strife, but this event also warns us of the ever-widening alienation between the Ambonese Muslims and Christians. And this has to do with the religious purification processes inside both communities, the one inspired by the universal Muslim brotherhood—motivated by the sentiment of being the majority in Indonesia—and the other by a well-established Protestant Moluccan Church. Some said that if the Moluccan *Nunusaku* primal religion were still present, no amount of provocation by outside forces would have succeeded in pitting the two groups against each other. Unfortunately, since *adat* ("customary law") has been nearly destroyed, it was easy for even a

---

9. See Sumartana, *Mission at the Crossroads*, 59–114.

10. Clifford Geertz's famous definition has influenced the semantics of Indonesian anthropologists: "By primordial loyalties is meant an attachment that stems from the subject's, not the observer's, sense of the 'givens' of social existence—speaking a particular language, following a particular religion, being born into a particular family, emerging out of a particular place; the basic facts of blood, speech, custom, faith, residence, history, physical appearance, and so on" (Geertz, "Primordial Loyalties," 7).

11. It was the combination of paramilitarism, local elites, and global enterprise that produced such a brutal civil strife in the Moluccas. For a complete report, see Salampessy and Husain, *Ketika Semerbak*.

slight provocation to stir up religious emotions.[12] Nunusaku religion unifies the Ambonese because they believe in a sacred mountain and one *Upa Lanite* ("Creator"). Since this primal religion has no structure, the people have a vehicle for a village alliance system (called *pela*) which links Muslim and Christian together. *Pela* is the brotherhood that spans religious differences, and it is also used for economic cooperation. In the recent reconciliation process, this *pela* is being renewed, and Christianity in the Moluccas is in a process of rethinking its identity in the context of this primal religiosity that has produced an important alliance system. To conclude, in the Moluccas as well as in other places, purification and dualism have led to a blind alley.

THE CONTRIBUTION OF PRIMAL RELIGION

The future of Christianity in these situations, however, will not be assured by the process of purification nor by a lasting dualism. It has been argued that the purification process in Indonesia will only incline the society toward a segregation process and stimulate fundamentalist tendencies in religion. As we have seen, communal strife flourished and cultural alliances broke up. My view, then, is from the converse perspective. Since a theological task is involved, this requires a kind of contextualization in which the primal aspect of local religiosity is reconciled and renewed through its encounter with the Christian faith. But this proposal will result in further complexities. We will use a case study to analyze this more carefully.

Something like a postcolonial text of Homi K. Bhabha[13] appeared in an area of Indonesia. Jaulung Wismar Saragih (1888–1968), a theologian of the Batak North Sumatra Church, became excited to translate the Bible. In his own expression, he translated the Bible with "my feeling, and although I don't know Greek nor Hebrew, I know the Batak-Simalungun language; and I think my translation is more correct than those of Western missionaries who know Greek and Hebrew but don't understand the feeling of my language."[14] His creativity focused on the translation of the name of God in

---

12. Dieter Bartels is the one who has this perspective; see his various notes about Moluccas-Ambon at Bartels, Nunusaku website.

13. Bhabha notes: "The native questions quite literally turn origin of the Book into an enigma. First: How can the word of God come from the flesh-eating mouth of the English?—a question that faces the unitary and universalist assumption of authority with the cultural difference of its historical moment of enunciation. And later: How can it be the European Book, when we believe it is God's gift to us?" *Location of Culture*, 102–3.

14. Saragih quoted in Swellengrebel, *In Leijdeckers*. Swellengrebel of the Dutch Bible Society named Jaulung Saragih as "een Simaloengeonse Luther," 165.

his own native language. He used the term *Naibata* for God. In this matter, we will see the summary of his critical contextualization of the gospel.

Naibata is a high god of Batak primal spirituality. Everyday life is carried out mostly with some specific deities, but they are nevertheless part of the family of Naibata. Naibata is the *arche* of human being, while the deities through their spirits bless the daily activities of humans.

Saragih chose Naibata for the biblical God while he rejected the deities as an aspect of Naibata. Here he made a rupture in the narrative of his primal religion. But the biblical God does not entirely dismiss the ingredients of primal religiosity in Naibata. He said that to become a Christian means "returning to the religion of our ancestors, to the religion of *Naibata!*" And for him, Naibata is a god who has liberated humans from the deities but at the same time is a god who can be understood rationally. However, Naibata "is also a part of our family, and we receive Him in the spirit of our *adat's* (customary law) hospitality; thus we know His Name that blesses us."[15]

For Jaulung Saragih to know "His Name" means especially to name his local social problems. And for him, the social problems primarily lie in the inability to name the reality through the people's own language. The Mission used another language—the language of conversion, the language of church institution and hierarchy, but also the language of another superior neighboring ethnic group, believing this to be the region's *lingua franca*. According to Saragih, "To use our language to translate God is the same as to use our language to name the realities."[16] Animated by this insight, he created a local Christian social movement. And based on this principle, he launched a larger movement of local ethnic dignity, trying to move his communities in the direction of liberation and autonomy. In the appropriation of Christianity, in which Saragih experienced his conversion, Bible translation and social engagement were at the same time a process of negotiating his primal world and life concerns.

This path of reconciling steps toward the primal spirituality has created a rich theological perspective. In this case, it is not only that the gospel transformed the primal cultural view but also that the primal culture has illuminated the gospel itself, both to the heart of the indigenous people and to their hand—i.e., a social movement of ethnic dignity. Indeed, this contextualization has promoted the vitality of the community for both resistance and identity formation.

However, this insight can produce other consequences; and if it is not tackled appropriately, it can grow into an "ethno-religious nationalism."

---

15. Ibid., 166.
16. Ibid.

In the case of Indonesia, Christianity has already received its seed, the *Volkskirche*.[17]

THE PRIMAL GEMEINSCHAFT

While theological dualism exists in the Church's religious life, sociologically we have here a quite bizarre social *gestalt* ("form") of Christianity: the *Volkskirchen* ("folk churches"). As we know, in Indonesia denominationalism disappeared, but ethnic churches flourished. Lothar Schreiner, a German scholar who lived in the Batak region for ten years, identified this bizarre form. First, he observed that the *traditio fidei* of the German Rhenish Missionary Society that established a mission in Sumatra in the nineteenth century was a salvation-conscious individualism, and the church was understood as a fellowship of reborn souls. But paradoxically, Schreiner observes that this German Pietist Mission also *doch verdeckt* ("stealthily") implanted a non-theological factor: a semi-mystical idea of the *Volk*, which had been associated with German national Protestantism.[18]

Here, church and Volk cannot be distinguished, and when the Volkskirche is established, it becomes a way to preserve a pre-modern primal way of life that is actually a part of the Romantic imagination. The German missionaries were working with this idea when they developed a *volkschristianisierung* method, where the ancient régime of the primal social structure was preserved and isolated from an open encounter with the new *Gesellschaft* ("society"). In the writings of the founder of German missiology, Gustav Warneck, we see some evidence of anti-modern thinking. Instead he promoted a regressive historical ideal of *Volk*—where Christianity is totally immersed.[19] This *gestalt* of the church in this very context of modern-global pluralism will appear as a conservative community; in other words, an ethnic-church and as an isolated primal *Gemeinschaft* ("community"). This sort of church is incompatible with the very idea of modern society, where plurality and conflicting ideas are openly recognized and accepted.

Dramatic events have been associated with this issue, for it has become a political issue[20] involving the biggest ethnic-church of Indonesia—the Hu-

17. The so-called (Batak) church movement for independence in Indonesia is colored by a regional-ethnic nationalism and not necessarily by an anticolonial movement. See Hutauruk, *Kemandirian Gereja*, 219.

18. See Schreiner, *Adat und Evangelium*, 286–87.

19. For a thorough analysis on *volkskirche*, see Ustorf, *Sailing on the Next Tide*, 18–29.

20. It is political since an international human rights institution made a complete report on this church. See Human Rights Watch/Asia, *Limits*, 88–108.

ria Kristen Batak Protestan (HKBP), or the Batak Church, that has around three million communicants. The incident started when a former head of the Indonesian Council of Churches, Dr. Nababan, was elected in 1987 as a Bishop in the HKBP. A social progressive, he asked the church to engage with broader social issues. He wanted to reshape this Volkskirche to take on more of a civil society form. But the traditionalists resisted this move since an open church at that time would collide with the authoritarian government of Indonesia. The traditionalist believed that the church should concern itself only with inner issues like *adat*, ordination, and other institutional formation matters. And the government was happy if the church remained a church of the Batak people—following the often-misunderstood theory of "two kingdoms"—by not concerning itself with critical social issues of the masses. The traditionalist wing then signed a pact with the authoritarian regime to expel Dr. Nababan. After ten years of conflict, with dozens of people being tortured and even developing a Civilian Militia, the HKBP realized that they were suffering from an incurable internal dissension. This Volkskirche remains passive, leading into a sort of cul-de-sac.

Yet we should not be blind to the process by which the *volkisch* mentality is extending itself into a broader and "ecumenical" sphere. The ongoing process of ethnic/primal-church in Indonesia nevertheless should also be scrutinized, especially in the context of their encounters with the various communities within the pluralist society. The focus will be on the possibilities of a new *gestalt* of Christianity, a *post*-ethnic church beyond Volkskirche. Only if this is the case can plurality give to Indonesian Christianity a beneficial input that could even enrich its life.

However, there is also promise of a new social form of Christianity in Indonesia that accepts the benefits of the pluralist society while still engaging creatively with elements of primal religion. A significant event occurred in 1962 when a large group from a *dusun* ("village") in central Java became Christian.[21] The culture of the *dusun*, however, is not in any sense truth-oriented, nor hierarchy-evoking. At its core is the Javanese primal sense of *abangan*. This involves the question of survival—not an abstract reflection but a concrete, everyday concern. Here we meet little preoccupation with "truth." The primacy of survival as a religious problem results in self-absorbing concern for one's own group. Nevertheless, everyday practice demands daily religious transcendence and also the art of "agreeing to differ."

The local church in Ngampel started in 1962 from a group of seven who searched for religious leadership. They set aside a year for this search.

---

21. From a report on Pradjarta's research by van Ufford and Nugroho, "Christians and Muslim," 12–23.

During this time they came into contact with mystics, Muslim *kiayis/mullah*, and a Catholic priest. They decided to join the Javanese Protestant Church, and it was in the *carik's* ("village secretary's") house where the faithful gathered every Sunday. The Christian congregation flourished.

After a few years, the question of a church building in Ngampel was raised. Some money could be received from Dutch churches, and the *carik* could possibly arrange "local initiatives" so the construction would be approved. Suddenly a problem appeared. The *carik* diverted the funds to another purpose: he built a school, and the entire *dusun*—Christians, Muslims, and Buddhists—went all out to contribute to the construction. A scandal of corruption began to spread. Soon the *carik* mobilized the entire village again, and a church was successfully constructed!

Gradually, the demarcation of Christian identity shifted. Relations between Christians and Muslims in the village took on a dynamism that involved a rather surprising turn: a number of youths from Christian homes had themselves circumcised. The pastor then visited the four families where a son had been circumcised. In each case, the pastor had a friendly chat with the family. He simply asked, "Have you been troubled by a rat plague in the rice field this season?" At no point did he discuss the matter of circumcision, but the congregation learned to accept the boundary—though not strictly enforced—that Christians do not practice circumcision.

This led to a remarkable event. During the Easter celebration, the church conducted a village ritual (*Pajatan*), and this ritual started by cleaning the village ancestors' graves.[22] This ritual was open and villagers from different religions joined in the meal. During the ritual, they also discussed and negotiated their political preference in anticipation of a national election in 2009. And yet in this Easter Pajatan ritual, the local cultural base of harmony was preserved. It is noteworthy that this was initiated by the church. This may be a sign of a Christian movement to form a new *koinonia*—an ecumenical expression that moves beyond the church's boundary. Here the church is becoming an open community, not the self-centered *gestalt* of a Volkskirche. It is important to recognize that this process exists because of the underlying local primal religiosity.

BIBLIOGRAPHY

Bartels, Dieter. Nunusaku website, 2010. http://nunusaku.com/research.htm.
Bhabha, Homi K. *The Location of Culture*. London: Routledge, 1994.

---

22. See report on this event by Nugroho and Kana, "Easter Pajatan Celebration," 163–69.

Geertz, Clifford. "Primordial Loyalties and Standing Ethnicities: Anthropological Reflections on the Politics of Identity." Collegium Budapest, Public Lecture 7 (April 1994).

Haire, James. *The Character and Theological Struggle of the Church in Halmahera, Indonesia, 1941–1979*. Frankfurt am Main: Lang, 1981.

Hirosue, Masahi. "Prophets and Followers in Batak: Millenarian Responses to the Colonial Order; Parmalim, Na Siak Bagi and Parhudamdam, 1890–1930." PhD diss., Australian National University, Canberra, 1988.

Human Rights Watch/Asia. *The Limits of Openness*. New York: Humans Right Watch, 1994.

Hutauruk, Jubil Raplan. *Kemandirian Gereja: Penelitian histories-sistematis tentang Gerakan Kemandirian Gereja di Sumatra Utara dalam Kancah Pergolakan Kolonialisme dan Gerakan Kebangsaan di Indonesia, 1899–1942*. Jakarta: BPK Gunung Mulia, 1992.

Nugroho, Singgih, and Nico L. Kana. "The Easter *Pajatan* Celebration: Identity Differences and Efforts to Restore Harmony." In *The Development of Religion/The Religion of Development: Liber Amicorum for Philip Quarles van Ufford*, edited by Ananta Kumar Giri et al., 163–69. Delft: Uitgeverij Eburon, 2004.

Partonadi, Sutarman Soediman. *Sadrach's Community and Its Contextual Roots: A Nineteenth Century Javanese Expression of Christianity*. Atlanta, GA: Rodopi, 1990.

Salampessy, Zairin, and Thamrin Husain, eds. *Ketika Semerbak Cengkih Tergusar Asap Mesiu: Tragedi Kemanusiaan Maluku di Balik konspirasi Militer, Kapitalis Birokrat dan Kepentingan Elit Politik*. Jakarta: Tapak Ambon, 2001.

Schrauwers, Albert. *Colonial "Reformation" in the Highlands of Central Sulawesi, 1892–1995*. Toronto: University of Toronto Press, 2000.

Schreiner, Lothar. *Adat und Evangelium. Zur bedeutung der altvoelkischen Lebensordungen fuer Kirche und Mission unter de Batak in Nordsumatra*. Gütersloh: Gütterslocher Verlagshaus, 1972.

Steedly, Mary Margaret. *Hanging without a Rope: Narrative Experience in Colonial and Postcolonial Karoland*. Princeton: Princeton University Press, 1993.

Sumartana, Th. *Mission at the Crossroads: Indigenous Churches, European Missionaries, Islamic Association and Socio-religious Change in Java, 1812–1936*. Jakarta: BPK Gunung Mulia, 1993.

Swellengrebel, J. L. *In Leijdeckers voetspoor: Anderhalve eeuw Bijbelvertaling en taalkunde in de Indonesische talen*. 's-Gravenhage: Martinus Nijhoff, 1978.

Ustorf, Werner. *Sailing on the Next Tide: Missions, Missiology, and the Third Reich*. Frankfurt am Main: Lang, 2000.

van Klinken, Gerry. *Minorities, Modernity and the Emerging Nation: Christians in Indonesia; A Biographical Approach*. Leiden: KITLV, 2003.

van Ufford, Philip Quarels, and Singgih Nugroho. "Christians and Muslims Live in Nothing but Harmony Here: Religion and Politics in a Javanese Village." *Renai* 3–4 (2002) 12–23.

Wessels, Anton. *Europe: Was it Ever Really Christian? The Interaction between Gospel and Culture*. London: SCM, 1994.

Chapter 10

Muslim Responses to Plurality in the Last 100 Years

J. Dudley Woodberry

THE FLAG OF THE Egyptian Independence Movement in the early twentieth century displayed a cross within a crescent, representing Muslims and Christians working together to get rid of their colonial masters. These foreigners, in turn, displayed a flag comprised of three overlapping crosses—those of St. George, St. Andrew, and St. Patrick—and a royal arms seal with a crown and the words *Dieu et mon Droit*—used by kings for their divine right to rule, a "Lion Rampant" ready to fight, and a unicorn—variously interpreted as reflecting pagan origins or being a sign of the incarnation. These symbols express divergent forces whose interaction determined the course of Muslim relations with the West, other faith communities, and Christians in particular.

Although the cross in the crescent on the flag of the Egyptian Independence Movement of 1919 was meant to represent Muslims and Christians working together, those represented by the cross have often felt that the crescent was clamping down on them like great jaws, while those represented by the crescent have often felt that those of the cross are an alien irritant in their throats. The crosses on the Union Jack often conveyed Crusader banners more than the sacrifice of Christ. The French motto for the divine right of kings to rule was a direct challenge to the Qur'anic, "Obey God and the Apostle" (3:132). The lion was in the posture indicating readiness to attack, rather than to lie down with the lamb. And the unicorn expresses the ambiguity of the Western culture that brought both missionaries, who sought to reflect the incarnation, and education, which facilitated secularization.

In this study, we shall first identify some Islamic and cultural roots of recent divergent opinions on plurality, and second, look at the historical contexts of the last one hundred years that facilitated the divergence. Third, we shall note representative examples of the spectrum of Muslim opinions on plurality, and fourth, official Muslim statements on freedom of religion. Fifth, we shall compare the attitudes that Muslims express concerning democracy and human rights, with the actual extent of freedom of religion and persecution in their countries. Then, after looking at the implications of the "Arab Spring"—which has moved on to the storms of the winter—we shall draw some conclusions.

Since some Muslims and non-Muslims claim categorically that Islam either is or is not compatible with pluralistic contexts, we need to raise two preliminary questions. Is Islam singular or plural; that is, is there an essential Islam or are there many "islams"? And, if there is an essential content in Islam, must it include the Law (*Sharia*) as developed in the early years of the community, or might it be a cluster of beliefs, practices, and values? To both of these questions, scholars from the secular academy give different answers, as do Muslims themselves. The traditional position of scholars in the field of Islamic studies holds that there is an essential Islam based on the literary tradition of the Qur'an, the canonical traditions (Sunna) of Muhammad, and the early companions (*salaf*) and law (*Sharia* and *fiqh*) as developed in the orthodox schools. Social scientists, such as anthropologists, in turn have tended to think of "islams" that represent the different views of people who claim to be Muslim. Among Muslim conservatives at one end of the spectrum would be "essentialists." Liberals on the other end would allow far more variety, though they would hold to certain Islamic values.[1]

ISLAMIC AND CULTURAL ROOTS OF DIVERGENT OPINIONS

To deal with the question of Muslims' attitudes toward living with those of other beliefs, we need to start with their roots in their sacred scripture and culture. It is possible to draw divergent opinions from the Qur'an, even on such basic issues as whether Christians and Jews are required to convert

---

1. See Rippin, *Defining Islam*.

to Islam for salvation and to attain paradise. Certain verses indicate that they, along with the hard-to-identify Sabians, have nothing to fear if they believe in God and the last day and do good (Qur'an 2:62; 5:69). One verse also includes the Magians (Zoroastrians) (22:17). Other verses indicate that these "People of the Book" are comprised of both those of faith who do good works and transgressors (3:110–15) and, thus, imply that some will be saved but not others. Finally, there is a verse frequently used to deny salvation to anyone who is not a Muslim, but it can also be understood in a less exclusivist sense: "Whoever desires a *din* [religion or profession] other than *islam* ['Islam' as a religion or 'submission' as an act] it will not be accepted of him, and in the hereafter he will be among the losers." Since there are not capital letters in Arabic, and the faith of Muslims in the Qur'an is at times associated with the faith of Christians (2:62; 5:111) and at other times not (2:190–193), exegetes draw different conclusions.

The different perspectives in the Qur'an are traditionally explained by the different periods in the Prophet's life. From 610–622 CE, he was preaching from a position of political weakness against the dominant Quraysh, although according to some authorities such as the eminent traditionist al-Tabari (873–971), Muhammad briefly sought accommodation with the pagans by including the "Satanic verses" in the Qur'anic recitation that gave some recognition to certain idols considered to be daughters of Allah.[2] During the first two to three years in Medina, as the Muslim community was gradually building strength, the community made attempts at accommodation with the Jews by adopting certain Jewish practices such as praying toward Jerusalem and fasting on *ashura*, which corresponded with the Jewish Day of Atonememt. After Muhammad's break with the Jews at the end of this period, the direction of prayer was changed toward Mecca and the obligatory fast to the month of Ramadan.

Qur'anic commentary (*tafsir*), traditions concerning Muhammad (*hadith*), and jurisprudence (*fiqh*) likewise render divergent opinions. Surah 2:62 of the Qur'an—which describes rewards and no fear for Jews, Christians, and Sabians who believe in God and the Last Day and do good works—is restricted to those who follow Muhammad and Islam by some of the works.[3] A little-known tradition that Jews and Christians belonged to the community of Muhammad is then strongly rejected.[4]

Whereas the Qur'an leaves punishment for apostasy until after death (47:25–28), the jurists range from demanding immediate executions to

2. al-Tabari quoted in M. J. De Goeje, *Ta'rikh al-rusul*, 29.
3. al-Tabari, *Commentary on the Qur'an*, 363–64.
4. Friedmann, *Tolerance and Coercion*, 32.

giving apostates forever to repent.[5] With respect to relations with non-Muslims, attitudes toward People of the Book became more rigorous while attitudes toward Zoroastrians became more tolerant as Muslims had to govern a large population of the latter in Persia. Nevertheless, in the Arabian Peninsula, where Muslims were the majority, attitudes toward pagans remained rigorous.[6] Yet in the medieval period, Muslim rulers were often more tolerant of Jews and Christians than Christian rulers were of Jews and Muslims.

There are cultural values as well as Islamic ones that influence the way Muslim peoples think about others. Ibn Khaldun (1332–1406) in his *Muqaddimah*[7] emphasized the concept of *'asabiya* (solidarity of the group) that is still applicable today. It is a bond based on such things as clan, ethnicity, and religion that firmly binds "insiders" together in contradistinction to the "other." The extent of the boundaries of the "insiders" is sometimes determined by who "the enemy" is. While a student in Beirut, I learned an Arab proverb: "Me against my brother; my brother and I against the non-relative." Likewise, when the Soviets invaded Afghanistan in 1979, the mujahideen groups—with contrasting ethnic and sectarian roots—fought alongside each other against the common enemy. After the Soviets were expelled in 1989, the holy war against the atheistic invaders became a civil war between the groups. As we shall see, when colonial powers drew the boundaries of future states dividing ethnic and religious groups from others of their "insiders" and forced them to live and ultimately develop governments with "outsiders," the roots of present national problems were inherent.

In Chapter 4 of this volume, Lamin Sanneh reviews Muslim and Christian interaction in history.[8] Here, we turn to the contexts in which Muslim views were formed in the modern period.

CONTEXT OF THE LAST ONE HUNDRED YEARS

The various contexts of Muslims in the twentieth century increased the diversity of their views with respect to living with those holding different beliefs. Early in the century, following World War I and the fall of the Ottoman Empire, much of the Muslim world was, or came under, colonial control or "protectorates" administered by European governments. The result was that Western systems of education and law were added to or superimposed upon

---

5. Ibid., 126–29; Bukhari, *Sahih*, IX, 42–43.
6. Friedmann, *Tolerance and Coercion*, 198–99.
7. See multiple index entries for "group feeling" in Khaldun, *Muqaddimah*, 3 vols.
8. See ch. 4 in this book, "Diversity and the Challenge of Difference."

Muslim and ethnic education, law, and traditional practices. As noted, the boundaries between emerging or future countries were drawn by European powers that, for example, divided Kurds between emerging Arab and Turkish countries without giving them a state of their own; and they divided Pashtuns between Afghanistan and the northern part of India that would ultimately become part of Pakistan. Turkey, however, was proclaimed a republic in 1923 and under Ataturk became a secular nation state—a status it maintained throughout the century. In fact, when I was privileged in 2004 to take part in a dialogue with the theological faculty of Samsun University in the city where Ataturk started the revolution, every Turkish dignitary, from the Minister of Religious Affairs to the dean of the theological faculty, affirmed the official secularity in their remarks.[9] However, the next year the Justice and Development Party with Islamist roots won the national elections and remains in power at the time of this writing.

Following World War II, most of the Muslim countries that had not received independence earlier became independent states. Now they needed to develop national identities with their diverse peoples and exposure to diverse religions and secular education and laws. One of the attempts to forge a nation based on ethno-linguistic identity was led by Gamal Abdul Nasser's Arab Socialist United Arab Republic in the late 1950s. But most of the Christian Lebanese students with whom my wife-to-be and I were studying at the time opposed it because they believed that the greater percentage of Muslims in it would reduce the rights they as Christians enjoyed in Lebanon. This was despite the fact that the earlier "Arab Awakening" received considerable impetus from Christians and the Syrian Protestant College (now the American University of Beirut).[10]

A few years later, in conjunction with my doctoral research, I was able to meet with leaders in Cairo of the then-underground Islamist Muslim Brotherhood, which was contending with the more secular movements, and feel their passion for a government based on Islam. Subsequently, in 1980 they were able to get Anwar Saddat, Nasser's secular successor, to hold a plebiscite which led to *Sharia* being adopted in Egypt as "the major source of legislation," though in reality it was not. After Sadat's assassination, another former general—Hosni Mubarak—carried on the more secular government of the roughly 90 percent Muslim and 10 percent Christian population.

Then in December of 2010, the "Arab Spring" started in Tunisia and swept through the Arab countries with its promise of greater democratic freedom as Arab strongmen were forced out. Egypt illustrates both the

---

9. See Woodberry et al., *Muslim and Christian Reflections on Peace*.
10. See Antonius, *Arab Awakening*.

general promise for human rights and its failure. Mubarak resigned February 11, 2011. Although Christians had joined Muslims in the hope of greater democratic freedom, by October they were protesting the destruction of a church and lack of protection for them. In subsequent elections, Mohammed Morsi of the Islamist Muslim Brotherhood won by a slight margin and was declared President in June 2012, but he gave himself power to legislate without judicial oversight, which led to a return to mass demonstrations. In July of 2013, Morsi was deposed by a coup. Former general Abdel Fattah el-Sisi was elected president in May of 2014, and the Muslim Brotherhood's Freedom and Justice Party was banned. Most Christians welcomed the return to the protection of a former general.

What has been described as the "Arab Winter" refers to the aftermath of the overthrow of strongmen, which morphed into ethnic and religious strife such as the Iraq insurgency and the Syrian Civil War. In the latter, the war that had deposed Saddam Hussein and his Sunni minority, and the subsequent American troop withdrawal, led to Shiite control and retaliation against the Sunni minority. In Syria fighting broke out between the Sunni majority and President Bashar al-Assad's minority Alawites (a Shiite sect). Since Assad protected the Christians and used them in government, many Syrian Christians supported him.

The turmoil in Iraq and Syria provided the opportunity for the Islamic State (ISIS) to conquer large areas of both countries and reestablish a caliphate with Abu Bakr al-Baghdadi as Caliph. ISIS has freely killed and enslaved non-Muslims, including beheading about twenty-one Egyptian Christians working in Libya. A video portraying them as "on the south of Rome on the land of Islam" refers to an expected apocalyptic event when the Caliph's army will defeat the forces of Rome. Moderate Muslims from Egypt to the United States are decrying this as a perversion of Islam. The Prime Minister of Egypt went to the village from which most of the Christians came and sat on the floor with their poor relatives to express the widespread empathy with them.

A few personal examples will illustrate the differing perspectives on plurality that have been evident around the Muslim world in the last half century. When, in 1976, I was privileged to go with my family as the first resident pastor to serve in Riyadh, Saudi Arabia, the government forbade Muslims to attend services.

Iran, with its Shiite majority, has had churches for centuries. Their Islamist movement came on the world stage in 1977–79 with the Khomeini Revolution against the modernist Shah. A government was established that adopted the "Governance of the Jurisconsult" (*vilayat-i faqih*), which gave ultimate authority over the administration and implementation of the divine law (Sharia) to the Chief Ayatollah and his advisors. Thus, even when citizens have elected a more liberal and moderate president such as the current Hassan Rouhani, the Judiciary and the Republican Guard answer to the Chief Ayatollah.

In 2014, the Iranian Foreign Minister invited ten of us from Academics for Peace to meet with government, academic, and religious leaders in Iran. We were taken to an Armenian Orthodox Church at the end of a Sunday worship service to show us that ethnic Christians, like Armenians and Assyrians, were allowed to worship freely. Protestants, however, faced more problems, and converts from Islam were not allowed to attend the recognized churches. With the religious leaders who were our hosts that day, we raised the case of Saeed Abedini, an Iranian-American convert who was jailed for helping to plant many house churches. They indicated that they lacked the authority to release him but that "it could be worked on."

In 1970, our family was living in Pakistan when the secular Zulfikar Ali Bhutto came to power on a platform of Islamic socialism. However, under pressure from the Islamist Jamait-i-Islami party, he had to add an Islamist agenda. What has been more disturbing is the Apostasy Law, which is meant to apply to the denigrating of God and is extended to include Muhammad but is sometimes used unjustly against Christians. Even if those who are wrongly accused are released from prison, they are sometimes killed on the street.

A much more restrictive form of Islamism was found in Afghanistan, where my family and I first moved in 1973 to pastor a church in Kabul. We were greeted with the announcement that a visiting Scandinavian family had been arrested for distributing four Gospels of Luke in the bazaar. In a subsequent court case, nothing from the Quran could be found against the Bible, so the family was just expelled. Years later, after the Taliban had taken over much of the country, they searched the guest home where my wife and I were staying, looking for Persian Bibles. Finding none, they then asked me to frisk them, so that we did not think they had stolen anything from us. They said they "did not want to lose their good name"—hence, viewing what they were doing as a moral task. When we returned to Kabul after the Taliban had been driven out, we found my old Bible with a bullet hole in it, indicating disrespect for the Jewish and Christian scriptures, even though the Quran recognizes the Torah, Psalms, and Gospel as being from God.

Three major trends in Islam—along with many subtrends—have been evident during the past one hundred years. Any of them can be peaceful or militant. First are the *adaptionists*, who have adapted their faith to new ideas with the result that they have become modernist, and in some cases, secular Muslims. Modernists have advocated against theocratic government and for democracy, the rights of women, freedom of thought, and freedom of religion. They want the door for individual interpretation (*ijtihad*) of the scriptural sources to be left open for Islam to continue to adapt to changing circumstances. There is a wealth of such modernist literature coming out today.[11]

Second are the *conservatives*, who have held to classical Islam as it developed during its first three hundred years when the major schools of law and theology were formed; they have wanted to keep the door to additional interpretation of the primary Islamic sources closed. However, these *ulama*—traditionally trained religious scholars—are subtly adapting the interpretation and application of *Sharia* to contemporary agendas.[12]

Finally, there are the *fundamentalistic reformers*, who want to return to the primary sources of the Qur'an and the Practice (Sunnah) of the Prophet and the early Muslim community (*salaf*) to meet present challenges, unbound by the interpretations of previous generations of Muslims, hence referred to as *salafis*.

Needless to say, the demarcation between these groups is not always clear. The Islamists (who emphasize that Islam is a religious and political system),[13] to the extent that they try to rely exclusively on the Qur'an and Sunnah, are drawn from fundamentalistic reformers; and to the extent that they emphasize *Sharia* and its development in classical Islam, are drawn from the conservatives.

Having looked at the multiple contexts that facilitate diversity of opinion, we turn to representative voices of these perspectives.

DIFFERING PERSPECTIVES ON PLURALITY

Given the divergent materials in the history of Islam, scholars have had plenty to draw on to support different perspectives. Some non-Muslim

---

11. See Kurzman, *Liberal Islam*; Mehran Kamrava, *New Voices of Islam*.
12. See Zaman, *Ulama in Contemporary Islam*.
13. See Euben and Zaman, *Readings in Islamist Thought*.

works have stressed the tolerance of Islam,[14] others its intolerance.[15] Many studies make generalizations about Islam's tolerance from very few examples.[16] On the one hand, the Turkish modernist Mahmud Aydin asserts that religious pluralism provides an opportunity to build peace, and argues against people who have exclusivist views.[17] On the other hand, Abu-l-'Ala Mawdudi (d. 1979), the late leader of the Pakistani Jamaat-i-Islami, said: "An Islamic state must, in all respects be formed on the law laid down by God through His Prophet."[18] And the late Egyptian theoretician of the Muslim Brotherhood, Sayyid Qutb (d. 1966), held a common position that because Islam includes all the true religions that came before it, it should be accepted by all peoples.[19]

However, since most negative responses to religious plurality tend to follow similar patterns of reasoning, we shall focus on more tolerant views. Mahmoud Mohamed Taha (1910–85) founded the Republican Brothers in Sudan and argued that the earlier Meccan passages of the Qur'an can abrogate later Medinan ones because they give the primary message rather than a later transitional one of the Prophet. The Meccan passages are often more tolerant and pluralistic when the Muslims had a minority status. These include such passages as 109:6, "To you your religion and to me mine;" and 2:62, "Surely they that believe and those of the Jews and Christians and the Sabians, who believe in God and the Last Day and work righteousness, their wages await them with their Lord and no fear shall be to them."[20] His reversal of the normal order for the abrogation of verses and his opposition to the Sudanese government policies led to his execution.

Others who did not reverse the order of abrogation also stressed toleration in Islam. Muhammad 'Abduh (d. 1905) and Rashid Rida (d. 1935) in their influential writings in *al-Manar* early in the century stressed Surah 2:256 ("There is no compulsion in religion") to plead their case for toleration in Islam.[21] Likewise, the eminent Shiite commentator Muhammad Husayn al-Tabataba'i (d. 1982) argued against the abrogation of Surah 2:62 (promising salvation to Jews, Christians, and Sabians who believe and do good

---

14. E.g., Arnold, *Preaching of Islam*.
15. E.g., Zwemer, *Law of Apostasy*; Spencer, *Myth of Islamic Tolerance*.
16. E.g., Issa J. Boullata, "Qur'anic Principle of Interfaith Relations," 43–53.
17. Aydin, "Religious Pluralism," 89–101.
18. Mawdudi, "Political Theory of Islam," 253.
19. Qutb, *Fi Zilal al-Qur'an*, I, 625–27; Sachedina, *Islamic Roots of Democratic Pluralism*, 39–40.
20. Taha, "Second Message of Islam," 270–83.
21. Jomier, *Commentair Coranique du Manar*, 282.

works) on the basis of Surah 6:88 ("God has promised those of them who believe and do good works, forgiveness and a great reward").[22] Abdulaziz Sachedina, Professor of Islamic Studies at the University of Virginia, in two significant studies lays great stress on verses such as Surah 5:48, which he says indicates that those of various faiths should work together toward justice and peace: "For every one of you [Jews, Christians, Muslims], we have appointed a path and a way. If God had willed He would have made you one community but . . . [He has not done so in order that] He may try you in what has come to you. So compete with one another in good works."[23] Lewis E. Winkler has found enough harmony in the views of Sachedina and the Christian theologian Wolfhart Pannenberg to suggest a potential bridge for cordial interaction over the troubled waters that have often divided us.[24]

It should be noted with reference to the verses cited by the above Muslim authors that although the Qur'an is the primary source for Islamic belief, some later Muslims have interpreted some of the verses in a variety of ways. Others claim they are abrogated by later revelation. And some have restricted the clear teaching of rewards for Jews, Christians, and Sabians who believe and do good works, to those who also accept Muhammad and Islam.[25]

It is beyond the scope of this essay to show the variety of ways that Muslims have adapted to pluralistic situations around the world. However, Osman bin Baker from Malaysia, who taught recently at Georgetown University, has pointed out how Muslims in Indonesia, for example, have expanded the Quranic category of People of the Book to include more people in this category of protected people.[26] The inclusion of the somewhat ambiguous Sabians in this category in the Qur'an (2:62; 5:69) facilitated this. Precedent for this might also be found in the inclusion of Zoroastrians into the protected category of *dhimmis* by a prophetic *hadith* in the first century of Islam, which subsequently in administration was broadened to include idol-worshiping Hindus.[27] This certainly did not make them equal to Muslims but did grant them an accepted place in the political system.

22. Tabataba'I, *Al-Mizan fi tafsir al-Qur'an*, quoted in Sachedina, *Islamic Roots* I, 193.

23 Sachedina, *Qur'an on Religious Pluralism*, 24–25. See also his more extensive *Islamic Roots* cited above.

24. See Winkler, *Contemporary Muslim and Christian Responses*.

25. See Friedmann, *Tolerance and Coercion*, 20–23, 24, 195.

26. Baker, "Pluralism and People of the Book," 99–112.

27. Friedmann, *Tolerance and Coercion*, 84–85. For a contemporary Muslim understanding of a normative religious and ethical pluralism, see Hassan, "Quranic Perspective on Religious Pluralism," 91–101.

Having looked at representative Muslim perspectives on plurality, we turn now to some major documents on Freedom of Religion.

PERSPECTIVES ON FREEDOM OF RELIGION IN DOCUMENTS

The International Bill of Human Rights treats freedom of religion as an unqualified right, and Muslim nations sign it when they join the United Nations. Muslim objections were raised in 1948 during deliberations on article 18, which states: "Everyone has the right of freedom of thought, conscience and religion; this right includes freedom to change his religion or belief, and freedom, either alone or in community with others in public or in private, to manifest his religion or belief in teaching, practice, worship and observance." A number of Muslim countries, Saudi Arabia in particular, tried to delete this. This debate and a subsequent one over its elaboration in the UN Resolution on the Elimination of Intolerance Based on Religion is discussed in David Little, John Kelsay, and Abdulaziz Sachedina, *Human Rights and the Conflict of Culture: Western and Islamic Perspectives on Religious Liberty*.[28]

In 1981, an alternative Universal Declaration of Human Rights was drawn up by representatives from Egypt, Pakistan, Saudi Arabia, and other countries under the auspices of the Islamic Council based in London and affiliated with the Muslim World League, an international, nongovernmental organization with headquarters in Saudi Arabia. The English version, at least superficially, seems close to the Universal Declaration of Human Rights, but it differs from the Arabic version. Also in 1993, the Cairo Declaration on Human Rights in Islam was presented at the World Conference on Human Rights in Vienna by the Saudi foreign minister. It had previously been presented to the United Nations by the Organization of the Islamic Conference.

The major areas of tension were three. The first focused on assumptions about human rights. Traditional Islam has said that human obligations are based on God's laws, whereas the UN held that religion is a matter of personal choice and implies values based on secularism.[29] Second, the UN made no distinction between people, but traditional Islam made distinctions based on religion and sex.[30] Third, the UN endorsed freedom of thought and conscience. Article 18 of the Universal Declaration of Human

---

28. Little et al., *Human Rights and Conflict of Culture*, 3–12, 101–5.
29. See Mayer, *Islam and Human Rights*, 52–53, 76–78.
30. Ibid., 89–94.

Rights includes for everyone "freedom to change his religion or belief."[31] But traditional Muslims held that "Islamic Law does not allow a Muslim to change his religion."[32] With reference to apostasy from Islam there is a spectrum of Muslim opinions. Although Abu'l A'la Mawdudi, the late founder of the Islamist Jamaat-i Islami, did not state his support for killing apostates in his pamphlet on human rights, he did support it in a Pakistan court in 1954.[33] On the other hand, liberal Muslims such as Mohamed Talbi and Subhi Mahmassani argue strongly against it, indicating that it is not warranted by the Qur'an, is contrary to the Qur'anic statement that "there is no compulsion in religion," and where found in the *hadith*, it refers to treason and sedition.[34]

We have noted the divergence of Muslim perspectives. We now turn to the divergence of Muslim attitudes and actions as found in two global studies.

TENSION BETWEEN ATTITUDES AND ACTIONS: TWO SURVEYS

In the last decade, two surveys were conducted that highlight the contrast between what a majority of Muslims say is their perspective on human rights and democracy in pluralistic contexts, and the exercise of these in their countries. They do not have identical foci, but they overlap sufficiently to show the contrast.

With respect to attitudes, the Gallup Poll of the Muslim World surveyed a sample representing more than 90 percent of the 1.3 billion Muslims in the world. John L. Espisoto and Dalia Mogahed in *Who Speaks for Islam? What a Billion Muslims Really Think*,[35] report on the findings in chapters titled: "Democracy or Theocracy?," "What Do Women Want?," and "Clash or Coexistence?"

With respect to actual actions, Brian J. Grim and Roger Finke, in turn, focus on actual religious freedom and persecution in *The Price of Freedom Denied: Religious Persecution and Conflict in the Twenty-First Century*. Using the databases of the Religious Data Archives and the International

---

31. Ibid., 149–50.
32. al-Marzouqi, *Human Rights and Islamic Law*, 437.
33. Mayer, *Islam*, 163, n. 39.
34. Ibid., 157–58.
35. Esposito and Mogahed, *Who Speaks?* Another survey with a smaller sample but similar results is Ahmed, *Journey into Islam*.

Religious Freedom Reports by the US State Department, they devote major attention to Muslim majority countries.

The overlap in the surveys allows us to contrast attitudes and practices with respect to governance in pluralistic contexts, the compatibility of Muslim and Western civilizations, and some human rights. The Gallup Poll indicated that[36] what Muslims most admired about the West was its technology and democracy, yet when they have exercised this democracy in recent years it has often included some form of *Sharia*. In Nigeria, seven out of ten say *Sharia* should be, at least, a source of legislation, while one in five say that it should be the only source—the same ratio as those who do not want it to be the source of legislation at all.[37] However, they have no uniform understanding of what that *Sharia* means.

A majority of Muslims in all countries surveyed—95 percent in Burkino Faso, 94 percent in Egypt, 93 percent in Iran, 99 percent in Indonesia—said that if they were drafting a constitution they would include freedom of speech, and a majority also want democracy to include religious values. In only a few countries did a majority say that *Sharia* should not have any role in society. However, in most countries only a small portion of those surveyed want it to be the only source of legislation. By contrast, in Jordan, Egypt, Pakistan, Afghanistan, and Bangladesh, a majority want Sharia as the "only source" of law. And male and female attitudes were very similar.[38] There were a variety of understandings of what *Sharia* means. These ranged from those who thought it includes the law as it developed in the various Sunni and Shiite schools through the classical periods, to those who felt it only meant the rejection of any legislation contrary to Quranic values.

Muslim scholars have found various historical concepts and practices to support democracy. These include *ijtihad*—independent, informed decisions based on Islamic sources. Whereas conservative Muslims have said that the "door of *ijtihad*" was closed at the end of the classical period—the first three hundred years of Islam—both liberals and fundamentalist reformers have called for the opening of the "door of *ijtihad*" for new interpretations of Islamic sources. Another classical practice used to support democracy is *shura* (consultations) practiced by the leaders of tribes and enjoined on Muhammad (Qur'an 3:159). *Ijma* (consensus of leaders or the community) approved as a source of legal decisions in three of the four Sunni schools of law, is also considered a democratic precedent.

---

36. Esposito and Mogahed, *Who Speaks for Islam?*, xii.
37. Ibid., 36.
38. Ibid., 48.

Most Muslims do not want a theocracy or a secular democracy but rather a democracy that includes religious values. Although a majority of Muslim men and women surveyed support *Sharia* as a source of legislation, they do not want religious leaders drafting their laws.[39]

Women's rights are the only human rights other than democracy that receive extensive treatment in the Esposito and Mogahed account of the Gallup Poll. According to the survey's findings, the majority of Muslims in most countries believe that women should have the same legal rights as men—85 percent in Iran; approximately 90 percent in Indonesia, Bangladesh, Turkey, and Lebanon; 77 percent in Pakistan; and 61 percent in Saudi Arabia—and that they should have the right to vote without influence from family—80 percent in Indonesia, 89 percent in Iran, 67 percent in Pakistan, 90 percent in Bangladesh, 93 percent in Turkey, 56 percent in Saudi Arabia, and 76 percent in Jordan. They also believe that women should have the right to hold a job for which they are qualified outside of the home—90 percent in Malaysia, Mauritania, and Lebanon, 85 percent in Egypt, 86 percent in Turkey, 82 percent in Morocco, 79 percent in Iran, 75 percent in Bangladesh, 69 percent in Saudi Arabia, 62 percent in Pakistan, and 61 percent in Jordan. Lastly, majorities in most countries—with the exceptions of Saudi Arabia (40 percent) and Egypt (50 percent)—said that women had the right to hold leadership at cabinet and national council levels.[40]

Whereas Muslim women wanted gender parity, they wanted it on their own terms and in their cultural context. They wanted equal rights but not Western values.[41] In Iraq, 58 percent of women were against the separation of religious and political power, and 81 percent said that religious authorities should take part in developing family law. A majority of women in most countries believe that *Sharia* should be a source of legislation.[42] The most successful way of challenging practices done in the name of *Sharia*—such as rape laws that can lead to the killing of the victim and the freeing of the perpetrator—has been to argue that they are against Islamic principles.[43] Many Muslims contend that women in *Sharia* have "complementary rights" rather than equal rights. They do not, for example, get an equal share of inheritance, because they do not have the same financial responsibilities as men do.[44]

39. Ibid., 63.
40. Ibid., 51–52.
41. Ibid., 107–8.
42. Ibid., 113–14.
43. Ibid., 116–17.
44. Ibid., 119.

The second world survey focuses on the actions of Muslim states—what religious freedoms are granted in their constitutions, and the extent and degree of religious persecution in these states. Grim and Finke describe the broad extent of religious persecution and denial of religious freedoms around the world today.[45] They argue that attempts to control religion by supporting a single one, or restricting religions or sects that are believed to be dangerous, leads to violent religious persecution. Building on views expressed historically by Voltaire, Adam Smith, and David Hume, they document their case by reports of religious freedom and persecution compiled by the Association of Religion Data Archives (ARDA), the annual International Religious Freedom Reports of the US State Department, and case studies.[46]

The restricting of religions or sects can be by governments or social movements that work with or against governments.[47] When one religious group has a monopoly of power so that it can restrict other religious groups, the temptation is to persecute competitors. When the state gives all religious groups identical privileges, none of them can claim state authority.[48] The data indicate that 33 percent of countries dominated by one religion have high levels of persecution in contrast to only 20 percent of countries where no religion dominates.[49] Although religious persecution is found in all regions, it is most severe in the Middle East and South Asia. In some cases, religious, ethnic, and regional ties are involved. In other cases, they are primarily religious. But on average, the number of cases is greater in Muslim countries or ones where a religion other than Christianity predominates. In fact, the rates of reported persecutions are more than twice as high in Muslim-majority countries than in Christian-majority counties or ones where no single religion includes more than 50 percent of the population.[50]

To explain why the levels of religious freedom are so low and the levels of violent religious persecution are so high, they propose that it is largely the result of religious social movements that challenge the state and restrict religious freedoms. They see these as attempts to revive and reclaim societies and lands that have been under Islamic rule. However, in contrast to Samuel Huntington's "Clash of Civilizations" thesis, they see the clashes

---

45. Grim and Finke, *Price of Freedom Denied*, 160.
46. Ibid., 3–6.
47. Ibid., 212–13.
48. Ibid., 8.
49. Ibid., 67.
50. Ibid., 18–22.

within Islam as being more important.[51] These internal clashes involve different views of what should be the type and role of Islamic law (*Sharia*) in the government and society. They note that "*governments in more than seven in ten Muslim-majority countries harass Muslims* compared with Muslims being harassed in only three in ten Christian-majority countries."[52]

To illustrate some of the problems in some Muslim-majority countries, the authors give the example of Afghan Abdul Rahman, who faced a possible death penalty for converting from Islam to Christianity in March 2006. One of the problems was a conflict in the Afghan constitution. Article 2 says that all citizens "are free to exercise their faith and perform their religious rights within the limits of the provisions of law." But Article 3 says, "No law can be contrary to the beliefs and provisions of the sacred religion of Islam." The Afghan government was torn between the international demands for Abdul Rahman's release and the local demands for his execution.[53] In this case, the American ambassador called me in to facilitate resolving the case as quietly as possible.

The Gallup Poll indicated that a majority of Muslims wanted democracy, but a significant percentage wanted it combined with some form of *Sharia*. Therein lies the rub. *Sharia* is viewed by some as only including divine principles like justice; hence, it is compatible with democracy. Others, however, view it as containing specific historical precedents, like death for apostasy and unequal treatment of men and women. Since historically Islam included faith and government, extreme Islamists may want to include some of these restrictions with their resultant implications for religious freedom and persecution. Yet, there has recently been considerable reflection and work in both Sunni and Shia contexts on negotiating and adapting *Sharia* to meet the challenges of modern societies.[54]

IMPLICATIONS OF THE "ARAB SPRING" AND "ARAB WINTER"

All of the elements for hope and concern were found in the "Arab Spring." Would it lead to the flowering of increased democracy, human rights, and religious freedom in the Muslim world? Or would these promising new shoots shrivel in the heat of sectarian, ethnic, and regional forces? As the year 2010 drew to a close, there was a sense of hopelessness in the Middle

---

51. Ibid., 161; Huntington, *Clash of Civilizations*.
52. Grim and Finke, *Price of Freedom*, 185, italics in the original.
53. Ibid., 1–2, 25, 41.
54. See Aymanat and Giffel, *Sharia*; and Na`im, *Islam and the Secular State*.

East and North Africa. About 60 percent of the population was under thirty years of age. There was widespread poverty, rampant corruption, and a lack of jobs, making it difficult for young people to marry; and most governments were led by strongmen or Islamists—though Iran and Saudi Arabia combined the two. The old structures had failed; the strongmen of Egypt, Libya, Yemen, and Syria were being challenged; the attempted balancing of the religious and ethnic communities in Lebanon and Iraq was tenuous, and the paternalism of the Gulf States was slow to respond to the changing times. Then, on December 17 in Tunisia, a fruit vender whose belongings had been confiscated and who had been slapped by a policewoman, set himself ablaze, and the fire of protest spread rapidly to Egypt, Yemen, Libya, Bahrain, Syria, and beyond.

What changed was a sense of hope sparked by a movement of youth who knew about the wider world, were able to organize through the Internet, were more concerned about jobs than religion, and wanted to be citizens, not subjects. There was, commonly, a symbolic person and event in each country with which the youth could identify: the insulted fruit vendor, Mohammed Bouazizi in Tunisia; Egyptian Khaled Said, who died at the hands of Egyptian police in Alexandria; thirteen-year-old protestor Hamza Ali al-Khateeb, who died in prison in Syria. In each country youth chanted: "We are" that person. And the impact spread across two continents—affecting such issues as the Palestine-Israel impasse, where Palestinians began largely peaceful demonstrations at the borders of Israel.

The significance of the uprisings is that the youth, at least for a time, got rid of the strongmen or obtained major concessions without the initial involvement of militants like al-Qaida—though, subsequently, the opposition became more militant in places like Libya and Syria. The original demonstrations were nonviolent, drawing from Eastern European models and the quiet advice of Americans like Gene Sharp.[55] The liberal and secular demonstrators were joined by conservative and religious ones. The 2/11 ousting of the Egyptian president accomplished what the United States's 9/11 response tried to accomplish, but without generating anti-United States feelings.

The uprisings, particularly in Egypt, started with great hopes of national and regional unity that transcended sectarian divides. It followed two years of increasing sectarian clashes, especially against Christians in Egypt. But during the demonstrations in Tahrir Square, when fighting broke out between demonstrators and pro-government forces, Christians held hands in a protective circle around Muslims when they prayed, and Muslims did

---

55. See Stolberg, "Shy U. S. Intellectual Created Playbook."

the same for Christians. The nearby Kasr al-Dobara Coptic Evangelical (Presbyterian) Church opened its doors for Muslims as well as Christians and preached and sang in the square without opposition when parishioners could not get to the church. In the square, people waved flags and banners and shouted that Muslims and Christians were one nation.

But the euphoria gave way to the underlying conflicts and problems of the regions involved—the Islamist-secularist divide in Tunisia, Muslim-Christian tensions in Egypt, Muslim branches and sects in Syria and Bahrain, and clans and tribes in Libya and Yemen. A unity rally in Tahrir Square on May 13, 2011, displayed the flags of Arab and Muslim nations, but many of the Christians held their own rally elsewhere. With the discredited police force becoming ineffective, sectarian conflicts continued to increase—though many Muslim leaders such as the Grand Mufti of Egypt gave strong support for harmony between Muslims and Christians, and the military and many Muslims began to help rebuild certain burned-down churches.

In Egypt, the Muslim Brotherhood won the elections, but it took the attitude that the winner takes all and was subsequently forced out by the military, and the former general al-Sisi was elected president. In Iraq, when the Shiites came to power they too took the attitude that the winner takes all. This and the Shiite-Sunni rivalry in Iraq created the vacuum for the Islamic State (ISIS) to gain ground. These are among the issues that have ushered in the "Arab Winter."

Behind these issues is the problem in much of the Muslim world of inadequate institutions to support democracy, such as the lack of independent judicial systems and a free press to check excesses of those in power and to protect and give voice to minorities. Meanwhile, conflicting voices remain: the Grand Mufti of Saudi Arabia called for the destruction of all churches in the Arabian Peninsula, while certain Muslim leaders objected.[56] The "Arab Spring" showed the potential of the power of common people, of freedom, and of national identity that transcends religious differences. This will remain a reminder of what can be.

CONCLUSION

A number of conclusions are evident. First of all, we need to recognize the divergence of Muslim views concerning how to live in contexts of plurality. Secondly, the divergence of examples in every major period of Islamic history should not only caution against making simplistic generalizations

---

56. Heneghan, "Europe Bishops Slam Saudi Fatwa." See also, "Mufti Ordered to Destroy All Churches."

about an Islamic perspective on plurality but should also provide a wealth of resources from which to draw for developing helpful models for living in contexts of plurality. Thirdly, we should not suggest that Muslims must choose between an Islamic political/social system and secularism. An alternative example is the Pancasila system in Indonesia that recognizes belief in God in a plurality of religions, even though it limits the number of acceptable religions.

This leads, fourthly, to the recognition that Muslims and Christians share some concerns, among them that rights be rooted in obligations to God. Fifthly, Muslims and Christians need to have ongoing dialogue over issues that affect both: for example, state-sponsored migration of Muslims to Christian areas, as in Indonesia, and Christians to Muslim areas, as in Mindanao in the Philippines; and the multidimensional nature of the fear of power, such as in Malaysia and Indonesia, where Muslims fear Chinese Christian economic power, and Chinese Christians in turn fear Muslim political power.

Finally, Christians and Muslims should recognize that both our scriptures have resources that call us to be peacemakers: "Blessed are the peacemakers" (Matt 5:8), and "If the enemy incline toward peace, do thou also incline toward peace" (Qur'an 8:61).

We started by reflecting on the symbol of the cross within the crescent on the flag of the Egyptian Independence Movement of 1919. And we noticed that when it reappeared in the recent "Arab Spring" something had changed. Now it is not only on flags and banners but also in the national colors displayed on the flesh of Muslim and Christian young people. These are the heads that can plan and speak and the hands that can work to bring to fruition what the joint symbol signifies in an Arab—and Muslim—Summer, after the Winter.

BIBLIOGRAPHY

Abu-Nimer, Mohammed, and David W. Augsburger, eds. *Peace-Building by, between, and beyond Muslims and Evangelical Christians.* Lanham, MD: Lexington, 2009.

Ahlul Bayt News Agency. "Saudi Grand Extremist Wahhabi Mufti Ordered to Destroy All Churches/Muslims, Christians Strongly Condemned It." March 26, 2012. Online: http://en.abna24.com/service/middle-east-west-asia/archive/2012/03/26/304564/story.html.

Ahmed, Akbar S. *Journey into Islam: The Crisis of Globalization.* Washington, DC: Brookings Institution, 2007.

Antonius, George. *The Arab Awakening.* London: Hamilton, 1938.

Arnold, Thomas Walker. *The Preaching of Islam: A History of the Propagation of the Muslim Faith.* Lahore: Muhammad Ashraf. Reprint in 1961.

Aydin, Mahmud. "Religious Pluralism as an Opportunity for Living Together in Diversity." In *Muslim and Christian Reflections on Peace: Divine and Human Dimensions*, edited by John Dudley Woodberry, Osman Zümrüt, and Mustafa Köylü, 89–101. Lanham, MD: Rowan & Littlefield, 2004.

Aymanat, Abbas, and Frank Giffel, eds. *Shari'a: Islamic Law in the Contemporary Context*. Stanford, CA: Stanford University Press, 2007.

Baker, Osman bin. "Pluralism and the 'People of the Book': An Islamic Faith Perspective.'" In *Religion and Security: The New Nexus in International Relations*, edited by Robert A. Seiple and Denis R. Hoover, 99–112. Lanham, MD: Rowan & Littlefield, 2004.

Boullata, Issa J. "Fa-stabiqu al-khayrat: A Qur'anic Principle of Interfaith Relations." In *Christian-Muslim Encounters*, edited by Yvonne Yazbeck Haddad and Wadi Zaydan Haddad, 43–53. Gainesville, FL: University Press of Florida, 1995.

Bukhari, al-. *Sahih, Kitab el Sawm*. Edited by Muhammad Muhsin Khan. Beirut: Dar al Arabia, 1979.

Donohue, John J., and John L. Esposito, eds. *Islam in Transition: Muslim Perspectives*. New York: Oxford University Press, 1982.

Esposito, John L., and Dalia Mogahed. *Who Speaks for Islam? What a Billion Muslims Really Think*. New York: Gallup, 2007.

Euben, Roxanne L., and Muhammad Qasim Zaman, eds. *Readings in Islamist Thought: Texts and Contexts from al-Bana to Bin Laden*. Princeton: Princeton University Press, 2009.

Friedmann, Yohanan. *Tolerance and Coercion in Islam: Interfaith Relations in the Muslim Tradition*. Cambridge, MA: Cambridge University Press, 2003.

Grim, Brian J., and Roger Finke. *The Price of Freedom Denied: Religious Persecution and Conflicts in the Twenty-First Century*. Cambridge, MA: Cambridge University Press, 2011.

Haddad, Yvonne Yazbeck, and Wadi Zaydan Haddad, eds. *Christian-Muslim Encounters*. Gainesville, FL: University Press of Florida, 1995.

Hassan, Riffat. "The Quranic Perspective on Religious Pluralism." In *Peace-Building by, between, and beyond Muslims and Evangelical Christians*, edited by Mohammed Abu-Nimer and David W. Augsburger, 91–101. Lanham, MD: Rowan & Littlefield, 2009.

Heneghan, Tom. "Europe Bishops Slam Saudi Fatwa against Gulf Churches." *Reuters*, March 26, 2012. Online: http://www.reuters.com/article/2012/03/26/uk-saudi-christians-fatwa-idUSLNE82P01220120326.

Huntington, Samuel P. *The Clash of Civilizations and the Remaking of World Order*. New York: Simon & Schuster, 1996.

Jomier, Jacques. *Le Commentaire coranique du Manâr: Tendances modernes de l'exégèse coranique en Égypte*. Paris: Maisonneuve, 1954.

Kamrava, Mehran, ed. *The New Voices of Islam: Rethinking Politics and Modernity*. Berkeley, CA: University of California Press, 2006.

Khaldun, Ibn. *The Muqaddimah: An Introduction to History*. Translated by Franz Rosenthal. 3 vols. New York: Ballinger, 1952.

Kurzman, Charles, ed. *Liberal Islam: A Sourcebook*. Oxford: Oxford University Press, 1998.

Little, David, et al. *Human Rights and the Conflicts of Culture: Western and Islamic Perspectives on Religious Liberty (Studies in Comparative Religion)*. Columbia, SC: University of South Carolina Press, 1988.
Marzouqi, Ibrahim Abdulla al-. *Human Rights in Islamic Law*. Abu Dhabi: published by author, 2001.
Mayer, Ann Elizabeth. *Islam and Human Rights: Tradition and Politics*. 3rd ed. Boulder, CO: Westview, 1999.
Mqawdudi, Abu-l-'Ala. "Political Theory of Islam." In *Islam in Transition: Muslim Perspectives*, edited by John J. Donohue and John L. Esposito, Part 4. New York: Oxford University Press, 1982.
Na'im, Abdullahi Ahmed an-. *Islam and the Secular State: Negotiating the Future of Shari'a*. Cambridge, MA: Harvard University Press, 2008.
Qutb, Sayyid. *Fi Zilal al-Qur'an*. Beirut: Dar al-Shuruq, 1973.
Rippin, Andrew. *Defining Islam: A Reader*. Oakville, CT: Equinox, 2007.
Sachedina, Abdulaziz A. *The Islamic Roots of Democratic Pluralism*. Oxford: Oxford University Press, 2001.
———. *The Qur'an on Religious Pluralism*. Washington, DC: Center for Muslim-Christian Understanding, History and International Affairs, Edmund A. Walsh School of Foreign Service. Georgetown, DC: Georgetown University Press, 1999.
Seiple, Robert A., and Denis R. Hoover, eds. *Religion and Security: The New Nexus in International Relations*. Lanham, MD: Rowan & Littlefield, 2004.
Spencer, Robert. *The Myth of Islamic Tolerance: How Islamic Law Treats Non-Muslims*. Amherst, NY: Prometheus, 2005.
Stolberg, Cheryl Gay. "Shy U. S. Intellectual Created Playbook Used by Revolution." *New York Times*, February 17, 2011 (A1, 11).
Tabari, al-. *The Commentary on the Qur'an (J'ami' al-Bayan'an ta 'wil ay al-Qur'an)*. Translated by J. Cooper. Oxford: Oxford University Press, 1989.
Taha, Mahmoud Mohamed. "The Second Message of Islam." In *Liberal Islam: A Sourcebook*, edited by Charles Kurzman, 270–83. Oxford: Oxford University Press, 1998.
Winkler, Lewis E. *Contemporary Muslim and Christian Responses to Religious Plurality: Wolfhart Pannenberg in Dialogue with Abdulaziz Sachedina*. Eugene, OR: Pickwick, 2011.
Woodberry, J. Dudley, et al., eds. *Muslim and Christian Reflections on Peace: Divine and Human Dimensions*. Lanham, MD: University Press of America, 2005.
Zaman, Muhammad Qasim. *The Ulama in Contemporary Islam: Custodians of Change*. Princeton: Princeton University Press, 2002.
Zwemer, Samuel M. *The Law of Apostasy in Islam*. London: Marshall Brothers, 1923.

Chapter 11

Hinduism in the Twentieth Century

Paul Cornelius

UNDERSTANDING HINDUISM IN THE twentieth century is a daunting task for two reasons: First, the "vast and intricate complex of deities, customs, philosophies, languages and holy books"[1] is not easily comprehended and can cause even the seasoned researcher to shy away from essaying a description or analysis of this religious phenomenon. Second, an enormous amount of scholarly work on Hinduism is readily available, and one more piece of writing risks redundancy. It is therefore necessary to state at the very outset that not all aspects of Hinduism can be dealt with in this essay. Current realities, however, draw our attention to the emergence and impact of *Hindutva* as the single most significant feature of Hinduism at the beginning of the twenty-first century in its nationalist or fundamentalist manifestations. Some historical interpretation is necessary to provide perspective and background, but the main focus will be on outlining the salient features of Hinduism in the areas mentioned above and describing how they impinge upon Christian witness in the context of religious plurality today.

It is also necessary to qualify the term "Hinduism." Hinduism is a relatively modern appellation owing its origins to the late eighteenth century. Its earlier cognate, "Hindu," specifically referred to anything "Indian" or "Native." Negatively it was used to denote those things that were not of the

---

1. Paul, "Cultural Core," 8.

"other"—"*not* Muslim, *not* Christian, *not* Jewish, or, hence, *not* Western."[2] In due course, Hinduism also came to describe the Brahmanical or Vedic religion of the earliest times. It was in this classical sense that the reformers and nationalist leaders of the nineteenth century understood and used it. It also refers to a variety of other religious practices such as "popular Hinduism" and "*bhakti* Hinduism." More recent usage, while covering all of the above, in particular refers to Hinduism as a syndicated movement organized around a core religion drawn from the early Brahmanical period and religious texts to authenticate its ideology and action. It is in this manner that "Hinduism" is used in this paper.[3]

Religions tend to intimidate each other, and nowhere is this more apparent than in contemporary India where the context of religious plurality is a given. The disturbing fact is that these "less-than-friendly" encounters are taking place in the political, economic, social, and cultural spheres of Indian public life.[4] In India, as in other parts of the world, the interaction between religions is both innocuous and aggressive. On the one hand, the daily social intercourse between individuals is relatively harmless. In fact, in some cases it enriches their faith lives.[5] On the other hand, religious encounters breed friction and hostility born out of a desire to create and protect distinct identities. The origins of these alarmingly hostile encounters are to be traced back to the policies of the erstwhile British Raj in India.

THE BRITISH RAJ AND THE EMERGENCE OF "HINDUISM"

There is no doubt that Hinduism as a religious entity began to emerge as the local belief system came into contact with both Islam and Christianity. As Romila Thapar, the eminent Indian historian, observes, "The first step towards the crystallization of what we today call Hinduism was born in the consciousness of being the amorphous, subordinate, other."[6] It can be argued, however, that the boundaries between the three religions prior to colonial rule were still blurred. Instances of benevolent patronage on the

2. Frykenberg, "Emergence of Modern," 85, italics in the original.
3. Thapar, "Syndicated," 54–81.
4. See Clarke, "Religious Liberty," 479.
5. See Young, "Enabling Encounters."
6. Thapar, "Syndicated," 63. Cf. Jaffrelot, *Hindu Nationalist*, who says that the process of identity building began to be crystallized in "reaction to a Hindu sense of inferiority or vulnerability which was directly related to stereotypes of the Others (the Muslims and the British)," 24.

part of local Indian rajahs are evident, stretching as far back as the early Thomas Christians, or to the Muslim rulers in the middle of the second millennium. Nonetheless, the Muslim invasion of the subcontinent resulting in widespread bloodshed, destruction of temples, and forced conversion left deep wounds that subsequent colonial policies reopened.

The beginning of the twentieth century was one of great political upheaval in India during which time the colonial construction of India took on a definite religious bent. The British censuses of India, beginning as early as 1871, enumerated the population in terms of religious affiliation. Thus, "Hindu" was officially recognized as referring to those who were not Christians, Muslims, Jains, Sikhs, or Buddhists. The *adivasis*, or native tribal groupings, were subsumed under the rubric of "Hindu," thereby statistically suggesting that the Hindus were the majority group. It must be noted that each census "regularly demonstrated an increasing proportion of the *Christian* population of India and a decreasing Hindu one."[7] The natural sentiment therefore at that time was that the Hindus were a "dying race." Various writings and predictions added to this feeling of insecurity. For example, in 1909 a certain U. N. Mukherji had calculated from census reports that "within the next 420 years Hindus would disappear because of their steady decline in numbers in comparison to Muslims and Christians."[8] Curiously, the fact that this has not been the case in no way deters Hindu fundamentalist entities from taking a hostile and aggressive stance toward Christians today.

Policies of the British Raj delineating the lines between Hindus and Muslims in the state of Bengal added fuel to a situation that was already beginning to take on a volatile state. After the Indian Mutiny of 1857, which the British believed was instigated by the Muslims, administrative jobs were increasingly entrusted to non-Muslims. Additionally, in Bengal where the poorer sections were largely Muslim, it was the high caste Hindus who benefited from Western education. Later attempts by the British to garner Muslim loyalty met with resistance from groups with a growing Hindu identity.

Further, one cannot ignore the impact of Western Orientalist discourse on the development of Hindu nationalism. This scholarly enterprise, initiated by Warren Hastings, the first governor-general of the East India Trading Company from 1772–86, brought "learned Europeans and Indians (Brahman pandits, Muslim hakims, Buddhists, Jains, and others)" together to recover and preserve India's cultural heritage.[9] These studies gave this

---

7. Bhatt, *Hindu Nationalism*, 21; italics in the original.
8. Mukherji quoted in Jaffrelot, *Hindu Nationalist*, 24.
9. Frykenberg, "Hindu Fundamentalism," 238.

emerging "Hinduism" respectability as well as a philosophical orientation. Subsequently, drawing heavily upon the Orientalist perception of Hinduism as tolerant and nonviolent, Vivekananda gained for it the formal recognition as a world religion at the 1893 Parliament of World Religions in Chicago.

HINDUTVA AS A TWENTIETH-CENTURY PHENOMENON OF HINDUISM

The socioeconomic, political, and religious reform movements of the nineteenth century birthed a "community" that became increasingly self-conscious, fearful, and militantly aggressive, beginning to view itself as the "majority community."[10] At its core was the issue of identity, which continues into the present. This consciousness emerged simultaneously with the development of a single state system during British rule. Pre-modern India did not have any form of inclusive Hinduism. It is more appropriate, as Thapar states, to understand that "the reality perhaps lay in looking at it as a cluster of distinctive sects and cults, observing common civilizational symbols, but with belief and ritual ranging from atheism to animism and a variety of religious organizations identifying themselves by location, language and caste."[11] Notions of a single monolithic Hindu community as a later phenomenon emerged out of the competition between various groups for political and economic resources as the Raj attempted to unify India into a single state entity.

Vinayak Damodar Savarkar's influential text *Hindutva: Who is a Hindu?* (1923) provided the impetus for the emergence of Hindutva or "Hindu-ness." Prior to this, Savarkar was intent on developing a revolutionary nationalism aimed at violent insurrection against colonial rule and interests in India to which end he founded—on the lines of revolutionary groups in Europe—Mithra Mela (Friends Group), later known as Abhinav Bharat (Young India). It is not clear under what circumstances his ideology underwent change, but his 1923 publication clearly moves in the direction of religious nationalism.[12] The Hindu Sabha (Assembly) founded in 1907 in the Punjab was the beginning of an overtly fundamentalist Hinduism. They considered themselves "ardent and watchful in the interest of the Hindu community."[13] It must be remembered that the Indian National Congress,

---

10. Ibid., 237–38.

11. Thapar, "Imagined Religious," 229.

12. See Bhatt, *Hindu Nationalism*, 8, for a fuller description of the forces that shaped Savarkar's ideologies.

13. Frykenberg, "Hindu Fundamentalism," 239.

especially under the leadership of Nehru, tried to develop a broadly secular identity. The leaders of the Congress distanced themselves from any definition of nationality that "constructed a hierarchy dominated by the Hindus—which was the ideal of the Hindu nationalists."[14] Hindutva therefore emerged distinctly as a form of religious nationalism, as opposed to Nehru's secular nationalism.

Hindutva ideology extends its influence across a broad spectrum of groups, both those overtly political in nature and those inclined to be more "cultural." It is concerned with defining a true "Hindu" identity and the practices and beliefs that are indicative of "Hindu-ness." Chakravarthi Ram-Prasad observes that its definition of Hindu is based upon three claims:

1. There are certain essential commonalities that characterize Hindu religious traditions.
2. These essentials are constitutive of the religion of India.
3. Being an Indian is to be a Hindu in some sense.[15]

Essentially for Savarkar, Hindutva was a concept that was meant to convey and include all aspects of Hindu life and belief, covering centuries of tradition and socioreligious life. Accordingly, he writes:

> Let Hinduism concern itself with the salvation of life after death, the concept of God, and the Universe. Let individuals be free to form opinions about the trio. . . . But so far as the materialistic and secular aspect is concerned, the Hindus are a nation bound by a *common culture*, a *common history*, a *common language*, a *common country*, and a *common religion*.[16] (italics added)

Matters of religion, the classical philosophy-theology, and all aspects of folk Hinduism as well as the totality of the Indian cultural and social inheritance were included in this ideology. In Savarkar's mind, irrespective of one's religious belief or creed, an individual was tied to the fatherland by a religious ethos and cultural tradition, the inheritance of which makes the person a Hindu. For him, the Hindu *Rashtra* (Hindu Nation) was both an ancient entity and a modern state, existing long before the era of the modern nation-state. Common territory, common blood, and common civilization together constitute Hindutva and form the bedrock of the Hindu *rashtra*. The brahmanical essence is also not to be missed here. The Brahmans, notes G. Aloysius, "as the dominant and leading class, reworked and

14. Jaffrelot, *Hindu Nationalist*, 83.
15. Ram-Prasad, "Being Hindu," 160.
16. Savarkar quoted in Ashby, *Modern Trends*, 98.

recast Brahminic ideology, from the vantage position of social dominance, to suit the times as an ideology of state power, simultaneous to their claim to appropriate the state itself. . . . [Thus] the emergent Hinduism was both Brahminical as well as national."[17] Brahminic hegemony was in place well before the advent of Western colonialism, albeit in a subtle form, as the upper castes sought to subordinate all the other groups.

A conceptual difficulty, however, arises from the above. Unlike Christianity and Islam, Hindutva has no definitive literary corpus that is accepted as authoritative for all Hindus and from which essential and nonnegotiable doctrines are derived. For this reason it is also difficult to view Hindutva as fundamental. However, if by fundamentalism we mean those strategies by which certain groups attempt to preserve and strengthen their distinctive identities, there can be no doubt that Hindutva ideology and methods do fit the pattern. According to Martin Marty and Scott Appleby, fundamentalists seek to strengthen their identity by drawing on doctrinal elements and practices from their "sacred past."[18] These are then reworked and improved to fit current requirements and needs. While the desire for a return to an earlier, golden era is a characteristic of fundamental movements, it is not simply an "artificial imposition of archaic practices and lifestyles. . ."[19] A renewal of identity based on certain essential religious beliefs and practices provides the underpinnings for a new political and social order that is both opportunistic and futuristic. Additionally, any fundamentalist enterprise is built around a significant charismatic, authoritarian leader and a core of disciplined adherents, and establishes a strict social and ethical code for its supporters. Based on these aspects, the Hindutva manifestation of Hinduism can be termed fundamentalist.

Current scholarship, both Indian and Western, demonstrates that the idea of "Hinduism" as a single religion and "Hindus" as a single people is essentially a nineteenth- and twentieth-century development, calling into question the very basis of Hindu unity. Be that as it may, the indubitable fact is that modern Hindus have attempted to define Hinduism with the help of a unifying feature. Ironically, that very aspect within Hinduism that created the need for unity—the problem of the plurality of texts, rituals, beliefs, and customs—provided the means of a self-definition that promoted oneness. Ram Prasad calls it the "doctrine of plurality," where Hindus "looking to find a common value or belief that would provide them with the determinant

---

17 Aloysius, *Nationalism*, 104.
18. Marty and Appleby, "Introduction," 1.
19. Ibid.

of Hindu identity, have by and large settled on the very fact of irreducible Hindu plurality and made a singular virtue of it."[20]

This doctrine of plurality helps define what Hinduism is and in fact becomes an essential value. Acceptance of the doctrine of plurality moves Hinduism beyond simply being a religion of tolerance. There is a larger claim that is implied and made here, for tolerance signifies a belief in the right of others to hold differing views. Rather, with the doctrine of plurality, Hinduism can go further and accept the rightness of all other beliefs and religions. Ram-Prasad extends the argument to its logical conclusion—the larger claim that Hinduism alone professes the rightness of other religions and therefore is higher than them because of its liberality toward them. Clearly, Hindu attempts to locate a value or attitude or belief to help define itself in the face of its religious diversity, reach their pinnacle here. It would be misleading to suggest that all Hindus hold to the doctrine of plurality or that those who accept it are sympathetic to Hindutva ideology. But one cannot deny the ambiguity of the relationship between the modern Hindu's search for identity and the Hindutva articulation of it. Nonetheless, there is a certain appeal in it for the general Hindu who wishes to perceive Hinduism as a universal religion on par, if not superior to, other world religions.

THE OUTCOMES OF A HINDUTVA READING OF HISTORY

The alarming fact, however, is the "specifically political extension" of this doctrine of plurality where Hinduism and the nation-state are seen to converge. The Indian National Congress, as already indicated earlier, sought to construct a nation that was "at once constituted by all religions but transcended them."[21] But the damage created by British policy was not easily undone. Religious identities had already been demarcated, and the Muslims voiced their concerns that the demographic dominance of the Hindu majority would in time make Congress's claims to secularism void. They maintained that a Hindu majority would always assure that the nation remained Hindu. Thus, wittingly or unwittingly, the partition of India ending in the creation of Muslim Pakistan paved the way for a Hindu India.

Issues of identity are crucial to the Hindutva ideology and are based upon a particularistic reading of history, ignoring the fact that *the British subjugated both Hindus and Muslims*. In broad strokes, the Hindutva understanding of history is as follows: 1) pre-Muslim India had a single

20. Ram-Prasad, "Being Hindu," 165.
21. Ibid., 173.

religion—namely, Hinduism—and all other movements are derivations; 2) first Islam and then Christianity, under the auspices of colonial rule, entered and dominated the native religion; 3) in spite of political independence from Britain, foreign traditions formed the basis of the new nation-state; and 4) this nation-state must become the successor to the ancient notion of a single-culture land.

It is not possible at this point to elaborate on the complex developments that have led to the current religiopolitical situation in India today. The various interpretations of Hindutva have spawned several organizations and groups that have come under the umbrella of the *Sangh Parivar*, or "family of organizations." These include the Rashtriya Swayamsevak Sangh (RSS), which claims to be nonpolitical; the Shiv Sena, or "Army of Shiva," with its strong political base in the state of Maharashtra; and the Vishwa Hindu Parishad (World Hindu Council). The Hindu Mahasabha, founded by Savarkar at the turn of the twentieth century, was reconstituted as the Jana Sangh group in post-Independence India and then became the Bharatiya Janata Party (BJP), which attained power in the 1990s with the help of the groups under the Sangh Parivar. The relation between these various groups and parties is problematic on two counts. The first is ideological and revolves around issues of whether Hindutva ideals should be focused on developing national culture and society or governance of the state.

The second concerns strategy and the "hard-soft" divide. Typically the leaders of most political parties sympathetic to Hindutva ideals have maintained hard strategies while in opposition and soft ones while in power. The RSS on the other hand has always followed "hard" strategies, resulting in violence against those who do not share their Hindu-derived values; namely, the Muslims, Christians, and sometimes the Dalits.[22]

Clarke helpfully delineates two strands of this type of Hinduism as it relates to present realities. He terms these (1) "the disciplining left hand of Hindu nationalism: ideological and physical violence," and (2) "the disciplining right hand of Hindu nationalism: coercive mechanisms of Indian-Hindu integration."[23] The first is violent, both ideologically and physically. It is prescriptive in its demands for a unified nation, language, culture, and religion, and all those who oppose this are dealt with in the severest fashion. The will of those communities who consider themselves part of the Indian nation but who do not wish to conform or subscribe to *Hindutva* ideology is not respected. In the second, Hindu nationalism attempts to restore the Hindu-Indian identity through the means of primary education

22. Ibid., 177.
23. Clarke, "Religious Liberty," 479.

in schools. Thus, the Hinduization of India is to be undertaken. A report by a commission of educational experts in October 1998 recommended that Sanskrit be made mandatory so that the "primary to the highest education should be Indianized, nationalized and spiritualized." Further, "Hindutva is a way of life and not a religion. . . . India's invaluable heritage of the Vedas and the Upanishads should find a place in the curriculum from primary to higher level courses, including the vocational courses."[24]

The role of the Vishwa Hindu Parishad (VHP) must not be minimized here. The VHP was founded in 1964 with the express purpose of representing all Hindus. Officers of political parties were discouraged from membership, ostensibly to indicate its nonpolitical orientation. The VHP, however, has sought to extend its influence by legitimizing itself as the body that directs both the "secular and religious conduct of all Hindus."[25] In 1996, the VHP declared its intent with certain resolutions that made Sanskrit compulsory in secondary education, banned the slaughter of cows, and approved reconversion of those who had left Hinduism. Particular mention was made of Christian activities among the tribals. Further, the VHP revealed its international character by resolving to strengthen ties and promote *dharma* (religion) among Hindus abroad.

One of the pivotal aspects of the success of the VHP has been its articulation of *bhakti* (devotion). Chetan Bhatt says, "The appeal to and at the same time modification of the bhakti affect is central to VHP technologies of hegemony, especially in conditions of limited literacy."[26] Indeed, even L. K. Advani manipulated religious feeling with dexterous use of religious icons and symbols, and with telling effect, as the BJP worked itself toward gaining central power in the government in the 1990s. The problem, however, was deciding which religious symbol was suitable to the plurality of sects and groups within the populace. The VHP circumvented this problem by historicizing Ram, claiming that Ayodhya in North India was his birthplace and whipping up religious frenzy in a push to build a temple to Ram where the Babri Masjid stood. The two epics *Mahabharata* and *Ramayana* were screened on national television on Sundays and superimposed with slogans of "strength, honour, obligation, violence and war."[27] Further, as Bhatt observes, where the *Bhagavad Gita* is intrinsically a discourse on ethics and morals, it was used to preach the primitive message that "any kind of violence, if undertaken for the protection of dharma, is a bounden obliga-

24. "Joshi Agenda," 1.
25. Bhatt, *Hindu Nationalism*, 182.
26. Ibid., 192.
27. Ibid., 193.

tion, regardless of the abhorrence of violence for any individual sensibility. Hence, violence becomes an unavoidable religious duty under *dharmic* principles for anyone who claims to be a Hindu."[28]

The Hindutva brand of Hinduism is distinctly expansionist and missionary in its outlook as well. In his well-researched book, C. V. Mathew draws upon his study of current movements and their interpretation of early texts, to clearly demonstrate the militant and missionary nature of twentieth-century Hinduism.[29] These are fueled by the desire to defend as well as the insatiable thirst to grow. The first is grounded in a fear of the "other's" dominance, whereas the second is based on the belief of the rightness and validity of the Hindu value system as expounded in its texts and practiced in daily life. The proliferation of gurus and their form of devotional and meditative Hinduism can be construed as a softer version of twentieth-century Hinduism, but potent nonetheless.

SOME ADDITIONAL OBSERVATIONS

Before considering how Hindutva impinges upon the Christian witness, some observations are in order here. First, we must remember that the Hindutva argument and rhetoric was initially directed more against the "secularists" within the Hindu polity than those of other faiths. It was meant to strengthen from within and therefore concentrated on spreading the Hindu "spirit" and consciousness among the peoples. The tirade was directed against those who sought to erode Hindu civilization, culture, and religion. By extension, in its current mode, it seeks to bring all those who would call themselves Indian under the overarching umbrella of being "Hindu." It is rejection of this call to become subordinate to the Hindu culture that ensues in violent demonstrations of religious nationalism.

Second, the fallout of the doctrine of plurality is negatively felt by those faiths that make exclusive claims, such as Christianity and Islam. The argument is as follows. If, according to Hindutva ideology, being Indian is synonymous with being Hindu, to be an Indian then is to accept the rightness of all religions and not claim exclusive uniqueness for any one particular faith. Conversion, therefore, is considered a subversive activity that must be extirpated.

Third, it is a fallacy to assume that the type of religious nationalism promoted by the hardliners is "anti-modern" in its religious discourse. This would be too simplistic. As Vinoth Ramachandra points out, these

28. Ibid.
29. See Mathew, *Saffron Mission*.

organizations and parties are "anti-secularist, anti-pluralist, but not anti-democratic. Their understanding of democracy is of 'majority rule.' They want both God and nuclear warheads."[30] H. D. S. Greenway, a noted columnist and former editor of the *Boston Globe*, at the end of his article titled "Religious Nationalism Clouds the Face of India" writes:

> The battle between Nehru's secular India and what the historian Burton Stein called the "distorted particularisms and intolerance" of religious-based nationalism comes just as a new, market-oriented and technologically minded India is trying to be born from the old socialist and inward-looking country that was, ironically, also Nehru's legacy.[31]

The struggle is a bitter one and not easily solved. On the one hand, the desire to compete with other nations at a global level prods India toward embracing modernity in all its fullness, while on the other hand, the "distorted particularisms and intolerance" of religious nationalism fight for an equal place in this modern construct. Ram-Prasad suggests that anxiety and ambition are twin concerns for the BJP and, by implication, Hindutva supporters.[32] On the one hand, the urban middle class for whom the notion of Hindu identity has begun to be widely accepted is anxious for the benefits of global competitiveness and for India's role as a world player. On the other hand, there is considerable worry on the cultural front aroused by the perceived threat from the import of Western patterns of lifestyle, such as sexual ethics, food and clothing trends, and worship practices. Hindutva ideology here is seen as protecting and defending the country from outside cultural and religious infiltration. It is this latter threat that is often linked with Indian Christians and is seen as an outcome of conversion to Christianity.

Fourth, even though the BJP and its "hardliner" allies were defeated in the 2004 elections, it would be naive to assume that Hindutva has been overthrown. If history is known to repeat itself, we can be assured that the religiously fundamentalist groups within Hinduism will take the hard stance to regain power at the center. This could mean only one thing for the minorities: increased aggression against their communities.

---

30. Ramachandra, *Faiths in Conflict*, 55.
31. Greenway, "Religious Nationalism," 89.
32. Ram-Prasad, "Being Hindu," 186.

IMPLICATIONS FOR HINDU-CHRISTIAN RELATIONS

The attempts by the Hindu right to reconstruct Indian history exhibit a desire to dominate and control not just the religious but also the social, political, and cultural affairs of all who would claim to be Indians. Such reconstructions view India as a homogenous cultural and religious entity, leaving very little room for diversity and differences. Scholarly consensus rejects such an imagining of India, arguing that plurality has always characterized Indian-ness.[33] These arguments, however, are drowned in populist and political rhetoric vilifying Islam and Christianity as purveyors of foreign cultures that threaten the "Hindu-ness" of India.

Historically, the Muslim community has been the "threatening other" in Hindu Nationalist discourse.[34] This was the direct consequence of the feeling that the notion of India as a "Hindu nation" would be lost if the Muslims were left unchecked in their attempts to convert the Indian populace to Islam. Beginning in the 1990s, similar sentiment was directed against the Christian community for its "divisive and subversive" activities carried out under the guise of community and welfare projects. Sustained propaganda undermining Christian mission, especially in the tribal areas, fueled widespread hostilities against the Christian community.

Although from a political standpoint the pro-Hindu BJP is no longer in power, various state-led governments continue the rhetoric and aggression toward the religious minorities. It would be foolhardy and premature to predict the demise of Hindu nationalism in Indian politics.[35] Recent events that led to severe persecution of Christians in the North Indian state of Orissa suggest quite the opposite.[36] The Hindutva brigade continues to view itself as the protector of fundamentalist Hinduism, and the earlier BJP-led government's acquiescence to the atrocities of the fundamentalists has provided the platform from which it intimidates and threatens those forces—forces that it maintains are destroying the fabric of Hindu society and culture.[37] This scenario, along with the understanding of Hindutva

---

33. For example, see Sen, *Argumentative Indian*.

34. Froerer, "Emphasizing 'Others,'" 40.

35. Chaudhury, "Ripping Up," 14–17.

36. In August 2008, Christian homes were burnt and churches destroyed by Hindu fundamentalist elements who justified their actions by claiming that Swami Laxmananda and four of his disciples were murdered by Christian missionaries. While the government was quick to point out that this was the act of Maoists, the Sangh Parivar claimed that Christian missionaries in Orissa were the culprits.

37. "Hindu" is used here in the sense of Indian, since for the fundamentalist Hindu, being Indian means being Hindu.

outlined above, leads us to consider some implications for Hindu-Christian relations.

First, in the tribal areas of the states of Orissa, Gujarat, and Karnataka, Hindu-Christian relations are marked by fear and suspicion. For the Christian as well as the Hindu fundamentalist, "fear" is the operative word in the struggle to create and maintain identity. It is convenient therefore to take up positions of rigidity and inflexibility, invariably eliciting the same response from the "other." Lines are drawn, and the gulf between communities grows deeper. As Clarke notes, "The general temptation is to fight one form of exclusivism with another form of the same, leading to a situation of competing fundamentalist or essentialist paradigms."[38] In most cases, this leads to what may be called a "mission compound mentality."

Second, there is no doubt that the educated urban middle class of India has bought into the notion of a Hindu identity. Various projections buttressed by current statistics hint that this group will soon constitute close to 40 percent of the Indian population.[39] Lancy Lobo argues that support for the BJP's nationalistic agenda is highest among the middle- to high-income group—namely, the strong urban middle class.[40] It follows logically then that this rather influential part of the population will actively be involved in the promotion of the Hindutva cause. But such fears may yet prove to be unfounded, given the uninhibited support of the saner voices among this segment of the citizenry.[41] The mounting dislike against the heavy-handed posturing of the radical elements within the Hindu right bodes well for communal harmony. The Christian community therefore must not eschew the opportunity to reach out and build bridges. As with all relationships, there must be give and take, and it is time for the Christian community to be proactive in developing relationships where it matters most—among their neighbors in the community and colleagues in the work place.

---

38. Clarke, "Religious Liberty," 479.

39. Puri, "Regulars," 16. See also Farrell and Beinhocker, "Next Big Spenders"; Rao, "India's Growing Middle Class"; and Lobo, *Globalisation*, 133.

40. Lobo, *Globalisation*, 133.

41. It is abundantly clear that in the majority of protests held across the country in response to the mindless violence, participants from all walks of life and from diverse religious backgrounds, including Hindus, raised their voice against the destructive ideology of Hindutva. For example, see *The Hindu* (online edition of India's National Newspaper), February 2, 2008.

TOWARD A CONSTRUCTIVE CHRISTIAN RESPONSE

First, a beneficial way perhaps to approach this problem is to respect the plurality of faith expressions that one is faced with. Respect of another's faith experience does not necessarily mean making a value judgment of whether it is right or wrong. It is simply acknowledging the variety of religious beliefs and allowing the "other" to hold to particular beliefs as a matter of his or her choice. Such a response is not imperialistic or exclusivistic and does not idolize one religion against another but rather opens up room for dialogue and respectful exchange of ideas. The challenge here is to maintain that delicate balance between retaining the uniqueness of Christ and slipping into reductionist pluralism. As Ramachandra states, "Respect for the beliefs of another entails that we take the trouble to explore what those beliefs mean for the believer in the wider context of his or her own life in a believing community, not arbitrarily assigning one's own private meanings to them."[42]

Second, we might ask the question: At what points on the boundaries between religions can we place ourselves so as to allow for thoughtful, meaningful, and respectful engagement? Part of the answer may lie in Indian Christians exploring what Richard Fox Young, borrowing from author Anne Fadiman, calls "the point of tangency."[43] He makes the case that Nehemiah Goreh, the Indian Christian theologian, was one who stood at the point of tangency between Hinduism and Christianity and understood his conversion experience. In his case, Young argues, through a series of intellectual exercises while standing on the edges of Hinduism and Christianity, Goreh came to view his conversion in the more cultural idiom from *ajnana* ("foolishness") to *jnana* ("wisdom"), and not the "Evangelical conversion paradigm" where one goes from "*sin* or *darkness* or *death* to *grace* or *light* or *life*."[44] Young goes on to state, "Thus he began to remake himself in the image of a Benares pandit, transformed by the *Christian* wisdom and called by God to make that wisdom *Indian* wisdom."[45] The point is that Christians must attempt to become aware of the faith convictions or the conceptual affirmations of the "other" so as to engage reflectively with cultural and religious

---

42. Ramachandra, *Faiths in Conflict*, 126.

43. Young, "Enabling Encounters," 14. Young quotes Anne Fadiman who says, "I have always felt that the action most worth watching is not at the center of things but where the edges meet. . . . There are interesting frictions and incongruities in these places, and often, if you stand at the point of tangency, you can see both sides better than if you were in the middle of either one" (in "Enabling Encounters," 14).

44. Ibid., 16.

45. Ibid., 17.

traditions that are not their own. This calls for a modicum of objectivity in examining both Christianity and—in the case of India—Hinduism, Islam, or any of the other faiths in order to construct a meaningful approach to the "other." Is it not possible that the point of tangency can eventually become the "point of convergence"? Goreh's example also highlights the crucial issue of the Indian-ness of the church and its continued captivity in many cases to Western models and approaches. Movement forward necessitates breaking free of this bondage and building an authentic Indian identity.

Third, any theological reflection on the foregoing begs a series of questions: (1) How can a "theology of religious plurality" foster positive and significant relationships or partnerships with the "other"? (2) Is it possible that we have misunderstood traditional and ecclesiastical identity to be the true identity that we cherish and fight hard to keep at the expense of isolating and distancing the other? (3) Can a re-reading of 1 Cor 9:19–23 provide fresh insight into understanding identity and how and where it is found?[46] These are not easy questions to deal with, but it might well be that a willingness to creatively answer them will bring about transformation in the church's witness and cause it to find greater acceptance with the "other."

BIBLIOGRAPHY

Aloysius, G. *Nationalism without a Nation in India*. New Delhi: Oxford University Press, 1997.

Ashby, Philip. *Modern Trends in Hinduism*. New York: Columbia University Press, 1974.

Bhatt, Chetan. *Hindu Nationalism: Origins, Ideologies and Modern Myths*. New York: Berg, 2001.

Chaudhury, Shoma. "Ripping Up the Rainbow." *New Internationalist* 142 (2006) 14–17.

Clarke, Sathianathan. "Religious Liberty in Contemporary India: The Human Right to Be Religiously Different." *The Ecumenical Review* 52 (2000) 479–89. Online: http://www.highbeam.com/library.

Fadiman, Anne. *The Spirit Catches You and You Fall Down: A Hmong Child, Her American Doctors, and the Collision of Two Cultures*, viii. New York: Farrar, Straus and Giroux, 1998.

Farrell, Diana, and Eric Beinhocker. "Next Big Spenders: India's Middle Class." *McKinsey Global Institute* (May 19, 2007). Online: http://www.mckinsey.com/mgi/mginews/bigspenders.asp.

---

46 "Though I am free and belong to no one, I have made myself a slave to everyone, to win as many as possible. To the Jews I became like a Jew, to win the Jews. To those under the law I became like one under the law . . . so as to win those under the law. To those not having the law I became like one not having the law . . . so as to win those not having the law" (1 Cor 9:19–21 TNIV).

Froerer, Peggy. "Emphasizing 'Others': The Emergence of Hindu Nationalism in a Central Indian Tribal Community." *Journal of the Royal Anthropological Institute* 12.1 (2006) 39–59.

Frykenberg, Robert Eric. "The Emergence of Modern 'Hinduism' as a Concept and an Institution: An Appraisal with Special Reference to South India." In *Hinduism Reconsidered*, edited by Gunther Sontheimer and Hermann Kulke, 1–29. Heidelberg: South Asia Institute, 1989; reprint, Delhi: Manohar, 2005.

———. "Hindu Fundamentalism and the Structural Stability of India." In *Fundamentalisms and the State: Remaking Polities, Economies, and Militance*, edited by Martin E. Marty and R. Scott Appleby, 233–55. Chicago: University of Chicago Press, 1993.

Greenway, H. D. S. "Hindu Nationalism Clouds the Face of India." *World Policy Journal* 18.1 (2001) 89.

Jaffrelot, Christophe. *The Hindu Nationalist Movement in India*. New York: Columbia University Press, 1995.

"Joshi Agenda: Sanskrit—Must in All Schools." *Asian Age* 17 (October 1998) 1.

Lobo, Lancy. *Globalisation, Hindu Nationalism and Christians in India*. New Delhi: Rawat, 2002.

Marty, Martin E., and R. Scott Appleby. "Introduction." In *Accounting for Fundamentalisms: The Dynamic Character of Movements*, edited by Martin E. Marty and R. Scott Appleby, 1–9. Chicago: University of Chicago Press, 1994.

Mathew, C. V. *The Saffron Mission: A Historical Analysis of Modern Hindu Missionary Ideologies and Practices*. New Delhi: Indian Society for Promoting Knowledge, 2001.

Paul, Timothy. "The Cultural Core of Hinduism." In *Rethinking Hindu Ministry: Papers from the Rethinking Forum*, 8. Pasadena, CA: Rethinking Forum, 2004.

Puri, Rajinder. "Bull's Eye." *Outlook* (October 11, 2004) 16.

Ram-Prasad, Chakravarthi. "Being Hindu and/or Governing India? Religion, Social Change and the State." In *The Freedom to Do God's Will: Religious Fundamentalism and Social Change*, edited by Gerrie ter Haar and James J. Busuttil, 159–96. London: Routledge, 2003.

Ramachandra, Vinoth. *Faiths in Conflict?: Christian Integrity in a Multicultural World*. Downers Grove, IL: InterVarsity, 1999.

Rao, Prem. "India's Growing Middle Class." *People at Work and Play*, October 29, 2007. Online: https://bprao.wordpress.com//?s=India%27s+Growing+Middle+Class&search=Go.

Samuel, Dibin. "Over 5,000 Christians Take Protest against Orissa Violence to India's Capital." *The Christian Post*. March 6, 2012. Online: http://www.christianpost.com/news/over-5-000-christians-take-protest-against-orissa-violence-to-indias-capital-34073/.

Savarkar, Vinayak Damodar. *Hindutva: Who is a Hindu?* Poona City: S. P. Gokhale, 1923.

Sen, Amartya. *The Argumentative Indian: Writings on Indian History, Culture and Identity*. New York: Picador, 2005.

Thapar, Romila. "Imagined Religious Communities?: Ancient History and the Modern Search for a Hindu Identity." *Modern Asian Studies* 23.2 (1989) 209–31.

———. "Syndicated Hinduism." In *Hinduism Reconsidered*, edited by Günther-Dietz Sontheimer and Hermann Kulke, 54–81. Reprint, Delhi: Manohar, 2005.

The Times of India. "11 More Churches Torched in Orissa." December 27, 2007. Online: http://timesofindia.indiatimes.com/India/11-more-churches-torched-in-Orissa/articleshow/2654765.cms#ixzz0w6MtYUEP.

Young, Richard Fox. "Enabling Encounters: The Case of Nilakanth-Nehemiah Goreh, Brahmin Convert." *International Bulletin of Missionary Research* 29.1 (2005) 14–20.

Chapter 12

Keeping Faith

Immigration, Religion, and the Unmaking of a Global Culture

Jehu J. Hanciles

IN THE LATE 1960s, the secularization thesis was at the height of influence in Western academic institutions. Propounded by a relatively small group of powerful Western academics extrapolating from an assessment of trends in Western Europe and North America, this thesis maintained that modernization and the inexorable spread of scientific rationality would inevitably cause an irreversible decline in religious belief and practice throughout the world. Foundational to this theory was the entrenched, if unstated, conviction that Western ideals and experiences are paradigmatic and sufficient for global projections and calculations. Even though concrete evidence indicative of comparable erosion in formal religious observance and allegiance within the non-Western world was lacking, the theory remained unchallenged.[1] We might call this tendency to ascribe global significance to Western particularity the "World Series" approach!

---

1. In fact, at about the same time, a handful of scholars versed in the study of non-Western Christianity were pointing to trends, including the phenomenal growth and unprecedented dynamism of Christianity in Africa, which sharply contradicted the claims of the secularization thesis. See Barrett, *Schism and Renewal*, 194; Turner, "Contribution of Studies," 170.

Not for the first time, but more patently than usual, academic pronouncements proved to be out of touch with reality. Contrary to the prognosis inherent in the secularization thesis, the world we live in today is as inundated by religious novelty, flux, and dynamism as it has ever been; and the rate of religious upsurge appears to be intensifying. All the major religions—Christianity, Islam, Judaism, Hinduism, Buddhism—are resurgent and have all produced vibrant renewal movements.

Indeed, far from undermining religious beliefs, the global spread of economic and social modernization has actually triggered "a global revival of religion" on every continent.[2] Perversely, from a secular rationalist point of view, Islamic fundamentalist movements have been strong in the more advanced and seemingly more secular Muslim societies such as Algeria, Iran, Egypt, Lebanon, and Tunisia[3]—fostering the view that Islamism increases with modernization. Christianity, also, is experiencing explosive growth in non-Western societies, often in contexts of abject poverty but also drawing considerable stimulus from increased middle class participation. Certainly in South Korea, remarkable Christian growth from the 1970s coincided with economic prosperity and modernization. And in other rapidly Westernizing Asian countries like Japan, Taiwan, Hong Kong, and Malaysia, folk religion and traditional faiths are also thriving.[4] Clearly, the gods have not retired in the face of scientific modernity.

Not surprisingly, by the end of the twentieth century, a growing number of notable Western intellectuals had firmly rejected the secularization thesis and declared it to be false even in the case of the Western world.[5] Among the most prominent defectors was American sociologist Peter Berger who averred that "strongly felt religion has always been around [and] what needs explanation is its absence rather than its presence."[6] Not unlike converts to a new faith, others were even more severe in their denunciation of the old religion. In an *Atlantic Monthly* article titled "Kicking the Secularist Habit: A Six-Step Program," David Brooks, who describes himself as a "recovering secularist," recommended six steps for other recovering secularists:[7]

---

2. Huntington, *Clash of Civilizations*, 97.

3. Ibid., 101. Islamism, adds Daniel Pipes, has often surged in countries experiencing rapid economic growth—including Jordan, Tunisia, and Morocco. Pipes, "God and Mammon," 14.

4. Stark and Finke, *Acts of Faith*, 75f.

5. See Berger, *Desecularization*; Stark and Finke, *Acts of Faith*; Stark, "Secularization," 1–19; Davie, *Europe*; also Brooks, "Kicking," 26–27.

6. Berger, "Desecularization," 11f; also Berger, "Four Faces," 419–27.

7. Brooks, "Kicking," 26–28.

1. Accept the fact that you are not the norm.
2. Confront your fear (of uncontrolled religious conflict).
3. Get angry (at secular fundamentalists) for their parochialism and ignorant convictions.[8]
4. Resist the impulse to find a materialistic explanation for everything.
5. Acknowledge that you have been too easy on religion.
6. Understand that America was never very secular anyway.

Note, however, that the falsification of the secularization thesis has done little to deflate the air of academic respectability that shrouds secular rationalism.[9] Indeed, one could argue that Western secularism, rather paradoxically, remains a force to be reckoned with precisely because it is a de facto "religion" with universalistic claims, utopian hopes, promises of salvation, strongly held creeds—including individual rights, gay rights, liberal democracy, liberal progressivism, and committed proselytization—especially through the media, active "congregants" in academic institutions, and its own fundamentalist core.[10] While the secular movement remains a predominantly European phenomenon, it is also enjoying some growth in the United States where self-confessed adherents represent more than 7.5 percent of the population.[11]

THE CULTURAL PARADIGM

But a more significant and pertinent point must be made. The discrediting of the secularization thesis has left intact the fundamental and entrenched

---

8. Brooks adds that "a great Niagara of religious fervor is cascading down around them while they stand obtuse and dry in the little cave of their parochialism—and many of them are journalists and policy analysts, who are paid to keep up with these things," ibid., 26.

9. A vocal minority of scholars in Europe and America has managed to keep up the debate surrounding the secularization theory, constantly sparring with rational choice theorists over the significance of religious pluralism. Davie, *Europe*, 15–16, 42–45, helpfully summarizes the debate. Advocates of secularization insist that "growing religious pluralism . . . necessarily undermines the plausibility of all forms of religious belief," while rational choice theorists counter that religious pluralism stimulates rather than depresses religious vitality by enabling the religious needs of increasingly diverse populations to be met.

10. Secular rationalism, observes Kenneth Minogue, is "the appropriate meta-religion for humanity as a whole" ("Religion," 131).

11. Klinghofer,"That Other," 62. They are known, insists Klinghoffer, to "use aggressive means in advancing their political agenda and spreading their faith."

epistemological notion that Western models, experiences, and values continue to set the standard for the rest of the world and will therefore inevitably enjoy global dominance. With a few notable exceptions, the crude notion of "West is best" is no longer explicit in public discourse, but in the United States and elsewhere, more sophisticated versions of this claim are well established in academic discourse. An increasingly common view attributes human progress—defined in terms of economic development, material well-being, and political democracy—to superior cultural values. This proposition, termed the "cultural paradigm," is posited as furnishing a more plausible model for explaining or addressing poverty and development around the world than previous explanatory constructs like colonialism, dependency, or racism. As one proponent put it, the United States can ill afford to ignore culture "as it attempts to find solutions for black and Hispanic underachievement."[12]

This approach was championed by distinguished scholars in a Harvard-sponsored symposium on "Cultural Values and Human Progress" held in April 1999, and subsequently published as *Culture Matters: How Values Shape Human Progress* (2000), edited by Lawrence E. Harrison and Samuel P. Huntington. Harrison noted that "a growing number of scholars, journalists, politicians, and development practitioners are focusing on the role of cultural values and attitudes as facilitators of, or obstacles to, progress."[13] With few dissenting voices, notably that of an anthropologist who described himself as a heretic at a revival meeting, the contributors to the volume, including the obligatory sample of non-Western scholars, upheld the link between Western cultural values or Westernization—the adoption of Western values, ideals, norms, etc.—and economic prosperity.

Among the most prominent arguments was the view that corruption is lowest in Protestant societies in Europe and North America—which stressed individualism and concern for self over communitarian and familial ties—and highest among Asian nations, which emphasize strong family ties.[14] Equally explicit was the conclusion by the African contributor that "if Europe . . . has been able to impose itself on the planet, dominating it and organizing it for its exclusive profit, it is only because it developed a conquering culture of rigor and work, removed from the influence of invisible forces. We [Africans] must do the same."[15]

---

12. Harrison, "Introduction," xvii–xxxiv.
13. Ibid., xxi.
14. Lipsett and Lenz, "Corruption, Culture," 112–24.
15. Etounga-Manguelle, "Does Africa Need," 65–77.

It would be quite mistaken to assume that these voices represent the sum total of views in the academic marketplace. But they represent a major strand. It is not the first time that a particular nation or region has staked claims to cultural supremacy by virtue of economic ascendancy. As Richard Shweder observes, "Throughout history, whoever is wealthiest and the most technologically advanced thinks that their way of life is the best, the most natural, the God-given, the surest means to salvation, or at least the fast lane to well-being in this world."[16] But due to the processes of contemporary globalization—the deepening experiences of global interconnectedness and the growing consciousness that the world is a single social place in which local experience is shaped by distant events and vice versa—the stakes have never been higher.

To make the point more clearly, even the globalization phenomenon is widely understood as a one-directional process, aided by technological innovations produced in the West, and synonymous for the most part with American capitalist expansion and cultural imperialism. This understanding of the single most important transformative force shaping human existence today is as problematic as it is commonplace.[17] But not only does it reflect the core assumption underlying the secularization theory, it also has fostered the parallel and even more consequential prognosis that we are witnessing the emergence of a single global culture or universal civilization.

This global culture or cultural homogenization thesis turns on at least two convictions: first, that economic dominance and technological supremacy are driving the inexorable spread of Western modernization, particularly American consumer culture, in a way that erodes local cultures and indigenous identities around the world; and second, that non-Western peoples aspire to be more like northern Europeans. The current reasoning, comments Huntington, is that the West "as the first civilization to modernize . . . leads in the acquisition of the culture of modernity" and "as other societies acquire similar patterns of education, work, wealth, and class structure . . . this modern Western culture will become the universal culture of the world."[18] As British Prime Minister Tony Blair put it ever so disarmingly in

---

16. Shweder, "Moral Maps," 158–76.

17. Undoubtedly, some vital aspects of contemporary globalization reflect American economic dominance. But, far from being a one-directional, single unified phenomenon, globalization is a multi-directional, inherently paradoxical movement that incorporates movement and counter-movement, hegemony and resistance. To depict it as a managed process with a fixed ideal ignores its ambiguities and complexities. As a number of scholars note, much about the phenomenon's impact remains open ended and indeterminate.

18. Huntington, *Clash of Civilizations*, 68.

an address before the United States Congress, "Ours are not Western values; they are the universal values of the human spirit."[19]

This essay focuses on the global culture argument and examines its claims in the light of contemporary patterns of immigration which constitute a major driving force behind cultural change and religious plurality in Europe and North America. With Islam as the main focus, two interrelated considerations inform the discussion: first, that contrary to entrenched notions of Western provenance and dominance within the globalization discourse, non-Western initiatives and movements are among the most powerful forces shaping the contemporary world order. Second, that the massive upsurge of people movements associated with contemporary globalization already implicate the West as a site of new religious interactions and ideologies that portend radical transformations of the religio-cultural landscape of Western societies.

WHITE MAN'S BURDEN

The single global culture theory is hostage to the prevalent view of globalization as an economic phenomenon driven by market forces and controlled by Western-dominated institutions and corporations.[20] Proponents note that a small group of around twenty to thirty large multinational corporations—the majority of which are US-based—dominate global markets for entertainment, news, television, and other industries and have acquired a significant cultural and economic presence on virtually every continent. Thus, for instance, the transnationalization of the music industry has simultaneously been the story of the diffusion and export of American-style popular music, artists, and genres and a range of associated aspects of culture and subcultures from which it grew.[21] The United States, it is also noted, dominates world trade in films and is the biggest exporter of television programs.[22] Even the Internet—widely hailed as the ultimate instrument of globalization—is largely controlled by two American giants: AOL Time Warner and Microsoft.

---

19. Blair, "Address."

20. For a useful summary of the main assumptions and arguments of the "global culture" argument, see Held et al., *Global Transformations*, 342–63.

21. Ibid., 352.

22. It has more than triple the combined exports of the next three biggest exporters, all the while maintaining an extremely low level of foreign imported programming; ibid., 359.

This "hyper-imperial American culture," some insist, is not only "laying waste to indigenous cultures" but also "represents an onslaught on indigenous identities."[23] As such, with the possible exception of countries where fundamentalist Islam provides the dominant ideology, few parts of the world have escaped the flooding of certain global brands or icons of mass cultural production—Nike, Coca-Cola, IBM, Michael Jordan, Levi's jeans, and others. Intrinsic to this process of cultural homogenization is the spread of the English language, considered by proponents to be the indisputable language of the future or the dominant language of the new global order.[24] "Never in human history," notes Joshua Fisher, "has one language been spoken (let alone semi-spoken) so widely and by so many."[25]

THE END OF HISTORY?

The more extreme forms of this single global culture argument not only celebrate Western cultural ascendancy but also insist on the futility or bankruptcy of alternative worldviews. Francis Fukuyama's "the end of history" thesis is a notable example.[26] Fukuyama argues that the end of the Cold War, and the collapse of Soviet communism, signified the triumph of Western liberal democracy as "the ideal that will govern the material world in the long run."[27] Drawing, ironically enough, on Marxist analysis, Fukuyama maintained that precisely because "the basic *principles* of the liberal democratic state could not be improved upon," the inevitable "universalization of Western liberal democracy as the final form of government" represented "the end point of mankind's ideological evolution." In a phrase: the end of history.[28]

---

23. Sardar and Davies, *Why Do People Hate*, 124–25.

24. Held et al., *Global Transformations*, 346.

25. Fishman, "New Linguistic Order," 435.

26. Fukuyama's arguments first appeared in the article "The End of History?" and were subsequently developed in his book *The End of History*. The points and quotations mentioned here are from the article.

27. In Fukuyama's view, the threat posed by Communist China to liberalism had already begun to lose its potency. Though that country could not as yet be described as a liberal democracy, at least by 1989 the pull of the liberal idea was gaining strength with the total discrediting of Marxist-Leninism as an economic system and the Chinese economy's growing openness to the outside world.

28. This outcome is signified by the emergence of the "universal homogenous state," which Fukuyama defines as "liberal democracy in the political sphere combined with easy access to vcrs and stereos in the economic," ibid., n.p.

For Fukuyama, the universal triumph of this Western ideal is not confined to politics; indeed, its impact is already evident in "the ineluctable spread of consumerist Western culture" that will underpin the "universal homogenous state," a Marxist concept.[29] And, in the long run, the desires stimulated by this consumer culture will allow liberalism to displace indigenous cultures in the non-European world. Highlighting Japan as a case study, he argues that the essential elements of economic and political liberalism have been "successfully grafted onto uniquely Japanese traditions and institutions" and that the "desire for access to the consumer culture, created in large measure by Japan, has played a crucial role in fostering the spread of economic liberalism throughout Asia and hence in promoting political liberalism as well."[30]

Importantly, Fukuyama discounts both religion and nationalism as viable challenges to modern liberalism. We must note in passing that his treatment of both draws mainly on the European experience in which modern liberalism emerged out of the ashes of bitter nationalist-religious conflicts. In the case of religion, he points to its shortcomings as a public or political instrument and notes that past experiments in religiously based societies, presumably European, have failed miserably to provide peace and stability. Nationalism, he argues, is not incompatible with the liberalism project. Ethnic and nationalist tensions arise not so much from liberalism itself as from the fact that the liberalism project is incomplete. The unabashedly Eurocentric nature of Fukuyama's arguments and the core claims of his thesis provoked a spirited debate and storm of criticism in the Fall 1989 issue of *The National Interest*.[31] There is no point in rehashing that debate here.

It is necessary, however, to briefly interrogate the core claims and arguments of the cultural homogenization thesis. First, we do well to remind ourselves that the concept of a single global culture or "universal civilization" is peculiarly Western.[32] This is one among many critical assumptions, as Meic Pearse notes, that distinguishes the Western worldview from that of every other major culture.[33] Nor is it new. Recent global culture arguments essentially reprise a Eurocentric notion of "civilization" that dates back to the eighteenth century and represented a critical lens through which non-European cultures—deemed "barbarian" or backward—were

---

29. In the original Marxist understanding, the universal autonomous state represents a utopian entity in which "all prior contradictions are resolved and all human needs are satisfied," ibid.

30. Ibid.

31. Ibid.

32. Huntington, *Clash of Civilizations*, 66.

33. Pearse, *Why the Rest*, 15–16.

judged.³⁴ Thus, the concept of the "white man's burden," in tandem with notions of "manifest destiny" or "divine providence," provided ideological rationalization for the belief that the superior values, ideals, and material benefits of this civilization, crucially identified with Christianity, should be spread around the world—a process of expansion that lasted for over four centuries.

Huntington's comment that this expansion represented "the unidirectional impact of one civilization on all others" is a typical but questionable historical assessment.³⁵ The combined impact of the European colonial and Christian expansion projects generated massive transformations and radical social change in many parts of the world, but the encounter with the non-Western world also had profound and often paradoxical consequences for Western societies.

Among other things, it uncovered the hollowness of many universalistic claims associated with enlightenment thinking³⁶ and bankrupted the Christendom construct.³⁷ Moreover, the missionary encounter with Africa and Asia contributed to the revitalization of older religions like Hinduism, revolutionized Western scholarship, and led to the establishment of new disciplines. It also exposed the contextual nature of theological reflection and laid the foundation for major transformations within global Christianity. And, most pertinent, it led to prolonged encounter with other major religious systems like Islam, Hinduism, and Buddhism. These encounters highlighted the very nature of religious plurality, raising important questions about Western understandings of the Christian faith and Scriptures and impacting Western theological reflections.

In the new global context, relationships of dominance, exploitation, and dependency remain entrenched and Western hegemony in various forms and disguises represents a major strand of globalization. Yet, its long pedigree notwithstanding, the single global culture thesis is deeply flawed in crucial respects. To start with, it ignores the profound complexity of cultural interaction and encounter and "fails to take into account the ways in which cultural products are locally consumed, locally read, and transformed in

---

34. "Civilization" meant Western civilization, understood as an advanced and sophisticated cultural entity.

35. Huntington, *Clash of Civilizations*, 53.

36. "The ideal of a universal human subject," writes Dorinda Outram, "could not easily be reconciled with ideals of the inferiority of the negro races, or with the justification of slavery, nor with the idea that pacific islanders lived in different time from Westerners.... Conflict and contradiction thus marked most Enlightenment thinking about race, as it did other aspects of the 'exotic.'" Cf. Outram, *Enlightenment*, 76.

37 Walls, *Cross-Cultural Process*, 195.

the process."[38] Sociologist John Tomlinson also points out that to equate the worldwide presence of certain cultural goods with the emergence of a global culture implies a rather "impoverished concept of culture."[39] Culture, he adds, "simply does not transfer in [a] unilinear way" immune to forces of interpretation, indigenization, or translation.[40]

It is also striking that most of the experiences implied in the so-called global culture bespeak elite interaction and participation.[41] In other words, such interaction is confined to the more affluent sectors of the developing and developed world—arguably less than 5 percent of the global population—whose education, tastes, aspirations, and purchasing power mean that they have more in common with each other than with others in their own countries. Their livelihood and modes of existence are far removed from vast populations in both the developed and developing world for whom fast-food chains, television, genuine Levi's jeans, Nike shoes, and even telephones are outside the frame of daily existence and the struggle to "make ends meet" is the foremost preoccupation. The genuine partakers of American cultural symbols and consumer products embody not so much cultural homogenization as the menacing divisions engendered by economic globalization.

In the case of genuine globalizing movements like Pentecostalism, which impact the local order in societies throughout the world, the interpenetrative conjunction of the global and the local is prominent. The face of the global is in the local. Transnational products, from McDonald's to evangelical worship, must be adapted to local taste and requirement in order to reflect global appeal. As a case in point, the increasing global use of English is subject to powerful local cultural and linguistic influences that impact its structure, syntax, vocabulary, and word sounds.[42] Moreover, as Huntington points out, the emergence of English as a global *lingua franca* actually "helps to maintain and, indeed, reinforces peoples' separate cultural identities."

38. Held et al., *Global Transformations*, 373.

39. Tomlinson, *Globalization and Culture*, 83–84; also Appadurai, "Disjuncture and Difference," 324.

40. In all cultural interactions, people interpret and appropriate new concepts and experiences in terms of preexisting views and values. Pentecostalism, for instance, enjoys a global appeal precisely because it "has been the quintessential indigenous religion, adapting easily to a variety of [local] cultures." Klaus, "Pentecostalism," 127.

41. This is evident, for instance, in Berger's "four faces of global culture" analysis; see Berger, "Cultural Dynamics," 1–16.

42. Americans and the English are not the only peoples divided by the same language. Outside of elite circles—where advanced educational attainments produce a certain affinity—English speakers from different parts of the world, say Japan and Jamaica, would struggle to understand each other fully.

Many people use English to communicate with peoples of other cultures precisely because they want to preserve their own culture.[43] And, given the issues under consideration, it is also relevant to note that the spread of English (and French to a lesser extent) greatly facilitates international migrant movement and the capacity of non-Westen cultural movements to impact the Western world.

In truth, many individuals and groups around the world embrace Westernization at the expense of indigenous identity. Accessibility to Western education and the pull of Western norms often play a critical role in decisions to migrate. And many immigrants in the West are only too eager to discard restrictive or exploitative traditional customs in favor of secular liberal values—though they soon discover that such assimilative moves do not immunize them from xenophobic intolerance or racial rejection. For still many others, maybe for most, the harsh reality of cultural alienation serves to strengthen cultural identity. Thus, for Africans living in Western societies, the cross-cultural experience evokes a profound appreciation for and attachment to aspects of their indigenous culture; and this revitalized appreciation can be reinforced both by enduring homeland ties and the recreation of a distinctive transnational identity.

More broadly speaking, however, many around the world use or partake in Western/American products while rejecting the values they represent or turning them to different ends. Berger, a proponent of an emerging global culture, concedes that "in principle an individual could wear jeans and running shoes, eat hamburgers, even watch a Disney cartoon, and remain fully embedded in this or that traditional culture."[44] In Huntington's evocative phrase, "somewhere in the Middle East a half-dozen young men could well be dressed in jeans, drinking Coke, listening to rap, and, between their bows to Mecca, putting together a bomb to blow up an American airliner."[45]

Conceptually, the cultural homogenization thesis implicitly discounts the persistent and increasing importance of cultural distinctions and competing ideological worldviews as well as the salience of cultural resistance. Alternative analyses—notably Huntington's "clash of civilizations" thesis—suggest that the processes of modernization and attendant market consumerism have triggered or bolstered profound cultural, often religious, movements stimulated by acute concerns about indigenous identity. Analyses of such divergent global trends render the singular vision of cultural

---

43. Huntington, *Clash of Civilizations*, 62.
44. Berger, "Cultural Dynamics," 7.
45. Huntington, *Clash of Civilizations*, 58.

homogenization—whether embodied by liberal democracy or Western capitalist consumerism—highly problematic.

In the final analysis, the cultural homogenization thesis fundamentally ignores the ambiguity, flux, and paradox that characterizes global processes and exchange and overlooks the capacity of non-Western elements to adapt or resist Western flows and project alternative movements with potential global impact. Quite simply, the forces of globalization do not move in only one direction. More nuanced interpretative perspectives allow for what Berger describes as "globalization from below" or "alternative globalizations"—that is, "cultural movements with a global outreach originating outside the Western world and indeed impacting the latter."[46] In this regard, contemporary migration movements embody the most significant trends.

CONTEMPORARY MIGRATIONS

Migration is integral to the processes of globalization and a prime factor in global religious expansion. It is therefore of no small importance that the current stage of history is characterized by unprecedented population transfers and associated displacements, fostering the claim that we are living in an "age of migration." It is also increasingly obvious that current patterns of migration will potentially have an incalculable impact on religious interactions in the course of the twenty-first century.

By the early 1990s, UN records indicated that there were about seventeen million refugees and asylum seekers in the world, twenty million internally displaced people, thirty million "regular" migrants, and another thirty million migrants with an "irregular" status. For obvious reasons, these numbers involve best guesses and continue to escalate—stimulated in large measure by demographic imbalances and global economic inequalities.

The attendant increase in migration research and study has also challenged old paradigms and furnished new conceptual tools. The traditional distinction between "refugees"—those forced to move—and "migrants"—those who chose to move—for instance, has lost credibility. Motives for migration are much too complex and variegated for such a simple dichotomy—even economic migration is "forced" in some sense. More helpful perhaps is the fairly generic definition of migrants as people who have lived outside their homeland for one year or more. In 2005 there were an estimated 191 million international migrants in the world, according to the UN—more than double the numbers three decades earlier. In what follows,

---

46. Berger, "Cultural Dynamics," 12.

the term "migration" is used in the broadest sense as descriptive of different forms of transience involving degrees of choice and compulsion.

Most importantly, transformations in global communications and transport infrastructure have had a profound impact on the nature and dynamic of international migration in the last five decades, enabling fixed social and religious networks and interactions that transcend national boundaries and geographical distance. In other words, for new migrant communities, identity formation and cultural distinctiveness are no longer bounded by geographical location or social space. Becoming migrants or permanent residents outside the homeland does not necessarily translate into complete cultural isolation, severed ties, and erosion of identity.[47] International migrants make accommodations with, and invest in, the "host"—better still, "target"—society to varying degrees, but a good many also maintain strong connection and some degree of participation in their society of origin.

This reality has led to two important modifications to dominant explanatory theories within migration studies. In the first place, it has led some scholars to adopt the terms "transnational migration" or "transmigration" as affording a better conceptual framework for understanding current trends.[48] Transmigrants are often bilingual, able to lead dual lives, move easily between cultures, frequently maintain a home in two countries, and are incorporated as social actors in both. In short, they help to link the fate of distant communities. Secondly, the overwhelmingly non-Western composition of international migration means that their communities remain ethnically distinguishable in many Western societies regardless of acculturation. This, argues Alejandro Portes, has led to the diminishing likelihood of uniform processes of assimilation and rapid integration within Western society.[49] He employs the term "segmented assimilation" or "selective assimilation" to indicate that the new immigrants and their offspring retain aspects of ethnic identity while often assimilating in some areas like the educational and social.

WANTED, NOT WELCOME

For wealthy developed countries, immigration will remain one of the most perplexing sociopolitical issues for a long time to come. While aging populations and low birth rates have intensified the need for substantial

47. Schiller, "Transmigrants," 94–119.
48. Cf. Portes, "Immigration Theory," 29.
49. Cf. ibid., 30; Ebaugh and Chafetz, *Religion*, 456.

immigration to meet huge labor demands, populist backlash against immigration—non-white immigration in particular—remains politically explosive. Essentially, the new immigrants are "wanted but not welcome"; and many a government is trapped in purposeful ambivalence on the immigration question.[50] We should note, in passing, that despite excited xenophobic foreboding that Western societies are being overwhelmed by immigrants, an estimated 90 percent of global migration takes place *within* the non-Western world in the form of South-to-South migration. Even so, it is noteworthy that South-to-North migration accounts for 40 percent of trans-boundary flows.[51] Indeed, it is conjectured that many movements that start as South-to-South transfers end up as South-to-North flows. It is this South-to-North flow that is of interest here, with the main focus on aspects of the religious encounter.

The nature and extent of religious decline within Western societies—particularly that of the once-dominant Christian faith—under the enduring onslaught of secularization remains complex. Yet, current trends indicate a significant depreciation not only of the church's privileged position in Western societies but also of the ability of Christian institutions to influence individual lifestyles and societal norms. In September 2001, the head of the Catholic Church in England and Wales publicly declared that Christianity has been "all but eliminated" as a source of moral guidance in people's lives.[52] In the United States, where levels of overt Christian religiosity remain much higher, assessment of the rate of decline remains a contested issue; but George Hunter makes the telling observation that much of what passes as Christianity in America is "Christo-paganism," a form of civil religion blending patriotism, morality, materialism, contemporary wisdom, and idolatry of culture, etc."[53]

THE EUROPEAN EXPERIENCE

It is an interesting historical coincidence that, "at precisely the moment when the historic religions in Europe are losing control of both the belief systems and lifestyles of many modern Europeans,"[54] Europe is confronted with the growing presence of immigrants, who bring with them both religious plurality and religious dynamism. This process is transforming the

50. For an excellent study on this issue, see Cornelius et al., *Controlling Immigration*.
51. Uçarer,"Coming Era," 1–16.
52. "Christianity," BBC News.
53. Hunter, *How to Reach*, 24.
54. Davie, *Europe*, 38f.

West itself into a frontline of cultural confrontation and compromise with long-term implications for its self-understandings and engagement with the rest of the world. This is true even of the encounter between post-Western Christianities and the post-Christian West. There are over three million African Christian migrants in Europe. Their presence and the dynamism of their churches—also characterized by intense spirituality—provide a sharp contrast with moribund homegrown models and challenge European understandings of the Christian faith.[55] As I argue elsewhere, these trends also signify a new missionary engagement.[56]

Perhaps of even greater consequence is the growing presence and robustness of Islam and the challenge it poses to Europe's secularized culture. Islam is the second largest religion in France,[57] and more Muslims attend mosque every week in England than Anglicans attend church. The growth of Muslim populations in Europe has stimulated vigorous debates about cultural identity, attended by evocative appeals to national myths and strident calls for more aggressive integration of newcomers. Dramatic events like the murder of prominent Dutch filmmaker Theo van Gogh by an Islamic radical generate genuine fears about religious extremism and harden xenophobic hostility.[58] In reality, Muslims constitute less than 3 percent of the European Union's total population (thirteen million of 457 million).[59] But in countries with significant Muslim populations—France, Germany, Britain, and the Netherlands among them—calls for "a more aggressive insistence on western liberal values" are growing amid widespread disavowal of multiculturalism as a viable alternative.[60]

But even as the public mood in countries like the Netherlands reflects mounting intolerance for cultural accommodation, the integration approach, which basically calls for the Europeanization of Muslims, faces complex challenges. Keen observers note that Theo van Gogh's alleged killer, Mohammed Bouyeri, was not a marginalized individual but a student who did well at school, spoke excellent Dutch, and was active in community

---

55. Some of the largest churches in Europe today were established by African immigrants—notably the Nigerian-led Embassy for the Blessed Kingdom of God to all Nations, in Kiev (Ukraine), which boasts a membership of 20,000.

56. Hanciles, *Beyond Christendom*.

57. "Islamic Terrorism," 55–56.

58. Van Gogh's movie had outraged Muslims with his inflammatory depictions of Islam. His death was followed by a period of recriminatory violence involving the burning of schools and places of worship. Cf. "New Dutch," 24–26.

59. "Civil War," 56.

60. Ibid.

affairs.⁶¹ He also was part of a larger cell that included two Dutch-American converts to Islam. Even more significant, recent research into Dutch Islam showed that cultural and religious practices—including mosque attendance, choice of marriage partners, and general attitudes to the surrounding culture—changed little by the second generation.

Although most receiving countries claim to be liberal democracies, immigrants face cultural rejection, social stigma, racial discrimination, and human rights abuses. As traditional attitudes of tolerance are eroded further, the trend toward harsher policies in many European countries is likely to further undermine long-cherished liberal values and radicalize attitudes within immigrant communities. Thus, even an uncompromising integrationist approach to non-Western minorities will have implications for the host society. In the Netherlands, where the promotion of integration increasingly defines government policies, the change has necessitated unprecedented and unfamiliar steps, including the offer of subsidies to universities to open theological departments to train Muslim prayer-leaders; calls for the restoration of the death penalty; debate over strengthening the country's blasphemy laws to protect Islamic sensibilities; and consideration by Parliament of stringent antiterrorism laws intended to curb deeply cherished civil liberties.⁶²

Attitudes to immigrant culture vary considerably within particular European societies and between European countries. And despite the heated reactions that inevitably accompany actions by radical extremist groups, most non-Western immigrants accept some degree of accommodation, and many become model citizens without committing cultural suicide: Portes's "selective assimilation." Even when immigrants fully embrace Western liberal values, they can apply these newfound ideals in unexpected ways. A key figure in the current immigrant backlash in the Netherlands was Somali-born, former Muslim, and sometime Dutch liberal politician Ayaan Hirsi Ali. Fully embracing the liberalism of her adopted country, Ali collaborated with van Gogh in the making of the controversial movie that led to his murder—in the movie, Koranic verses were scrawled on the body of a naked woman—and to calls for a more aggressive integrationist policy centered on Western liberal values.⁶³ Her vigorous denunciation of immigrant culture not only alienated other Dutch Muslim women, whose cause she purportedly championed, but also invited criticism from other Dutch politicians.⁶⁴

61. "New Dutch," 24–26.
62. Ibid.
63. "Civil War," 56.
64. Cf. "Ayaan Hirsi Ali," 26.

A more dispassionate view suggests that meaningful long-term solutions to the current crisis will remain elusive without some adaptive compromise on both sides that involves cultural accommodation and a willingness to forge new collective identities. For Europeans this must necessarily involve a revisitation of some national myths and vigorous debate about what constitutes Western values—never mind claims to universality! Meanwhile, immigrant religions and cultures are also being transformed by the exigencies of life in Western societies and the pressures of transnationalism. These processes of change are forging within major world religions a pluriverse of new identities, ideologies, and cultural expressions that undermine the image of uniformity that tend to characterize Western perceptions.

For all the public angst generated by events surrounding new immigrant Muslim populations, the Islamic presence in Europe has a long history and, apparently, a growing future. Russia is home to an estimated twelve to twenty million Muslims, who account for approximately 14 percent of its population and constitute its largest religious minority. The recent creation of two new Muslim countries in Eastern Europe—Bosnia and Kosovo—not to mention the admittedly uncertain prospect of Turkey's 99 percent Muslim population being absorbed into the European Union,[65] all point to the fallacy of the prevalent notion that the Islamic world and the West are discrete geographical entities.

This deterritorialization of Islam—a trend attributable less to aggressive expansionism than the forces of migration—has witnessed increasing numbers of Muslims taking up permanent residence in non-Muslim societies. The fact that minority Muslim groups now account for a third of the world's Muslim population also raises acute questions about the traditional conception of the Muslim *ummah* as a bounded territorial reality.[66] As such, calls for the Europeanization of Islam overlook the very tangible possibility that Islam is already European. The same consideration applies to the American context.

---

65. For a thorough assessment of Turkey's prospects of European Union (EU) membership, see "Survey of Turkey." It is noteworthy that in May 2004, the EU experienced its biggest enlargement ever in terms of scope and diversity with the addition of ten new countries: Cyprus, the Czech Republic, Estonia, Hungary, Latvia, Lithuania, Malta, Poland, the Slovak Republic, and Slovenia—representing all together more than one hundred million citizens (see "History," *European Union*).

66. Roy, *Globalized Islam*, 18. Only about 18 percent of Muslims live in the Arab world.

Part 3: Contemporary and Global Perspectives

THE AMERICAN EXPERIENCE

America is the chief destination of the world's international migrants. By 2000, one in ten Americans was foreign born,[67] and the total "immigrant stock," including US-born children of immigrants, represents over one-fifth of the entire population.[68] Unlike previous waves of immigration, however, the overwhelming majority of current immigrants—90 percent of whom arrived after 1960—is of non-European stock and comes from over 150 countries.[69] Despite post-September 11, 2001, efforts to tighten immigration procedures, this pattern of immigration is set to continue. Already, children of immigrants make up the fastest growing component of the US population and represent 20 percent of all children.[70] These trends have immense implications not only for the future ethnic composition of the US population but also for the future shape of its sociocultural and religious landscape.

Not surprisingly, the nature and impact of the new immigration has generated much debate and nativist alarm.[71] Despite immense religio-cultural diversity and decades of substantial nonwhite immigration, the notion of America as an Anglo-Protestant culture—strongly evident in attitudes toward bilingual education—remains entrenched in the public mind.[72] This image is under severe threat. Data from the New Immigrant Survey (2001) indicates that while the majority of the new immigrants (65 percent) claim to be Christian, less than 19 percent identified themselves as Protestant and fully 15 percent reported themselves as Muslim, Buddhist, or Hindu.[73] In major cities throughout the country, immigrant religion is stimulating, in the words of one study, "a remarkable and exuberant expansion of churches, mosques, Buddhist temples, and synagogues, many of them designed to serve growing orthodox populations and new immigrants."[74]

67. Eck, *New Religious America*, 2.
68. Rumbaut and Portes, "Ethnogenesis," 1–19.
69. Ibid., 9. Slightly more than half (52 percent) come from Latin America and the Caribbean, and nearly a third (29 percent) come from Asia and the Middle East.
70. Jensen, "Demographic Diversity," 22.
71. Conservative political figures on the extreme right, like Pat Buchanan, already warn that Western European culture is endangered by depopulation, surrender of nationhood, and drowning in waves of Third World immigration—cf. Buchanan, *Death of the West*. "Only the AIDS epidemic," he surmises with remarkable callousness, "stands in the way of a Europe overshadowed and eventually overwhelmed by African peoples" (100).
72. Cf. Lexington, "How Anglo."
73. For a full analysis, see Jasso et al., "Exploring the Religious Preferences," 221.
74. Kotkin, "God," 35.

The immigrant infusion is rapidly changing the face of American Christianity. In thousands of churches and Christian communities across the country, the language of worship, theological orientation, and modes of interaction draw on decidedly foreign elements and seek to replicate non-Western preferences. Surely one reason why the Roman Catholic Church in the United States has avoided the fate of its counterparts in much of Europe is the huge boost it constantly receives from Hispanic immigration[75]—even given the possibility of large defections to vibrant Charismatic churches after arrival. Less well noticed is the impact of African immigrant churches whose vitality and dynamism cater for and draw on a widening base of immigrants hungry for the kind of spiritual orientation they represent. A seminal essay on the subject concluded that while "many immigrants adapt their religions to the social conditions of the host country the overall impact is what might be termed the *de-Europeanizing* of American Christianity."[76]

For analysts convinced that the end of the Cold War signifies the triumph of Western ideals and the inevitable surrender of non-Western cultures to the juggernaut of Western secularism or worldviews, the trends denoted by the new immigration must occasion discomfort. America's economic dominance clearly facilitates the global spread of American cultural goods—which, to reiterate an earlier point, does not in itself signify cultural homogenization—but equally important, if not more so, America's supremacy and democratic ideals also provide the ideal environment for the incubation, renewal, and global spread of minority faiths. This much is indicated by the case of Islam.

THE MAKING OF AMERICAN ISLAM

Of all the religious traditions associated with the new immigrants, Islam has experienced the most accelerated growth in recent years.[77] Estimates of the numbers of Muslims in the United States range from six to ten million. Of these, immigrant Muslims—two-thirds of whom are from South Asia—represent 70 to 75 percent, while American converts or indigenous Muslims account for the remaining 25 to 30 percent.[78] The latter includes

---

75. The new immigrants include a higher percentage of Catholics (42 percent) than the native population (22 percent) (Jasso et al., "Exploring the Religious Preferences," 218). By 1998, Mass was being celebrated in Spanish in at least 3,500 Catholic parishes throughout the country.

76. Yang and Ebaugh, "Transformations," 269–88, italics added.

77. Jasso et al., "Exploring the Religious Preferences," 221.

78. Khan, "Constructing," 176. The remaining one-third of immigrant Muslims come from the Middle East and Africa.

hundreds of thousands of white Americans, but the vast majority is African American. Even by the most conservative estimates, Muslims in America outnumber Episcopalian and Presbyterian Church USA adherents combined.[79] Indeed, Islam is poised to replace Judaism as the second-largest religion in the country. As in the case of Europe, America is now part of the Muslim world.

Partly because of this rapid growth, the formation of a cohesive Muslim community in America faces significant challenges in at least three areas.[80] First, though mainly Sunni, immigrant Islam is characterized by daunting ethnic, linguistic, racial, and sectarian diversity. With representatives from more than sixty nations,[81] it includes virtually every movement in the Muslim world, including those deemed "heretical." In reality, Islam in America is a microcosm of global Islam. Second, integrating this diverse immigrant body with indigenous Muslim communities has proven extremely difficult. Third, the climate of suspicion and antipathy engendered within the general public by the stereotypical and negative depictions of Islam and Muslims in the mainstream media deters many Muslims from fully identifying with their communities. Only the last two challenges will receive brief attention here.

The enduring tensions between the immigrant and indigenous Islamic communities have a lot to do with socioeconomic and ideological differences. On the one hand, immigrant Muslims in America tend to be among the best educated since restrictive immigration policies still favor highly skilled professionals. Reportedly, these Muslims have "at least ten times the wealth of the African, Hispanic, European, and Native American community"[82] and tend to be more focused on foreign policy issues and events overseas. Non-immigrant Muslims, on the other hand, are largely drawn from the poorer sections of American society, have inferior educational attainments as a whole, and are far more sensitive to experiences of racism and oppression within American society. These divisions remain difficult to bridge, and some suggest that the unilateral decision by immigrant Muslims to support George W. Bush in the 2000 presidential election may have caused irreparable and lasting damage.[83]

Both America's predominantly Christian ethos and the fact that many immigrant Muslims hail from countries Americans consider unfriendly

---

79. Eck, *New Religious America*, 2.
80. For a helpful overview, see McCloud, "Islam in America," 163–64, 167.
81. Haddad, "Make Room," 218.
82. Ibid., 172.
83. Ibid.

make integration and acceptance within American society a daunting prospect for serious Muslims. In turn, significant proportions of the Muslim community view America as an imperialistic, anti-Islam colossus intent on spreading its (immoral) values around the world. Yet, for the majority of Muslims, America's multicultural diversity, liberal democracy, and tolerance of religious plurality provides an environment that is far more conducive for building Islamic institutions and reconstituting Islamic movements than is conceivable in much of the Muslim world, where fixed ideologies and repressive political instruments militate against such initiatives. M. A. Muqtedar Khan points out that the hostility and prejudice many Muslims experience in America is nothing compared to the stifling character of despotic regimes in much of the Islamic world.[84]

In a word, the United States provides an enabling environment in which Islam is able to thrive and in which, thanks to the filtering process of immigration mechanisms, gifted Muslim professionals and intellectuals—some of whom came to the country as students—can pursue a revival of Islam and the reformulation of an Islamic identity.

To be sure, thousands of Muslims in America make rigorous efforts to assimilate: they Americanize their names—from Alhaji to Al, for example, give up Islamic habits in food and dress, and distance themselves from the Muslim community. But the growth of this community in the last three decades, the continued experience of hostility in the public domain, and increasing American involvement in the Islamic world have helped to stimulate a widespread determination among the new Muslim immigrant communities to preserve religious values and reconstruct an Islamic identity; and even make an impact on American society. To this end, there has been a huge drive toward institutional development. Islamic centers and schools have proliferated throughout the country. Over 2,000 centers and 1,200 schools have been established, and additional organizations provide intellectual vision, emphasize spiritual renewal, provide means of combating prejudice against Islam, generate copious publications, and encourage political mobilization.[85]

But all these developments are significantly shaped and influenced by the American context. Outside the cultural matrix that defines social organization and religious life in the Muslim world, major adaptations and remodeling of the practice of faith become mandatory. This process of selective adaptation and experimentation has been most conspicuous and extensive in the creation of Islamic centers or mosques, and communal

---

84. Khan, "Constructing," 180.
85. Cf. Ibid., 183–88.

life.[86] Adaptive changes have included the following: creation of a professionalized clergy;[87] the transformation of the mosque into a community center where marriage ceremonies and funerals take place, as well as non-mosque activities such as soup kitchens; the emergence of congregational membership; the adoption of Sunday for religious activities, including the implementation of Sunday schools for religious instruction; the adoption of evangelical phrases such as "'born-again' Muslims, 'salvation,' and realizing the 'Kingdom of God' on earth";[88] and a much expanded role for imams to include missionary activities not unlike that of Western evangelists.

Rogaia M. Abusharaf insists that such structural adaptation or institutional flexibility is not a novel phenomenon within Islam.[89] But even more important, this process of adaptation within immigrant communities in the United States has resulted in what is referred to as "the mosque movement," a movement that "promotes a vision of the mosque as the center for organized community activities"—understood as its original role—and aims to spread the new experiment in the Muslim world. Through the immigrant experience, therefore, the mosque has emerged "not so much as a transplant but a new creation with a revitalized function and role in society."[90] Far from being assimilated within a Western prism, Islam has experienced "new birth" and renewal through the immigrant encounter.

For this new generation of immigrant Muslims, the task of forging an identity as American Muslims has entailed experimenting not only with new institutional models but also major ideological shifts. Leading Muslim intellectuals, many of whom are alumni of American universities, promote a different kind of activism that is far removed from the media stereotypes of intolerant jihadists and terrorists. For them, the pressures and implacable constraints of the immigrant experience in America has enforced not mindless assimilation but a sophisticated ideological reorientation: a rethinking of ingrained hostility toward the West and a reinterpretation of Islamic ideals to meet the exigencies of life in a modern, predominantly non-Muslim context.

---

86. Cf. Abusharaf, "Structural Adaptations," 235–61; Haddad, "Make Room," 232–33.

87. Islam makes no provision for an official priesthood, and mosques in the Islamic world do not have professional ministers: imams are not professional religious leaders but rather "local leaders recognized for their extensive knowledge of the . . . Qur'an." Abusharaf, "Structural Adaptations," 253.

88. Haddad, "Make Room," 232.

89. Abusharaf, "Structural Adaptations," 251.

90. Haddad, "Make Room," 235.

In fact, argues Muqtedar Khan, this new generation of American Muslims is "not satisfied with the mere preservation of Islamic identity. They want it accepted and recognized as a constituent element of the American identity itself."[91] To this end, he elaborates:

> They have rejuvenated the tradition of *ijtihad* (independent thinking) among Muslims and now openly talk about . . . interpretation of the Shariah for places where Muslims are in the minority. They have emphasized Islamic principles of justice, religious tolerance, and cultural pluralism. They have Islamized Western values of freedom, human rights, and respect for tolerance by finding Islamic sources and precedents that justify them. . . .
>
> [They] are not Americans who are Muslims or Muslims who are born in America. They are American Muslims. They believe in Islam, they are democratic, they respect human rights and animal rights, and they share a concern for the environment. . . .
>
> [They] are as Islamic as any Muslim and as American as any American.

If previous generations sought to modernize Islam, confirms Yvonne Haddad, the current generation "seeks to Islamize modernity."[92] And the United States, by virtue of its determination to influence third world leadership and attract foreign students to its universities, has become a major center of Muslim intellectual activity, to the extent that it has replaced France as the primary center for Islamic intellectual reflection."[93] This development provides an even more cogent example of how non-Western immigrants can adopt and adapt the values and ideals obtained in a Western context and use them for unexpected ends.

THE CERTAINTY OF A RELIGIOUS FUTURE

Much about the processes of contemporary globalization calls for the use of new conceptual tools and critical models. The dynamism and flux of ongoing global transformations involve non-Western agents and elements and increasingly call into question the longstanding but Eurocentric dichotomies between secular and religious, modern and traditional, even global

---

91. Khan, "Constructing," 186.
92. Haddad, "Make Room," 231.
93. Ibid., 223.

and local. Grand theories that embody what I would term the myth of Western predestination and that depict globalization as a unidirectional process with a fixed set of outcomes are patently unhelpful. The best assessments allow for the unpredictability, ambiguity, and paradox that are intrinsic to global processes and exchange.

Whether the long-term resettlement of Muslim populations in Europe and North America makes Islam a "Western religion," as Olivier Roy asserts, must remain an open question.[94] Roy also makes the qualifying observation that "the dominant and final consensus in the West is about institutions, not values."[95] At the very least, self-satisfied claims about the global spread and imposition of Western culture and values look increasingly whimsical and myopic when massive migration movements steadily introduce non-Western cultures and religious expressions into European societies, transforming the collective image and religiosocial landscape. Importantly, the presence of these vibrant religious minorities in Europe and North America underlines the permanence of religion within global processes and its role as a central feature of social existence. It is a safe prediction therefore that whatever else the global future will be, it will be religious.

BIBLIOGRAPHY

Abusharaf, Rogaia M. "Structural Adaptations in an Immigrant Muslim Congregation in New York." In *Gatherings in Diaspora: Religious Communities and the New Immigration*, edited by R. Stephen Warner and Judith G. Wittner, 235–61. Philadelphia: Temple University Press, 1998.

Appadurai, Arjun. "Disjuncture and Difference in the Global Cultural Economy." In *The Globalization Reader*, edited by Frank J. Lechner and John Boli, 322–30. Malden, MA: Blackwell, 2000.

Barrett, David B. *Schism and Renewal in Africa: An Analysis of Six Thousand Contemporary Religious Movements*. Nairobi: Oxford University Press, 1968.

BBC News. "Christianity 'Almost Vanquished' in U.K.'" September 6, 2001. Online: http://news.bbc.co.uk/2/hi/uk_news/1527876.stm.

Berger, Peter L. "The Cultural Dynamics of Globalization." In *Many Globalizations: Cultural Diversity in the Contemporary World*, edited by Peter Berger and Samuel P. Huntington, 1–16. New York: Oxford University Press, 2002.

———. "The Desecularization of the World: A Global Overview." In *The Desecularization of the World: Resurgent Religion and World Politics*, edited by P. Berger, 1–18. Grand Rapids: Eerdmans, 1999.

———. "Four Faces of Global Culture." In *Globalization and the Challenges of a New Century: A Reader*, edited by Patrick O'Meara et al., 419–27. Indianapolis: Indiana University Press, 2000.

94. Roy, *Globalized Islam*, 17.
95. Ibid., 15.

———, ed. *The Desecularization of the World: Resurgent Religion and World Politics*. Grand Rapids: Eerdmans, 1999.

Berger, Peter L., and Samuel P. Huntington, eds. *Many Globalizations: Cultural Diversity in the Contemporary World*. New York: Oxford University Press, 2002.

Blair, Tony. "Address to the US Congress." *The Guardian*. July 18, 2003. Online: http://www.guardian.co.uk/politics/2003/jul/18/iraq.speeches.

Brooks, David. "Kicking the Secularist Habit: A Six-Step Program." *The Atlantic Monthly* 291.2 (2003) 26–28.

Buchanan, Pat. *The Death of the West: How Dying Populations and Immigrant Invasions Imperil Our Country and Civilization*. New York: St. Martin's, 2002.

Conser, Walter H., and Sumner B. Twiss, eds. *Religious Diversity and American Religious History: Studies in Traditions and Cultures*. Athens, GA: University of Georgia Press, 1997.

Cornelius, Wayne A., et. al., eds. *Controlling Immigration: A Global Perspective*. Stanford, CA: Stanford University Press, 2004.

Davie, Grace. *Europe, the Exceptional Case: Parameters of Faith in the Modern World*. London: Darton Longman & Todd, 2002.

Dempster, Murray W., et al., eds. *The Globalization of Pentecostalism: A Religion Made to Travel*. Irvine, CA: Regnum, 1999.

Ebaugh, Helen Rose., and Janet Saltzman Chafetz. *Religion and the New Immigrants: Continuities and Adaptations in Immigrant Congregations*. New York: AltaMira, 2000.

Eck, Diana L. *A New Religious America: How a "Christian Country" Has Now Become the World's Most Religiously Diverse Nation*. San Francisco, CA: Harper, 2001.

The Economist. "Ayaan Hirsi Ali: A Firebrand Under Cover." (April 2, 2005) 26.

———. "A Civil War on Terrorism." (Nov. 27, 2004) 56.

———. "Islamic Terrorism in Europe: After Van Gogh." (Nov. 11, 2004) 55–56.

———. "The New Dutch Model?" (April 2, 2005) 24–26.

———. "A Survey of Turkey." *The Economist* (March 19, 2005). No pages.

Etounga-Manguelle, Daniel. "Does Africa Need a Cultural Adjustment Program?" In *Culture Matters: How Values Shape Human Progress*, edited by Lawrence E. Harrison and Samuel P. Huntington, 65–77. New York: Basic, 2000.

European Union. "History." European Union, April 12, 2005. Online: http://europa.eu.int/abc/history/2004/index_en.html.

Fishman, Joshua A. "The New Linguistic Order." In *Globalization and the Challenges of a New Century: A Reader*, edited by Patrick O'Meara et al., 435–42. Indianapolis: Indiana University Press, 2000.

Fukuyama, Francis. "The End of History?" *The National Interest* Special Edition (Summer 1989). No pages.

Glasswell, Mark E., and Edward W. Fashole-Luke, eds. *New Testament Christianity for Africa and the World: Essays in Honour of Harry Sawyerr*. London: SPCK, 1974.

Haddad, Yvonne Yazbeck. "Make Room for the Muslims?" In *Religious Diversity and American Religious History: Studies in Traditions and Cultures*, edited by Walter H. Conser and Sumner B. Twiss, 218–61. Athens, GA: University of Georgia Press, 1997.

Haddad, Yvonne Yazbeck, et al., eds. *Religion and Immigration: Christian, Jewish, and Muslim Experiences in the United States*. Walnut Creek, CA: AltaMira, 2003.

Hanciles, Jehu J. *Beyond Christendom: Globalization, African Migration, and the Transformation of the West.* Maryknoll, NY: Orbis, 2008.

Harrison, Lawrence E. "Introduction." In *Culture Matters: How Values Shape Human Progress*, edited by Lawrence E. Harrison and Samuel P. Huntington, xvii–xxxiv. New York: Basic, 2000.

Harrison, Lawrence E., and Samuel P. Huntington, eds. *Culture Matters: How Values Shape Human Progress.* New York: Basic, 2000.

Held, David, et al., eds. *Global Transformations: Politics, Economics and Culture.* Stanford, CA: Stanford University Press, 1999.

Hirschman, Charles, et al., eds. *The Handbook of International Migration: The American Experience.* New York: Russell Sage Foundation, 1999.

Hunter, George G., III. *How to Reach Secular People.* Nashville, TN: Abingdon, 1992.

Huntington, Samuel P. *The Clash of Civilizations and the Remaking of World Order.* New York: Simon & Schuster, 1996.

Jasso, Guillermina, et al. "Exploring the Religious Preferences of Recent Immigrants to the United States: Evidence from the New Immigrant Survey Pilot." In *Religion and Immigration: Christian, Jewish, and Muslim Experiences in the United States*, edited by Yvonne Y. Haddad et al., 217–53. Walnut Creek, CA: AltaMira, 2003.

Jensen, Leif. "The Demographic Diversity of Immigrants and Their Children." In *Ethnicities: Children of Immigrants in America*, edited by Rubén G. Rumbaut and Alejandro Portes, 21–56.

Khan, M. A. Muqtedar. "Constructing the American Muslim Community." In *Religion and Immigration: Christian, Jewish, and Muslim Experiences in the United States*, edited by Yvonne Y. Haddad et al., 175–98.

Klaus, Byron D. "Pentecostalism as a Global Culture: An Introductory Overview." In *The Globalization of Pentecostalism: A Religion Made to Travel*, edited by Murray W. Dempster et al., 127–30. Irvine, CA: Regnum, 1999.

Klinghoffer, David. "That Other Church: Let's Face It: Secularism Is a Religion. Let's Treat It as Such." *Christianity Today* 49.1 (2005) 62.

Kotkin, Joel, and Karen Speicher. "God and the City." *The American Enterprise* (October/November 2003) 34–39.

Lechner, Frank J., and John Boli, eds. *The Globalization Reader.* Malden, MA: Blackwell, 2000.

Lexington. "How Anglo is America?" *The Economist* (November 13, 2004). No pages.

Lipset, Seymour Martin, and Gabriel Salman Lenz. "Corruption, Culture, and Markets." In *Culture Matters: How Values Shape Human Progress*, edited by Lawrence E. Harrison and Samuel P. Huntington, 112–24. New York: Basic, 2000.

McCloud, Aminah Beverly. "Islam in America: The Mosaic." In *Religion and Immigration: Christian, Jewish, and Muslim Experiences in the United States*, edited by Yvonne Yazbeck Haddad et al., 159–74. Walnut Creek, CA: AltaMira, 2003.

Minogue, Kenneth. "Religion, Reason and Conflict in the 21st Century." *The National Interest* (2003) 127–31.

O'Meara, Patrick, et al., eds. *Globalization and the Challenges of a New Century: A Reader.* Indianapolis: Indiana University Press, 2000.

Outram, Dorinda. *The Enlightenment.* New York: Cambridge University Press, 1995.

Pearse, Meic. *Why the Rest Hates the West: Understanding the Roots of Global Rage.* London: SPCK, 2004.

Pipes, Daniel. "God and Mammon: Does Poverty Cause Militant Islam?" *National Interest* 66 (Winter 2001/2002) 14–21.

Portes, Alejandro. "Immigration Theory for a New Century: Some Problems and Opportunities." In *The Handbook of International Migration: The American Experience*, edited by Charles Hirschman et al., 21–33. New York: Russell Sage Foundation, 1999.

Roy, Olivier. *Globalized Islam: The Search for a New Ummah*. New York: Columbia University Press, 2004.

Rumbaut, Rubén G., and Alejandro Portes, eds. *Ethnicities: Children of Immigrants in America*. Berkeley, CA: University of California Press, 2001.

———. "Ethnogenesis: Coming of Age in Immigrant America." In *Ethnicities: Children of Immigrants in America*, edited by Rubén G. Rumbaut and Alejandro Portes, 1–19. Berkeley, CA: University of California Press, 2001.

Sardar, Ziauddin, and Merryl Wyn Davies. *Why Do People Hate America?* New York: The Disinformation Company, 2002.

Schiller, Nina Glick. "Transmigrants and Nation-States: Something Old and Something New in the US Immigrant Experience." In *The Handbook of International Migration: The American Experience*, edited by Charles Hirschman et al., 94–119. New York: Russell Sage Foundation, 1999.

Shweder, Richard A. "Moral Maps, 'First World' Conceits, and the New Evangelists." In *Culture Matters: How Values Shape Human Progress*, edited by Lawrence E. Harrison and Samuel P. Huntington, 158–76. New York: Basic, 2000.

Stark, Rodney. "Secularization: The Myth of Religious Decline." *Fides et historia* 30.2 (1998) 1–19.

Stark, Rodney, and Roger Finke. *Acts of Faith: Explaining the Human Side of Religion*. Berkeley, CA: University of California Press, 2000.

Tomlinson, John. *Globalization and Culture*. Chicago: University of Chicago Press, 1999.

Turner, Harold W. "The Contribution of Studies on Religion in Africa to Western Religious Studies." In *New Testament Christianity for Africa and the World: Essays in Honour of Harry Sawyerr*, edited by Mark E. Glasswell and Edward W. Fashole-Luke, 169–78. London: SPCK, 1974.

Uçarer, Emek M. "The Coming Era of Human Uprootedness: A Global Challenge." In *Immigration into Western Societies: Problems and Policies*, edited by Emek M. Uçarer and Donald James Puchala, 1–16. Washington, DC: Pinter, 1997.

Walls, Andrew F. *The Cross-Cultural Process in Christian History: Studies in the Transmission and Appropriation of Faith*. New York: Orbis, 2002.

Warner, R. Stephen, and Judith G. Wittner, eds. *Gatherings in Diaspora: Religious Communities and the New Immigration*. Philadelphia: Temple University Press, 1998.

Yang, Fenggang, and Helen Rose Ebaugh. "Transformations in New Immigrant Religions and Their Global Implications." *American Sociological Review* 66 (April 2001) 269–88.

Chapter 13

The Future of Pluralisms— and Why They Likely Will Fail[1]

Veli-Matti Kärkkäinen

FOR ORIENTATION: VARIOUS "TURNS" IN THE CHRISTIAN THEOLOGY OF RELIGION

TO NEGOTIATE THE UNIQUENESS of Christian confession of the Triune God in relation to the "foundational" claims of other living faith traditions, Christian theologians have proposed several tactics in order to find common ground. At the cost of oversimplifying a complex set of developments, let us name these turns a movement from Christocentric to Theocentric to Pneumatocentric approaches. As long as Christian theology was based on a more or less exclusivist standpoint, the point of departure for the theology of religions discourse was the finality of Christ as the only way to God. A turn to Theocentrism seemed to give more space for opening up to other religions: while Christ is one way to the Father, he is not the only one. God is bigger than any single religion. Soon, among theologians from across the

---

1. This is a shortened version of Chapter 14 in my *Trinity and Revelation: A Constructive Christian Theology for the Pluralistic World* (Grand Rapids: Eerdmans, 2014). Adapted and reprinted by permission of the publisher; all rights reserved.

ecumenical spectrum, a turn to the "Spirit" was enthusiastically initiated.[2] The turn to pneumatology seemed to promise a lot. After all, doesn't the Spirit speak for universality while Christ speaks for particularity?

This essay argues that each of these turns in itself is inadequate and leads to insurmountable problems. It is not the case that earlier turns, particularly the turn to the Spirit, have been all wrong. It is just that, left on their own, they are not able to deliver the promises attached to them, such as openness, tolerance, and genuine dialogue. Briefly put, they fail in providing an attitude of hospitality and they end up denying both the otherness of the Other and one's own solid identity. Therefore, a more coherent framework is to be found in an effort to relate the Christian Trinitarian confession of faith with other living faiths in a genuinely and authentically *Trinitarian* approach.[3]

To make the discussion manageable and specific enough, the current essay focuses on the pluralistic theologies' conceptions of God, or the Divine, which of course in traditional Christian faith means belief in God as Trinity. One could also approach the question of religious pluralisms and their claims via Christology[4] or pneumatology[5] or, say, the doctrine of revelation.[6] Yet, many of the underlying theological and religious claims stay materially intact.

The first main section after this introduction will delve into a critical discussion of the "first generation" Christian theological pluralistic proposals, focusing on those coming from Asian soil as well as the well-known and widely debated proposal of John Hick. Following that discussion, an evaluative look at various recent *Trinitarian* approaches that seek to correct Hick's and similar-minded colleagues' modernist views will be offered. Before attempting a constructive Trinitarian proposal in defeat of pluralisms, a summative global assessment of the reasons why pluralisms may fail is offered. In the final main section, an outline of a constructive Trinitarian proposal will be set forth.

---

2. See, e.g., Yong, "Turn to Pneumatology."

3. For an up-to-date report, see Johnson, *Rethinking the Trinity*, 25–50. Also, Netland and McDermott, *Trinitarian Theology*.

4. For a critique and alternative constructive proposal concerning the turn from Christocentric to theocentric, see my *Christ and Reconciliation*, ch. 9.

5. For a critique and alternative constructive proposal to pneumatocentric approaches, see my *Spirit and Salvation* (forthcoming), ch. 5.

6. For a comparative study of the understanding of revelation and Scripture between Christian faith and four other living faith traditions—Jewish, Muslim, Hindu, and Buddhist, see my *Trinity and Revelation*, ch 8. There I also critique Christian pluralistic notions.

THE "FIRST GENERATION" PLURALISMS

God as "Mystery"

The somewhat clumsy expression "first generation" pluralisms is a convenient way of referring to the pluralistic Christian theologies of religions that arose in the second half of the last century, building on the modernist epistemology and ethos. These emerged both in the Global North—from Protestant John Hick and Roman Catholic Paul F. Knitter—and in Asia—from Protestant Stanley J. Samartha, Mar Thoma M. M. Thomas, and Roman Catholic Aloysius Pieris. Even those coming from Asian soil, while shaped by that continent's multireligious context, draw their main inspiration from the European Enlightenment and its subsequent developments, including Classical Liberalism. By and large, they represent the replacement of Christocentrism with Theocentrism. Unlike later versions of pluralisms to be discussed in the next subsection, these did not take the Trinity as the main framework but rather, more generally, the doctrine of God.[7]

In the context of India and other Asian countries, with the growing sense of religious tolerance but increased and intensified political and social intolerance, theologians such as Samartha saw clearly the impasse between the traditional exclusivist Christian confession and the plurality of religious claims. In keeping with the less categorical pan-Asian mindset—whose logic does not so predominantly operate with the Western either/or logic,[8] Samartha took as a clue the category of the Divine as "Mystery":

> This Mystery, the Truth of the Truth (*Satyasya Satyam*), *is* the transcendent Center that remains always beyond and greater than apprehensions of it even in the sum total of those apprehensions. It is beyond cognitive knowledge (*tarka*), but it is open to vision (*dristi*) and intuition (*anubhava*). It is near yet far, knowable yet unknowable, intimate yet ultimate, and according to one particular Hindu view, cannot even be described as "one." It is "not-two" (*advaita*), indicating thereby that diversity is within the heart of Being itself, and therefore may be intrinsic to human nature as well.[9]

The emphasis on Mystery is meant to make room also for the mystical and the aesthetic in theology. Samartha believes that Mystery lies beyond the

---

7. For an overview and exposition of these and other pluralistic proposals, see my *Introduction to the Theology*, esp. chapters 32–35.
8. See Jung, "Yin-Yang Way of Thinking," 87.
9. Samartha, "Cross and Rainbow," 111.

dichotomy of theistic versus nontheistic. "Mystery is an ontological status to be accepted, not an epistemological problem to be solved. Without a sense of Mystery, *Theos* [Greek term for god] cannot remain *Theos*, nor *Sat* [Hindi term for god] remain *Sat*, nor can Ultimate Reality remain ultimate."[10] Samartha believes that the nature of Mystery makes inadmissible any claim on the part of one religious community to have exclusive or unique knowledge. Exclusiveness creates dichotomies between different religious communities and leaves little room for the nonrational elements in religious life, such as the mystical, the aesthetic, meditation, and rituals.

While Christ remains central in this conception, for Samartha Christ is not exclusively so. "This Other [God as the Mysterious Other] relativizes everything else. In fact, the willingness to accept such relativization is probably the only guarantee that one has encountered the Other as ultimately real."[11] While Samartha is not naively assuming the equality of all religions, he also insists that "a particular religion can claim to be decisive for some people, and some people can claim that a particular religion is decisive for them, but no religion is justified in claiming that it is decisive for all."[12]

Rather than attempting a full critical response to Samartha at this point, let me add a couple more general comments before I discuss John Hick's version of a theocentric pluralism and engage him in a more thoroughgoing manner. While different in many aspects, Samartha's and Hick's theocentric pluralisms share a similar underlying logic. To speak of God as Mystery, which is nothing new in Christian tradition, is not necessarily to shy away from the claim to uniqueness. Beginning from early patristic traditions, when Christian theology insisted on the mysterious nature of the Triune God, it meant to say that we have to be humble and modest about how much we know of this "Unknowable One." To claim, as Samartha does, that from the mysterious nature logically follows the standpoint that refuses to consider Christ as the fullest and only true revelation of God, is of course a way to deny the logic of the statement itself! In other words, of total Mystery the human mind cannot say this or that. Likewise, the desire to "soften" the rational claims of theology and make room for aesthetic and mystical elements is also familiar in Christian tradition; but again, from this move it does not follow necessarily that one must reject the Christian claim for uniqueness.

---

10. Ibid.
11. Samartha, *Courage for Dialogue*, 151–52.
12. Ibid., 153; see also Samartha, "Unbound Christ," 146.

God as the "Ultimate Reality"

Having left behind much of the traditional Christian confession,[13] John Hick compares his turn to pluralistic theocentrism with the astronomical model of Copernicus that replaced the Ptolemaic view. In that model, at the center of all religions stands God, the Ultimate Truth around which all religions—including Christianity—as human interpretations of divine reality, revolve in the analogue of the planets.[14] The essence of theocentric pluralism hence is that there are "both the one unlimited transcendent divine Reality and also a plurality of human concepts, images, and experiences of and responses to that Reality."[15] All religions—whether Christian or Hindu[16] or Buddhist[17]—are challenged to move away from the "Ptolemaic" view.[18] To accomplish this task, Hick contends that the views of the adherents of religions cannot be taken at face value, but rather each religion has to be confronted by the challenge of deemphasizing its own absolute and exclusive claims.[19] Various conceptions of God/god(s)/divine, such as Yahweh, Allah, Krishna, Param Atma, or Holy Trinity, are but aspects of the Divine[20] or like maps or colors of the rainbow.[21]

While at first Hick was content to speak of *God*, later—in order to do justice to his understanding of the nature of religious language and respond to justified criticism that his pluralistic conception still favored theistic and even *mono*theistic religions—Hick shifted from speaking about God to speaking of the "Ultimate Reality." This term is more flexible than the personal term *God*. The Sanskrit term *sat* and the Islamic term *al-Haqq* are expressions of that personal term, as are *Yahweh* and the Christian *God*.[22]

In describing religions' access to and knowledge of the Ultimate Reality, Hick utilizes the Kantian distinction between *phaenoumena* (the way we see things) and *noumena* (the thing in itself, which is unknown to us), and maintains that there is a part of the Divine/Reality that is totally unknown to us and a part about which we know at least something. The Hindu concept

---

13. See Hick, "Reconstruction of Christian Belief," 339–45 and 399–405.

14. This is the main claim of Hick's widely read *God and the Universe*. For a succinct, summative statement, see his *Second Christianity*, 82.

15. Hick, *Second Christianity*, 83.

16. Hick, *God and the Universe*, 131; Hick, *God Has Many Names*, 83.

17. Hick, *Problems*, 48; Hick, *The Metaphor of God Incarnate*, 134.

18. Hick, *Rainbow of Faiths*, 44.

19. Hick, *Interpretation of Religion*, 2–3.

20. Hick, *God and the Universe*, 140–41.

21. Hick, *Problems*, 80.

22. Hick, *Interpretation of Religion*, 10–11.

of *nirguna Brahma*, in contrast to *saguna Brahma*, refers to something that cannot be fathomed at all by human means of knowledge. Similarly, the "eternal Tao" of Taoism about which we know nothing is distinguished from the "expressed Tao." Irrespective of these differing names and approaches to the Reality, in Hick's view there is only one Reality, the ultimate divine. This he postulates mainly on the basis of astonishingly similar concepts of the divine in various religions.[23] A key tool for Hick in constructing this Theocentric pluralism is his turn to metaphorical understanding of religious language.

What about Hick's view of the Trinity? He has not said much of that. He rightly notes that in the doctrinal system in which Christian thought was embedded from the beginning, the doctrines of incarnation, atonement, and Trinity cohere together.[24] Since he does not feel bound to a traditional view of Christ's incarnation or atonement,[25] he ends up affirming a modalistic or Unitarian view, which he describes himself in the following way:

> An inspiration christology coheres better with some ways of understanding trinitarian language than with others. It does not require or support the notion of three divine persons in the modern sense in which a person is a distinct center of consciousness, will, and emotion—so that one could speak of the Father, the Son, and the Holy Spirit as loving one another within the eternal family of the trinity, and of the Son coming down to earth to make atonement on behalf of human beings to his Father. An inspiration christology is, however, fully compatible with the conception of the trinity as affirming three distinguishable ways in which the one God is experienced as acting in relation to, and is accordingly known by, us—namely, as creator, redeemer, and inspirer. On this interpretation, the three persons are not three different centers of consciousness but three major aspects of the one divine nature.[26]

In line with his metaphorical understanding of religious talk, Hick can understand the doctrine of the Trinity "not as ontologically three but as three ways in which the one God is humanly thought and experienced."[27] In his view, this kind of modalistic version of the doctrine of the Trinity

23. Hick, *Rainbow of Faiths*, 69.
24. Hick, "The Non-absoluteness of Christianity," 30.
25. Discussed in some detail in my *Christ and Reconciliation*, 214–24.
26. Hick, "Non-absoluteness of Christianity," 32; also *Interpretation of Religion*, 170–72, 271–72.
27. Hick, *Metaphor of God Incarnate*, 149.

has parallels with other religions such as Islam's threefold name of God as omnipotent creator and ruler of the universe, God as gracious and forgiving, and God as intimately present to us.[28]

Even though Hick claims to present a kind of metatheory[29] of religions, he reminds us of the fact that his view is not based on some preconceived philosophical or theological standpoint but rather is a result of empirical, phenomenological observations. The pluralist, according to Hick, does not even claim to possess the final word about religions.[30] While the last claim might be true of any academic and theological scholar of religion, I find it highly problematic that Hick seeks to offer a world-embracing metatheory of religion.

There are a number of problems here, not the least of which is naive reliance on the grand stories of modernity! First, it could be argued that Hick's proposal is not a metatheory but rather yet another form of positive religion. Second, attempting a meta-religion takes quite a bit of pride and hubris since it means nothing less than lifting up oneself above existing religions and claiming to have a neutral—perhaps even God's—point of view. Third, such an enterprise leads to violence and denial of the right of the religious Other to be other. Indeed, Hick is telling the rest of humanity—most of whom are adherents of a particular religion—that their view (of the uniqueness and "salvific" power) of their own religion is "wrong" and should be replaced with another. Rightly, many critics have noted that ignoring the self-understanding of adherents of religions means nothing less than violating their religious rights.[31] It is "elitist" and "imperialistic."[32] Even some pluralists have critiqued Hick for the lack of respect for the religious Other.[33] In this context, it should also be asked, what gives the modern interpreter a superior knowledge concerning ancient religions?[34] Fourth, methodologically Hick's metatheory builds on the now-rejected

---

28. Hick, "Rethinking Christian Doctrine," 98.

29. See further, Hick, "Religious Pluralism," 417–20; 418; Hick, "Epistemological Challenge," 277–86.

30. Hick, *Problems of Religious Pluralism*, 37; Amnell, *Uskontojen Universumi*, 49.

31. See Kaufman's nuanced and important critique, "Religious Diversity," 143–64.

32. Amnell, *Uskontojen Universumi*, 63. One critic goes so far as to claim that Hick is guilty of "intellectual Stalinism." See McGrath, "Conclusion," 200–209; see Cobb's similar critique, *Beyond Dialogue*, 38–44.

33. Instead of this kind of "universal" pluralism, Panikkar calls for a deepening respect among religions in view of existing real differences. Panikkar, "Invisible Harmony," 120–25, 141.

34. Several authors have raised this question; e.g., Berger, *Heretical Imperative*, 119–20; Amnell, *Uskontojen Universumi*, 90.

older theory of the common core behind all religions. It is not self-evident at all that behind the diversity of manifestations of religions lies a common core. It can also be argued that regardless of the difference or similarity of the manifestations, behind them lie irreconcilable religious, philosophical, and worldview differences.[35] Fifth, while not totally non-cognitivist, Hick's way of conceiving the nature of religious language virtually rips it away from any serious truth claims—a "truth claim" most adherents of religions find impossible to accept.

With regard to Hick's view of the Divine/Ultimate Reality, these difficult questions must be raised: First, it seems to me his view of the Divine is formal, without any content. It has to be so lest it begin to favor unduly a certain kind of religion. The dilemma is simply this: on the one hand, the more Hick says about what kind of "god" the Ultimate Reality is, the more he begins to exclude religions; on the other hand, the less he says of what the Ultimate Reality is, the more meaningless and less interesting the claim becomes because it is virtually empty. Second, if it is a formal concept, how does Hick "know" that there are two aspects to the Divine— "phenomenological" (of which something can be known) and "noumenal" (of which nothing can be known)? Hick shares this deep dilemma with Kant.[36] Third, anyone following the classical canons of Christian tradition cannot be content with a modalistic view of the Divine.

Trinitarian pluralists are proposing theologically more interesting and, in terms of interfaith engagement, more fruitful ways of negotiating the Christian confession of God in response to religious pluralism and specific claims of living faiths. We turn next to their suggestions before attempting a constructive proposal for the purposes of this project.

THE "TURN" TO TRINITARIAN WAYS OF CONSTRUCTING PLURALISTIC THEOLOGIES

Trinity and a Cosmotheandric Vision

As mentioned above, after many moves, the turn to the Trinity as the way to negotiate the relation of the God of the Bible to religious pluralism and other living faiths has caught the attention of several contemporary theologians.[37] While these proposals differ in nature and orientation, they all build

---

35. I am indebted here to Risto Saarinen, "Eri uskonnot," 150–56.

36. I am indebted here to the nuanced, detailed, and insightful discussion throughout Amnell, *Uskontojen Universumi*.

37. A massive pioneering study by the late senior Roman Catholic theologian

on the conviction that apart from the Trinitarian framing of the doctrine of God, no lasting results will come.[38] The pioneer in the field is the Roman Catholic Raimundo Panikkar,[39] who places himself at the confluence of the four rivers: Hindu, Christian, Buddhist, and Secular.[40] In his small yet highly significant book *The Trinity and the Religious Experience of Man* (1973), Panikkar argued for the viability of a Trinitarian approach based on the groundbreaking idea not only that all religions reflect a Trinitarian substructure but also that there is a Trinitarian structure to reality. The underlying notion of Panikkar's theological vision in general and Trinitarian understanding in particular is the neologism "cosmotheandrism," defined thus: "The cosmotheandric principle could be formulated by saying that the divine, the human and the earthly—however we may prefer to call them—are the three irreducible dimensions which constitute the real, i.e., any reality inasmuch as it is real."[41] Or, "There is no God without Man and the World. There is no Man without God and the World. There is no World without God and Man."[42] In other words, in Panikkar's vision the cosmotheandric principle expresses the fundamental structure of reality in terms of an intimate interaction of God, humankind, and the world or cosmos.

A key insight for Panikkar is that the Trinity, while a distinctively Christian way of speaking of cosmotheandrism, is not an exclusively Christian reality.[43] The Trinity is the "junction where the authentic spiritual dimensions of all religions meet."[44] Hence, Christians alone cannot "own" the Trinity or its proper understanding; its appreciation requires constant interaction with other religions. Christianity can learn from others, but it also has a significant role to play in leading "to the plenitude and hence to the conversion of all religions."[45] In the final analysis, the end of this process (and the goal of Christianity) is "humanity's common good."[46]

Born to an Indian father and Spanish mother, Panikkar follows the typical Asian way of thinking and logic built on the principle of *advaita*,

---

Jacques Dupuis is *Toward a Christian Theology*. For a thoughtful account and proposal from a moderate Process perspective, see Suchocki, *Divinity and Diversity*.

38. For my critical engagement with the proposal in Smart and Konstantine, *Christian Systematic Theology*, see my book *Trinity*, ch. 16.

39. See Vanhoozer, "Does the Trinity Belong?," 58.

40. Panikkar, *Unknown Christ*, 30.

41. Panikkar, *Cosmotheandric Experience*, ix.

42. Ahlstrand, *Fundamental Openness*, 134.

43. See Panikkar, *Trinity*, viii.

44. Ibid., 42.

45. Ibid., 4.

46. Panikkar, "Jordan," 102.

which means "non-duality" (literally, not two). Wary of all dualisms, Panikkar surmises that there "are not two realities: God and man (or the world). . . . Reality itself is theandric; it is our way of looking that causes reality to appear to us sometimes under one aspect and sometimes under another."[47] Applied to the ancient problem of unity and diversity in the Trinitarian God, the advaitic principle implies that Father and Son are not two, but they are not one either; it is the Spirit who unites and distinguishes them.[48] Fittingly, a recent commentator names Panikkar's vision "Advaitic Trinitarianism."[49]

Following his advaitic logic, Panikkar constructs the Christian doctrine of the Trinity in a most unique way. The Father is "Nothing." This is the apophatic way—but even more than that, the way to approach the Absolute is without name.[50] There is no "Father" in himself; the "being of the Father" is "the Son." Panikkar comes to this conclusion on the basis of his interpretation of the Johannine saying that no one comes to the Father except through the Son (John 14:6).[51] In the incarnation, *kenosis*, the Father gives himself totally to the Son. Thus the Son is "God."[52] Panikkar believes this understanding is the needed bridge between Christianity and Buddhism as well as advaitic Hinduism. What *kenosis* ("self-emptying") is for Christianity, *nirvana* and *sunyata* are for these two other religions. "God is total Silence. This is affirmed by all the world religions. One is led toward the Absolute and in the end one finds nothing, because there *is* nothing, not even Being."[53] Consequently, the Son is the only "person" of the Trinity. For this statement to make sense, Panikkar notes that the term "person," when used of the internal life of the Trinity, is an equivocal term that has different meanings in each case. Since the "Father" is a different kind of "person" compared to the "Son," and the "Spirit" differs in nature from both, it is not advisable to use the same term "person" for these different meanings.[54] In that qualified sense, it is also understandable when Panikkar says that there is in fact "no God" in Christian theology in the generic sense of the term. There is only "the God of Jesus Christ"; thus, the God of theism is always the

47. Panikkar, *Trinity*, 73.
48. Ibid., 62.
49. Cousins, "Panikkar's Advaitic Trinitarianism"; for the term *advaitic*, see esp. 120.
50. Panikkar, *Trinity*, 46. Coming from a Hindu background, the Mahayana concept of *sunyata* looms large in the background.
51. Ibid., 47.
52. Ibid., *Trinity*, 45–47.
53. See Ramachandra, *Recovery of Mission*, 91, for discussion of Panikkar's proposal.
54. See further, Panikkar, *Trinity*, 51–52.

"Son," the only one with whom human beings can establish a relationship.[55] What about the Spirit? The Spirit is "immanence." To make more concrete the meaning of the Spirit as immanence is challenging (acknowledged in all theologies for that matter): "Immanence is incapable of revealing itself, for that would be a contradiction of terms; an immanence which needs to manifest itself, is no longer immanent." Panikkar uses images, paints pictures to say something more about the Spirit: "The Father is the source of the river, the Son the river that flows from the source, and the Spirit is the ocean in which the river ends."[56]

Everything said so far speaks of Panikkar's desire to facilitate the coming together of living faiths, yet without leaving behind the uniqueness of each. As mentioned, however, his pluralistic vision based on the doctrine of the Trinity is radically different from the typical pluralistic ideas of "rough parity" among religions. The Trinity speaks for diversity, not for uniformity or denial of differences.[57] "The mystery of the Trinity is the ultimate foundation for pluralism."[58] And "In the Trinity a true encounter of religions takes place, which results, not in a vague fusion or mutual dilution, but in an authentic enhancement of all the religious and even cultural elements that are contained in each."[59] Instead of pluralism, Panikkar prefers the term "parallelism": all religions run parallel to meet only in the Ultimate, at the end of time.[60]

Furthermore, for Panikkar, Christian understanding of the Trinity is in need of deepening from other religions; on the other hand, Christianity contributes to a fuller understanding of that vision among other religions. Exclusivism is avoided by maintaining that Christianity, no more than other religions, must never absolutize its current historical understanding. Panikkar firmly maintains that religions need each other and are mutually dependent.[61] His cosmotheandric vision sees the need to affirm diversity and posit mutuality on the basis of Trinitarian relations. All attempts toward universalization, so prevalent in Western culture as he sees it, are anathema to Panikkar.[62]

---

55. Ibid., 52.
56. Ibid., 63.
57. See Raj, *Raimon Panikkar's Cosmotheandric Vision*, 39.
58. Panikkar, "Jordan," 110.
59. Panikkar, *Trinity*, 42.
60. See further, Panikkar, *Intrareligious Dialogue*.
61. See further, Ahlstrand, *Fundamental Openness*, 184.
62. See further, Lanzetta, "Mystical Basis," 97.

One term Panikkar uses to speak of diversity and complementarity is *perichoresis*. For Panikkar, the idea of *perichoresis* implies the mutual conditioning and transformation of religions in their diversity on the way to convergence.[63] Another implication of the idea of *perichoresis* is that plurality as such is not a problem but rather an asset. The goal of pluralistic theologies is to not water down or dismiss plurality but enhance it. Therefore dialogue matters; through interaction, religions condition and enrich each other. Each religion comes out of the encounter with a deeper sense of its own identity, yet with the awareness of needing each other. Finally, in a very bold move, Panikkar places the world's religious traditions interior to the Godhead and depicts them as pluralistic self-revelations of divinity. "The Trinitarian life is one of pluralism in oneness, or distinction in unity, that is constantly replenishing itself."[64]

Panikkar's contribution to the development of Christian Trinitarian thinking cannot be undermined even if it also faces considerable challenges. In my understanding, his main contribution is elevating the doctrine of the Trinity to a central place not only in Christian theology in general but also in the theology of religions in particular. This is a healthy, badly needed corrective both in the theology of religions and comparative theology. With his bold move, Panikkar has offered a major critique of pluralisms. Another major asset of his Trinitarian doctrine is his insistence on diversity-in-unity. In addition, the fact that he has been able to not only "contextualize" the doctrine but also relate it to his own Asian context and religiosity is an admirable achievement.

What are the challenges?[65] Regarding the foundational question of whether Panikkar's revised vision of cosmotheandrism really represents a Christian doctrine of the Trinity, we must tackle a question he puts to himself: "Why do I persist, then, in still speaking of the Trinity when, on the one hand, the idea that I give of it goes beyond the traditional idea by Christianity?"[66] Without really giving substantial answers, he is content to insist on the continuity with Christian tradition.[67] His version of Trinitarianism, however, certainly elicits serious questions.

Panikkar's interpretation of the Johannine sayings that no one comes to the Father except through the Son (John 14:6) seems to go beyond any

63. See Ahlstrand, *Fundamental Openness*, 184.
64. Lanzetta, "Mystical Basis," 95.
65. For a more extensive engagement, see my *Trinity and Religious Pluralism*, 119–33. I engage Panikkar's pluralistic Christology in *Christ and Reconciliation*, 134–54.
66. Panikkar, *Trinity*, 43.
67. Ahlstrand, *Fundamental Openness*, expresses serious reservations, esp. 152–56.

exegetical warrants or any traditional Christian theological intuitions. In contrast to his interpretation, Christian theology has understood from this saying not that the Father does not exist but rather that the only way to know the Father is through the Son sent by his Father. I understand Panikkar's motive here—to relate the Father of Christianity to the godhead in the Buddhist concept of nirvana and sunyata—but I fear he is misrepresenting both Buddhist and Christian sources here.

Whatever similarities there might be with the basically a-theistic, nonpersonalist Buddhist notion of *nirvana*, in my opinion, no amount of stretching of the meaning of the concepts could make it compatible with the personalist, theistic notion of the Father in Christian faith. This is to confuse the way we talk about God (in apophatic terms) with how God exists (if in Buddhism there is any kind of concept of the divinity). Rather than trying to connect Buddhism and Christianity with the help of this most suspect twisting of terms, Panikkar should rather be faithful to his foundational idea of radical differences between religions and their concepts of the divine. So I think Panikkar has committed the most typical sin of pluralism—of which he is often critical—namely, dismissing the real differences among religions and their conceptions by assuming a similarity behind the terminology.[68]

Equally problematic is Panikkar's interpretation of the role and meaning of Son in his Trinitarian vision. In Christian theology, the Son is not the focus. Thus, ironically, Panikkar's version of Trinitarianism is to be judged as too "Christocentric": the biblical canon, especially the Gospel of John, makes clear that even the Son's equality to the Father never implies taking the place of the Father.

Also problematic is Panikkar's advaitic approach to logic and truth. While I think it is appropriate for him as a theologian to draw from Asian wells by using the thought forms available in those cultures, I fear that his quite uncritical—and selective—use of the *advaitic* principle becomes problematic. It seems to me an *advaitic* principle is called forth whenever serious logical or other intellectual problems are encountered. Resorting to either the advaitic or mystical principle can become an exercise in avoiding the core problem.[69] But, of course, Panikkar's own notion of pluralism cannot be a universal theory, and therefore truth itself is pluralistic.[70] Like any other relativistically oriented thinker, Panikkar cannot live up to his philosophical claims to relativism. His position, like those of many other pluralists, rests

---

68. Kärkkäinen, *Trinity and Religious Pluralism*, 130.
69. See also Larson, "Contra Pluralism," 72.
70. Ibid., 77.

on certain propositional claims and thus requires a propositional network and operates with truth/falsehood logic.[71]

Trinity and Diverse Religious Ends

The Trinitarian proposal of the American Baptist S. Mark Heim evades typical categorizations in that, on the one hand, it looks quite traditional in elevating the Trinity as the major theological topic, and on the other hand, while critical of existing pluralistic theologies of religions,[72] attempts to advance a radically pluralistic view of religious ends based on the idea of the diversity in the godhead. The launch pad for Heim's development of a distinctively Trinitarian pluralism is his 1995 work titled—surprisingly—*Salvations* (plural). The main argument of that book is that, rather than one common religious end for people of all faiths, there is a diversity of end goals willed by God. The sequel, *The Depth of the Riches: A Trinitarian Theology of Religious Ends* (2001), represents a full-blown vision of the Trinity as the guarantor of more than one goal for the followers of religions, including Christians, for whom communion with God is the highest aim.

The key idea in Heim's Trinitarian understanding of the theology of religions is simple and straightforward: "One set of ways may be valid for a given goal, and thus final for that end, while different ways are valid for other ends."[73] A twofold affirmation is included in this programmatic statement: not only that differences among religions are real but also that those differences should be honored and be made an asset rather than an obstacle. This means not only that *moksha* or *nirvana* of the Buddhist religion are legitimate ends for Buddhists but also that Buddhism as a particular religion is necessary to make those ends possible; the same applies to salvation as communion with God as promised for Christians.[74]

Heim champions a robust theology of communion that underwrites a relational and dynamic view of the Triune God. If relationality in the godhead speaks for communion—yet communion in diversity—then salvation also means varying degrees of being in communion with God or being related to God.[75] Salvation simply means being in relation. The following quotation makes this point succinctly:

71. Ibid., 81.
72. Heim's criticism concerning (other) pluralistic theologies lies in their denial of real differences among religions (*Salvations*, 3).
73. Ibid.
74. Heim, *Depth of the Riches*, 31.
75. Ibid., ch. 2.

> We can . . . see the connection between the Trinity and varied religious aims. The actual ends that various religious traditions offer as alternative human fulfillments diverge because they realize different relations with God. It is God's reality as Trinity that generates the multiplicity of dimensions that allow for that variety of relations. God's threefoldness means that salvation necessarily is a characteristic communion in diversity. It also permits human responses to God to limit themselves within the terms of one dimension. Trinity requires that salvation be communion. It makes possible, but not necessary, the realization of religious ends other than salvation.[76]

The implications of this approach are staggering: "The 'one way' to salvation, and the 'many ways' to religious ends are alike rooted in the Trinity."[77] Whether one looks for communion with God (as in Christian religion) or dissolution into the divine (as in the mainstream Hindu religion[s]), these goals are "grounded in God, in the coexisting relations in God's own nature."[78]

What about the differences between religions? How do the differences in how people in various religions are related to God play into the differences in the religious ends? Here Heim introduces an idea of a "hierarchy" of religious ends, an idea that helps him differentiate ends but is problematic in that hierarchy implies "higher" and "lower" ends. That kind of grading, however, can only be done from a particular perspective: what seems to be a "higher" end for, say, Christians might not appear as high to the devout Hindu. Therefore, I have suggested that perhaps a term like "taxonomy" would be more appropriate for his purposes.[79] Furthermore, Heim argues that his vision is in keeping with the traditional Christian eschatological vision based on the ancient idea of "plenitude." The principle of plenitude means simply that God's infinite nature entails the proliferation of the greatest variety of types (but, of course, not number) of beings.

While Heim's specific views about religious ends will be considered in the discussion of eschatology, for the purposes of this discussion, I will focus only on the question of the way Trinity is related to other faiths. If I have correctly understood Heim's nuanced and brilliant proposal, it seems to me that Heim fails to deal with the question of the unity in the godhead. He either takes the unity for granted—an assumption that is unwarranted

---

76. Ibid., 181.
77. Ibid., 209.
78. Ibid., 179.
79. Kärkkäinen, *Trinity and Religious Pluralism*, 134–54.

in the context of comparative theology—or wishes to highlight the diversity at the expense of the unity. So the question simply is: How does God's "communion-in-diversity" account for the unity?

One way to highlight the importance of tackling the question of the unity is to ask: To what extent can Heim's vision be considered to be in keeping with classical canons of Christian theology? The reason this question is legitimate is that Heim often makes the claim that his theological program is a faithful, albeit creative, interpretation of biblical and historical theology. As Heim himself notes, the main impetus for the rise of the doctrine of the Trinity in early Christian theology was to secure the closest possible union between Yahweh of the Old Testament and Jesus Christ.[80] Not only that, but the Trinity was also needed to negotiate the apparent tension between the transcendence of God and the historical particularity of the incarnated Son as the very revelation of God. So the original purpose of the doctrine of the Trinity was not so much to affirm diversity in God as it was to affirm belief in one God. In that sense, the way Heim works toward his theology of the Trinity is exactly the opposite. That in itself is of course not the problem, but unless the unity is secured, I fear that making the diversity the main theological asset is suspect.

The question of unity aside, the main critical question—again, in need of much more elaboration—has to do with the question of "So what?" Granted that there is diversity in the godhead—and all Trinitarian doctrines affirm it—one needs to ask what the implications are for our theology. The biggest challenge to Heim's way of linking the diversity in the godhead to the question of the diversity of religious ends can be formulated this way: To make a jump from the principle of the diversity in the godhead to the diversity in the religious ends willed by the Triune God is both unwarranted and logically less than convincing. Logically the claim may or may not be true; biblically and theologically the claim is not, I fear, a legitimate move. Indeed, it seems to me that it speaks against the very idea of communion: in the biblical vision, the purpose of humanity, created in the image of God, is to (re)turn to eternal communion with the Triune God. Even when that does not happen, Christian theology affirms that it is not because God has not willed it but rather because God honors the freedom given to humanity.

To allow the possibility of lack of communion—as with the doctrine of hell or annihilation—is radically different from making the failure to reach communion a theological program. It seems that Heim's use of the Trinitarian doctrine conflicts with the biblical vision of the gathering of all people in the New Jerusalem under one God (Rev 21–22). Somewhat ironically,

---

80. Heim, *Depth of the Riches*, 131.

it takes another pluralist, the Catholic Paul F. Knitter, to bring to light the problem I am trying to highlight here:

> Christians have always taken for granted, and still do, that because there is one God, there is one final destination. Heim's efforts to draw out the possibility of many salvations from the Christian doctrine of the Trinity go only half-circle.... The other half swings back to oneness: the three divine persons... have something in common that enables them to relate to each other, enhance each other, achieve ever greater unity among themselves.[81]

Yet another significant challenge to Heim's position also makes it less pluralistic than it claims to be: it is hardly good news to the Hindu or Buddhist to be told that their nirvana is an end willed by the Christian God and that it is "lower" than communion with the Triune God. How pluralistic is such a claim? How much does it differ from a typical inclusivistic approach?[82]

Having now investigated and critiqued several leading Christian pluralistic approaches, let me subject them to a "global" assessment by looking at the reasons why I believe they fail to deliver the promises they typically announce, namely, openness, tolerance, and equality.[83]

BROKEN PROMISES OF PLURALISMS

The leading Roman Catholic theologian of religions from England, Gavin D'Costa, has offered a sharp criticism of pluralisms, which he considers merely representations of modernity's "hidden gods," a species of Enlightenment modernity. What is the main reason for the failure of pluralisms then? "Despite their [pluralists'] intentions to encourage openness, tolerance, and equality they fail to attain these goals—on their own definition—because of the tradition-specific nature of their positions. Their particular shaping tradition is the Enlightenment.... The Enlightenment, in granting a type of equality to all religions, ended up denying public truth to any and all of them.... [And the end result is that the pluralists'] 'god is modernity's god.'"[84] D'Costa laments the fact that even though pluralists present

---

81. Knitter, *Introducing Theologies of Religions*, 231.
82. See Kärkkäinen, *Trinity and Religious Pluralism*, 151.
83. The rest of this chapter is heavily indebted to my earlier essays: "Uniqueness of Christ," 111–35; "'Trinitarian Prolegomena,'" 47–70; "Trinitarian 'Rules,'" 121–27;
84. D'Costa, *Meeting of Religions and the Trinity*, 1–2.

themselves as honest "brokers to disputing parties," they in fact conceal the fact "that they represent yet another party which invites the disputants actually to leave their parties and join the pluralist one"; namely, "liberal modernity." Therefore, ironically, pluralists end up being "exclusivists," even guilty—as in Hick's case—of "liberal intolerance."[85] An antidote to pluralisms, D'Costa argues, is not exclusivism but rather an attitude that takes delight in the potential of an encounter with the Other without denying either parties' distinctive features. "The Other is always interesting in their difference and may be the possible face of God, or the face of violence, greed, and death. Furthermore, the Other may teach Christians to know and worship their own trinitarian God more truthfully and richly."[86]

I agree with D'Costa's criticism of the failures of modernist pluralisms as well as its goal for making room for a "critical, reverent, and open engagement with otherness, without any predictable outcome."[87] In order for this to happen, we must reconceive the three cardinal virtues of pluralism that modernity-based ideology fails to deliver: equality, justice, and tolerance. The reason pluralism fails is because it waters down real differences among religions and regards all of them as the same below the surface. As noted above, Hick's version of pluralism is an example of the approach that denies the otherness and difference of the Other. Consequently, it does not take the dialogue with Other seriously since basically all religions teach the same thing, differing doctrines notwithstanding. Why should one engage in serious dialogue with the Other whose difference has already been mythologized and subsumed under one's own world explanation? Doing so, pluralism denies the self-definitions of particular religions and from a distance tells the followers of other religions what is the truth.[88]

In contrast, with D'Costa this project argues that openness becomes "taking history seriously," and not dismissing it as "pluralism" seems to do. Differences do matter and should not be suspended. Tolerance, rather than denying the tradition-specific claims for truth—which in itself, ironically, is one more truth claim among others—becomes the "qualified establishment of civic religious freedom for all on the basis of Christian revelation and natural law." Equality becomes the "equal and inviolable dignity of all persons," which naturally leads to taking the Other seriously, dialoguing with the Other with willingness to learn from the Other and teach the

---

85. Ibid., 20, 22, 24.

86. Ibid., 9.

87. Ibid.

88. See further, D'Costa, "Christian Theology and Other Religions," 161–78, and Hick's response: "Possibility of Religious Pluralism," 161–66.

Other.[89] On the "foundation" of this open-minded, tolerant, and equalitarian attitude toward the religious Other, an integrally Trinitarian approach to religions builds in five interrelated movements. For brevity's sake, let us call them "Trinitarian Sign-posts."

SOME TRINITARIAN "SIGN-POSTS" ON THE WAY TOWARD A HOSPITABLE INTERRELIGIOUS CO-HABITATION

Trinitarian Faith as the Christian Criterion[90]

It was no less a theological giant than Karl Barth who made this programmatic statement: "The doctrine of the Trinity is what basically distinguishes the Christian doctrine of God as Christian, and therefore what already distinguishes the Christian concept of revelation as Christian, in contrast to all other possible doctrines of God or concepts of revelation."[91] Indeed, the most foundational tenet of faith for all Christian churches is the Trinitarian confession of Father, Son, and Spirit. The one God of the Old Testament, *Yahweh*, is the Father of Jesus Christ who came to save us in the power of the Spirit.

The Trinity not only determines the Christian view of God, it also shapes our understanding of Christ. Only when Christ is confessed as truly divine and truly human, following the ancient symbols (creeds) of faith confessed by all Christian churches, can the Christian doctrine of the Trinity be maintained. Making Jesus merely an ethical teacher, as in Classical Liberalism, or only one "incarnation" among others—as in extreme Pluralisms, an embodiment of the Deity, a.k.a. Hindu *avataras*—truncates not only the confession of the Trinity but also the biblical understanding of Christ. While there is of course no reason to limit the knowledge of God to the particularity of Jesus of Nazareth, it also is true, to quote Heim, that "the Trinity is unavoidably Christocentric."[92] It is one of the tendencies of current pluralistic—and also some nonpluralistic pneumatological—theologies of religions to seek release from the contours of history, and as they believe, of particularity. That will not do or else the Christian identity is lost.

---

89. For a brief statement, see D'Costa, *Meeting of Religions*, 9.

90. This section borrows directly from my two earlier essays titled "Theologies of Religions," in *Evangelical Interfaith Dialogue*, and "Theologies of Religions," in *Witnessing to Christ*, 110–18;

91. Barth, *Church Dogmatics*, 1/1, 301.

92. Heim, *Depth of the Riches*, 134.

As noted above, many problems in theologies of religions derive from a less than satisfactory conception of the Trinity, including the typical pluralistic pitfalls of the turn to "theocentrism" in an effort to replace Jesus as *the* Way or the turn to the "Spirit" in order to get around the centrality of Jesus and Father, as if the Spirit's ministry were independent from other Trinitarian members. Approaches to other religions and mission similarly fail, in their tendency to minimize the church and only speak of the kingdom of God and the building of the kingdom as the only goal.[93] That is to fail to recognize the fact that the kingdom, the rule of God, is in itself a Trinitarian process: the Son comes in the power of the Spirit to usher in the Father's righteous rule, graciously allowing the Church, the body of Christ, to participate in its coming. Of course, the kingdom is far wider than the church; but the church serves as sign, anticipation, and tool of the coming rule of God.

"'Othering' with Grace and Courage"

For Christians, the confession of the Triune God is not an abstract statement. It is "economic" language based on the revelatory presence and embodiment of God in Christ with us. The Trinity speaks of relationality, communion, and belonging. The Divine communion exists in the form of an eternal mutual love. Out of that love, Father reaches out to men and women in his Son through the Holy Spirit. God has not only spoken; God has also become one of us—without leaving behind the deity. Thereby, the Trinity introduces history and time into the divine life. God's relation—reaching out—to the world in incarnation, salvation, and consummation is not something external to the divine life. Borrowing from the biblical scholar Walter Brueggemann, I make the term "other" a verb to remind us of the importance of not seeing the religious Other as a counter-object but rather "the risky, demanding, dynamic process of relating to one that is not us."[94] What matters is the capacity to listen to the distinctive testimony of the Other, to patiently wait upon the Other, and make for him or her a safe space. Similarly, that kind of encounter gives the Christian an opportunity to share the distinctive testimony of the love of God.

An important aspect of the process of "othering" is to resist the tendency, so prevalent in secular societies of the Global North and in the various forms of religious pluralisms, to draw the Other under one's own

---

93. For a critique of the Roman Catholic pluralist Paul F. Knitter in this respect, see my *Christ and Reconciliation*, 231–35.

94. Brueggemann, *Covenanted Self*, 1.

world-explanation and thus deny the existence and possibility of genuine differences among religions. It is an act of insult rather than a sign of tolerance to tell the believer of another faith that, contrary to his or her own self-understanding, no real differences exist in beliefs, doctrines, and ultimate ends.

When the Other is allowed to be Other in his or her own distinctive way, a genuine interfaith encounter has the potential of facilitating both the receiving and giving of gifts. One of the Christian gifts is the sharing of an authentic, personal testimony to Christ, the Lord and Savior, with a view to inviting people of other faiths to submit their lives to the God of the Bible. At the same time, the Christian receives the twofold gift; namely, learning about the Other and at times learning more about one's own faith in the mirror of another faith. This is what the Roman Catholic Gavin D'Costa calls the Holy Spirit's "invitation for mutual engagement."[95]

With this in mind, Christians, along with representatives of other faiths of good will, should do their best to help governments and other authorities to secure a safe, noncoercive place for adherents of religions to present their testimonies without fear. The late missionary bishop Lesslie Newbigin reminded us of the fact that while for Christians the gospel is a "public truth," it has nothing to do with a desire to return to the Christendom model in which the state seeks to enforce beliefs.[96] That should be unacceptable to all religions. In a truly pluralist society, decision for beliefs can never be a matter of power-based enforcement. When Christians, Muslims, Hindus, Buddhists, Sikhs, Confucians, and followers of other faiths can without fear and threat meet each other in a free "marketplace" of beliefs and ideologies, genuinely missionary encounters are possible.

A powerful metaphor that has been adopted in many contemporary discourses on interfaith encounters is that of "hospitality," a concept well represented in the biblical canon as well as in various cultural contexts. The above-cited ecumenical document "Religious Plurality and Christian Self-Understanding" reminds us that "in the New Testament, the incarnation of the Word of God is spoken of by St. Paul in terms of hospitality and of a life turned toward the 'other' [Phil 2:6–8]."[97]

---

95. D'Costa, *Meeting of Religions*, 109–17.
96. For details, see my "Church in the Post-Christian Society," 125–54.
97. World Council of Churches, "Religious Plurality," 27.

Dialogue, Mission, and Tolerance

The recent Catholic interreligious document titled "Dialogue and Proclamation" encapsulates in a few pregnant sentences a holistic understanding by listing the principal elements of mission in terms of Christian "presence and witness; commitment to social development and human liberation; liturgical life, prayer, and contemplation; interreligious dialogue; and finally, proclamation and catechesis." The document stresses that "proclamation and dialogue are thus both viewed, each in its own place, as component elements and authentic forms of the one evangelizing mission of the Church. They are both oriented toward the communication of salvific truth."[98] In other words, interfaith dialogue includes and makes space both for proclamation, with a view to persuading by the power of truth and love, and for dialogue, with a view to facilitating mutual understanding, reconciliation, and harmony.

For the representatives of those religions that are missionary by nature, such as Christianity and Islam, any dialogue engagement also provides a legitimate opportunity to try to persuade the other parties of the supremacy of one's own beliefs. Bishop Newbigin tirelessly reminded us that Christian faith—or any other missionary faith—that is not eager and willing to share its deepest convictions in the hope of being able to convince the Other, does not really believe in the truthfulness and value of its faith!

For the dialogue to be meaningful it takes both commitment to one's own beliefs and openness to listen carefully to the Other. A true dialogue does not mean giving up one's truth claims but rather entails patient and painstaking investigation of real differences and similarities. The purpose of the dialogue is not necessarily to soften the differences among religions but rather to clarify similarities and differences as well as issues of potential convergence and impasse. A successful and fruitful dialogue often ends up in mutual affirmation of differences, different viewpoints, and varying interpretations.

The contemporary secular mindset often mistakenly confuses tolerance for lack of commitment to any belief or opinion. That is to misunderstand the meaning of the term *tolerance*. Derived from the Latin term meaning "to bear a burden," tolerance is needed when real differences are allowed. Tolerance means patient and painstaking sharing, listening, and comparing notes—as well as the willingness to respectfully and lovingly make space for continuing differences.

---

98. Pontifical Council, "Dialogue and Proclamation."

A religiously pluralistic environment and society calls for tolerance that makes room for differences and facilitates mutual missionary enterprises as long as those arise from the self-understanding of each religion.

BIBLIOGRAPHY

Ahlstrand, Kajsa. *Fundamental Openness: An Enquiry into Raimundo Panikkar's Theological Vision and Its Presuppositions*. Uppsala: Swedish Institute for Missiological Research, 1993.

Amnell, Matti T. *Uskontojen Universumi: John Hickin uskonnollisen pluralismin haaste ja siitä käyty keskustelu*. Suomalaisen Teologisen Kirjallisuusseuran Julkaisuja 217. Helsinki: STK, 1999.

Barth, Karl. *Church Dogmatics*, vol. 1.1. Edited by Geoffrey W. Bromiley and Thomas F. Torrance, and translated by Geoffrey W. Bromiley. Edinburgh: T. & T. Clark, 1956.

Berger, Peter. *The Heretical Imperative: Contemporary Possibilities of Religious Affirmation*. Garden City, NY: Anchor, 1980.

Brueggemann, Walter. *The Covenanted Self: Explorations in Law and Covenant*. Minneapolis: Augsburg Fortress, 1999.

Cobb, John B., Jr. *Beyond Dialogue: Toward a Mutual Transformation of Christianity and Buddhism*. Philadelphia: Fortress, 1982.

Cousins, Ewert H. "Panikkar's Advaitic Trinitarianism." In *The Intercultural Challenge of Raimon Panikkar*, edited by Joseph Prabhu, 119–30. Maryknoll, NY: Orbis, 1996.

D'Costa, Gavin. "Christian Theology and Other Religions: An Evaluation of John Hick and Paul Knitter," *Studia Missionalia* 42 (1993) 161–78.

———. *The Meeting of Religions and the Trinity*. Maryknoll, NY: Orbis, 2000.

Dupuis, Jacques. *Toward a Christian Theology of Religious Pluralism*. Maryknoll, NY: Orbis, 1997.

Elwood, Douglas J., ed. *Asian Christian Theology: Emerging Themes*. Philadelphia: Westminster, 1980.

Heim, S. Mark. *The Depth of the Riches: A Trinitarian Theology of Religious Ends*. Grand Rapids: Eerdmans, 2001.

———. *Salvations: Truth and Difference in Religion*. Maryknoll, NY: Orbis, 1995.

Hick, John. "The Epistemological Challenge of Religious Pluralism." *Faith and Philosophy* 14 (1997) 277–86.

———. *God and the Universe of Faiths: Essays in the Philosophy of Religion*. 2nd ed. London: Macmillan, 1977.

———. *God Has Many Names*. Philadelphia: Westminster, 1982.

———. *An Interpretation of Religion: Human Responses to the Transcendent*. Gifford Lecturers, 1986–87. New Haven, CT: Yale University Press, 1989.

———. *The Metaphor of God Incarnate: Christology in a Pluralistic Age*. London: SCM, 1993.

———. "The Non-absoluteness of Christianity." In *The Myth of Christian Uniqueness: Toward a Pluralistic Theology of Religions*, edited by John Hick and Paul F. Knitter, 16–36. Maryknoll, NY: Orbis, 1987.

———. "The Possibility of Religious Pluralism: A Reply to Gavin D'Costa." *Religious Studies* 33 (1997) 161–66.

---. *Problems of Religious Pluralism*. London: Macmillan, 1988.
---. *The Rainbow of Faiths: Critical Dialogues on Religious Pluralism*. London: SCM, 1995.
---. "Reconstruction of Christian Belief for Today and Tomorrow: 1." *Theology* 73 (1970) 339–45.
---. "Reconstruction of Christian Belief for Today and Tomorrow: 2." *Theology* 73 (1970) 399–405.
---. "Religious Pluralism and the Divine: A Response to Paul Eddy." *Religious Studies* 31 (1995) 417–20.
---. "Rethinking Christian Doctrine in the Light of Religious Pluralism." In *Christianity and the Wider Ecumenism*, edited by Peter C. Phan, 89–102. New York: Paragon, 1990.
---. *The Second Christianity*. London: SCM, 1983.
Hick, John, and Paul F. Knitter, eds. *The Myth of Christian Uniqueness: Toward a Pluralistic Theology of Religions*. Maryknoll, NY: Orbis, 1987.
Johnson, Keith E. *Rethinking the Trinity and Religious Pluralism: An Augustinian Assessment*. Downers Grove, IL: InterVarsity Academic, 2011.
Kärkkäinen, Veli-Matti. *Christ and Reconciliation: A Constructive Christian Theology for the Pluralistic World*. Grand Rapids: Eerdmans, 2013.
---. "The Church in the Post-Christian Society between Modernity and Late Modernity: Lesslie Newbigin's Post-critical Missional Ecclesiology." In *Theology in Missionary Perspective: Lesslie Newbigin's Legacy*, edited by Mark T. B. Laing and Paul Weston, 125–54. Eugene, OR: Pickwick, 2013.
---. "'How to Speak of the Spirit among Religions': Trinitarian Prolegomena for a Pneumatological Theology of Religions." In *The Work of the Spirit: Pneumatology and Pentecostalism*, edited by Michael Welker, 47–70. Grand Rapids: Eerdmans, 2006.
---. "How to Speak of the Spirit among Religions': Trinitarian 'Rules' for a Pneumatological Theology of Religions." *International Bulletin of Missionary Research* 30.3 (July 2006) 121–27.
---. *An Introduction to the Theology of Religions: Biblical, Historical, and Contemporary Perspectives*. Downers Grove, IL: InterVarsity, 2003.
---. *Spirit and Salvation: A Constructive Christian Theology for the Pluralistic World*. Grand Rapids: Eerdmans, forthcoming.
---. "Theologies of Religions." *Evangelical Interfaith Dialogue* 1.2 (2010) 3–7. Online: http://cms.fuller.edu/EIFD/issues/Spring_2010/Theologies_of_Religions.aspx.
---. "Theologies of Religions." In *Witnessing to Christ in a Pluralistic World. Christian Mission among Other Faiths*, edited by Lalsangkima Pachau and Knud Jørgensen, 110–18. Edinburgh 2010 Studies. London: Regnum, 2011.
---. *Trinity and Religious Pluralism: The Doctrine of the Trinity in Christian Theology of Religions*. Aldershot, England: Ashgate, 2004.
---. *Trinity and Revelation: A Constructive Christian Theology for the Pluralistic World*. Grand Rapids: Eerdmans, 2014.
---. *The Trinity: Global Perspectives*. Louisville, KY: Westminster John Knox, 2007.
---. "The Uniqueness of Christ and Trinitarian Faith." In *Christ the One and Only: A Global Affirmation of the Uniqueness of Jesus Christ*, edited by Sung Wook Chung, 111–35. Exeter, UK: Paternoster, 2005.

Kaufman, Gordon D. "Religious Diversity and Religious Truth." In *God, Truth, and Reality: Essays in Honour of John Hick*, edited by Arvind Sharma, 143–64. New York: St. Martin's, 1993.

Knitter, Paul F. *Introducing Theologies of Religions*. Maryknoll, NY: Orbis, 2002.

Lanzetta, Beverly J. "The Mystical Basis of Panikkar's Thought." In *The Intercultural Challenge of Raimon Panikkar*, edited by Joseph Prabhu, 91–105. Maryknoll, NY: Orbis, 1996.

Larson, Gerald James. "Contra Pluralism." In *The Intercultural Challenge of Raimon Panikkar*, edited by Joseph Prahu, 71–90. Maryknoll: Orbis, 1996.

Lee, Jung Young. "The Yin-Yang Way of Thinking." In *Asian Christian Theology: Emerging Themes*, edited by Douglas J. Elwood, 81–88. Philadelphia: Westminster, 1980.

McGrath, Alister E. "Conclusion." *Four Views on Salvation in a Pluralistic World*, edited by Dennis L. Okholm and Timothy R. Phillips, 200–9. Grand Rapids: Zondervan, 1995.

Netland, Harold A., and Gerald R. McDermott. *A Trinitarian Theology of Religions: An Evangelical Proposal*. Oxford: Oxford University Press, 2014.

Panikkar, Raimundo. *The Cosmotheandric Experience: Emerging Religious Consciousness*. Maryknoll, NY: Orbis, 1993.

———. *The Intrareligious Dialogue*. New York: Paulist, 1978.

———. "The Invisible Harmony: A Universal Theory of Religion or a Cosmic Confidence in Reality?" In *Toward a Universal Theology of Religion*, edited by Leonard Swidler, 120–25, 141. Maryknoll, NY: Orbis, 1987.

———. "The Jordan, the Tiber and the Ganges: Three Kairological Moments of Christic Self-Consciousness." In *The Myth of Christian Uniqueness: Toward a Pluralistic Theology of Religions*, edited by John Hick and Paul F. Knitter, 89–116. Maryknoll, NY: Orbis, 1987.

———. *The Trinity and the Religious Experience of Man: Icon-Person-Mystery*. Maryknoll, NY: Orbis, 1973.

———. *The Unknown Christ of Hinduism*. London: Darton, Longman & Todd, 1964.

Pontifical Council for Inter-Religious Dialogue. "Dialogue and Proclamation." 2. May 19, 1991. Online: http://www.vatican.va/roman_curia/pontifical_councils/interelg/documents/rc_pc_intereleg_doc_19091991_dialogue-and-proclamatio_en-html.

Prabhu, Joseph, ed. *The Intercultural Challenge of Raimon Panikkar*. Maryknoll, NY: Orbis, 1996.

Raj, Anthony Savari. *A New Hermeneutic of Reality: Raimon Panikkar's Cosmotheandric Vision*. Bern: Lang, 1998.

Ramachandra, Vinoth. *The Recovery of Mission: Beyond the Pluralist Paradigm*. Grand Rapids: Eerdmans, 1996.

Saarinen, Risto. "Eri uskonnot—sama Jumala?: Jumalakuva uskontojen välisessä dialogissa." In *Jumalan kasvot: Jumalan ihmisen todellisuudessa*, edited by Risto A. Ahonen and Hans-Olof Kvist, 150–56. Tampere: Kirkon Tutkimuskeskus, 1995.

Samartha, Stanley J. *Courage for Dialogue: Ecumenical Issues in Inter-Religious Relationships*. Maryknoll, NY: Orbis, 1982.

———. "The Cross and the Rainbow: Christ in a Multireligious Culture." In *Asian Faces of Jesus*, edited by R. S. Sugirtharajah, 104–23. Maryknoll, NY: Orbis, 1995

———. "The Unbound Christ: Toward a Christology in India Today." In *Asian Christian Theology: Emerging Themes*, edited by Douglas J. Elwood, 145–60. Philadelphia: Westminster, 1980.
Smart, Ninian, and Steven Konstantine. *Christian Systematic Theology in a World Context*. Minneapolis: Fortress, 1991.
Suchocki, Marjorie Hewett. *Divinity and Diversity: A Christian Affirmation of Religious Pluralism*. Nashville: Abingdon, 2003.
Swidler, Leonard J., ed. *Toward a Universal Theology of Religion*. Maryknoll, NY: Orbis, 1987.
Vanhoozer, Kevin J. "Does the Trinity Belong in a Theology of Religions?: On Angling in the Rubicon and the 'Identity' of God." In *The Trinity in a Pluralistic Age: Theological Essays on Culture and Religion*, edited by Kevin J. Vanhoozer, 41–71. Grand Rapids: Eerdmans, 1997.
World Council of Churches. "Religious Plurality and Christian Self-Understanding." February 14, 2006. Online: http://www.oikoumene.org/en/resources/documents/assembly/2006-porto-alegre/3-preparatory-and-background-documents/religious-plurality-and-christian-self-understanding.
Yong, Amos. "The Turn to Pneumatology in Christian Theology of Religions: Conduit or Detour?" *Journal of Ecumenical Studies* 35 (1998) 437–54.

Chapter 14

Afterword
Looking Back with an Eye to the Conversational Future

Richard J. Plantinga

THIS VOLUME OF ESSAYS came to be through conversations among scholars, missionaries, and pastors from various parts of the globe. Despite different backgrounds and perspectives (some academic-scholarly and others ecclesial-popular), these servants of the worldwide church were unified in their focus on the matter of what the original conference conveners called "Christianity and religious plurality in global and historical perspective." As the foregoing essays have made clear, Christianity has changed significantly during the last one hundred or so years of history, taking root in parts of the globe where it had not had a pronounced presence earlier. In this brief, concluding essay, I will seek to specify some thematic lessons that this collaboration offers and thereby indicate the possible direction of future conversation.

To begin, I will point to the fundamental matter of religious plurality. The world of the twenty-first century shows tremendous diversity of religious orientations and perspectives, both *across* religious traditions and *within* them. The focus in the present volume falls on intra-Christian matters, although it is clear that Christianity in various parts of the world finds itself engaging non-Christian religious traditions (especially Islam). As the contributions by Wilbert Shenk and Veli-Matti Kärkkäinen especially make clear, plurality is not pluralism (and there are several pluralisms). Simply put for the present purpose, plurality is the recognition of the fact of religious manyness; pluralism, often taken as a synonym for plurality (but not in this volume), is a philosophical and theological judgment about the fact of religious manyness (and this judgment can vary, depending on the articulator). The matter of Christianity's relationship to the religious traditions of the world is a matter of deep concern to Christians in the West, where Christianity is defensive in nature and in a state of decline. It is also a matter of some concern to Christians outside the West, where Christianity is not as defensive in nature and generally more robust. Perhaps the plural "Christianities" should be employed in recognition of this diversity. The historically grounded global perspective presented in the foregoing suggests that the Christianities emerging across the globe today are something rather different than the post-Enlightenment version that is struggling in the West.

How are these emergent Christianities different from their Western counterpart? The essays in this volume suggest that Christianity in its new situations—although locally grounded—is global (and therefore hardly confined to the West). That fact in itself merits pause and reflection. Indeed, today there is—increasingly—a post-Christian West. But there are also post-Western Christianities. The old territorial conception of Christianity, as that set of beliefs and practices that characterized a geographical region (i.e., Europe and North America), has run its course. The operative term for this problematic territorial conception of Christianity is, of course, Christendom. Several of the contributors to this volume make this point forcefully (see especially the essays by Wilbert Shenk and Jehu Hanciles).

Connected to the post-Christendom nature of Christianity across the globe today is a new emphasis on its dynamic, translational character. As the fine contribution by the late Kwame Bediako makes particularly clear, Christianity has from the beginning been a faith that can be expressed in various idioms and contexts. Christianity's founder, Jesus, can be thought of as divinity translated into humanity.[1] The teachings of Jesus, who spoke Aramaic, were expressed in the writings of the New Testament, which were written in Greek. This originally Jewish conception of God, humanity, and the world came to be expressed—or translated—into the idiom of the Greco-Roman world. For many centuries, a certain kind of Christianity that descended from the Greeks and Romans (the West) was dominant in the world. But this particular Christianity is not normative. Nor should it be privileged. The growth of Christianity across the globe in the last cen-

---

1. See Walls, *Missionary Movement*, xvii.

tury has provided a timely reminder of Christianity's dynamic and translational—and diverse—nature. New Christianities are emerging. The essays in this volume are keen to emphasize this understanding of Christianity's dynamic, translational character.

Key in the consideration of translation is the matter of the pre-Christian beliefs and practices that are the subject of Christian conversion (from the Latin *verto*—to turn). In this volume, this matter is referred to as "primal religion" (see in particular the essay by Gillian Bediako). What is the pre-Christian religious experience from which converts turn? Clearly, that *from* which one turns plays a key role in apprehending that *to* which one turns. If one thinks of the transition from pre-Christian experience (metaphorically, the Old Testament) to Christian experience (metaphorically, the New Testament), one could ask about a plurality of "Old Testaments" (in this connection, see the essay by John Goldingay). The collective vision of this volume implies that taking primal religion more seriously than has heretofore been done is crucial for understanding the changes taking place on the landscape of global Christianity.

As Christianity has grown and grows dynamically and moves across the contemporary globe, it does so in reflection of different sociopolitical locations, as the essay by Wilbert Shenk illustrates well. Affluent Christians in the modern West are generally focused on rationality, intellectual coherence, existential meaning, secularism, relation to science, and the like.[2] These are hardly the primary concerns of poor Christians in Africa, to name but one different group in a radically different sociopolitical location from the modern West. The contextual matter of sociopolitical location is not only a reality globally today; it has also been a reality historically. For example, pre-Constantinian (pre-Christendom) Christianity was rather more marginal *vis-à-vis* the surrounding culture than its post-Constantinian (Christendom) successor. And equally clearly, Christianity in Christendom was a powerful force *vis-à-vis* its surrounding culture, especially as seen in comparison with Christianity after Christendom, in which a rather more marginalized, privatized existence has become the order of the day (i.e., in the West).

To invoke the world of pre-Constantinian Christianity is to touch on another theme in this volume—namely, the instructive parallel between the Christianity of the early church (prior to the fourth century, pre-Christendom) and the emergent Christianity seen around the globe today (post-Christendom). As Andrew Walls has noted, he once went to Sierra Leone on behalf of "older" churches to instruct the "younger" ones about the early

---

2. See Tracy, *Analogical Imagination*.

church—only to discover that these younger churches (and to his increasing astonishment, their would-be instructor) were actually *living* in a situation much like the early church.³

As it sought to be faithful to its charge to carry the gospel to the ends of the earth, the Christian church has had many encounters with other systems of belief and practice. In the foregoing chapters in this volume, there are many helpful and learned historical overviews of Christianity's encounter with primal religions, "old testaments," indigenous cultures, and the like. These essays—e.g., by Lamin Sanneh, Gerald Pillay, Peter Phan, Kim-Kwong Chan and Daniel Bays, Gillian Bediako, Martin Sinaga, J. Dudley Woodberry, and Paul Cornelius—illustrate many of themes that impinge on religious plurality. The reader is reminded how long Christianity has been a "world" religion, even though this truth has only come into purview and wider acceptance rather more recently. The essay by Jehu Hanciles furthermore reminds us that the Western secularization thesis cannot be presumed to apply to global Christianity, which is moreover complicated by the realities of global migration. Old wineskins eventually burst. New wineskins— new assumptions and concepts—are needed. This recognition is one of the convictions of the present collaborators.As the development of Christianity has been examined in this volume a question that has surely presented itself is this: What precisely *is* Christianity? Does it have a core or an essence? Is there something that binds all of the different Christianities together and is incumbent upon all Christians? This is a difficult and elusive matter. Andrew Walls gives something of an answer to this question in a well-known essay,⁴ emphasizing historical connection across the various Christianities. Central to this historical connection is the person of Jesus, who is made known by scripture. Christian Scripture is, of course, differently conceived, read, translated, and interpreted by various Christian communities in their particular linguistic and cultural contexts. But scripture is, in any case, key for knowing the Triune God revealed in the history of Israel and particularly made known in Jesus Christ. Later patristic Christianity spent much time on conceptual precision as it sought to (re)articulate the biblical portrait of the God made known in Christ to whom scripture bears witness. In other words, part of the Christian tradition's work and responsibility historically has been clarification of its faith and its talk about God (*logos* about *theos*). This mandate for ongoing theological work was nicely captured by Anselm in his memorable expression "faith seeks understanding" (*fides quaerens*

---

3. See Walls, "Introduction," *Missionary Movement*, xiii–xv.
4. See Walls, "Gospel as Prisoner and Liberator," *Missionary Movement*, 3–15.

intellectum).[5] That is, as Christians live their lives and think about their beliefs and practices, they wonder about the nature of the God in whom they believe, the meaning of life, the nature of suffering, the question of justice, and the like. This pattern will surely continue as Christianity takes up residence in different parts of the globe. But Christians in, say, sub-Saharan Africa are likely to ask quite different questions of their faith than, say, Christians in the United States. Nonetheless, as Christianity moves beyond the West, it will not move beyond theology. As theological inquiry is central to and vital for Christian existence, theology will continue to be an ongoing undertaking of the church. The kind of theology, however, that emerges over the next century is likely to look rather different in content and temperament than the Western theology that preceded it.

Differences among the Christianities aside, one of the common, contemporary challenges for global Christianity is the presence and growth of Islam, the world's second largest religion numerically speaking (after Christianity). Increasingly, post-Christian Europe seems ripe for Islamic missionary activity, a reality encountered by Christianities in other parts of the globe as well (e.g., Indonesia and parts of Africa). Given the realities of commonality and difference, as well as various challenges (both common and particular), what is vitally important for global Christianity moving forward is commitment to dialogue among the Christianities. Western Christianity, which was long the chief custodian of much of Christian tradition's treasures, is no longer in the position that it once was. Although it still has things to contribute to the global conversation, it also has things to learn—and learn it must. Non-Western Christianity also has things to contribute to the conversation as well as things to learn. The vision that gave rise to this volume is grounded in the need for healthy and ongoing dialogue among the Christianities. In this emerging dialogue, no one Christianity has the dominant, or even the upper, hand. The idea of wiser, older churches and less wise, younger ones must be surrendered, if it has not been jettisoned already. Christians and churches in the West, however, have not been left behind or rendered irrelevant because of Christianity's global march forward; all have a seat at the table and a voice in the dialogue. The authors of this volume collectively cherish the hope of a continuing real and meaningful global Christian conversation in the decades to come. May it be so.

---

5. See Anselm of Canterbury, *Proslogion*, 243–44.

BIBLIOGRAPHY

Anselm of Canterbury. *Proslogion*. In *The Prayers and Meditations of Saint Anselm*, translated by Sister Benedicta Ward, 238–67. Harmondsworth: Penguin, 1973.

Tracy, David. *The Analogical Imagination: Christian Theology and the Culture of Pluralism*. New York: Crossroad, 1981.

Walls, Andrew F. *The Missionary Movement in Christian History: Studies in the Transmission of Faith*. Maryknoll, NY: Orbis, 1996.

www.ingramcontent.com/pod-product-compliance
Lightning Source LLC
Chambersburg PA
CBHW021345300426
44114CB00012B/1082